JOHN HAY,
FRIEND OF GIANTS

JOHN HAY, FRIEND OF GIANTS

*The Man and Life Connecting
Abraham Lincoln, Mark Twain, Henry James,
and Theodore Roosevelt*

Philip McFarland

ROWMAN & LITTLEFIELD
Lanham • Boulder • New York • London

Published by Rowman & Littlefield
A wholly owned subsidiary of The Rowman & Littlefield Publishing Group, Inc.
4501 Forbes Boulevard, Suite 200, Lanham, Maryland 20706
www.rowman.com
Unit A, Whitacre Mews, 26–34 Stannary Street, London SE11 4AB
Distributed by NATIONAL BOOK NETWORK

British Library Cataloguing in Publication Information Available

Library of Congress Cataloging-in-Publication Data

978-1-4422-2281-6 (cloth)
978-1-4422-2283-0 (electronic)

♾ ™ The paper used in this publication meets the minimum requirements of American
National Standard for Information Sciences—Permanence of Paper for Printed Library
Materials, ANSI/NISO Z39.48–1992.

Printed in the United States of America

IN MEMORIAM

Patricia Connors McFarland

1932–2013

"I have been extraordinarily happy all my life. Good luck has pursued me like my shadow. . . ."

—John Hay to Henry Adams, July 11, 1901

CONTENTS

LIST OF ILLUSTRATIONS

JOHN HAY,
FRIEND OF GIANTS

John Hay at thirty-five. Wedding picture taken in early 1874. Courtesy of John Hay Papers (Call no. Ms. Hay), John Hay Library, Brown University, Providence, Rhode Island.

PROLOGUE: JOHN HAY, 1838–1905

Now, perhaps, only those enmeshed in nineteenth-century American history know his name; but when John Hay died in 1905, in his sixty-seventh year, of a coronary thrombosis at his home near Newbury, New Hampshire, he was one of the most famous men in the world. And one of the most highly regarded. "I am so happy," wrote the steel baron Andrew Carnegie, "(& proud, excuse me) that I have known you John Hay. You make the Republic what its Founders intended—something higher than the governments that preceded its birth." Theodore Roosevelt, president of the United States, who knew Hay well, thought that "he was the most delightful man to talk to I ever met, for in his conversation he continually made out of hand those delightful epigrammatic remarks which we would all like to make"—and don't think of until we're out the door. Then added: "He was moreover, I think without exception, the best letter-writer of his age." In sum, Hay's "dignity, his remarkable literary ability, his personal charm, and the respect his high character and long service commanded thruout the country, together with his wide acquaintance with foreign statesmen and foreign capitals, made him one of the public servants of real value to the United States."

As for the respect in which his country held this particular cabinet secretary, Mark Twain conveyed in 1904 (anonymously, so that the busy recipient would not feel obliged to respond) his own high view of Secretary Hay, then added: "There are majorities that are proud of more than one of the nation's great servants, but I believe, & think I know, that you are the only one of whom the entire nation is proud. Proud and thankful."

Yet even before those late years of esteemed public service, Hay had earned wide respect, although from quite different endeavors. From the mid-1870s and far into the 1880s, for instance, he and a close friend and collaborator labored on a massive work of history and biography that, when published—in ten volumes, in 1890—was hailed by our leading critic of the time, William Dean Howells, as not only "the most important work yet accomplished in American history," but as "one of the noblest achievements of literary art"— that is, as history *and* literature. And, through the next half-century, Hay and Nicolay's *Abraham Lincoln: A History* would remain the one indispensable source for studying our greatest president.

Earlier still, in the 1870s, Hay distinguished himself as an editor of a then-leading newspaper, the *New York Tribune*. For five years he held the position, during which time he earned the approbation of the newspaper's founder, the legendary, irascible Horace Greeley, as the best editor the *Tribune* ever had. And at the very start of his journalistic career, in 1870, Hay dashed off a poem, in the dialect of his Illinois childhood, that became enormously popular throughout the United States—it made "John Hay" a household name, rather to the author's amazement—and a second poem, a second Pike County ballad, followed that was perhaps even more popular than the first; so that, modest though he was about his poetic gifts, Hay was counted from then on to the end of his life and beyond as among a select group of best-loved American poets.

In the 1860s, starting in his late twenties, Hay had served as a diplomat overseas, successively—and successfully—in Paris, Vienna, and Madrid, acquiring a cosmopolitan polish as he perfected his knowledge of French and German and developed a competence in Spanish. He had, in addition, throughout his life a great capacity for friendship. And no wonder: testimony survives from people who thought Hay the best storyteller they had ever listened to. Not a glad-hander, or a back-slapper, or a hail-fellow-well-met, he nevertheless won the loyalty and devotion of great numbers of friends as the most agreeable of companions, easy-going, full of engaging anecdotes, a wonderful listener, and a generous, good-humored host. And he was lucky. From the first, good luck pursued John Hay, as he said, like his shadow—until one dreadful year late in life (in 1901) when it didn't. But mostly the sun shone down on this capable gentleman; and although prone to various indeterminate illnesses, he tried not to let them hinder him from cherishing his days: exercising his several gifts, relishing his family amid their abundant creature comforts, enjoying his friends immensely, finding ample time for leisure, and marveling at his lifelong good fortune.

Yet one more example of that last: at the start of the 1860s—or just before— young Hay, fresh out of college, dejected, unsettled in life, had the rare good fortune (no doubt the greatest luck that ever befell him) at age twenty of finding himself, for lack of anything better to do, reading law in a lawyer uncle's office in Illinois. Lucky for Hay that the year was the one it was; and lucky that his Uncle Milton's practice was on the same floor and next door to that of a couple of other lawyers—specifically, of Lincoln & Herndon, Attorneys. And extremely lucky for John Hay that the senior member of the neighboring firm was just then coming into his own on the national stage.

The not-yet-bearded Abraham Lincoln as the Republican presidential nominee in mid-June 1860. When they first met the previous fall, Hay would have known Lincoln thus. Courtesy of the Library of Congress

1

HAY AND ABRAHAM LINCOLN: THE 1860S

1. RISING POLITICIAN

Abraham Lincoln was fifty years old and a lawyer in Springfield, Illinois, when young John Hay met him for the first time, in 1859. Well before then, Mr. Lincoln's practice had grown extensive; if the attorney hadn't got rich from it, that was in part because he could write such a letter as this, to a George P. Floyd of Quincy, Illinois: "Dear Sir: I have just received yours of 10th, with check on Flagg & Savage for twenty-five dollars. You must think I am a high-priced man. You are too liberal with your money. Fifteen dollars is enough for the job. I send you a receipt for fifteen dollars, and return to you a ten-dollar bill. Yours truly, A. Lincoln."

So the senior partner at Lincoln & Herndon wasn't rich by September 1859, but he was highly regarded in Springfield—among the best lawyers in attorney-dense Illinois—and busy enough to provide comfortably for his family. Moreover, all this occurred while his reputation as a midwestern political leader kept rising. Precisely a year earlier, newspapers had been full of the contents of debates between Mr. Lincoln and one of Illinois's two senators, Stephen A. Douglas, transcribed from shorthand notes of reporters at the various sites. Seven such joint discussions had unfolded all over the state through nearly two months during late last summer and into the fall, and each debate had been well and enthusiastically attended. As many, for instance, as fifteen thousand spectators had crowded as close as they could to the speakers' platform at Galesburg, in west-central Illinois; and even down south, in tiny Jonesboro with a population of no more than nine hundred, the smallest audience of the seven numbered a respectable 1,200 people: farmers, artisans, tradesmen, and others, there and elsewhere, eagerly standing in fairgrounds or

---

1

town squares through the heat of summer afternoons, standing while it rained as well, or when in October it turned chilly, those near enough keeping as quiet as possible so as to catch whatever the speakers might say, until some sally or other would strike a response from partisans ("Good," "hear, hear," "Hit him on the woolly side," "Hurrah for Douglas!" LOUD CHEERS, APPLAUSE AND LAUGHTER) through the three hours that each debate consumed.

Who would do that now, stand in a mob under shadeless summer sun straining for hours to make out distant, unamplified political argument? But in the long monotonies of agrarian America in the 1850s, the Lincoln-Douglas debates provided stimulating and pretty much unprecedented diversion. By the 2 P.M. commencement of the speeches, spectators had already passed a lively morning, and sometimes the evening before, rallying for their candidates. A torchlight procession would have greeted Illinois's famous senator, arriving on his special train that brought along supporters and his own cannon to be fired off emphatically as called for; and the following morning dignitaries would have beamed down upon the local parade with its elaborate floats, on the military band marching under banners strung overhead, on a wagon bearing smiling young ladies who represented the thirty-two states of the Union, on flags fluttering and townsfolk following and peddlers hawking their wares alongside the pageantry, with porches and storefronts draped in bunting and a couple of four-horse carriages standing ready to transport the candidates from their respective hotels to the mobbed debate site.

Lew Wallace, thirty-one-year-old Democratic state senator over from neighboring Indiana (who two decades later would write *Ben-Hur: A Tale of the Christ*, which sold more copies than any other novel published in nineteenth-century America, Mrs. Stowe's *Uncle Tom's Cabin* not excepted), in mid-September had gazed in wonder over one such site in Charleston, in Coles County: "The platform for the speakers reminded me of an island barely visible in a restless sea—so great was the gathering." And Carl Schurz at twenty-nine, German immigrant only six years in our country but himself destined for distinction (minister to Spain, Civil War general, senator from Missouri, secretary of the interior, editor of the *New York Evening Post*) would remember into old age having attended the sixth Lincoln-Douglas debate at Quincy, in Adams County, on October 13—"the Democratic displays were much more elaborate and gorgeous than those of the Republicans"—and would recall the principals on the platform: the senator himself, the "Little Giant" (a national figure, by far the more noteworthy of the two), round-faced, stout, standing a diminutive five feet four but with a deep, sonorous voice and gestures of theatrical grace, in sharp contrast to gaunt Mr. Lincoln, at six four a full foot taller, his voice high-pitched, his gestures awkwardly jerky. Yet the sincerity of the attorney from Springfield—and his eloquence—compensated, in Schurz's opinion, for any deficiencies he might exhibit as an orator.

What the two were arguing about concerned the fate of American land lying west of the Mississippi. As soon as designated territories of that vast acreage attracted enough settlers, they could join the Union; but would they come in as slave states or free? Congress had dealt with the question nearly forty years earlier, as long ago as 1820, with a compromise arrived at between the North and the South that let Maine enter as a free state while the new state of Missouri permitted slavery; that way the numbers of slave- and free-state senators in Congress remained in balance. Moreover, by extending Missouri's southern border in an imaginary line due westward toward the Pacific, the disposition of any future states had been agreed upon: territory south of the line was to be opened to slavery; what was north of it would be free soil.

For a while, the Missouri Compromise appeared to have dealt with the slavery issue to general satisfaction. But then Texas broke away from Mexico and, in 1845, entered the Union as a slave state—an acquisition large enough that two slave states, or three, or four, might yet be carved from it, with two senators apiece to help assure that the South dominated Congress. And four months after Texas became the twenty-eighth state, America found itself at war with Mexico, a conflict that ended by our acquiring even more land, much more, roughly a third of the whole of our vanquished adversary. From the conquest would eventually be fashioned California, Nevada, and Utah, as well as parts of Wyoming, Colorado, Arizona, and New Mexico.

But when they entered the Union, any states made from those spoils of war would further jeopardize the delicate equilibrium of the earlier Missouri Compromise. A new arrangement had to be worked out, and was, laboriously, in 1850 (Senator Douglas of Illinois playing a leading role in getting the controversial legislation through Congress). California—its population fortuitously swollen with Forty-Niners—was allowed to come in at once as a free state, whereas the sprawling territories of Utah and New Mexico were left to wait until their populations had achieved the requisite size, when they themselves would make the choice for or against slavery.

Nobody North or South much liked the Compromise of 1850; but those provisions, along with a couple of others to appease southern sensibilities (a stricter fugitive slave law, slavery retained in the District of Columbia), were hoped to have settled the issue once and for all.

Abruptly, however, in 1854, Senator Douglas as chairman of the Committee on Territories shepherded through Congress a bill that effectively nullified the compromises of 1820 and 1850 both. Douglas's Kansas-Nebraska Act extended to all territories yet to be settled the same terms that New Mexico and Utah had been granted four years earlier. Approaching statehood, settlers in whatever incipient state, north of the former compromise line or south of it, would be left to determine for themselves how they wanted to join the Union, with slavery or without it.

This new doctrine of "popular sovereignty," which had the effect of opening to slavery territory north of latitude 36° 30′ where it had been prohibited before, lay at the heart of what Senator Douglas and Mr. Lincoln were contesting all over Illinois in the summer and fall of 1858. "A house divided against itself cannot stand," Lincoln had pronounced near the start of a much-noted address in Springfield just last June, shortly before the first of the debates. His scriptural reference, to Mark 3:25, conveyed the speaker's conviction that the United States, in the wake of the Kansas-Nebraska Act, could not continue as it was, half slave and half free. The house would not fall; the Union would not break up. But it would become all one thing or the other: either slavery would disappear, or it would spread inexorably throughout the western territories and at last over free soil northward. "Have we no *tendency* to the latter condition?" Always in need of more land, did not the South appear bent on spreading its peculiar institution ever farther outward: already into Texas, with talk of making states out of Cuba and Santo Domingo while moving steadily westward into the new territories acquired from Mexico and north beyond the earlier east-west compromise line of 1820 into the free-soil territory of Kansas and from there on into Nebraska? Were not slavery's advocates even now striving to "push it forward, till it shall become alike lawful in all the States, old as well as new—North as well as South"?

Senator Douglas dismissed any such fears that slavery would ever intrude into free states up North. At the Jonesboro debate in mid-September, on the platform with Mr. Lincoln seated behind him, the Little Giant protested, "Why cannot this Union exist forever divided into free and slave States as our fathers made it?" Mr. Lincoln had said that a house divided cannot stand, but the Union had stood half slave and half free from the beginning, and had expanded and thrived and grown strong. "If we live upon the principle of State rights and State sovereignty, each State regulating its own affairs and minding its own business, we can go on and extend indefinitely, just as fast and as far as we need the territory." We are about to acquire Cuba, the senator announced to terrific applause, and when we do, "We must take it as we find it, leaving the people to decide the question of slavery for themselves, without interference on the part of the federal government, or of any State of this Union." So with additional lands—from Mexico, or from Canada, or from islands beyond our shores—that may become future states: "We must take them as we find them, leaving the people free to do as they please, to have slavery or not, as they choose." That is popular sovereignty; that is democracy; that is what will accommodate all the variety and rapid growth that are even now making "this confederacy one grand ocean-bound republic." Over such spaciousness Mr. Lincoln would impose a dreary uniformity and, Senator Douglas charged, was urging regional warfare—free states against slave states—to attain his ends. Douglas for his part would let each state decide for itself, and cared not at all whether settlers voted slavery up or down. That was *their* business. *Our* great mission should be to "restore peace and quiet by teaching each State to mind its own business, and regulate its own domestic affairs, and all to unite carrying out the constitution as our fathers made it, and thus to preserve the Union and render it perpetual in all time to come."

The two candidates alternated through the seven debates, one speaking first for an hour, the second responding for an hour and a half, then the first allowed an additional half hour to conclude. Here at Jonesboro, Lincoln in reply was concurring with much of what Judge Douglas had just said. "In so far as he has insisted that all the States have the right to do exactly as they please about all their domestic relations including that of slavery, I agree entirely with him. He places me wrong in spite of all I can tell him, though I repeat it again and again, insisting that I have no difference with him upon this subject." The Constitution sanctions slavery; thus, in those states where it already exists, Lincoln would let it alone. But Judge Douglas has asked in effect why we can't let the Union stand as our fathers made it. "That," his opponent explained, "is the exact difficulty between us." By the Northwest Ordinance of 1787, reaffirmed in 1789, the founding fathers barred slavery from the territory north and west of the Ohio River clear out to the Mississippi. "I say when this government was first established it was the policy of its founders to prohibit the spread of slavery into the new Territories of the United States, where it had not existed. But Judge Douglas and his friends have broken up that policy and placed it upon a new basis by which it is to become national and perpetual." Thus slavery is turned into a federal matter, a concern of all the states. Moreover, when Senator Douglas says he is indifferent to whether settlers in the territories vote slavery up or down, he ignores what is the essence of the institution: that it is wrong. In effect, his indifference aims at dulling northern sensibilities, accustoming the North to regard slaves not as human beings but as chattel, as mere property.

At the seventh and final debate, in Alton in mid-October, Lincoln returned to the point: Senator Douglas's nonchalance about whether settlers vote for or against slavery reveals his feeling that there is nothing wrong with people casting other people into bondage. "That is the real issue," his opponent insisted. "That is the issue that will continue in this country when these poor tongues of Judge Douglas and myself shall be silent. It is the eternal struggle between these two principles—right and wrong—throughout the world. They are the two principles that have stood face to face from the beginning of time. The one is the common right of humanity"—what the same speaker would later call government of the people, by the people, for the people—"and the other the divine right of kings. It is the spirit that says, 'You work and toil and earn bread, and I'll eat it.'" Loud applause broke out with that, and after the applause died down: "No matter in what shape it comes," Lincoln went on, "whether from the mouth of a king who seeks to bestride the people of his nation and live by the fruit of their labor, or from one race of men as an apology for enslaving another race, it is the same tyrannical principle." Yet Senator Douglas has said *that he looks to no end of the institution of slavery.* At Quincy day before yesterday Mr. Lincoln had thanked him for saying as much, and he thanks him again here and now, in Alton. "That will help the people to see where the struggle really is." The one side would make slavery perpetual; the other side sees it as wrong. And when the people at large understand it as wrong, "there will soon be an end of it."

Election Day in Illinois fell on a rainy Tuesday, November 2, 1858, and the results were very close. Out of 250,000 votes cast, Lincoln won a plurality of 4,000; but because of the number of congressmen not up for reelection and the way the congressional districts for those who were were drawn, Democrats retained control of the legislature. The Constitution (until the passage of the Seventeenth Amendment in 1913) made it the duty of state legislators to choose senators. In this case, by 54 to 46, legislators chose the Democratic candidate to be senator from Illinois for the coming six-year term. Thus Stephen A. Douglas returned to Washington, and Abraham Lincoln went back to Springfield, but with his political stature much enhanced.

2. A POET IN EXILE

John Hay met Mr. Lincoln ten months later. Twenty years old at the time, about to turn twenty-one, Hay had been reading law in Springfield, although unenthusiastically. What the young man really wanted to be was a poet.

He was, in fact, a poet of promise already, having a little more than a year earlier performed as senior class poet at college back East. There, on Class Day, June 10, 1858, at Brown University in Providence, Rhode Island, John M. Hay of Warsaw, Illinois, delivered to much acclaim his poem "Erato," a nineteen-year-old's quite dazzling display of verbal flair, wit, and classical learning (Erato is the Greek muse of lyric poetry), celebrating the power of verse in twelve printed pages of some 450 lines that ended aptly enough for an audience of new graduates commencing their postcollege journeys:

> As we go forth, the smiling world before us
>   Shouts to our youth the old inspiring tune;
> The same blue sky of God is bending o'er us,
>   The green earth sparkles in the joy of June.
> Where'er afar the beck of fate shall call us,
>   'Mid winter's boreal chill or summer's blaze,
> Fond memory's chain of flowers shall still enthrall us,
>   Wreathed by the spirits of these vanished days.
> Our hearts shall bear them safe through life's commotion,
>   Their fading gleam shall light us to our graves;
> As in the shell, the memories of ocean
>   Murmur forever of the sounding waves.

Three golden years this westerner had spent at Brown, and had loved all of it, in a world unlike any he had known. Born in October 1838 in tiny Salem, an Indiana village down near the Ohio River, raised in an even tinier village on a bluff overlooking the Mississippi in western Illinois, Hay had early displayed scholastic aptitudes in meager surroundings—learned effortlessly, could read with ease, had a fine memory—so that his doting family sent their prodigy off at age thirteen sixty miles to a private academy in larger Pittsfield, Illinois, there to live with an uncle, his father's brother Milton. But within a couple of years young John Hay had exhausted Pittsfield's educational resources, where-upon his fond uncle arranged that he continue his studies in the capital city, Springfield, at Illinois State University. *University* rather overstated what that newly founded institution had to offer; so that in the fall of 1855, again through Uncle Milton's generosity, John, just shy of seventeen, set out for New England to pursue his learning at far-off Brown University in Rhode Island. At that same Brown, Hay's maternal grandfather—dead twenty-two years when the grandson was born—had been senior class poet himself, in 1792. Thus a child of the frontier was blessed with the luck not only of a loving family and a very generous uncle to stand behind him but also of an illustrious ancestral example to guide him forward.

Hay was lucky all his life, and knew it right up to the end. Lucky, if by no means invariably happy. For one thing, his health was not always to be relied on. At Brown, for instance, he was sick thirty days during his first year and forty-two in his second, although no more than six days of the third, the last. During that final spring, of 1858, the senior joined the Providence Athenaeum, where he made friends with local poetical celebrities who included Nora Perry and Sarah Helen Whitman. The latter, his mother's age, had earlier, briefly, been the fiancée of Edgar Allan Poe. Mrs. Whitman's poems appeared in the *Providence Journal* and the *New York Tribune*; a book of them was published in 1853. In addition to such stimulating extracurricular connections, Hay, who possessed a gift for making friends, relished his several friendships with congenial classmates and a warmer attachment to the younger sister of a favorite professor, as well as that triumph in Manning Hall at the end of three glorious years: John M. Hay of Warsaw, Illinois, reading his poem "Erato" to the Brown community assembled, which agreed in judging it the university's best class poem in memory.

But with college days behind him, the young man back in Warsaw fell into despondency. "In spite of the praise which you continually lavish upon the West," he wrote to his poet friend Miss Perry not long after returning to Illinois, "I must respectfully assert that I find only a dreary waste of heartless materialism, where great and heroic qualities may indeed bully their way up into the glare, but the flowers of existence inevitably droop and wither." Of what use were a poet's flowers out West? And what else might such a sensibility find to do in these raw surroundings? Hay's mother and his older brother Augustus ("my first friend and my best") were opposed to the young man's becoming a schoolmaster. Gus wanted John to go back East for further study, but where was the money for that? By invitation in the fall of 1858, this recent college graduate, still only nineteen, did deliver to appreciative villagers a lecture he had worked hard on: "The History of the Jesuits." Warsaw's newspaper praised it highly, as "a very able and eloquent effort" in a church filled to overflowing. The lecturer's "voice was strong and clear, and his manner of delivery excellent—far surpassing that of any person we have before heard in our city." Yet more: "The parents of this young man may justly feel proud of him, as do the citizens of our city, for his intelligence and manly bearing. He has the talents, and if he does not make his mark in the world as a bright and shining light, the fault is with himself."

How to make that mark, though? Some in his audience, impressed, had urged Hay to be a preacher, but he felt no calling to the religious life. Should he become a doctor? John's father was the village physician, beloved by all. Yet it was an arduous life that Dr. Charles Hay lived, making his rounds on horseback in Warsaw, up and down the river, and out to ailing families in the countryside. Graduate of Transylvania Medical School in Lexington, Kentucky, Dr. Hay had brought his wife and children to the village in 1841 and remained there the rest of his days, rarely venturing far through forty-three years of ill-paid ministrations before dying in 1884. Was that the life his gifted son aspired to?

There was the law. Here, near the frontier, lawyers were always in demand: wills, deeds, and bills of sale to draw up, titles to search, certificates of survey to prepare, boundary disputes to settle, along with appeals, slander suits, assaults, and other such matters to be adjudicated. Uncle Milton had been practicing law over in Pittsfield while his nephew attended the academy there. Married, Milton Hay and his wife had two children, both of whom died early. When his young wife died as well, Milton moved back to Springfield, in 1858, as partner in the firm of Logan & Hay. Logan was Stephen T. Logan, a wizened advocate who was among the best lawyers in the state, and who fifteen years before had had for a junior partner Abraham Lincoln. Indeed, Milton Hay had read law in the offices of Logan & Lincoln before setting up his own practice in Pittsfield. Now returned to the capital late in the 1850s, Attorney Hay located upstairs in the three-story brick building on Capitol Square, adjacent, as it happened, to the shabby though well-respected offices of what by then was the partnership of Abraham Lincoln and William Herndon, attorneys at law.

As for Milton Hay's talented nephew John back in Warsaw: "A few months of exile has worn the luster from my dreams and well-nigh quenched all liberal aspirations," the young man was complaining to Nora Perry. "I do not see how I could gain either honor or profit by writing, so I suppose the sooner I turn my attention to those practical studies which are to minister to the material wants in the West, the better it will be." "Erato" had sung of poetry's precious beauty in a prosaic world—of its flowers that

> . . . bloom forever in the paths of trade,
> These heavenly asphodels that shall not fade,
> Nor let earth's cares crush, in their rude career,
> These bright memorials of a higher sphere;
> Let not the whirling incense-clouds of steam
> Dim the pure radiance of the poet's dream . . .

Yet Hay's own dream, of passing his days among asphodels, was dimming. "John is now at home," Dr. Hay had written earlier to his brother Milton, "and I am somewhat undecided as to what course I will advise him to pursue." One course under consideration: "Upon what terms can he enter your office and spend twelve months as a student?" Milton Hay had already taken to his nephew with the warmth of a father deprived of his own two children, so the terms were soon settled on. Young John Hay found himself back in Springfield in the spring of 1859 reading law.

"I am stranded at last," the law student wrote to a college chum that May, "like a weather-beaten hulk, on the dreary wastes of Springfield, a city combining the meanness of the North with the barbarism of the South." The capital of Illinois boasted some nine thousand generally unpoetical souls, many of its streets unlit and unpaved as yet, and the mud deep. "There is no land so sad as this," Hay wrote. "The sky is forever leaden with gloomy clouds, or glowing with torrid fervors. But the Aborigines are contented & happy. If the air is a furnace, they say 'Powerful nice weather for the wheat.' If the day weeps in sad-coloured showers they shake the rain from their hats & grin, 'This is given to send the corn up amazin'.'"

Thus one cultured Brown alumnus to another. Exiled in Illinois, meanwhile, where he kept such disparagements to himself, accomplished John Hay was making his way toward becoming a general favorite in Springfield: youthfully attractive in appearance, smooth-faced, self-confident, of an easy disposition, dapper, a lively conversationalist full of anecdotes and puns, a regular at church fairs and sociables, the college man who attended lectures and helped the ladies with their French or German, all the while so well read and witty, such good company. Again to Nora Perry, in this same spring of 1859: "Never before have I been so much in society. Yet into every parlor my Daemon has pursued me. When the air has been fainting with prisoned perfumes, when every spirit thrilled to the delicate touch of airy harmonies, when"—he is describing attendance at a local dance—"perfect forms moved in unison with perfect music, and mocked with their voluptuous grace the tortured aspirations of poetry, I have felt, coming over my soul colder than a northern wind, a conviction of the hideous unreality of all that moved and swayed and throbbed before me." Poet Perry back East would have understood her correspondent's melancholy, his frustrating search for the eternal real along the edges of an evanescent western frolic.

Among John Hay's circle in Springfield was a friend from earlier times, from Pittsfield academy days, before Hay had gone on to Illinois State University and his three years at Brown. John George Nicolay had been born in

Bavaria in 1832, had come with his family to America in 1838 (the year of Hay's birth), had attended school briefly in Cincinnati, then immigrated on to Illinois, to Pittsfield, as a printer's devil, then a printer, then editor of Pittsfield's *Pike County Free Press* and soon a force in local politics. Nicolay, six years Hay's senior, had gotten to know and (as many did) admire the young academy student at the start of the 1850s. Later, the printer had met Lincoln, in 1856—while Hay was at Brown—when the attorney came into the *Free Press* offices to get some job printing done. A couple of years after that Nicolay moved the seventy miles east to Springfield, to be librarian at the capitol and clerk to the secretary of state of Illinois. There he became a devoted adherent to Mr. Lincoln's political views.

Those views had been widely circulated in newspapers covering the Lincoln-Douglas debates over the previous summer and fall. The midterm elections that followed returned Stephen A. Douglas to the Senate; but ever since then, Abraham Lincoln had been keeping busy as well. The Springfield lawyer rode his last of many circuits in 1859, along with fellow attorneys bringing justice to towns and villages in central Illinois through arduous, weeks-long, semiannual buggy and horseback travel over two hundred miles of primitive roads and prairie trails, at one-room courthouses in agrarian America performing a taxing duty that the uncomplaining Lincoln loved for its companionship and variety. Yet this Illinois lawyer was increasingly called to other, political work, leaving it to his partner, Billy Herndon, to attend to legal matters back in Springfield.

In September 1859 Lincoln did meet John Hay, Milton Hay's nephew and John G. Nicolay's friend; but with his rising reputation the senior partner of Lincoln & Herndon was out of town much of the time now, invited to share his antislavery views with audiences in Columbus, in Cincinnati, in Milwaukee, in distant Kansas. He got busy seeing to the publication in book form of the debates with Judge Douglas, so that they might reach a wider audience. An autobiography was called for, and Lincoln obliged, briefly and to the best of his recollection. For he had become the sought-after regional spokesman for the new Republican Party, to the extent that even people as far off as back East were growing eager to hear from him directly. Thus, in October 1859 Mr. Lincoln received an invitation to address the Rev. Henry Ward Beecher's large congregation in Brooklyn, New York, although when the date came round the following February, others had taken charge of the affair and moved it across the river to the Cooper Institute, on East Seventh Street in Manhattan.

At Cooper Union, then, on February 27, 1860, Abraham Lincoln was introduced to a crowd of 1,500 easterners curious to assess the presidential qualities of this little known westerner from the humblest of backgrounds. The hall where he spoke survives: one who was sitting inside it on that earlier occasion puts us back there, back then: "When Lincoln rose to speak, I was greatly disappointed. He was tall, tall,—oh, how tall! and so angular and awkward that I had, for an instant, a feeling of pity for so ungainly a man." The lecturer's voice emerged pitched higher than expected, and he spoke in an Indiana accent different from what his auditors were used to: *heerd* for *heard*. A little way into the speech, however, "his face lighted up as with an inward fire; the whole man was transfigured. I forgot his clothes, his personal appearance, and his individual peculiarities," this eyewitness set down. "Presently, forgetting myself, I was on my feet like the rest, yelling like a wild Indian, cheering this wonderful man."

The speech proved to be a triumph of lucidity and logic. About slavery, Senator Douglas had proclaimed in an address last fall: "Our fathers, when they framed the Government under which we live, understood this question just as well, and even better, than we do now." Indeed they did, and Mr. Lincoln seized upon Douglas's autumn comment to explain to his listeners in February, irrefutably, that a clear majority of those fathers—those thirty-nine signers of the Constitution—found nothing in that document that forbade Congress from prohibiting slavery in federal territory. The Constitution sanctioned slavery (if only implicitly; *slavery* is never mentioned) in states where it then existed. Votes in Congress, however, concerning the then Northwest Territories of 1787; the land later deeded by North Carolina and Georgia from which would be formed Tennessee, Alabama, and Mississippi; and the territory acquired in the Louisiana Purchase of 1803 all clearly attested to the fact that the founding fathers judged slavery the way Republicans judged it at this later time, "as an evil not to be extended, but to be tolerated and protected only because of and so far as its actual presence among us makes that toleration and protection a necessity."

In the course of his Cooper Union speech, Lincoln spoke directly to the southern people, "if they would listen—as I suppose they will not." What is it you charge against the Republican Party? "You say we are sectional. We deny it." If our party does not yet appeal down South, our getting "no votes in your section, is a fact of your making, and not of ours"—of your incessantly demonizing "Black Republicanism." We *will* get votes in the South, and within this very election year. Meanwhile, nothing in our principles wrongs the South in any way. "Again, you say we have made the slavery question more prominent than it formerly was. We deny it." It *is* more prominent, but the South has made it so. "It was not we, but you, who discarded the old policy of the fathers. We resisted, and still resist, your innovation; and thence comes the greater prominence of the question." For it is you who are striving to extend slavery beyond its constitutional boundaries. Moreover, you threaten to destroy the Union "unless you be allowed to construe and enforce the Constitution as you please, on all points in dispute between you and us." Then, you say, with the Union in pieces the fault will be ours! "That is cool. A highwayman holds a pistol to my ear, and mutters through his teeth, 'Stand and deliver, or I shall kill you, and then you will be a murderer!'"

Having developed his argument fully, the speaker closed with words to his fellow Republicans. *"Even though much provoked, let us do nothing through passion and ill temper. Even though the southern people will not so much as listen to us, let us calmly consider their demands, and yield to them if, in our deliberate view of our duty, we possibly can."* True, what will satisfy them appears to be "this, and this only: cease to call slavery *wrong*, and join them in calling it *right*." All else will follow. "Holding, as they do, that slavery is morally right, and socially elevating, they cannot cease to demand a full national recognition of it, as a legal right, and a social blessing. Nor can we justifiably withhold this, on any ground save our conviction that slavery is wrong."

But it *is* wrong. And yet wrong as slavery is, we must let it alone where its presence is constitutionally permitted. That said, we stand by our conviction that it must not spread. And we must not be diverted from our duty "by false accusations against us, nor frightened from it by menaces of destruction to the Government nor of dungeons to ourselves. LET US HAVE FAITH THAT RIGHT MAKES MIGHT, AND IN THAT FAITH, LET US, TO THE END, DARE TO DO OUR DUTY AS WE UNDERSTAND IT."

Lincoln's carefully wrought, 7,700-word speech contains much that a condensation such as this can only hint at. As delivered, it was a sensation. The undeclared presidential candidate went on to speak in Manchester and Concord, in Hartford and Meriden, in New Haven, in Woonsocket, Rhode Island, so that by the time he got back home, Illinois's favorite son had become a politician of near-national stature.

The Republican nominating convention assembled in the spring, in Lincoln-friendly Chicago as it happened, in crucial Illinois, on May 16, 1860, with New York's senator William H. Seward favored to prevail. But on the third ballot delegates chose instead former Representative Abraham Lincoln to be their standard bearer, and Lincoln's hometown went wild. "As the events of the last week have rendered Springfield, in one respect at least, the central city of the north, I have thought"—it is John Hay, swept up in the excitement, requested to write for the *Providence Journal*—"that some mention of the occurrences that have recently disturbed its monotonous quietude, might not be devoid of interest to the readers of the Journal." At the first news of victory, a cannon from the Mexican War had been dragged out of the Capitol here in Illinois and fired off to rouse the somnolent prairies, and "Lincoln banners, decked in every style of rude splendor, fluttered in the high west wind, and the very church bells signalled the triumph of stainless honor and pure conservatism by clangor that was unecclesiastically merry." That same triumphant night a huge, happy crowd gathered in the Capitol rotunda and listened to speeches of several gentlemen "who were kind enough to furnish a thread to hang shouts and cheers on; then proceeded with banners and music to the residence of the illustrious nominee. Soon the tall, gaunt form of the future anchor of the republic appeared. . . ."

In the thrill of the moment the young law student has put verse aside. Hay is writing in his baroque style—poet turned journalist—which was not unfamiliar to newspaper readers of the era, a style quite in contrast to Lincoln's own crisp, clear, methodical, and at proper times eloquent prose. Through the summer and fall, Hay's good friend John G. Nicolay will become deeply involved in Lincoln's presidential campaign, and John Hay will pitch in. A couple of decades back, the Hays had immigrated from slaveholding Kentucky north and westward to the free soil of Indiana and Illinois, so Dr. Hay's family were all of antislavery leanings; young John could get behind this present candidate and speak and scribble on his behalf, sorting letters, writing articles, helping to keep the new flow of visitors orderly, running errands as needed, and shaping himself into the staunch Republican he remained for the rest of his life.

Opposition to the candidate had meanwhile split: northern Democrats for Stephen A. Douglas, southern Democrats for Kentucky's John Breckinridge, and yet a third party, the Constitutional Union Party, for Tennessee's John Bell, who hoped to avoid the slavery issue altogether. In the election that November Republicans voted as one, while Democrats sliced up their votes three ways, allowing Abraham Lincoln to gain if not a majority, at least an adequate plurality of just under 40 percent of the canvass. In only its second run at the office, a new political party would be moving into the White House next March.

Early on, the president-elect out in Springfield appointed John G. Nicolay to be his personal secretary, a burdensome post that the election triumph had made far more so. A hundred letters a day were pouring in, soon up to two hundred. Friends, colleagues, relatives, and office-seekers were at the door, all wanting only five minutes of the victor's time. Nicolay would need an assistant, and he and Lincoln's friend Milton Hay had someone in mind. So, having seven days earlier passed the bar to practice law in Illinois, twenty-two-year-old John Hay—lucky man—found himself in the presidential traveling party at the Great Western depot as Abraham Lincoln's time in Springfield drew to a close. Around 8 A.M. on a drizzly Monday morning, February 11, 1861, Hay encountered a scene, he tells us, that was "impressive and touching in the last degree." Upward of a thousand fellow citizens had turned out despite the dismal weather. Mr. Lincoln met with several hundred of them in the station waiting room, bidding each one farewell "with an affectionate grasp of the hand." His usual cheerful manner in public had forsaken him. When it came time for the train to leave, their townsman mounted the platform of the rear car and spoke to the people solemnly, "a brief and touching speech, which left hardly a dry eye in the assemblage."

"My friends," the president-elect began, barely controlling his emotions:

> no one, not in my situation, can appreciate my feeling of sadness at this parting. To this place, and the kindness of these people, I owe everything. Here I have lived a quarter of a century, and have passed from a young to an old man. Here my children have been born, and one is buried. I now leave, not knowing when, or whether ever, I may return, with a task before me greater than that which rested upon Washington. Without the assistance of the Divine Being who ever attended him, I cannot succeed. With that assistance I cannot fail. Trusting in Him who can go with me, and remain with you, and be everywhere for good, let us confidently hope that all will yet be well. To His care commending you, as I hope in your prayers you will commend me, I bid you an affectionate farewell.

Their tall neighbor turned and disappeared inside the yellow railroad car bedecked in its patriotic bunting. Accompanying Lincoln east to Washington were various dignitaries, military personnel, reporters, his eldest son Robert, and his new private secretaries, one official, the other unofficial. Mrs. Lincoln and the two younger children would be joining the party by special train tomorrow, in Indianapolis; but now, here at the Springfield station, three rousing cheers had just rung out, and "every hat in the assemblage was lifted, and the crowd stood silent as the train moved slowly from the depot."

3. FROM SPRINGFIELD TO WASHINGTON, D.C.

Funds had been authorized for only one presidential secretary, for Mr. Nicolay. Lincoln's friend Milton Hay offered to cover a much-needed assistant secretary's expenses through the first six months, but the president-elect insisted on meeting that additional cost himself. In the event, once in Washington, a position was devised for Nicolay's helper, Milton's young nephew John Hay, as clerk in the Department of the Interior, from which posting he was promptly detailed to the White House, where he served through all but the final weeks of Lincoln's presidency.

Yet finding a source for Secretary Hay's salary was among the least of the problems facing the president-elect on a drizzly February morning as the train left Springfield bound east. It stopped first, briefly, for fueling and watering at Decatur, forty-five miles along the way. Young Hay, acting for now as traveling journalist filing reports for the newspapers, tells us that at Decatur several thousand people from the surrounding countryside had assembled at the depot, "and the air rung with cheer on cheer" as the train bowled in and pulled to a stop. "Mr. Lincoln left the car, moving rapidly through the crowd, shaking hands vigorously, and incurring embraces and blessings." Already the assistant secretary was impressed. "No one could witness this frank, hearty display of enthusiasm and affection on the one side, and cordial, generous fraternity on the other," Hay wrote for the *New York World*, "without recognizing in the tall, stalwart Illinoisan the genuine Son of the West, as perfectly *en rapport* with its people now, with his purple honors and his imperial cares upon him, as when he was the simple advocate, the kindly neighbor, the beloved and respected citizen. Having spent his life in the very heart of the mighty West, having mingled with its people for a lifetime, the sympathy between the constituent and the elect is as perfect as that between near kindred."

Along most of the long journey unfolding, from Springfield almost to the end of its roundabout route along two thousand miles through seven states and eleven days to the nation's capital, the crowds proved large and enthusiastic. Americans wanted to lay eyes on the one-time farmer, former riverboat man, failed storekeeper, surveyor, and one-term member of the House of Representatives, on this prairie lawyer so suddenly elevated to the highest office in the land. Honest Abe the Rail-Splitter: invitations had been extended to him from state capitals—from Indianapolis, Columbus, Albany, Trenton, Harrisburg, each one accepted—and the presidential party would stop at other cities, towns, and villages as well. As at this present stop, at Decatur, where the crowd had come from a distance on foot and on horseback, in buggies, wagons, and carriages, so many as couldn't all expect to hear, just see, just be there and catch a glimpse when the train passed through. In days ahead they would read in their newspapers and be moved by Mr. Lincoln's farewell remarks at Springfield; they may have seen a photograph of him, or a chromolithograph of a portrait; but they wanted to be part of history and lay eyes on the new president in person. As at tiny Tolono, the next stop, where cannon boomed and the flag-waving, handkerchief-waving multitude erupted in cheers of their own. Amid such fanfare, the presidential train passed the state line into Indiana around noon, crowds at village stations all along the way, and by five that afternoon it was pulling into Indianapolis.

Yet of those first hours "the gloom of parting with neighbors and friends," Hay tells us, "of bidding farewell to the community in the midst of which he has lived for a quarter of a century, seemed to rest upon the President during the greater part of the day. He was abstracted, sad, thoughtful, and spent much of his time in the private car appropriated to his use." At the Indianapolis depot the party was greeted by a thirty-four-gun salute for each of the states in the Union (Oregon and Kansas having recently been added), and by Governor Morton with a procession that included both chambers of the Indiana legislature, various civic dignitaries, and volunteer firemen to escort their honored guest—Mr. Lincoln uncovered in the barouche and "bowing to the cheering multitudes"—to the Bates House, for festivities and overnight rest.

So it went. After supper and a speech that evening, breakfast at the hotel next morning, although necessarily brief, "was brilliant, convivial, and elegant. Mr. Lincoln," Hay records, "charmed all whom he met with his graceful *bonhomie*, his quaint western wit and his adroit repartee. He has shaken off the despondency which was noticed during the first day's journey, and now, as his friends say, looks and talks like himself." Mrs. Lincoln, with little Willie and Tad, arrived by special train by mid-morning, and at eleven the journey resumed. "All the towns along the route were gayly decorated with flags and streamers; in some places guns were fired, and the train seemed to ride upon the crest of one continued wave of cheers." Reaching Cincinnati by 3 P.M. of the second day out, Mr. Lincoln was escorted to the Burnet House in a carriage drawn by six horses, along streets "populous as the cities of the Orient. Every window was thronged, every balcony glittered with bright colors and fluttered with handkerchiefs; the sidewalks were packed; even the ledges and cornices of the houses swarmed with intrepid lookers-on."

The reception in Cincinnati was, Hay tells us, "a thorough and magnificent success." And the warmth and enthusiasm continued, in Columbus, in Pittsburgh, in Cleveland, in Euclid, Wickliffe, Willoughby, Painesville—

vociferous, joyful crowds all along. At Westfield, Mr. Lincoln asked if among his hearers was the young lady who had written him as a candidate that he should grow a beard. "There was a momentary commotion, in the midst of which an old man, struggling through the crowd, approached, leading his daughter, a girl of apparently twelve or thirteen years of age." She was eleven, Grace Bedell, and the candidate's note answering her from Springfield, October 19, 1860, survives: "My dear little Miss . . ." Now here in her home village, "Mr. Lincoln stooped down and kissed the child, and talked with her for some minutes," on his compliant chin the beard of four months' growth that she had suggested he cultivate. Then on to Ashtabula, to Girard, "where a profound sensation was created by the sudden, unscheduled appearance of Mr. Horace Greeley," wearing his familiar white coat, carrying the yellow bag that bore his name in letters large enough that they "might be read across Lake Erie." The editor of the *New York Tribune* expressed chagrin at having mistaken this special train for the general one, but Secretary Nicolay led him at once to the president's car, where the great editor met Mrs. Lincoln for the first time and rode on with Mr. Lincoln, of whose Republican Party Greeley, according to Hay, "was one of the most powerful and least judicious supporters." When the train next stopped, at Erie, the *Tribune* editor disappeared as mysteriously as he had arrived, leaving behind him "an amusing topic of conversation during the rest of the journey."

The train pulled into Buffalo at 5 P.M. to a welcome "unprecedented in the history of popular gatherings in this part of the country. It is estimated that at least seventy-five thousand persons must have participated in the turbulent ceremonials which greeted the arrival of the President elect." Here and elsewhere: dignitaries, deputations, processions, legislatures to address, dinners to partake of, balconies to speak from, torchlight parades, bonfires, fireworks, ladies' levees to appear before—festivities everywhere, and all the while pushing ever forward. A very early departure from Buffalo next morning, on to Albany, and always the "wild arrival of crowds past which we are whirled" en route. "The echo of acclamation scarcely dying behind us, before that far onward breaks upon our ears. But," our reporter observes late in the journey, "any iteration whatever wearies at length. Crowds are singularly alike. They are always seen from an elevated point of view, dotted with a bright, almost tropical arabesque of color, and they always bellow. They invariably call for speeches, and then make such a row that the speaker's voice is inaudible. They are curiously wavy and undulating, like tides which rise and fall." And, having dealt with one, and the next, and the next, and the next, the train chugs onward, its passengers increasingly fatigued—all of them, apparently, except for Mr. Lincoln—through New York City, Jersey City, Trenton, Philadelphia and a flag-raising ceremony at Independence Hall, on to Harrisburg. And here at last a change.

In the capital of Pennsylvania on February 22, 1861: "All along the route from Philadelphia," Hay reports, "and especially at Lancaster, receptions seemed more the result of curiosity than enthusiasm. Even at Harrisburg, not one man in a hundred cheered. The crowds everywhere were uniformly rough, unruly, and ill bred." And that same night, a "drunken, fighting, noisy crowd infested the city all the evening, cheering, calling for 'Old Abe,' and giving him all sorts of unmelodious serenades. No terms are too severe to characterize the conduct of the crowd about the hotel and the arrangements there."

But what a journey it had been until then! The diligent scholar Harold Holzer has counted out the achievement: more than 1,900 miles covered on eighteen different railroad lines, the president-elect having delivered no fewer than 101 known (if intentionally uninformative) speeches along the way, including addresses to legislatures in five state capitals and briefer remarks at depots, in hotel lobbies, from balconies, from train platforms, and as part of at least twenty-four parades and processions, in addition to shaking thousands of hands at more than a dozen formal receptions and appearing in the flesh before perhaps three-quarters of a million people. An unprecedented feat, and an astounding test of endurance, which Mr. Lincoln appeared to be thriving on.

Ahead of him, between here and the party's arrival at Washington, lay only Baltimore and Annapolis. But those two cities were in the slaveholding state of Maryland, which had given Lincoln less than 3 percent of its vote last November—and more recently no invitation for the president-elect to visit on his way east, from either the mayor of Baltimore or the governor in Annapolis. Now, here in Harrisburg, Detective Pinkerton, hired by the Philadelphia, Wilmington & Baltimore Railroad to assure the safety of the presidential party, was reporting darkly of an assassination plot laid athwart the tracks ahead. Mr. Lincoln didn't credit it. Despite numerous scrawled, often semi-literate and obscene death threats amid the piles of mail that Secretary Nicolay had lately been dealing with, no president had ever been assassinated; it wasn't in the American character. Yet independent sources confirmed such a plan: Maryland had assaulted local Republican candidates during the fall, and even now gangs of plug-uglies were massing in Baltimore, making ready. Reluctantly Lincoln acceded to his advisors' urgings. With Pinkerton and a bodyguard he slipped out of his Harrisburg hotel, boarded a sleeper well before the presidential train was due to depart, changed at Philadelphia, and on a different train reached Baltimore in the early hours, there to have his railroad car detached and pulled by horses over tracks the slow, vulnerable way across town from one depot to another, to be hooked up to yet one more train and dispatched toward the nation's capital. Thus, covertly, at daybreak on Saturday, February 23, 1861, twelve hours ahead of schedule, Abraham Lincoln, undetected in a felt hat and borrowed overcoat, hunching to reduce his height, arrived at Washington aswirl in rumor, mistrust, and fear. Five days earlier (as the long train journey just ended was traveling between Buffalo and Albany), Jefferson Davis, colonel of the Mississippi Rifles in the Mexican War, former U.S. secretary of war, former senator from Mississippi, had stood on the steps of Alabama's capitol building in Montgomery and taken the oath as president of the newly formed Confederate States of America.

4. INAUGURATION

As soon as the Republican Lincoln won election to the White House, in late 1860, South Carolina had moved to leave the Union. Delegates to a convention in Charleston on December 20 unanimously approved an Ordinance of Secession: the Palmetto State, the *Charleston Mercury* exulted at the time, "has resumed her entire sovereign powers, and, unshackled, has become one of the nations of the earth." Mississippi followed South Carolina's defiant lead on January 9, 1861, Florida on the tenth, Alabama on the eleventh, Georgia on the nineteenth, Louisiana on the twenty-sixth, and Texas on the first of February—in those fast-moving days hardly a fortnight before Jefferson Davis was inaugurated provisional president of the new, now seven-state Confederacy.

But what else could the South do? Back in 1787, six sovereign states from Maryland to Georgia had voluntarily united with the other former British colonies in signing the Constitution; and from that bright beginning in an agrarian world, the plantation economy below the Mason-Dixon Line had prospered. Its sons and daughters crossed the Alleghenies and settled lands to the west. Its legislators thrived in the halls of the U.S. Congress. Its fields of rice, tobacco, and cotton flourished, and the great waterways of the Mississippi Valley flowing generally north to south through the heart of the continent transported wealth that bade fair to make New Orleans at the Gulf of Mexico the commercial capital of the Western Hemisphere.

In those earlier times South and North had been, as it were, equal partners in the American enterprise. But that had changed. By 1820 textile factories

had risen in New England, in imitation of those in old England. Both loca-
tions provided markets for southern cotton, but the new industries here at
home rapidly multiplied eastern wealth. Within five years New York had
opened the Erie Canal and a waterborne passage west to east that diverted
some of the profits previously flowing south along the Mississippi. By the
1840s traffic on rivers and canals was giving way to the newfangled railroads,
twice as many miles of rail being laid in the more densely populated North
than in the rural, more leisurely South. The money made in building those
rails, like the money made manufacturing cotton clothing, found its way to
bankers in the East, specifically in New York City at the mouth of the Hudson,
into which the Erie Canal continued to pour its lucrative trade. Planters down
South had to go where the money was, to bankers up North, to meet their
expenses at seedtime, running up debts that they hoped to pay off when the
harvest came in. And the new wealth in the East could advocate successfully
for high tariff walls to protect its young industries from foreign competition—
exactly what the South didn't want, with its cotton to sell overseas and its taste
for overseas manufactured goods now bearing the additional costs that tariffs
imposed.

Moreover, increasingly, the North had grown hostile to slavery, the peculiar
institution on which the southern economy depended. As early as 1808 Americans were barred from participating in the African slave trade. By the late
1830s northerners were organizing to help shelter slaves who had fled the
labor they owed to their southern masters. The Compromise of 1850, while
continuing to tolerate slavery in the District of Columbia, had shut down the
slave trade there as a blight on the nation's capital. And despite the finding of
the Supreme Court in the *Dred Scott* decision of 1857—that slaves were not
citizens and had none of the rights or privileges of citizens (and, besides, the
Constitution granted the federal government no authority to ban slavery from
the western territories)—here came the Black Republican Lincoln, sneaking
into Washington at 6 A.M. one recent Saturday morning, bound for the White
House via Willard's Hotel and bearing planks of a party platform that not only
would bar slavery from entering those western territories that the Supreme
Court had unequivocally opened it up to but also would confine the institution
to states where it currently existed. The South needed no crystal ball to foretell
a Republican future. Soon, slavery would be outlawed altogether in the District of Columbia. Next, owners would be told they couldn't move their slaves
from state to state down South. Then, southern ordinances sanctioning slavery
would be declared unconstitutional. And from there slavery would be abolished in all the states of the Union.

What were southerners to do? One by one, through January 1861 and into early February, states in a South that had voluntarily joined the Union after 1787 clamorously withdrew from it. In mid-February they set up a nation of their own: a confederacy of sovereign states that protected the institution of slavery in perpetuity and that had its own constitution, its capital at Montgomery, and its president: Jefferson Davis of Mississippi. Not long after, travelers passing through the South reached Washington to tell of the excitement encountered on their way: the widespread fervor in the new nation, southern regiments and brigades forming down there, its soldiers drilling.

The Washington that learned of such doings was itself a southern city, most of its inhabitants Virginians and Marylanders, slaveholders among them, the land it sat on donated by the latter state. In 1860 Washington's population was somewhere around seventy thousand people, on the verge of wartime a figure soon to be augmented—to as high as two hundred thousand—by the opportunities that a new political party in power offered. Office-seekers in droves, politicians, lobbyists, jobbers, sharpers imposing on the transients, adventurers, speculators, blacks fleeing northward, soldiers, and too soon the wounded and caregivers all flooding in: all that human deluge lay not far ahead. For now, however, Abraham Lincoln was seated beside his predecessor, the feckless, aged Democrat James Buchanan of Pennsylvania, self-styled Old Public Functionary, two passengers in an open black carriage in this half-formed city of magnificent distances, riding mostly in silence along Pennsylvania Avenue from Willard's on their way to Capitol Hill. It was March 4, 1861, Monday, rain earlier having given way to sunshine and increasing mildness by noon. At the east portico of the Capitol, under the unfinished dome through which a crane protruded, Mr. Lincoln stood on the inaugural platform before a crowd of perhaps ten thousand gathered in the plaza below. He was looking for a surface on which to rest his stovepipe hat. Among the dignitaries behind him sat Senator Stephen A. Douglas, who reached forward and took the hat and held it for the incoming president throughout what immediately followed. Ancient Roger Taney of slaveholding Maryland, chief justice of the Supreme Court since 1836, author of the lengthy *Dred Scott* decision that our times have come to regard as the worst ever handed down by that august body, awaited the end of the address when he would administer, as he had for six predecessors, the oath of office to Abraham Lincoln as sixteenth president. "Fellow citizens of the United States," the ungainly westerner was beginning in his tenor voice with its curious pronunciations, "In compliance with a custom as old as the government itself, I appear before you to address you briefly, and to take, in your presence, the oath prescribed by the Constitution of the United States."

The speaker didn't intend, he said, to discuss this afternoon matters "about which there is no special anxiety, or excitement." Rather, he would speak of what was on everybody's mind: fears among southerners that a Republican administration endangered "their property, and their peace, and personal security." Such fears had no basis in fact. Mr. Lincoln's views were amply on record, as in an earlier speech from which he now quoted: "I have no purpose, directly or indirectly, to interfere with the institution of slavery in the states where it exists. I believe I have no lawful right to do so, and I have no inclination to do so." He read, as well, from the platform of the Republican Party: "*Resolved*. That the maintenance inviolate of the rights of the States, and especially the right of each State to order and control its own domestic institutions according to its own judgment exclusively, is essential to that balance of power on which the perfection and endurance of our political fabric depends, and we denounce the lawless invasion by armed force of the soil of any state or Territory, no matter under what pretext, as among the gravest of crimes."

Even so, and bearing in mind the precedent that seventy-two years and fifteen distinguished predecessors since the inauguration of the first president have provided, "I now enter upon the same task," the speaker continued, "for the brief constitutional term of four years, under great and peculiar difficulty. A disruption of the Federal Union heretofore only menaced, is now formidably attempted," rebellion against the lawful government at Washington in fact and uniquely under way.

Yet, Lincoln insisted, the Union remains perpetual. No government would provide for its own end. Thus, under our Constitution, "the Union will endure forever—it being impossible to destroy it, except by some action not provided for in the instrument itself." But even if the Union were no more than an association of states, merely a contractual arrangement, a contract cannot be negated, the tall lawyer at the lectern argued, "by less than all the parties who made it." One party may break the contract, but all are required lawfully to rescind it. Anyway, our present Union was formed not by the Constitutional Convention of 1787, which the South says it voluntarily joined and can thus leave at will, but by the earlier Articles of Association in 1774, by the Declaration of Independence in 1776, and by the Articles of Confederation in 1778, with "the faith of all the then thirteen States expressly plighted and engaged that it should be perpetual." Thus, "no State, upon its own mere motion, can lawfully get out of the Union."

Accordingly, "to the extent of my abilities," the incoming president vowed, "I shall take care, as the Constitution expressly enjoins upon me, that the laws of the Union be faithfully executed in all the States." There need be no violence accompanying this resolve, and there will be none unless forced upon the national authority. "The power confided to me," Lincoln reassured the nation, "will be used to hold, occupy, and possess the property, and places belonging to the government, and to collect the duties and imposts, but beyond what may be necessary for these objects, there will be no invasion—no using of force against, or among the people anywhere."

He had not quite finished. Some, the speaker granted, may be bent upon destroying the Union; "if there be such, I need address no word to them. To those, however, who really love the Union may I not speak?" Will you risk so desperate a step "while there is any possibility that any portion of the ills you fly from, have no real existence? Will you, while certain ills you fly to"—a civil war and its horrific consequences—"are greater than all the real ones you fly from? Will you risk the commission of so fearful a mistake?"

Whatever the event, the chief executive derives his power from the people, "and they have conferred none upon him to fix terms for the separation of the States. The people themselves can do this also if they choose, but the executive, as such, has nothing to do with it. His duty is to administer the present government, as it came to his hands, and to transmit it, unimpaired by him, to his successor." Thus: "In *your* hands, my dissatisfied fellow countrymen, and not in *mine*, is the momentous issue of civil war." The South had registered no oath in Heaven to destroy the Constitution, "while *I* shall have the most solemn one to 'preserve, protect and defend' it."

He had clarified his policy for all to hear—since Election Day way back in November having declined, while not yet in office, to do so further than was evident in his public utterances and writings already on record. Yet something else felt needed at the last. Earlier Lincoln had shown his inaugural speech to a few close associates, one of them his archrival for the Republican nomination last May in Chicago, Senator Seward of New York. Seward, whom the president-elect (in a typically generous yet shrewd gesture) had since chosen to be his secretary of state, felt that a concluding, conciliatory paragraph was called for. Perhaps along these lines? The New Yorker jotted down his thoughts: "I close. We are not we must not be aliens or enemies but fellow countrymen and brethren. Although passion has strained our bonds of affection too hardly they must not, I am sure they will not be broken. The mystic chords which proceeding from so many battle fields and so many patriot graves pass through all the hearts and all the hearths in this broad continent of ours will yet again harmonize in their ancient music when breathed upon by the guardian angel of the nation."

Lincoln had attended to the recommendation, saw the justice of the impulse, took Seward's awkward prose and transmuted it—this self-taught prairie lawyer—into an eloquence rarely matched in all the pages of our history. "I am loth to close," he told the multitude gathered around him at the capitol on that fateful March afternoon.

> We are not enemies, but friends. We must not be enemies. Though passion may have strained, it must not break our bonds of affection. The mystic chords of memory, stretching from every battle-field, and patriot grave, to every living heart and hearthstone, all over this broad land, will yet swell the chorus of the Union, when again touched, as surely they will be, by the better angels of our nature.

5. WARTIME

President Lincoln's private secretary, John G. Nicolay, wrote to his fiancée, Therena Bates, back in Pittsfield, Illinois, on March 5: "As you see from the heading of my letter, I am fairly installed in the 'White House.' We had a gratifying and glorious inauguration yesterday—a fine day, and a fine display and everything went off as nicely as it could have possibly been devised." But, as with so many others just then, Therena was more likely interested in news of the crisis down South, concerning which, even a full month later, Nicolay remained reassuring. Despite all the current talk of war, "which the newspapers and the gossiping public insist is near at hand," his love need not worry, he reported on April 7. Oh, a "brush at Charleston or Pensacola is quite possible but that any general hostilities will result from it I have not the least fear." And four days further on, on April 11: "Don't," Nicolay persisted, "get alarmed at the 'rumors of war' which you hear from this direction." He assured Miss Bates out in Illinois that most of it was mere idle talk—an insight from the seat of federal power offered on the very eve (as it turned out) of an early morning in South Carolina, in Charleston Harbor, where Fort Sumter came under vigorous assault. Shelling had erupted at 4:30 A.M.: fifty rebel cannons firing from all sides at federal troops trapped at dawn in their island fortress, an initial engagement that, thirty-four hours later, forced the ill-supplied Union garrison to surrender and evacuate the premises.

War had begun. "On the 12th day of April, 1861," President Lincoln noted in recapitulation, "the insurgents committed the flagrant act of civil war by the bombardment and capture of Fort Sumter, which cut off the hope of immediate conciliation." For an attentive Congress a year later, the Chief Executive went on to summarize what had followed. Immediately after the shelling, "all the roads and avenues to this city were obstructed, and the capital was put into the position of a siege. The mails in every direction were stopped, and the lines of telegraph cut off by the insurgents, and military and naval forces, which had been called out by the government for the defence of Washington, were prevented from reaching the city by organized and combined treasonable resistance in the State of Maryland." That state, rife with secessionists, all but surrounded the capital, a city full of disloyalty anyhow, where southern army officers were hastily resigning and heading off to fight against the Union. The army was in a bad way to start with, only sixteen thousand strong, most of those under the command of southerners and spread along far-flung borders or dealing with Indians out West as far away as California.

Near at hand, Virginia just across the Potomac—wealthiest and most populous of the southern states—resounded, as did Maryland, with rebel clamor. Lincoln must act promptly. By a proclamation dated three days after the first shell fell on Sumter, the president summoned forth "the militia of the several States of the Union, to the aggregate number of seventy-five thousand, in order to suppress" combinations, as he called them, grown too powerful to be dealt with otherwise, "and to cause the laws to be duly executed." But Virginia rejected such a levy outright, flatly refusing to fill its assigned quota or to provide any fighting men at all. "Your object," its governor John Letcher instructed the secretary of war in Washington via a response dated April 16, the day after receiving Lincoln's proclamation, "is to subjugate the Southern States, and a requisition made upon me for such an object"—which Governor Letcher deemed unconstitutional in any case—"will not be complied with. You have chosen to inaugurate civil war, and, having done so, we will meet it in a spirit as determined as the administration has exhibited toward the South." Two days later the Old Dominion, the Mother of Presidents, left the Union, followed in weeks just ahead by Arkansas, Tennessee, and North Carolina. Eleven states that included Virginia now constituted this enlarged Confederacy, its capital moved forthwith from Montgomery north to Richmond, a mere ninety-five miles from the federal capital. Exuberant rebels meanwhile were taking possession of the arsenal at Harpers Ferry, Virginia—federals having blown up as much as they could before abandoning it—and of the abandoned naval base at Norfolk. Elsewhere throughout the South, insurgents set about appropriating ships, occupying forts, taking charge of customhouses, and commandeering federal weapons wherever they found them.

Northern states by then had responded to the president's call for volunteers with a zeal that led everywhere to quotas handsomely oversubscribed, as exultation raged on both sides in those early days: both sides complacent, amid their bonfires, patriotic speeches, songs and shouts and high hearts, with the North reveling in prospects of prompt vengeance for the outrage of Sumter and the South glorying, as one Richmond newspaper exclaimed, in the triumph "of truth and justice over wrong and attempted insult," evidenced by this spontaneous uprising against the northern oppressor, so that soon "the Southern wind will sweep away with the resistless force of a tornado, all vestige of sympathy or desire of co-operation with a tyrant who, under false pretences, in the name of a once glorious, but now broken and destroyed Union, attempts to rivet on us the chains of a despicable and ignoble vassalage."

During those same frenetic, bombastic days, Hay and Nicolay found work and distractions enough wherever they looked. The secretaries shared sleeping quarters upstairs in a room in the White House in the northeast corner opposite the president's office. Nicolay had an office of his own across the hall, and Hay a smaller one adjoining. Now throughout the long workday, in the stairs, corridors, and anterooms, they dealt with anxious petitioners of all stripes, who pushed forward, jostling, calling out for notice, importunate to lay their appeals or warnings or counsel before the president. The Teutonic Nicolay, twenty-nine, served as stern gatekeeper, Hay at twenty-two as more the diplomat, charged with venturing forth into the crowds to summon or, as needed, turn away visitors with gentle words that sought to leave feelings unbruised. So it went from morning to night, until Nicolay convinced the Chief, the Ancient, the Tycoon (as he and his friend Hay variously, privately referred to the president) to cut back overgenerous, day-long visiting hours to the more manageable length of from ten in the morning to three in the afternoon, soon—still overwhelmed—from ten to one. And all the while letters poured in, piles of them for the secretaries to sort out, read, distribute as appropriate, respond to as instructed, the sifted excess finally to be burned as a barrier to mosquitoes beyond the mansion's southern lawn, down toward the undeveloped flats and marsh and river and fetid canal.

As the president saw it, his initial task was threefold: to "defend Washington: Blockade the Ports: and retake Government property." The last named, pertaining to federal forts that the South had seized, would have to wait a while; but the rebel ports could be ordered closed at once, still in April, by proclamation on the 19th, even before Washington was secure. Thus, Charleston, Savannah, and the other such southern coastal cities were soon to feel the pinch of trade denied, no ships with their cargoes allowed in or out. Yet up the Potomac, hemmed in by rebellion, the other side's capital was subjected to the same pinch. "Housekeepers here are beginning to dread famine," Hay recorded on Monday, April 22. "Flour has made a sudden spring to $18.00 a bl and corn meal . . . $2.50 a bushel." Politicians were getting a taste of hardship as well: Willard's Hotel had trimmed its dinner menu, Hay added, and limited teatime refreshments to pound cake only.

But soon Washington learned that relief was on the way, from the newly formed Sixth Massachusetts Volunteer Militia, although those New England infantrymen would have to pass through Maryland to get here. Such a route caused Baltimore's mayor and the state's governor at Annapolis both to warn of dire consequences if, during the present crisis, Yankee boots trod Maryland soil. Still the volunteers came on; and in the streets of Baltimore on April 19 a jeering, bawling, armed secessionist mob assailed them. Shots rang out, and at least four soldiers and nine townsmen lay dead at the end of the mêlée, many more wounded—the first blood spilled, the first casualties of the Civil War (about where an assassination plot against President-elect Lincoln was said to have lain in wait two months earlier, and on precisely the date eighty-six years before when blood had first flowed, at Lexington and Concord, in the American Revolution). During this later day, the battered Massachusetts reinforcements did pass on through, and New York's Seventh Regiment reached Washington soon after, on the morning of the 25th, ending (as Nicolay noted) "a very anxious suspense we had been in, ever since last Sunday," through six long, uncertain days and nights. "We had during all that time but about 2000 men in the City that we could really *count on.*" Another three thousand were under arms, but—amid rumors of the enemy massing over the southern horizon—no one could trust that lot not to turn their weapons on Unionists if rebels charged the capital. Now though, by Sunday the 26th, more loyal regiments were reported to have skirted Baltimore and arrived at Annapolis heading south, so that "we shall have no trouble," Nicolay was able to report, "either to keep a communication open or to get a sufficient number of men here to place the safety of the Capitol beyond a doubt."

Days ahead saw Union confidence rising, as the blockade of federal ships formed and took station off the southern coast, as foreign powers withheld recognition of this new so-called Confederate States of America, and as the supply of northern recruits grew larger. The raw Army of Northeastern Virginia, as it came to be called, encamped on Washington's outskirts through the late spring and early summer of 1861 to drill and learn to be soldiers. By July the troops appeared more or less battle-ready. They would meet a force (presumably no better prepared) that the rebels had gathered together twenty-five miles southwest near Manassas Junction, by a stream called Bull Run, where Yanks meant to thrash those unseasoned southern farm boys, then march on to Richmond and put a prompt end to the uprising.

John Hay, in his role as occasional journalist, reported for the press on what happened there, then. It was high summer, before dawn of July 21, 1861. Townspeople had come out to see. "The solemn midnight march of the grand army across the Potomac," Hay wrote at the time, "roused an intensity of feeling and expectancy. The popular heart was moved to its deepest depths. The marching regiments so long encamped here were cheered on their departure with a lusty enthusiasm and hopefulness unprecedented in war annals." Civilians on hand presumed it was the start of brilliant victories, "that the enemy would be routed from their fastnesses among the mountainous ravines and glens, their cannon captured, and intrenchments demolished." Sure enough: "At an early hour in the morning the thundering roar of the distant artillery was first heard." Spectators lingering at the camp felt the thrill. "Senators, congressmen, heads of departments, and civilians of every rank and degree showed eagerness to go to the battle field." Many set out on horseback, in carriages, afoot, some with picnic baskets. Others waited anxiously where they were, through the morning into the afternoon, until early reports came in at last: "the enemy completely routed. This caused universal demonstrations of delight."

But in time word arrived that tempered the jubilation, turned it into astonishment and dismay and grief and shame. "It was terrible," Hay reported, "to witness the effect" that this later, more reliable account produced far and wide. The following day furnished a "continuation of the excitement of yesterday although different in kind," in the aftermath of major armies North and South clashing for the first time, at Bull Run. "There was never such a day here before—it is to be hoped there will never be such another. With the ushering in of daylight there came pouring into the city crowds of soldiers, some with muskets, some without muskets, some with knapsacks, and some without knapsack, or canteen, or anything but their soiled and dirty uniform, burned faces and eyes, that looked as they had seen no sleep for days, to indicate that they were soldiers." Wagons followed the vanquished from the battlefield, one by one, "filled with the dead and wounded. Most horrible were the sights presented to view, and never to be forgotten by those who witnessed them. The bodies of the dead," Hay writes, "were piled on top of one another; the pallid faces and blood-stained garments telling a fearfully mute but sad story of the horrors of war. And the appearance of the wounded, bereft of arms, of legs, eyes put out, flesh wounds in the face and body, and uniforms crimsoned with blood." Civilians clustered around each wagon, "and those of the wounded who were able to talk were questioned as to the incidents of the battle. To the hospital the crowd followed, and it was with difficulty the physicians in attendance could keep them back, so earnest were many to learn the fate of relatives and friends."

Brigadier General Irvin McDowell, commanding the Union army so soundly mauled yesterday, would be replaced; and the figure generally agreed on to lead the chastened troops, in a war that was clearly to last longer than anyone had foreseen, was Major General George B. McClellan. Young at thirty-four, near the top of his class at West Point, Mexican War veteran, chief engineer and vice president of the Illinois Central Railroad in peacetime, McClellan had reentered the service at the start of the present crisis and led troops in western Virginia through a couple of skirmishes to early, rare, and much welcomed victories, thus winning wide acclaim. Lincoln summoned this commander of the Department of the Ohio to Washington and, to broad approval, gave him the higher command. And that summer and fall of 1861, the general did wonders with his renamed Army of the Potomac, elevating morale while shaping his soldiers into a sharp, well-trained, and disciplined force, in the process earning their devotion as the ranks grew from 50,000 in July to 168,000 by November.

But Little Mac, as his men called him affectionately—the Young Napoleon—had his failings. He was vain, overly cautious (accepting intelligence that wildly exaggerated the strength of the enemy), and much better at logistical tasks relating to organization than as a commander in the field. Moreover, he was frequently scornful of his superiors to the point of insubordination. Lincoln consulted with his general often, McClellan having a home near the White House; and in the historically priceless diary that John Hay kept (if not always faithfully) through the war, the president's secretary reports on those consultations, as on November 1, 1861: "we went over to McClellans," Hay and the president, on an occasion when the general, having built up Washington's defenses and reorganized his demoralized veterans of Bull Run into a first-rate fighting force, was promoted to general in chief of all the Union armies. "In addition to your present command," Lincoln remarked during that visit, "the supreme command of the army will entail a vast labor upon you." Hay records McClellan's response to assuming overall command of the western theater as well as the eastern: "I can do it all," the young leader answered coolly.

Twelve days later, Hay described another such call, on Wednesday, November 13. "I wish here to record what I consider a portent of evil to come," he wrote. "The President, Governor Seward and I went over to McClellan's house tonight. The Servant at the door said the General was at the wedding of Col. Wheaton at General Buell's, and would soon return. We went in, and after we had waited about an hour McC. came in and without paying any particular attention to the porter who told him the President was waiting to see him, went up stairs," passing the doorway beyond which his guests were seated. "They waited about half-an-hour, and sent once more a servant to tell the General they were there, and the answer came that the General had gone to bed." Hay adds: "I merely record this unparrallelled insolence of epaulettes without comment"—though he does note that it is the first instance encountered "of the threatened supremacy of the military authorities." On the way back to the White House, "I spoke to the President about the matter," the diarist continues, "but he seemed not to have noticed it specially, saying it was better at this time not to be making points of etiquette & personal dignity."

Some ninety years further along, during the Korean War, a president in a similar situation behaved differently. Never having seen the five-star general, Harry Truman came on October 15, 1950, to confer in person with Douglas MacArthur at Wake Island in the Pacific. President Truman later recalled that the two shook hands on the tarmac and arranged a meeting. "I got there on time, but he was forty-five minutes late, and this meeting—it was just between the two of us you understand." The tardiness had left the president seething. When MacArthur finally entered, "I took one look at him and I said, 'Now you look here. I've come halfway across the world to meet you, but don't worry about that. I just want you to know I don't give a good goddamn what you do or think about Harry Truman, but don't you ever again keep your Commander in Chief waiting. Is that clear?'" According to Truman's recollection, the general's "face got as red as a beet, but he said, he indicated that he understood what I was talking about, and we went on from there." From then on, MacArthur "was just like a little puppy at that meeting. I don't know which was worse, the way he acted in public or the way he kissed my ass at that meeting."

We might have welcomed some such forceful response to McClellan's outrageous snub on a November evening in 1861. But in the midst of all the burdens of his office, and the griefs (not far ahead, the nearly twenty-four thousand casualties at Shiloh in April 1862 and the costly and demoralizing failure of McClellan's Peninsular Campaign to take Richmond and end the war that same spring and summer), Lincoln was unwavering, and never averse to speaking bluntly when he felt the occasion called for it. In those same grim months, for instance, to Major General Hunter, on December 31, 1861: "Dear Sir: Yours of the 23rd. is received, and I am constrained to say it is difficult to answer so ugly a letter in good temper." To McClellan on March 31, 1862, after issuing an order that he knew the general would resent: "If you could know the full pressure of the case, I am confident you would justify it—even beyond a mere acknowledgment that the Commander-in-chief, may order what he pleases." To McClellan again, on April 9, 1862: "And, once more let me tell you, it is indispensable to *you* that you strike a blow. . . . I beg to assure you that I have never written you, or spoken to you, in greater kindness of feeling than now, nor with a fuller purpose to sustain you, so far as in my most anxious judgment, I consistently can. *But you must act.*" To the governor and state treasurer of Illinois, who had solicited a promotion for a constituent, on April 10, 1862: "I fully appreciate Gen. Pope's splendid achievements with their invaluable results; but you must know that Major Generalships in the Regular Army, are not as plenty as blackberries." To the ever fretting and dilatory McClellan, yet again, on May 1, 1862: "Your call for Parrott guns from Washington alarms me—chiefly because it argues indefinite procrastination. Is anything to be done?" Again to McClellan, on May 25: "I think the time is near when you must either attack Richmond or give up the job and come to the defence of Washington. Let me hear from you instantly." (He did.) And on July 26, to Reverdy Johnson, who had forwarded complaints about the Union General Phelps's harsh military rule in New Orleans. Those afflicted "know the remedy—know how to be cured of General Phelps. Remove the necessity of his presence. And might it not be well for them to consider whether they have not already had *time* enough to do this? If they can conceive of anything worse than General Phelps, within my power," Lincoln wrote, "would they not better be looking out for it? They very well know the way to avert all this is simply to take their place in the Union upon the old terms. If they will not do this, should they not receive harder blows rather than lighter ones?"

One more example of this man's way of speaking plainly: his iron fist in a velvet glove, as Lincoln biographer Carl Sandburg put it: Washington, August 22, 1862. To Hon. Horace Greeley. "Dear Sir, I have just read yours of the 10th, addressed to myself through the New York Tribune." The president was responding to an open letter in that influential newspaper headed "The Prayer of Twenty Millions." The editor had begun peremptorily: "I do not intrude to tell you," wrote Greeley, "—for you must know already—that a great proportion of those who triumphed in your election, and of all who desire the unqualified suppression of the rebellion now desolating our country, are sorely disappointed and deeply pained by the policy you seem to be pursuing with regard to the slaves of rebels. I write only to set succinctly and unmistakably before you what we require, what we think we have a right to expect, and of what we complain." Lincoln's ire had risen as he read on. Editor Greeley's open letter was accusing the president of being "strangely and disastrously remiss in the discharge of your official and imperative duty" to free the slaves. "Had you, sir, in your Inaugural Address, unmistakably given notice that, in case the rebellion already commenced, were persisted in, and your efforts to preserve the Union and enforce the laws should be resisted by armed force, you would recognize no loyal person as rightfully held in Slavery by a traitor, we believe the rebellion would therein have received a staggering if not fatal blow."

Greeley went on with considerably more of the same, which was based, Lincoln knew, on inaccurate facts and ill-informed inferences, the whole put forward in a tone that was obnoxious. Yet hear his response to it, which says all that, but deftly. I have read yours of the 10th, he wrote to Greeley, and "If there be in it any statements, or assumptions of fact, which I may know to be erroneous, I do not, now and here, controvert them. If there be in it any inferences which I may believe to be falsely drawn, I do not now and here, argue against them. If there be perceptable in it an impatient and dictatorial tone, I waive it in deference to an old friend, whose heart I have always supposed to be right. As to the policy I 'seem to be pursuing' as you say, I have not meant to leave any one in doubt. I would save the Union."

Would save it—Lincoln went on—under the Constitution, in "the shortest way" I can. If some would not save the Union unless they could at the same time preserve slavery, "I do not agree with them." If others would not save the Union unless they could destroy slavery, "I do not agree with them. My paramount object in this struggle *is* to save the Union, and is *not* either to save or to destroy slavery. If I could save the Union without freeing *any* slave I would do it, and if I could save it by freeing *all* the slaves I would do it; and if I could save it by freeing some and leaving others alone I would also do that." Could a policy be laid out more clearly? "I shall try," the president added, "to correct errors when shown to be errors; and I shall adopt new views as fast as they shall appear to be true views." That said: "I have here stated my purpose according to my view of *official* duty; and I intend no modification of my oft-expressed *personal* wish that all men every where could be free. Yours, A. LINCOLN."

Lincoln's reply, which appeared in the *Tribune*, was widely read. What his letter didn't say was that, precisely one month earlier, on July 22, 1862, he had shown his Cabinet, not for their approval—he was not seeking that—but only for their information, his initial draft of the Emancipation Proclamation. Few in the Cabinet had any idea that such an epochal shift was in the offing. Nor could such a step as that document decreed have been ventured upon much earlier. Horace Greeley had founded his *New York Tribune* as far back as 1841 as a reform journal, committed to avoiding the sensationalism and salaciousness of the penny press of its time while advocating for such measures as vegetarianism, temperance, and abolition. But if, in the inaugural address these two decades later that Greeley referred to, Lincoln had heeded the reformer's advice and announced that all slaveholding insurgents who took up arms against the Union forfeited their slaves to freedom, such a step would assuredly have propelled the border states not only of Virginia (still in the Union then) but also of Maryland, Kentucky, and Missouri into the Confederacy—very likely a fatal blow to any hope the Federals had of prevailing. Most of the Mississippi would then be in southern hands, virtually all of the left bank of the Ohio, and Washington—totally surrounded—would perforce have been abandoned, the Union capital moved to Harrisburg or wherever. Northerners as well, who at the start of the conflict had shown themselves eager to join in a struggle to save the Union, would have exhibited no such zeal in a fight to free the slaves. By and large, whites up North despised African Americans about as much as white southerners did, maybe more—not knowing them as well; in 1853, *Lincoln's home state* had passed a law (and not for the first time) that blacks, *free* blacks, couldn't settle in Illinois. Think of that—and what it says about the age. And if the liveliest issue of those antebellum years concerned the western territories' right to admit or prohibit slavery, free-soilers striving to exclude the South's peculiar institution from Kansas, Nebraska, and other western lands did so less out of concern for slaves than in order to keep those lands free for white settlers to profit from, so that homesteading families wouldn't have to compete with southern whites exploiting the coerced labor of blacks in bondage—free-soil calculations concerned far less with slavery's burdens as they fell on blacks than as they fell on whites.

All that said, Lincoln had grown in the presidency; his views had changed. Back in 1858, during the Lincoln-Douglas debates, he had conceded (as indeed he was obliged to concede if he had any hopes of winning the Senate seat) that blacks were inferior to whites. African Americans were entitled to life, liberty, and the pursuit of happiness—and to the bread they labored for—but "I am not," he asserted at Quincy, "nor ever have been, in favor of bringing about in any way the social and political equality of the white and black races . . . and I will say in addition to this that there is a physical difference between the white and black races which will ever forbid the two races living together on terms of social and political equality."

He was, after all, a nineteenth-century American politician, alert to the views of his constituents and bound by the perspectives of his era. As president he remained a politician, as well as a strategist highly sensitive to the importance in the present crisis of keeping the border states loyal. Maryland, for instance, after Sumter at the start of the war, "was made to *seem* against the Union. Our soldiers were assaulted, bridges were burned, and railroads torn up, within her limits; and we were many days, at one time, without the ability to bring a single regiment over her soil to the capital." However, as President Lincoln reminded Congress in his first Annual Message, in December 1861, all that of last April had changed. "Now, her bridges and railroads are repaired and open to the government; she already gives seven regiments to the cause of the Union and none to the enemy; and her people, at a regular election, have sustained the Union, by a larger majority, and a larger aggregate vote than they ever before gave to any candidate or any question."

Lincoln would save the Union. As a war measure, then, in order to rob the South of a formidable weapon in its possession—the manpower of slaves who were being used in camps and behind southern lines to support the Confederate military—the president as Commander in Chief of the Union forces felt ready by July 1862 to act upon his deep conviction that slavery was wrong. Secretary of State Seward urged him to wait until the North, whose fortunes were at a low point, had scored a military victory, so that such a radical assault on southern social custom as was being proposed would appear to be something other than a flailing adversary's act of desperation. The battlefield victory, such as it was, came finally two months later, in Maryland, at Antietam, when McClellan's troops, at dreadful cost to both sides, finally fought the Army of Northern Virginia to a standstill, and Lee retreated. That one day of conflict, on September 17, 1862, took more lives than any other twenty-four hours in American history before or since: 22,720 dead, wounded, or missing in a single day. But within a week of the bloodshed, the president of the United States had issued his preliminary Emancipation Proclamation as a military order, not needing Congress's approval: "That on the first day of January in the year of our Lord, one thousand eight hundred and sixty-three, all persons held as slaves within any state, or designated part of a state, the people whereof shall then be in rebellion against the United States shall be then, thenceforward, and forever free."

6. DOMESTIC MATTERS

Above all, he would save the Union. More important to Lincoln than the issue of slavery had been the preservation of what he called "the last best hope of earth." John Hay very early in his years as assistant secretary, on a Tuesday morning, May 7, 1861, had gone in "to give the President some little items of Illinois news" and share with him suggestions that the many correspondents to the White House were offering on how to deal with the South. "For my own part," Hay quotes Lincoln as saying on that occasion, "I consider the central idea pervading this struggle is the necessity that is upon us, of proving that popular government is not an absurdity." Are the people capable of governing themselves, without king or emperor or strongman to do it for them? At the time, it appeared by no means certain that they were. "We must settle this question now," Lincoln told Hay, "whether in a free government the minority have the right to break up the government whenever they choose." If so, the nation that our Constitution has uniquely established will have failed. "Taking the government as we found it," the president added, "we will see if the majority can preserve it."

Preserve the Union as it was at his inaugural, when our sixteenth president had sworn an oath to uphold the Constitution. That document, as of March 1861, sanctioned slavery within the limits over which the practice had existed in 1787. Lincoln meant to enforce what he had sworn to defend—including the Constitution's support of slavery—even though he had always hated slavery. "I am naturally anti-slavery," he remarked in 1864. "If slavery is not wrong, nothing is wrong. I can not remember when I did not so think, and feel."

Such vigorous opposition to the institution might seem unusual in one born in slaveholding Kentucky (this particular southerner on February 12, 1809) who had gone on to spend formative years, from seven to twenty-one, in southern Indiana, where white people were hardly less antipathetic to blacks than were those in Lincoln's native state across the Ohio River. Thomas Lincoln, Abraham's father, was left an orphan in poverty when he was eight. Thus, as his famous son explained, the elder Lincoln "even in childhood was a wandering laboring boy, and grew up litterally without education. He never did more in the way of writing than to bunglingly sign his own name." Nor, apparently, did the older man value book learning. As for the son, we can know little of Abraham's childhood, obscure as it was, glanced at in the couple of brief accounts that the subject himself provided and elaborated on in reminiscences long after the fact (often as dubious as are our own recollections) by those who shared that childhood with him. But the surviving pieces of evidence concur in confirming that the father was virtually illiterate, that son and father didn't get along, that the boy disliked farm labor ("Lincoln said to me one day that his father taught him to work but never learned him to love it"—in itself reason for tension between them), and that the son moved away from father, and farm, and farm life, and manual labor when he could. "I suppose that Abe is still fooling hisself with eddication," Thomas is reported to have remarked when his son was twenty-seven and had long lived apart from him. "I tried to stop it, but he has got that fool idea in his head, and it can't be got out. Now I hain't got no eddication, but I get along far better than ef I had."

In such uncongenial circumstances, the farm boy had borrowed books and taught himself to read: the Bible, Shakespeare, history, Euclid, and books of grammar, rhetoric, and law. The family had migrated from Kentucky to Indiana in 1816, when Abe was seven years old. By the time he had reached his early twenties and his father was making another of his several moves, always farther west, in Illinois by then, on to yet another farm, in Coles County, young Lincoln ventured instead to the village of New Salem, on the Sangamon River in the central part of the state. That was in 1831, when he was twenty-two, by which time he had worked as a farm laborer and twice as flatboatman down the Mississippi to carry produce for sale to New Orleans. In years just ahead, in New Salem, he would try his hand as storekeeper, as volunteer in the Black Hawk War for a little under three months, as postmaster, as deputy surveyor, and as a Whig elected to the state Assembly. By 1836, when he was twenty-seven, he had earned his license to practice law and was winning reelection to the Assembly, first in a field of seventeen for the seven seats from Sangamon County. During the following year, he led a drive to move the capital of Illinois from Vandalia northwest to the more centrally located Springfield (both little more than villages then), and in 1838 Lincoln was once again returned to the state legislature by a sizable margin, a clear indication of the lawyer's popularity in his community.

He was twenty-nine that year, the year in which John Hay was born, on October 8, 1838, in a different Salem, in Indiana. Hay's background and youth share similarities with Lincoln's of the generation before: forebears of both at their separate times on their separate tracks moving from the east westward across frontiers into Kentucky, on into Indiana, then into Illinois. But Hay's father was not a farmer, nor was he illiterate. Charles Hay was trained as a physician, and all his life he coveted books to the extent that his relatively modest means allowed—a founder and lifetime trustee of the public library in the Illinois village of Warsaw, where the Hay family finally came to rest before John was three. The boy remained close to and admiring of his father throughout his life, and of his mother, and of his brothers and sisters, and of his uncle—his father's brother Milton in Pittsfield and Springfield. Thus John grew up in an environment full of books and well supported, his way made smoother by wise, generous adults. Lincoln along his way three decades earlier had encountered many more obstacles to overcome; so that by 1859, when Hay at twenty (already a cultured young poet and star of his college class back East) returned to raw, prosaic Springfield and met his uncle's friend—Abraham Lincoln of growing fame, age fifty—the dapper young sophisticate beheld what looked to him like little more than a gangly country lawyer, rumpled in the manner of the frontier. As late as January 1861, shortly before the suddenly supremely successful politician and his two secretaries started on their train trip to Washington, the younger of the two wrote of the president-elect to a college friend: "I am beginning to respect him more than formerly. He maintains a very dignified attitude before all strangers"—a passing remark that implies earlier impressions not altogether favorable. Yet by the time the long train trip was done, Hay had learned to admire his new employer every bit as much as friend Nicolay had all along.

On the other hand, neither young man cared for Mr. Lincoln's wife. Mary Todd had been born near the end of 1818, the third of seven children to distinguished parents—friends of Lincoln's political idol Henry Clay—in slaveholding Lexington, Kentucky. Slaveowners themselves, the Todds had thrived prominently in that Athens of the West, where, when she was six, Mary endured the wrenching experience of losing her mother in childbirth. Her father, a banker, soon remarried, to a woman by whom he had nine more children, and with whom Mary never got along (any more than did her siblings by the first Mrs. Todd). In Lexington this able daughter of the local aristocracy was sent to finishing school and there learned French and perfected skills in music, dance, drama, and other social graces. Her family was Whig, and Mary proved to be more politically attuned than was usual in young women of her era. At twenty, partly to get away from a disagreeable stepmother whose attentions were lavished on her own numerous children, she set out on an extended visit to her oldest sister, Elizabeth, by then the wife of a prominent lawyer, Ninian Edwards, in Springfield, Illinois. The Edwardses were at the center of Springfield society, into whose midst Mary Todd of Lexington, Kentucky, brought conversational and terpsichorean skills that let her shine at the town's frequent suppers and soirées.

At one such, Mary met a friend of the Edwardses, Mr. Lincoln, a local attorney. He was in his early thirties, nine years older than Mary. They became engaged. At the new year 1841 Lincoln broke off the engagement and fell into a deep depression. The relationship was resumed; and in November 1842, in the Edwardses' parlor, the two were married.

What can we know about other people's marriages? That of the Lincolns seems an unlikely one, maybe not least because of the indicative physical contrast between the two: he tall, gaunt, careless of appearance; she short, plump, vain, and fixed on fashion. True, both were political, both Whigs, and both were ambitious. But in so many other ways far beyond the physical they differed. He was rational, deliberate; she was highly emotional. She bore grudges; he did not. Lincoln kept on good terms with just about everybody; Mrs. Lincoln had fallings-out with whoever got in her way. His sense of humor was lively; hers was all but nonexistent. And his background—kept to the forefront for its political usefulness—was humble (he said that Gray's "short and simple annals of the Poor" described it fully), while his wife preened herself on her superior ancestry and her connections with the upper classes in both Lexington and Springfield. Finally, whereas Lincoln relished what he called the plain people, his wife was a snob.

The self-taught, socially awkward, ambitious lawyer would have been grateful for a well-bred helpmate's adeptness in dealing with the proprieties, even if Mary's new husband did lead her unwittingly into years of household drudgery that a finishing-school education hardly prepared her for. Lincoln himself proved not easy to live with: often absent from home, leaving his wife to her chores, and when at home often distracted—as well as overindulgent with the children (of whom they would have four, all boys). After their marriage the couple lived in rooming houses, then in 1844 bought a cottage in Springfield at Eighth and Jackson, the first and last home that Lincoln ever owned. There, the refined Todd daughter ("What would my poor father say if he found me doing this kind of work?") slogged through her housekeeping with minimal help and only modest funds in, by Lexington standards, near-frontier conditions: cooking, baking, somewhat casually looking after the boys, mending their clothes, dusting and dusting some more, fetching water and always cleaning, for the cleanliness of a house was thought in large part to determine the health of the children.

Robert was the first of the Lincoln children, born nine months after the wedding, in August 1843. He was the only one of the four boys to grow to adulthood, and indeed would live out a long life of affluence and high respectability, dying in his eighties, a quarter way into the twentieth century. Eddie, born in 1846, died a month before his fourth birthday, of what was thought to be diphtheria but, given the fifty-two days of suffering the much-loved child endured at the end, was more likely pulmonary tuberculosis. Both of Eddie's parents were left desolate at his passing, both all but inconsolable. (Lincoln had long been susceptible to depression in any case, his wife more likely to manifest her grief through frenzy and hysteria.)

Willie, the third son, was born ten months after Eddie's death—that is, in December of 1850—and Tad, the last of the children, in April 1853. Three years on, with her husband prospering through legal fees from such clients as the Illinois Central Railroad and Mary in possession of a legacy from her late father's estate, she was able to oversee the enlargement of the now crowded one-and-a-half-story cottage, the Lincoln home for twelve years, into a more spacious two-story dwelling in the Greek Revival style (as it stands today): residence suitable at last to the needs of a rising political star.

For the Springfield attorney must entertain more lavishly now, something Mrs. Lincoln's finishing-school training had prepared her to do well. More-over, she enjoyed being in the limelight—indeed, had chosen her homely husband, she once confessed, over another, suaver Springfield suitor (Stephen A. Douglas, in fact) because she judged the former to have a better chance of becoming president, so early had her ambition been astir. In Springfield, then, as Mr. Lincoln's own ambition moved him closer to what both of them wanted, his wife found herself frequently entertaining in their remodeled home at Eighth and Jackson, where her efforts were regarded favorably—as, for instance, by a social committee in agreement that their hostess was "amiable and accomplished, gracious, and a sparkling talker."

Those valuable traits she brought to Washington, to the Executive Mansion, and won plaudits there as well. The esteemed historian George Bancroft, for one, was impressed by the range of the First Lady's interests and her ease in discussing them sensibly, in a conversation that ended by her "giving me a gracious invitation to repeat my visit and saying she would send me a bouquet. I came home entranced." Through such means Mary Lincoln discharged her social obligations at public receptions and state dinners that came with her husband's high office. Nor did wartime deter the First Lady (earliest to be so called) from introducing the innovation of an elaborate White House *party*, not for the public at large but rather for a select group of invited guests, to be held on February 5, 1862. By then, through nine months into a war that was going miserably for the Union, Mrs. Lincoln had refurbished the presidential mansion (much in need of it, but at an expense well over the budget that Congress allowed) and had established herself as undisputed mistress of the premises—even intruding on the president's official responsibilities by delving into patronage matters (to general dissatisfaction), in addition to reviewing the troops and visiting the wounded in area hospitals. Now, in the depths of winter, she would direct her considerable energies to cheering up the elite of Washington with an evening affair by invitation only: diplomats, admirals, generals, Supreme Court justices, congressmen and senators to the number of five hundred. Even so, the guest list remained a select one, everyone on it (including Theodore Roosevelt Sr., father of a future president) bearing Mrs. Lincoln's approval, leaving the uninvited to grumble about the poor taste of indulging in such frivolities in wartime.

It all went off handsomely, though: the president and his wife receiving in the East Room, the Marine Band playing, doors opened at midnight on a magnificent supper—finest of Washington's caterers providing the fare. To be sure, fewer guests appeared than had been invited, and one who did complained about the hostess's imperial airs, more appropriate to Empress Eugénie overseas: "*her bosom* on exhibition, and a flower pot on her head," a Democratic senator noted sourly, with great yards of silk trailing from the too youthful gown on a lady of forty-three. The observer bemoaned as well the absence of republican simplicity all about, the "weak minded Mrs. Lincoln" having degenerated "from the industrious and unpretending woman that she *was* in the days when she used to cook Old Abes dinner, and milk the cows with her own hands, now her only ambition seems to be to exhibit her own milking apparatus to the public gaze."

Such testiness was muted, however, amid the general revelry. Yet the bustle and excitement that had preceded what was to have been a social triumph had turned to ashes for the host and hostess. All this while upstairs in the White House their son Willie lay ill with typhoid fever. Two sons had come down with it earlier, but the younger, Tad, had got better and appeared out of danger. Willie, though—eleven years old—lay dreadfully ill. Thus, through much of the festive and eagerly anticipated evening in progress below, Willie's mother and father lingered at the child's bedside upstairs. A fortnight after the last of the guests had gone, Willie—perhaps the favorite of the Lincoln children, a serious boy on whom they had pinned high hopes—was dead.

So much grief to bear, even here at the pinnacle of Mary Todd Lincoln's glory, and after so long at her lowly, lonely chores back in Springfield. And the griefs ahead for the woman! One must feel for her; yet to Nicolay and Hay on the scene, dealing with Mrs. Lincoln day by day, she had made herself into a "Hell-Cat," into "Her Satanic Majesty." They couldn't stand her. A colleague of theirs, William Stoddard, brought on to help with the cascades of mail pouring in, got along better with the president's wife, yet even he was led to wonder, in looking back some years later, "why a lady who could be one day so kindly, so considerate, so generous, so thoughtful and so hopeful, could, upon another day, appear so unreasonable, so irritable, so despondent, so even niggardly, and so prone to see the dark, the wrong side of men and women and events."

Mary Lincoln earned herself a great many critics in Springfield and Washington both. For one thing, she displayed a volatile, sometimes violent temper, so that visitors and neighbors in both cities might overhear—and report on—her shrill voice belaboring servants, workmen, tradespeople, even the patient Lincoln himself. Add to that that she shopped on credit, compulsively, without money to pay—determined that no one would think her rustic simply because she came out of the West—chose materials for costly gowns and bought numberless gloves, shoes, and household furnishings, running up debts and keeping quiet about them, profligate when buying for herself, she who was stingy with others. And what was most lamentable—what Hay and Nicolay couldn't forgive, for it provided the starkest of her many contrasts with her husband—unlike Honest Abe, Mary Lincoln was (the record confirms it repeatedly) dishonest.

She would be off—all this in wartime, and other ladies knitting socks for the soldiers, knitting the troops mittens and mufflers—to watering places, or to New York or Boston or Philadelphia on shopping expeditions, then have to scrounge where she could to get money to pay for the charges. She came to Secretary Hay; or, as he put it in a mock query two months after the White House party, reporting to frail Nicolay, out West by then for well-earned rest: "Madame has mounted me to pay her the Stewards salary. I told her to kiss mine. Was I right?" And next day, April 5, elaborating: "The devil is abroad, having great wrath. His daughter, the Hell-Cat, sent Stackpole in to blackguard me about the feed of her horses. She thinks there is cheating round the board and with that candor so charming in the young does not hesitate to say so. I declined opening communications on the subject." These hundred and fifty years later, the secretary's disdain glows undimmed. He goes on: "She is in 'a state of mind' about the Steward's salary. There is no steward. Mrs. Watt has gone off and there is no *locum tenens*"—nobody at present holding the position and collecting the salary, the disposition of which was in Secretary Hay's hands. Mrs. Lincoln wanted the salary passed quietly on to her, leaving the post vacant. "She thinks she will blackguard your angelic representative into giving it to her 'which I dont think she'll do it. Hallelujah!' " And four days later: "The Hellcat is getting more Hellcattical day by day."

Mary padded household expenses and pocketed the difference. She used her influence with the president to gain benefits for those who would then reward her clandestinely. She was gossiped about for yet more serious offenses, her name connected with a White House gardener here, a self-styled chevalier there. Because many of her slaveholding Lexington relatives were fighting alongside the rebels, she was accused of being a Confederate sympathizer. Such talk caused her husband embarrassment, for which neither Nicolay nor Hay could forgive her. Worse, gossip about his wife caused the president grief, he with much else to worry him in grievous times.

Yet what can we know of other people's marriages? Lincoln loved Mary, apparently to the end. At a White House reception, for instance, he was heard to remark (sentiment expressed not for the first or the last time): "My wife is as handsome as when she was a girl and I a poor nobody then, fell in love with her and once more, have never fallen out."

7. "WHAT A MAN HE IS!"

Of the four Lincoln children, Eddie, who had died at age three in 1850, was buried back in Springfield. Willie, born in the year of Eddie's death, died in the White House in February 1862, before the first anniversary of his father's inauguration. Soon after Willie's death, the youngest of the children, Thomas, or Tad, turned nine: the last, lively—if verbally impaired—voice of a Lincoln offspring to be regularly heard in the mansion during the rest of the family's living there.

The oldest son, Robert, nineteen when Willie passed away, was off at college through the bulk of Lincoln's time in office. Robert wasn't close to his father in any case. "I scarcely even had ten minutes of talk with him during his Presidency," the son recollected, "on account of his constant devotion to business." Nor had it been much different earlier on: "During my childhood and early youth he was almost constantly away from home, attending courts or making political speeches." At sixteen, the boy went off to Phillips Exeter Academy in New Hampshire and from there to Harvard. Thus removed, and with Mr. Lincoln's elevation to the presidency, "any great intimacy between us became impossible."

The distance separating the two, a father and his first born, was the more regrettable because Lincoln reveled in fatherhood, as he did in the surrogate fatherhood of serving as mentor to young men generally. He served in that capacity in his law office—for, among others, Billy Herndon and Elmer Ellsworth—and in kindly fashion for young lawyers in courts along the circuit. Lincoln had been kind to Jonathan Birch, applicant to the bar, leaving Birch later to remark that "somehow—probably because of the recollection of his own early struggles—his heart seemed especially filled with sympathy and concern for the young man whose footsteps took him in the direction of the law." One such was John Hay, who at twenty-two had been admitted to the Illinois bar in February 1861, a week before boarding the train at Springfield that started the presidential party on its eleven-day journey to Washington. Robert Lincoln was aboard on that trip, during which he and Hay (both having attended Illinois State University in Springfield) became friends, Hay the elder by five years; and they enjoyed each other's company after reaching the federal capital, in evenings visiting haunts in town together before Bob Lincoln returned to college.

The friendship between the two endured, with consequences in decades ahead. As noted, Hay had a gift for friendships—impressively so (for another example) with Robert's father. Less surprising, perhaps, because the president and his young secretary shared a number of tastes. Each had a keen sense of humor, both gifted tellers of jokes and anecdotes. Both relished dialect poems such as Lowell's *Biglow Papers* and Burns's verse in general. Both loved Shakespeare, Lincoln's love less broad than deep (*Hamlet*, *Macbeth*, some of the history plays); so that the two could entertain each other with literary talk and specimens to read aloud through the leisurely interludes they managed to find together. And both were capable of working hard and long without fuss, Hay having been that way from an early age, back at least through school days, when his classmates marveled at his ability to master studies all but effortlessly. At the White House, one who saw him just about daily commented on Hay's possession of "a silent power of work, doing a great deal and saying little about it," even as "his spirit was ever of unruffled serenity, his manner of invariable sweetness and charm," and his talk "apt, varied, refined, and of a markedly literary quality."

Work seemed relentless for the president and his secretaries. "I find," wrote Hay, "I can put in twenty-four hours out of every day very easily, in the present state of affairs at the Executive Mansion." Lincoln could, too—and sometimes on concerns that may have appeared tangential to the all-engrossing war effort: matters of historic import nevertheless, such as seeing fulfilled an 1860 Republican platform promise to enact a homestead law, by means of which settlers could lay easy claim to public land out West. Also the platform pledged to build a railroad (dream of so many years) over those same vast lands to the Pacific. What had held that latter project back was deciding whether such a massive undertaking should follow a southern route, as the Union's former secretary of war, Jefferson Davis, had argued for. But Davis and fellow southerners once high in the federal government had left to set up a government of their own, permitting legislators who remained to drive forward the claims of a more northern route, a matter of no small interest to the present tenant in the White House. For Lincoln, the railroad lawyer, had picked out the very spot—at Council Bluffs (a monument commemorates it now) in Iowa on the Missouri River opposite Omaha—where such a line should begin. On May 20, 1862, the president signed the Homestead Act, and signed the Pacific Railroad Act on July 2. One consequence of those two pieces of legislation was to bind West and North more closely together, to momentous effect in years to come.

Meanwhile, the generally dismal showing of Union armies on eastern battlefields during that same spring and summer of 1862 was furnishing their commander in chief with a source of continual distress. Federals had suffered a crushing defeat at Bull Run a year before, in July 1861. The president forthwith replaced McDowell, in command at that disaster, with General McClellan. Through the fall and into the subsequent winter, Lincoln grappled with McClellan's delays, ordering the general at last, with his now much larger, more formidable Army of the Potomac, to advance toward Richmond before the end of February. The general's Peninsular Campaign was the cumbersome result. While his army maneuvered in the East, Grant out west in Tennessee barely won, at tremendous cost, the battle of Shiloh in April 1862. McClellan near Richmond in late May fought inconclusively at Seven Pines with the rebels' Joe Johnston; but a month later, Robert E. Lee, though outnumbered in the Battle of the Seven Days, put an end decisively to the vaunted Peninsular Campaign. Union forces were obliged to withdraw toward Washington in early July.

By August the president and Stanton of the War Department were placing their hopes for favorable battlefield news on a major general summoned east from successes out West. In command of the newly formed Army of Virginia, John Pope late that month engaged the enemy once more alongside Bull Run, at Manassas Junction. "Every thing seemed to be going well and hilarious on Saturday," Hay recorded in his diary, "& we went to bed, expecting glad tidings at sunrise. But about Eight oclock the President came to my room as I was dressing and calling me out said, 'Well John we are whipped again, I am afraid. The enemy reinforced on Pope and drove back his left wing and he has retired to Centerville.'" Second Bull Run thus joined the growing, dismal roll call of Union defeats; and almost immediately, Lee's jubilant Army of Northern Virginia launched an invasion into Maryland.

Away from the battlefield, quotidian life went on in its minor key, of course, as it does for most of us even while thunderous events nearby rumble toward their fateful conclusions. A glimpse of one such unguarded interlude from within the White House in this same season, on a hot Sunday morning in the summer of 1862, upstairs in the president's office. Stoddard, newest of the secretaries, is sorting mail in there in his shirtsleeves. From his room across the hall, Hay enters full of a comical story he's bursting to tell—and John Hay famously knows how to tell a story. Only this time, as Stoddard attends, the teller breaks up near the middle of it, can't go on for laughing, which sets the other off as well, so that Nicolay overhearing joins them, eager to get in on the merriment. For Nicolay's benefit Hay starts over, and again breaks down partway through, as all three erupt into guffaws.

Beyond the laughter the White House living quarters have been hushed on this Sabbath morning, until a voice at the office door interrupts: "Now John, just tell that thing again." The Tycoon—Japanese, by the way, for "great prince," a term that the first diplomatic mission from Japan to America had introduced in the spring of 1860—enters and takes a seat expectantly in Andrew Jackson's chair, one long leg propped over the other. For a third time Hay at the mantel begins his story, improving on it "up to its first explosive place," Stoddard tells us, "but right there a quartette explosion went off. Down came the President's foot from across his knee, with a heavy stamp on the floor, and out through the hall went an uproarious peal of fun." Just at that moment, though, the doorman appears from below to inform Mr. Lincoln that Secretary Stanton and Senator Trumbull are waiting for him; so the laughter must trail off as the war intrudes, leaving the rest of the story untold, and the White House mail yet to be sorted.

By late August 1862, the president had goaded McClellan into pursuing Lee's invading army with his own Army of the Potomac. The two forces met in Maryland, near Sharpsburg at Antietam Creek on September 17, the first battle of the war on Union soil—and (it bears repeating) the bloodiest day in American history—fought to a stalemate. But although outnumbered two to one, Lee and his rebels, unhindered by an overcautious adversary, were able at the end to withdraw safely across the Potomac into Virginia. Both sides claimed victory, yet the invader had been driven out of the North, which counted as success enough for the president to issue his Emancipation Proclamation, effective on the first day of the new year 1863.

McClellan had let the rebel army get away, though. For that and other negligences, Lincoln was finally moved to replace his commanding general for good, this time with Ambrose Burnside. In December, General Burnside's forces met Lee's in the town and on the battlefield at Fredericksburg, Virginia. Again the Federals were roundly, soundly beaten. The outnumbered enemy inflicted nearly thirteen thousand Union casualties while sustaining just over five thousand losses themselves: eighteen thousand dead, wounded, or missing in all, each single number of that sorrowful total denoting human flesh and blood.

The weary commander in chief would try again, in late January 1863, replacing Burnside with General "Fighting Joe" Hooker. Hooker in his turn met Lee on the battlefield that spring, in the early days of May, at Chancellorsville. Again the Union's Army of the Potomac suffered a crushing defeat, by a force it outnumbered more than two to one. And promptly in June, General Lee led his victorious rebels back onto northern soil, in Pennsylvania.

Foreign observers wondered, as did many at home: Why was the North, with its greater population and resources, so often beaten by an outnumbered enemy? Lincoln attempted an explanation for one European correspondent, supposing it owing to the "facts that the enemy holds the interior, and we the exterior lines, and that we operate where the people convey information to the enemy, while he operates where they convey none to us." But it was military leadership, too, as the commander in chief knew well. In late June of this same 1863 Lincoln accepted the resignation of "Fighting Joe" Hooker, vanquished at Chancellorsville, and replaced him with yet one more general: George Gordon Meade.

Promptly, Meade pressed into Pennsylvania in pursuit of the invader Lee. The two armies clashed at Gettysburg in early July. Three days of bloody fighting ensued before the rebels retreated, Lee heading south toward the safety of Virginia. At last a Union victory, a huge one; and, moreover, at the Maryland border the battered rebels met with a Potomac River too swollen to cross. On July 11, Hay's diary reports that the "President seemed in a specially good humor today, as he had pretty good evidence that the enemy were still on the North side of the Potomac," with Meade making known that he meant to attack. "The Prest. seemed very happy in the prospect of a brilliant success," Hay goes on: a "Coup de grace upon the flying rebels." Do that—seize the moment to wound Lee's army fatally—and this terrible war will be over.

But the Union general hesitated, as though uneasy about tangling with Lee again. An exhausted Meade dawdled, allowing the rebels to get safely across the Potomac to fight another day. Gettysburg, which might have marked the end of the war, was to become rather the turning point of a conflict that would drag on for twenty more months, with grievous loss on both sides. At that turning point, on July 14, Hay commented on his chief's reaction to Meade's temporizing: "Every day he has watched the progress of the Army with agonizing impatience, hopes struggling with fear. He has never been easy in his own mind about Gen Meade since Meades General Order in which he called on his troops to drive the invader from our soil." Such a charge sounded too much like McClellan: "The same spirit that moved McC.," after Antietam, "to claim a great victory because Pa & Md were safe." Neither Pennsylvania nor Maryland nor the Union itself could be safe as long as Bobby Lee's army remained intact; and although Gettysburg was a victory for which the president felt profound gratitude, "Will our Generals never get that idea out of their heads" that the *North* is our soil? For, as Lincoln insisted: "The whole country is *our* soil."

One officer out West appeared to understand well enough. At this very time, on July 4, 1863—almost simultaneously with the victory at Gettysburg and after a grueling campaign and a siege that had lasted nearly two months— General Ulysses Grant accepted the surrender of a rebel army of 29,491 officers and men holed up inside Vicksburg, last stronghold on the Mississippi of the self-styled Confederate States of America. The entire length of the great river was thus restored to the Union, land that was still in rebellion effectively cut in two. The dogged Grant and his men had achieved a strategically vital triumph; and by the following year, after further successes out West, it was Grant whom Lincoln turned to, bringing the western leader to Washington and, on March 9, 1864, putting him in charge as general in chief of the Union armies overall.

But the crucial shift of command lay in the future. For now, immediately after Gettysburg, for all the gratitude and all the relief that Lincoln felt for General Meade's victory and for the Union soldiers' valor in battle, Hay sets down the president's private feelings, as reported by his son Robert: "R. T. L. says the Tycoon is grieved silently but deeply about the escape of Lee."

The war would go on, and its costs had to be reckoned with. Two weeks after Gettysburg, Hay reports himself "in a state of entire collapse after yesterday's work": six hours sequestered with Lincoln and Judge Holt reviewing courts martial. The solemn, taxing labor had its occasional pleasures even so, as Hay's entry for that yesterday—Saturday, July 18, 1863—discloses: "I was amused at the eagerness with which the President caught at any fact which would justify him in saving the life of a condemned soldier. He was only merciless in cases where meanness or cruelty were shown." Cowardice in particular Lincoln had felt "averse to punishing with death. He said it would frighten the poor devils too terribly, to shoot them. On the case of a soldier who had once deserted & reenlisted he endorsed, 'Let him fight instead of shooting him.' "

In these summer months the Tycoon and his secretary were spending much time together, both in the White House and, in evenings, at more elevated, cooler, more salubrious quarters three miles to the northwest, at a stone cottage on the grounds of the Soldiers' Home. Lincoln and Hay would often ride to and from there side by side, chatting along the way, the president speaking with candor and complete trust in his young friend's discretion. Mrs. Lincoln had been injured in a carriage accident in July. Recuperating, she had taken Tad with her out of the noxiousness of summertime Washington to vacation with son Robert in New Hampshire's White Mountains. "They will be gone some time," Hay wrote of the absence to Nicolay, also away, back home with his fiancée in Pittsfield. And Stoddard was gone, "a conscript bold," Hay reported. So Lincoln and his young secretary were left pretty much to themselves in the White House living quarters. "The Tycoon is in fine whack," Hay could tell Nicolay that August, on the 7th. "I have rarely seen him more serene & busy. He is managing this war, the draft, foreign relations, and planning a reconstruction of the Union, all at once. I never knew with what tyrannous authority he rules the Cabinet, till now." Most matters the president decided on his own and let the Cabinet know of afterward. "I am growing more and more firmly convinced," Hay wrote, "that the good of the country absolutely demands that he should be kept where he is till this thing is over. There is no man in the country, so wise so gentle and so firm. I believe the hand of God placed him where he is."

On one Saturday night in late August, Lincoln and his secretary "went to the Observatory with Mrs Young. They were very kind and attentive. The Presdt. took a look at the moon & Arcturus. I went with him to the Soldiers' Home & he read Shakespeare to me, the end of Henry VI and the beginning of Richard III till my heavy eye-lids caught his considerate notice & he sent me to bed. This morning we ate an egg and came in very early"—rode the three miles back to the White House together, to one more day among weeks with their far-reaching significance that were passing by.

Passing into other seasons, other labors and recreations. The theater then filled much the role of movies now; so that with the coming of fall and cooler weather, and Mary Lincoln back from her travels: "Spent the evening at the theatre with the President Mrs Lincoln, Mrs Hunter Cameron and Nicolay," Hay notes in an entry for November 9, 1863. "J Wilkes Booth was doing the 'Marble Heart.' Rather tame than otherwise." And nine days afterward a lengthy diary entry, on Wednesday, the 18th: "We started from Washington to go to the Consecration of the Soldiers' Cemetery at Gettysburg. On our train were the President Seward Usher & Blair: Nicolay & Myself: Mercier & Admiral Reynaud," along with a few others. "We had a pleasant sort of a trip. At Baltimore Schenck's staff joined us."

Reaching Gettysburg around five, the parties rapidly broke up, Hay says, "like a drop of quicksilver spilt." He and some companions "foraged around for a while—walked out to the College got a chafing dish of oysters then some supper and finally loafing around to the Court House," there running into a knowledgeable older friend, the Pennsylvania editor John Forney, who told him: "Hay you are a fortunate man. You have kept yourself aloof from your office"—unlike an old fellow of seventy, an acquaintance of the editor's, once President Madison's private secretary who had been living solemnly off the recollection ever since. Hay, by contrast, "has laughed through his term," Forney was telling him, as they followed along toward music ahead where the president was staying, waited while Lincoln was serenaded, heard him cheered when he came to the door to say a few innocuous words. Then the group of friends repaired to Forney's quarters nearby, did some singing themselves and some drinking; and the editor chose to reproach serenaders gathered before his own door, who drunkenly cheered him when he appeared: "You gave no such cheers to your President down the street. Do you know what you owe to that Great man? You owe your country—you owe your name as American citizens." More such patriotic sentiments found expression among the high spirits of that bibulous evening, and more music was sung, and speechifying offered, and more drinking undertaken, before the group back upstairs after a bit "sang John Brown and went home."

Next morning, likely hung over, "I got a beast," Hay records succinctly of an immortal Thursday, the 19th of November 1863, "and rode out with the President's suite to the Cemetery in the procession." There, "after a little delay Mr. Everett took his place on the stand—and Mr Stockton made a prayer which thought it was an oration—and Mr Everett spoke as he always does perfectly"—for two hours—"and the President in a firm free way, with more grace than is his wont said his half dozen lines of consecration"—in two minutes—"and the music wailed and we went home through crowded and cheering streets. And all the particulars are in the daily papers."

The president's 272 words were no briefer than they should have been, he there not to commemorate—that was Everett's elaborately comprehensive task—but only to dedicate, to consecrate this spot that sacrifice had made solemn unto sacredness. In the short time they took to deliver, Lincoln's ten sentences did precisely what they were meant to do—and in addition shaped

From Hay's Civil War Diary, November 8, 1863: "We had a great many pictures taken. Some of the Presdt. the best I have seen. Nico & I immortalized ourselves by having ourselves done in group with the Presdt." Within two weeks of the date, Lincoln would deliver his remarks at Gettysburg. Photo by Alexander Gardner. Courtesy of the Library of Congress.

themselves into one of the two or three greatest utterances in all of American thought.

The party returned to Washington. On the first of December the Army of the Potomac went into winter quarters at Culpeper, Virginia. By mid-month, on the 15th during the lull of a somewhat less active wintertime, Lincoln and young Hay (recently turned twenty-five) were back at the theater, at Ford's, with Nicolay "to see Falstaff in Henry IV." The celebrated Hackett was performing the role, admirably, although the "President criticised H's reading of a passage where Hackett said, 'Mainly *thrust* at me' the President thinking it should read 'mainly thrust at *me*.' I told the Presdt. I tho't he was wrong, that 'mainly' merely meant 'strongly' 'fiercely.'"—about which the secretary was right, in this fair indication of the ease of their talk together.

Here is another glimpse: at the end of April 1864, with Grant now placed in command of all Union armies east and west. Upstairs in the White House a little after midnight, Hay sat writing in his diary when "the President came into the office laughing, with a volume of Hood's works in his hand to show Nicolay & me the little Caricature 'An unfortunate Bee-ing'"—a hapless fellow tripping and overturning an angry beehive—"seemingly utterly unconscious that he"—Lincoln—"with his short shirt hanging about his long legs & setting out behind like the tail feathers of an enormous ostrich was infinitely funnier than anything in the book he was laughing at." The diarist continues: "What a man he is! Occupied all day with matters of vast moment, deeply anxious about the fate of the greatest army of the world, with his own fame & fortune hanging on the events of the passing hour, he yet has such a wealth of simple bonhommie & good fellowship that he gets out of bed & perambulates the house in his shirt to find us that we may share with him the fun of one of poor Hoods queer little conceits."

Lincoln's fortune and fame, which Hay refers to, did appear in jeopardy as that grim summer of the election year 1864 advanced. Ever larger numbers of the president's constituents were feeling dispirited. Grant near Richmond had launched his spring-summer campaign directly against Lee's army, as the commander in chief had wanted: in the Wilderness, at Cold Harbor, at Petersburg, but with appalling loss of life in what turned sometimes into hand-to-hand combat, thousands and thousands newly dead with little apparently to show for it. Lee's rebel forces remained intact, still threatening. The North, meanwhile, had long since grown sick of the bloodletting. Along with many others, Greeley of the *Tribune* clamored loudly for peace. Volunteers had stopped rallying to fight for the Union, so that states were unable to meet their quotas. But more fighting men were needed; so in 1863 the president in desperation had established, for the first time in our history, a national draft, a hugely unpopular federal conscription of civilians into the service. A free people's resistance to the despotic novelty was fierce, horrifyingly so in New York City over four ghastly, blood-soaked days in July: violent, murderous rioting that it took soldiers back from Gettysburg to put down. Now, a year later, the government was calling for five hundred thousand additional draftees to serve. Meanwhile, radical Republicans in the North remained vexed with the president's slow pace in freeing the slaves, while Democrats and other conservatives were outraged that he had gone as far as to turn a war to save the Union into what appeared now to be all about blacks. Anyway, by this time Old Abe should know he was beaten. Sue for peace and staunch the blood.

Democrats convening in Chicago that summer nominated as their presidential candidate the hero of Antietam, General George McClellan, on a platform calling for peace with our southern brothers. As for Republicans, so tenuous had Mr. Lincoln's hold on power appeared that one or two Republicans—Secretary Chase, General Frémont—complied with what their supporters were urging and set about seeking the nomination for themselves. In June, however, the Party at Baltimore in convention assembled named Abraham Lincoln its choice for a second time, even as many thoughtful people in the war-weary Union (Lincoln among them) harbored strong doubts that he could win.

That August, off for a visit with his family in Illinois, in Warsaw, John Hay grew irritated confronting the locals' views. "I lose my temper sometimes talking to growling Republicans," he wrote back to Nicolay. "There is a diseased restlessness about men in these times that unfits them for the steady support of an administration." Republicans for Chase, for Frémont, for union at any cost, for abolition, for peace, for pursuing the war with more vigor; and malcontents everywhere. "It seems as if there were appearing in the Republican party the elements of disorganization that destroyed the whigs." Hay was reminded of stupid beasts and the plagues that come as their torment. "If the dumb cattle are not worthy of another term of Lincoln," he wrote in disgust, "then let the will of God be done & the murrain of McClellan fall on them."

8. PEACE OVERTURE

The bloodletting didn't slack off, flowing copiously at Cold Harbor, for instance, through two horrific weeks in early June 1864, when a determined Grant—the fumbling butcher Grant—threw his men, wave after wave, against entrenched rebels to disastrous effect: as many as 13,000 Union casualties to maybe 2,500 on the defenders' side. Such slaughter further demoralized northerners, although—less obvious at the time—Grant's offensive managed to seize the initiative, forcing General Lee thereafter to stay put, defend Richmond, and with other southerners wait for results of November's presidential election up North, where the tyrant Lincoln appeared about to be replaced by somebody more amenable to talking peace between the two warring nations.

The president of the United States during those fraught months and years remains the most eloquent we've ever had; and of the many examples of Lincoln's eloquence—of his finding the apt and affecting expressions to utter on crucial occasions—three stand out. One is the Gettysburg Address. A second, which relates to the cost in lives that the Civil War was exacting, takes the form, less momentously, of a private letter:

EXECUTIVE MANSION

Washington, Nov. 21, 1864

Dear Madam,—

I have been shown in the files of the War Department a statement of the Adjutant General of Massachusetts, that you are the mother of five sons who have died gloriously on the field of battle.

I feel how weak and fruitless must be any words of mine which should attempt to beguile you from the grief of a loss so overwhelming. But I cannot refrain from tendering to you the consolation that may be found in the thanks of the Republic they died to save.

I pray that our Heavenly Father may assuage the anguish of your bereavement, and leave you only the cherished memory of the loved and lost, and the solemn pride that must be yours, to have laid so costly a sacrifice upon the altar of Freedom.

Yours, very sincerely and respectfully,
A. LINCOLN

Imagine the writerly task—as commander in chief and to that extent responsible—of saying something consoling to a mother of five sons killed in battle. Try to think of what phrasings you would resort to that hadn't been robbed of meaning by being written and said so many times before. Then, please, read the letter again.

It is perfection: the tact of its brevity, the simple flow and logic of the structure, the tender befitting diction, the cadences in each sentence that let emphases fall invariably where they should, all in a tone that conveys profound sincerity—and not a word too many, none to add and not one that could be removed without detriment.

Nor does it matter that the president had been misinformed. Nor that three of Mrs. Bixby's five sons still lived, one a deserter to the enemy. Nor that this particular mother appears to have been a Confederate sympathizer who ran a brothel. Lincoln couldn't have known any of that. It hardly matters, even, that he may not have written the letter himself, so Lincolnesque does it sound on early readings and so moving in what it achieves, however the feat came about.

Most scholars agree that Lincoln did write the Bixby letter (and would want to think so anyway—would they not?—keeping this glittering gem as part of the canon), although a few have argued, compellingly, that Lincoln's secretary wrote the letter to Mrs. Bixby, that John Hay wrote it; and here are their reasons.

The holograph doesn't survive. According to her descendants, the Boston matron of rebel sympathies threw it away ("destroyed it in anger," her great grandson was told, "shortly after receipt without realizing its value": a pity; that single sheet of paper would be worth millions now). The text does survive in newspapers of the time, and clippings of it are pasted in two of Hay's scrapbooks, where he kept little if anything that he hadn't written himself. That alone, on the part of a man of such rectitude, is indicative. Why would Hay twice have put the Bixby clipping among his own writings? Moreover, Lincoln in the White House seems to have seen few of the letters addressed to him. Stoddard implies as much; and in 1866 Hay assured Billy Herndon, who was gathering information about his martyred law partner, that the president had written "very few letters. He did not read one in fifty that he received. At first we tried to bring them to his notice, but at last he gave the whole thing over to me, and signed without reading them the letters I wrote in his name." As part of that duty, the secretary learned to reproduce Lincoln's signature so accurately that collectors still have trouble distinguishing the authentic from the forged; and the Tycoon's prose style, of which Hay had read sizable quantities, he could imitate, too. In addition, Lincoln was unusually harried by office-seekers and congratulatory friends in the election month when the Bixby letter was composed; "the crush here just now is beyond endurance," Hay remarked at the time. Moreover, in later years others of repute spoke of John Hay's having told them (although this is hearsay) that he was the author of the letter, told them no doubt in passing, privately, not as a boast but merely as an interesting fact.

BOUDOIR PROPHECIES.

One day in the Tuileries,
When a south-west Spanish breeze
    Brought scandalous news of the Queen,
The fair, proud Empress said,
" My good friend loses her head
If matters go on this way,
I shall see her shopping some day
    In the Boulevart-Capucines."

The saying swiftly went
To the Place of the Orient,
    And the stout Queen sneered " ah well !
You are proud and prude, ma belle !
But I think I will hazard a guess,
I shall see you one day playing chess
    With the curé of Carabauchel."

Both ladies, though not over wise,
Were lucky in prophecies.
    For the Boulevart shopmen well
Know the form of stout Isabel,
    As she buys her *modes de Paris ;*
And after Sedan, in despair,
The Empress, prude and fair,
Went to visit *Madame sa Mère*
    In her villa at Carabauchel—
    But the Queen was not there to see.

GOD'S VENGEANCE.

[The following quaint and powerful lines are from
the pen of Major John Hay, late Private Secretary
to Mr. Lincoln, and now a distinguished attaché of the
Paris Legation. They were evidently thrown off in
the first anguish of our national bereavement—a bereavement which took from Mr. Hay one who loved
him as a son; and as a cry of grief *de profundis*, they
are marked by a stern and terrible earnestness. Their
first appearance was in the columns of the *Independent.*
—ED. CITIZEN.]

Saith the Lord, " Vengeance is mine;
    I will repay," saith the Lord;
Ours be the anger Divine,
    Lit by the flash of His word.

How shall His vengeance be done?
    How, when His purpose is clear?
Must He come down from His throne?
    Hath He no instruments here?

Sleep not in imbecile trust,
    Waiting for God to begin,
While, growing strong in the dust,
    Rests the bruised serpent of sin.

Right and Wrong—both cannot live
    Death-grappled. Which shall it be?
Strike! Only Justice can give
    Safety to all that shall be.

Shame! to stand paltering thus,
    Tricked by the balancing odds ;
Strike! God is waiting for us!
    STRIKE! FOR THE VENGEANCE IS GOD'S!

THE ADVANCE GUARD.

In the dream of the Northern poets—
    The brave who in battle die
Fight on in shadowy phalanx
    In the field of the upper sky;
And as we read the sounding rhyme,
    The reverent fancy hears
The ghostly ring of the viewless swords
    And the clash of the spectral spears.

We think with imperious questionings
    Of the brothers that we have lost,
And we strive to track in death's mystery
    The flight of each valiant ghost.
The Northern myth comes back to us,
    And we feel through our sorrow's night
That those young souls are striving still
    Somewhere for the truth and light.

It was not their time for rest and sleep;
    Their hearts beat high and strong;
In their fresh veins the blood of youth
    Was singing its hot, sweet song.
The open heaven bent over them,
    'Mid flowers their little feet trod,
Their lives lay vivid, light, and blest
    By the smiles of women and God.

Again they come! Again I hear
    The tread of that goodly band.
I know the flash of Ellsworth's eye
    And the grasp of his hard, warm hand;
And Putman, and Shaw, of the fine heart,
    With an eye like a Boston girl's;
And I see the light of heaven which shone
    On Ulric Dalghren's curls.

There is no power in the gloom of hell
    To quench those spirits' fire;
There is no charm in the bliss of heaven
    To bid them not aspire.
But, somewhere in the eternal plan
    That strength, that life survive,
And like the files on Lookout's crest,
    Above death's clouds they strive.

A chosen corps—they are marching on
    In a wider field than ours;
Those bright battalions still fulfil
    The scheme of the heavenly powers.
And high, brave thoughts float down to us,
    The echoes of that far fight,
Like the flash of a distant picket's gun
    Through the shades of the severing night.

No fear for them! In our lower field
    Let us keep our arms unstained,
That at last we be worthy to stand with them
    On the shining heights they've gained.
We shall meet and greet in closing ranks,
    In Time's declining sun,
When the bugles of God shall sound recall
    And the battle of life be won!

Pathetic Letter of the President to a Poor Widow.

BOSTON, Nov. 25.—Mrs. Bixby, the recipient
of the following letter from President Lincoln,
is a poor widow living in the Eleventh ward of
this city. Her sixth son, who was severely
wounded in a recent battle, is now lying in the
Readville hospital:

" EXECUTIVE MANSION, }
" WASHINGTON, Nov. 21, 1864. }

" DEAR MADAM: I have been shown on the
file of the War Department a statement of the
Adjutant General of Massachusetts, that you
are the mother of five sons who have died gloriously on the field of battle.

"I feel how weak and fruitless must be any
word of mine which should attempt to beguile
you from the grief of a loss so overwhelming;
but I cannot refrain from tendering to you the
consolation that may be found in the thanks of
the republic they died to save.

"I pray that our Heavenly Father may assuage the anguish of your bereavements, and
leave only the cherished memory of the loved
and lost, and the solemn pride, that must be
yours, to have laid so costly a sacrifice upon
the altar of freedom.

"Yours, very sincerely and respectfully,
" A. LINCOLN.
"To Mrs. BIXBY, Boston, Mass."

A page of Hay's Civil War scrapbook, containing newspaper clippings of three of his poems as well as the text of the Bixby letter. Courtesy of John Hay Library.

Textual clues provide further suggestive evidence, in our age when computers can furnish such data. That lovely word *beguile*: the fruitlessness of attempting "to beguile you from the grief of a loss so overwhelming." Hay uses it elsewhere in his writing some thirty times; Lincoln never does. Similarly with words and phrases such as *assuage, cherished, gloriously, cannot refrain from tendering, pray that our Heavenly Father*: all several times echoed in Hay's prose and rarely if at all in Lincoln's. None of this is conclusive, and maybe it doesn't matter. But what is certain is that both Nicolay and Hay—utterly loyal to their chief—very early earned his total trust (more than enough by 1864 to make such alternate authorship plausible), and they never lost it.

As promptly as in the late summer and early fall of 1861, for instance, with the Civil War not five months old, the president had demonstrated his trust in young Hay, twenty-two then, by sending him on two errands that Lincoln cared about: one personal, the other diplomatic. The personal—in part awarded to a hard-working secretary as a break from summertime Washington—was to accompany Mrs. Lincoln and her two young children on holiday to the fashionable resort of Long Branch, New Jersey. Hay got away from that assignment as soon as he could; but in early September he set out for St. Louis bearing a letter of consequence from the president to deliver by hand to the celebrated Pathfinder, to John C. Frémont. Frémont was a western explorer and trailblazer, surveyor of a railroad route to the Pacific, first senator from California, first candidate for president on the Republican ticket, of 1856, and now, as a political general, commander of the Union's Department of the West. But General Frémont was also self-important, arrogant, and impetuous: without consulting his Commander in Chief he had on August 30 issued an order emancipating the slaves of all rebels in Missouri. Lincoln couldn't have that: certainly not in a border state, not by a Union army officer, not as early as 1861. Thus on September 2, Hay entrained for St. Louis to put in the general's hands the president's letter saying so, and while there the envoy was to size up the situation before bringing his impressions back to Washington. Young Hay found Frémont, whom he saw much of during the visit, "quiet earnest industrious, imperious." But whatever the president's deputy reported in confidence to the White House, Lincoln countermanded the popular general's order and, in October, transferred him from the sensitive border state of Missouri to a less controversial command among the mountains of western Virginia.

Throughout the war, both Hay and Nicolay undertook responsible errands for their chief. In March 1863, as another instance, Hay, invested at twenty-four with the brevet rank of colonel, boarded a ship bound for Union fortifications at Hilton Head, South Carolina. On that occasion, Lincoln's deputy remained in the South among federal troops for two months. ("They have made a d'd burlesque of the thing," he wrote, "by giving me so much rank"; yet he jokingly instructed Nicolay, "Write to me when you have nothing else to do & be good enough to remember that I have a pretty extensive handle to my name"—alluding, as well, to his additional title of Assistant Adjutant-General, A.A.-G., nor would he raise any objection for the rest of his life to being addressed as Colonel Hay.)

Still later, in 1864, that darkest summer, as blood continued to flow over battlefields near Richmond while growing numbers of northerners were crying out for peace, the president entrusted Hay—by then a major, of lower rank but more securely held—with a mission that called for high-level diplomacy. The South, along with others, had accused this president of being a tyrant for having assumed—while Congress was in recess at the start of the war—powers that none of his predecessors exercised (although none had faced widespread rebellion, either). Among his wartime acts, Lincoln selectively established martial law, suspended writs of habeas corpus, arrested seditious legislators, and finally instituted a national and very unpopular draft. Extraordinary measures for extraordinary times; and in addition to enforcing such tyrannies, King Abraham Africanus was charged, as well, with bloodthirstiness in prolonging the war, unwilling to meet with southern emissaries seeking peace as the slaughter dragged on.

The sticking point for Lincoln was this: from the beginning he had regarded what the South proclaimed as a new nation to be merely states of the Union in rebellion. Thus he declined to negotiate with a Confederate States of America, for no such sovereignty legitimately existed. The enemy were not Confederates but rather rebels, insurgents (the term he preferred) who had strayed from their loyalty to the Union, which was perpetual. But should any delegates authorized to speak for Jefferson Davis arrive with the intent first of all of rejoining the Union, the president of the United States would most willingly hear them out.

By early July 1864, Horace Greeley thought he had found such a delegation. Gentlemen high in southern councils, whom the *New York Tribune* editor had been told were sent by Mr. Davis, hovered just on the far side of the Canadian border ready to talk. Greeley wrote to the president about them, enclosing correspondence from a certain William Jewett, acting as intermediary. "I am authorized," Jewett at Niagara Falls had informed the editor on July 5, "to state to you, for your use only, not the public, that two ambassadors of Davis & Co. are now in Canada, with full and complete powers for a peace." What could be plainer than that? Editor Greeley reminded Mr. Lincoln of a strong yearning down South that the killing cease, while adding "that our bleeding, bankrupt, almost dying country also longs for peace—shudders at the prospect of fresh conscriptions, of further wholesale devastations, and of new rivers of human blood." He ventured to refer as well to "a widespread conviction that the Government and its prominent supporters are not anxious for peace, and do not improve proffered opportunities to achieve it," thus doing harm that is bound "to do far greater in the approaching elections." By which was meant that Lincoln would lose the November election unless he made a conspicuous effort to end the war. For those reasons the editor implored his president to talk with the southern commissioners, in his own time and manner but the sooner the better: give safe conduct to Washington, specifically, to Honorable Clement C. Clay, former U.S. senator from Alabama; to Honorable Jacob Thompson, former secretary of the interior in President Buchanan's cabinet; and to Honorable James P. Holcombe, representative in the Confederate Congress and professor at the University of Virginia. Nor did Greeley shirk at spelling out the very terms—six, which he numbers—that the president should offer the distinguished rebel emissaries.

To all which counsel Lincoln responded promptly, July 9, 1864, to Hon. Horace Greeley: "If you can find any person anywhere professing to have any proposition of Jefferson Davis, in writing, for peace, embracing the restoration of the Union and abandonment of slavery, whatever else it embraces, say to him he may come to me with you; and that if he really brings such proposition, he shall, at the least, have safe conduct with the paper (and without publicity, if he chooses) to the point where you shall have met him. The same if there be two or more persons. Yours truly, A. Lincoln."

It wasn't what the editor wanted to hear. The burden that was to have been shifted to the president was being returned to Greeley's own busy shoulders: "he may come to me *with you*." The New Yorker tarried a bit before framing his reply, on the 12th, one that provoked a prompt telegram from the White House: "I was not expecting you to send me a letter, but to bring me a man, or men. Mr. Hay goes to you with an answer to yours of the 13th. A. Lincoln."

Adjutant Hay set out at 11:15 next morning, "by way of Baltimore, around by Boat to Perryville & thence by rail, the vilest route known to travel." Reaching New York at 6 A.M. on Saturday, the 16th, the weary messenger was washing his face in his room at the Astor House when up came "G.'s card. I went down to the parlor delivered the letter," and observed that Greeley didn't much like what he read. Lincoln's response had been brief, under the date July 15: "My Dear Sir:—Yours of the 13th just received, and I am disappointed that you have not already reached here with those commissioners. If they would consent to come, on being shown my letter to you of the 9th instant, show that and this to them, and if they will come on the terms stated in the former, bring them. I not only intend a sincere effort for peace, but I intend that you shall be a personal witness that it is made."

The terms in the president's letter of the 9th, already quoted, stipulated that any such envoys must have with them Jefferson Davis's written agreement that the South would give up slavery and rejoin the Union, all else being negotiable. But Greeley, through Jewett the intermediary, had neglected to mention those terms to the gentlemen at Niagara Falls. And about this business of his conducting the same gentlemen personally to Washington: Editor Greeley, Hay notes, protested in the Astor House parlor that "he was the worst man that could be taken for the purpose: that as soon as he arrived there, the newspapers would be full of it: that he would be abused & blackguarded &c &c" for dealing with rebels. But he would go if required to, even though "all along opposed to the President proposing terms. He was in favor of some palaver any how—wanted them," the emissaries, "to propose terms which we could not accept" but would then "go to the country on—wanted the government to appear anxious for peace & yet strenuous in demanding as our ultimatum proper terms."

Those views Hay telegraphed to Lincoln at once: the editor was willing to go, although "he thinks some one less known would create less excitement." And he needs absolute safe conduct, so as not to have to explain his business to every officer who stops him. "If this meets with your approbation, I can write the order in your name as A.A.-G., or you can send it by mail." Within hours Hay had his reply: "Yours received. Write the safe-conduct as you propose, without waiting for one by mail from me. If there is or is not any thing in the affair, I wish to know it without unnecessary delay."

Thus armed, Greeley left for Niagara Falls. There, on Sunday the 17th, the *Tribune* editor, through Jewett, sent the rebel envoys a message announcing his arrival: "Gentlemen:—I am informed that you are duly accredited from Richmond as the bearers of propositions looking to the establishment of peace" and "that you desire to visit Washington in the fulfilment of your mission." Assuming this information to be accurate, "I am authorized by the President of the United States to tender you his safe-conduct on the journey proposed, and to accompany you at the earliest time that will be agreeable to you."

But despite what the intermediary Jewett had said, the southerners weren't accredited at all. Hay, meanwhile, had returned to the White House, reaching there Monday morning, the 18th. That same evening, at Lincoln's direction, he set out, again via New York, for Niagara Falls, arriving shortly before noon on Wednesday, the 20th. There, at the International Hotel, he rejoined the unhappy Greeley, "a good deal cut up at what he called the President's great mistake in refusing to enter at once into negotiations without conditions." By that time the rebel envoys on the other side of the Falls had admitted in a note to the editor that they weren't actually Jefferson Davis's representatives, although confident, because of their high standing in the Confederacy, that any terms they agreed on would be honored in Richmond. The new turn of affairs led Greeley to urge that Jewett be brought into the proceedings directly; but Major Hay had formed an aversion to Jewett, "an odd, half-witted adventurer," as described in Hay's diary, who had already written "interminable letters of advice to Mr. Lincoln"—and to Mr. Davis, too—leaving it to be inferred that he was intimate with the highest levels of government on both sides. Hay would have nothing to do with Jewett.

Greeley, for his part, didn't intend to be caught alone with rebels; Hay must come with him then, to deliver Mr. Lincoln's message himself. So the two Americans took a carriage over to the Canadian side, to the Clifton House. "Our arrival," Hay writes, with "Greeleys well known person created a good deal of interest: the barroom rapidly filling with the curious & the halls blooming suddenly with wide eyed & pretty women. We went up to Holcombe's room," where they found the representative to the Confederate Congress at tea and toast, "a tall solemn spare false looking man with false teeth false eyes & false hair." Courtesies were exchanged and the president's note delivered, along with another that Hay had brought with him from the White House, in Lincoln's handwriting, dated July 18 and addressed "To Whom It May Concern": "Any proposition which embraces the restoration of peace, the integrity of the whole Union, and the abandonment of slavery, and which comes by and with an authority that can control the armies now at war against the United States, will be received and considered by the executive government of the United States, and will be met by liberal terms on substantial and collateral points, and the bearer or bearers thereof shall have safe conduct both ways."

Honorable Clement Clay had absented himself for the day, but Professor Holcombe assured his visitors that an answer to Mr. Lincoln's messages signed by both emissaries would be ready in the morning. Major Hay expressed his willingness to bear back to Washington whatever the gentlemen were pleased to impart.

There matters stood. The two Americans returned to the New York side of the Falls. Hay spent the night in nearby Buffalo, expecting on the morrow to receive the southerners' reply. Nothing came. In due course and in full diplomatic mode, he respectfully inquired "whether Professor Holcombe and the gentlemen associated with him desire to send to Washington by Major Hay any messages in reference to the communication delivered to him on yesterday, and in that case when he may expect to be favored with such messages." The query stirred a like formality in its recipient: "Mr. Holcombe presents his compliments to Major Hay, and greatly regrets if his return to Washington has been delayed by any expectation of an answer to the communication which Mr. Holcombe received from him yesterday." The message inquired about "was accepted as the response to a letter of Messrs. Clay and Holcombe to the Honorable H. Greeley, and to that gentleman answer has been transmitted."

But by then Greeley, the duped Greeley, was on his way back to the *Tribune* offices in New York City, the emissaries' reply in Jewett's hands for delivery. And a blistering reply it was. "Instead of the safe-conduct which we solicited," the ornately outraged, very long missive reads in part, "and which your"—editor Greeley's—"first letter gave us every reason to suppose would be extended for the purpose of initiating a negotiation in which neither Government would compromise its rights or its dignity, a document has been presented which provokes as much indignation as surprise." The haughty syntax and florid verbiage would seem shaped less for Greeley or Mr. Lincoln than for the readership of northern newspapers, and indeed Jewett saw to it that the Confederates' letter was soon published far and wide on the other side of Niagara Falls. (Yet it was "incomprehensible," Hay reflected years later, "that a man of Mr. Greeley's experience should not have recognized at once the purport of this proposal"—that Holcombe and Clay, uncredentialed, negotiate directly with Abraham Lincoln. "It simply meant that Mr. Lincoln should take the initiative in suing the Richmond authorities for peace, on terms to be proposed by them.") Their letter to Greeley rumbles on: President Lincoln's manifesto, "Addressed 'to whom it may concern'"—which appears to have particularly rankled the honorable southern gentlemen—"precludes negotiation, and prescribes in advance the terms and conditions of peace." How to explain its author's insulting manner and his "fresh blasts of war to the bitter end, we leave for the speculation of those who have the means or inclination to penetrate the mysteries of his cabinet, or fathom the caprice of his imperial will. It is enough for us to say that we have no use whatever for the paper which has been placed in our hands. We could not transmit it to the President of the Confederate States without offering him an indignity, dishonoring ourselves, and incurring the well-merited scorn of our countrymen."

Much more in that vein followed: "if there be any patriots or Christians in your land"—in the United States—"who shrink appalled from the illimitable vista of private misery and public calamity which stretches before them, we pray that in their bosoms a resolution may be quickened to recall the abused authority" at the polls in November "and vindicate the outraged civilization of their country." Vote Abraham Africanus the First out of office—the gist of the emissaries' missive as a whole definitively ending Greeley's efforts toward peace pretty much as President Lincoln thought they would end. What the go-between got for his pains was a note Hay had dated July 18 to Wm. Cornell Jewett, Etc, Etc, Etc., before setting out for Niagara and while busy with his White House duties managing Lincoln's mail. To the pestiferous Mr. Jewett, Hay had written that, in discharging those duties, "it is necessary for me to use a certain discretion in the choice of letters to be submitted to the personal inspection of the President. In order to avoid a further waste of time on your part, I have to inform you that your letters are never so submitted. My proceeding in this matter has the sanction of the President. I am, Sir, very truly your obedient servant."

Thus the parley fizzled, the uncredentialed southerners presumably less intent on making peace than on affecting northern opinion against a stubborn autocrat up for reelection. Major Hay had got some additional practice in diplomacy that might serve him in years ahead; but portentous events in Niagara, as is often the case behind the scenes of wartime, turned out at the last not to matter that much.

What did matter burst forth at summer's end, in September, on the 2nd, when Atlanta fell. Sherman's conquest changed everything. Morale in the North shot skyward, Lincoln's standing as wise leader solidified, and events went on breaking in the Union's favor. Before the month was out, Sheridan's cavalry had defeated the rebel Early in the Shenandoah Valley, and Frémont withdrew from the presidential race. That race came to an end in November, on the 8th—remarkably, without turmoil at the polls—Lincoln winning it by 400,000 popular votes, 212 electoral votes to McClellan's 45. Sherman occupied South Carolina's capital in mid-February, and Charleston and Fort Sumter were retaken a day later. On the 4th of March, Abraham Lincoln, at the East Portico under the completed dome of the Capitol, was sworn in for his second term as president, delivering an inaugural address that constitutes his third supreme specimen of rhetorical grace: "With malice toward none, with charity for all, with firmness in the right as God gives us to see the right, let us strive on to finish the work we are in, to bind up the nation's wounds." And within weeks, on April 1, Grant had broken through Lee's lines at Petersburg, driving the rebel army westward. The next day the Confederate government fled Richmond. By the 8th, Sheridan had reached a crossroads that let him cut off the rebel general's retreat; and at that spot in the afternoon following, on April 9, 1865, Ulysses S. Grant accepted Robert E. Lee's surrender of his Army of Northern Virginia, at Appomattox.

9. APRIL 1865

Bob Lincoln was at Appomattox, outside on the steps of the brick residence (which still stands) while within, in the parlor, the two generals signed papers that effectively ended the Civil War. The president's son and recent Harvard graduate had longed to get into the fight before it was over, but his mother was terrified of losing yet another child, this one on the battlefield. Robert pleaded; Mary Lincoln protested and cried; and the Commander in Chief compromised by attaching his eldest (or rather by then, with the death of two sons already, his elder) to Grant's staff late in the war.

Captain Lincoln was back from Appomattox within the week, the fighting virtually done, and he free to visit with family and friends in Washington, including with John Hay upstairs in the White House on Friday evening, April 14.

Hay and young Lincoln would have found much to talk about. There was the surrender, of course, and the captain's having met General Lee at Appomattox; he had already told his father about that at breakfast. And this very noon, down in South Carolina, at Fort Sumter in Charleston Harbor, the conflict came full circle. On this day, precisely four years after its federal commander had saluted Old Glory being lowered in surrender to rebel forces, the hands of that same commander raised the identical flag in celebration of a Union restored, near the end of the war that rebel shore batteries firing on Sumter at an earlier dawn had begun.

As for Hay, his situation had changed over recent weeks as well, and he and Bob Lincoln would have talked about that. Hay would no longer be serving as the president's private secretary through this second term. The young man had his reasons, although not all of them for sharing, inasmuch as one concerned the younger Lincoln's mother. Hay had had enough of the Hell-Cat; and anyway, she had her own favored candidate for the position he was leaving. For another, Hay was sick up to here of petitioners; some years afterward, in 1880, when a later president-elect asked him to take on the same role he had filled for Lincoln, Colonel Hay respectfully declined, gorge rising at the memory: "The contact with the greed and selfishness of office-seekers and the bull-dozing Congressmen is unspeakably repulsive," he told his old Civil War acquaintance James A. Garfield, now bound for the White House. "The constant contact with envy, meanness, ignorance, and the swinish selfishness which ignorance breeds needs a stronger heart and a more obedient nervous system than I can boast."

So Hay would be relinquishing the duties he had capably discharged throughout the Civil War, never to resume them, as would Nicolay, intent on going home and marrying Therena Bates. Both secretaries would leave as early as was convenient for Mr. Lincoln. To his brother Charles, Hay wrote about it: "I am thoroughly sick of certain aspects of life here, which you will understand without my putting them on paper." He would have quit soon anyhow, and meanwhile Secretary Seward had found a post for Hay in the State Department—"entirely unsolicited and unexpected"—at the U.S. Legation in Paris. Mr. Seward was one whom the secretary worked with almost daily and in whose nearby home he had frequently been a visitor on White House business, or to play whist, or to dine. The two, in fact, felt real affection for each other, the Secretary of State now offering Hay a position for which his young friend was eminently qualified. And Mr. Lincoln acquiesced, although he "requested me to stay with him a month or so longer to get him started with the reorganized office, which I shall do, and shall sail probably in June."

Meanwhile (with Mr. Nicolay "absent at Charleston, at the flag-raising over Sumter"), Hay and Bob Lincoln were "gossiping in an upper room" of the White House, as the former recalled some two decades later, gossiping sometime around 10:30 on that first Friday evening after Appomattox, neither one distracted by the persistent revelry that the weather outside only somewhat dampened: the city's ongoing, raucous rejoicing, with bright bunting strung everywhere, celebratory weaponry firing off, street crowds genially shouting out their often inebriated cheer, illuminations alight in windows—of eagles, of stars and stripes, of Peace, Peace. Until suddenly—in an older Hay's later words, recollecting the horrid instant—from a catastrophe among the audience at Ford's Theatre on Tenth Street four or five blocks away "a crowd of people rushed instinctively to the White House and, bursting through the doors, shouted the dreadful news to Robert Lincoln and Major Hay." The president has been shot! Or was it a messenger Mrs. Lincoln dispatched from the site who brought the appalling word? Or the doorman from downstairs? And what precisely had he or they called out? In an instant all was confusion. Something has happened to the president!

Lincoln's son and his friend—Hay continues in the third person—"ran downstairs. Finding a carriage at the door, they entered it to go to Tenth street. As they were driving away, a friend came up and told them that Mr. Seward and most of the Cabinet had been murdered. The news was all so improbable that they could not help hoping it was all untrue. But when they got to Tenth street and found every thoroughfare blocked by the swiftly gathering thousands, agitated by tumultuous excitement, they were prepared for the worst. In a few minutes those who had been sent for, and many others, were gathered in the little chamber where the chief of state lay in his agony."

Secretary Seward had indeed—at about the same time—been violently attacked in his bed at home, a knife-bearing intruder wounding him and his adult son grievously; and Vice President Andrew Johnson was slated for murder as well, his picked assassin losing his nerve, however, and slinking away. But the murderer of the president, in a box at Ford's Theatre with Mrs. Lincoln seated alongside as horrified witness, had managed to accomplish what he set out to do that fatal night: entering the presidential presence unimpeded not long after ten, in the midst of the play in progress below, and from behind firing a bullet into the brains of Abraham Lincoln, who slumped forward senseless. The murderer Booth—the handsome twenty-six-year-old theatrical star John Wilkes Booth—paused, witnesses from across the theater reported, as though awaiting applause; and indeed, amazingly, the assassin anticipated gratitude from the nation for what he had done, although at the moment he was fighting off another man in the box and, nimble as the trained young actor he was, was vaulting over the railing the ten feet down to the stage. *Sic semper tyrannis*, some heard the assassin cry out—Virginia's state motto: "Thus always to tyrants!"—all gaping astounded as, despite breaking an ankle bone in the fall, Booth limped hastily toward and past an actor fleeing in incomprehension and disappeared backstage out a rear door onto a waiting horse and into the alleyway darkness before anybody could stop him.

A doctor had got up to the crowded box. The president must be moved. They carried Mr. Lincoln's long form through the corridor, down the stairs, out into the damp night, and across the street to a rooming house opposite. A bedroom had been hastily made ready, and in there on a bed too short the brain-shattered body was laid. "The wound would have brought instant death to most men," Hay surmised, but Lincoln's strength "was extraordinary. He was, of course, unconscious from the first moment; but he breathed with slow and regular respiration throughout the night." Behind the headboard Robert Lincoln and John Hay stood among others listening to the breathing in the packed little room. (How tiny it seems to the visitor now! Can such a cramped space ever have held the twenty-nine somber witnesses whom Hay records as present during Lincoln's final hours?)

About all this the secretary's invaluable diary is silent, its final entry on December 18, 1864, well before the fatal night. But some two decades afterward Hay set down an account, doubtless making use of sources to prod his memory, of a scene he had been part of himself. Near him, at the head of the bed through their vigil into the morning hours of the 15th of April, had stood Gideon Welles, Secretary of the Navy, who recorded soon after in his own diary what he saw. Welles brings the scene into sharper focus. "The giant sufferer lay extended diagonally across the bed, which was not long enough for him. He had been stripped of his clothes. His large arms, which were occasionally exposed, were of a size which one would scarce have expected from his spare appearance. His slow, full respiration lifted the clothes with each breath that he took. His features were calm and striking. I had never seen them appear to better advantage than for the first hour, perhaps, that I was there. After that, his right eye began to swell and that part of his face became discolored." Guards were stationed at the front door and on the sidewalk to control the crowd, "which was of course highly excited and anxious," Welles goes on. "The room was small and overcrowded. The surgeons and members of the Cabinet were as many as should have been in the room, but there were many more, and the hall and other rooms in the front or main house were full. One of these rooms was occupied by Mrs. Lincoln and her attendants, with Miss Harris," the latter a guest of the Lincolns in their theater box that evening: Clara Harris, whose fiancé Major Rathbone had grappled with Booth and was badly cut doing so. Across Tenth Street this short time later, "once an hour Mrs. Lincoln would repair to the bedside of her dying husband," Welles writes, "and with lamentation and tears remain until overcome by emotion." Or until her hysterics led others to press her to leave.

And what thoughts must have been going through John Hay's mind as he waited behind the headboard during that long, slow watch? He had noted, and years later would write about, changes that came over his chief in the course of the war: Lincoln "was in mind, body and nerves a very different man at the second inauguration from the one who had taken the oath in 1861." Although his kindness persisted, there was less laughter, fewer funny stories. The president had been called on to bear so much. Hay enumerates: disappointments, treachery, hope deferred, the open assaults of enemies and the sincere anger of discontented friends, as well as the "affliction which flowed from the great conflict in which he was engaged and which he could not evade. One of the most tender and compassionate of men, he was forced to give orders which cost thousands of lives; by nature a man of order and thrift, he saw the daily spectacle of unutterable waste and destruction which he could not prevent. The cry of the widow and the orphan was always in his ears; the awful responsibility resting upon him as the protector of an imperilled republic kept him true to his duty, but could not make him unmindful of the intimate details of that vast sum of human misery involved in civil war."

The vigil allowed Hay ample time to ponder such burdens and changes. To brood as well on his friend Mr. Seward's condition, horribly wounded. To feel what must have been an overwhelming sadness in the sound of the president's tenacious breathing, with so much that would never be said to him now, so much that the magnanimous, kind Springfield attorney and politician had done for a young poet-cum-lawyer from Warsaw, Illinois, which now could never be acknowledged.

There was a consolation. The president had been allowed to live long enough to see last November's election successfully concluded, when a republic had done what no such republic had managed before, what many had thought a government by the people couldn't do: in the midst of horrendous civil strife—and without violence, even though feelings ran high—had conducted a federal canvass, Lincoln *vs.* McClellan, with bonfires, torchlight parades, marching bands, and full-throated oratory, testing whether the Constitution could endure amid such desperate contentions, whether a republic so conceived could survive such a continental ordeal. It *had* survived: the election had gone off peacefully. The people's will had been registered. The war was won. Slaves were free. And the Union was saved.

This dying man had saved the Union. Years later—in words that recollection touches with lyricism—Hay writes of the ineradicable scene when the regular breathing of him who had served his country so well finally stopped. "As the dawn came, and the lamplight grew pale in the fresher beams," nearly nine hours after the mortally wounded body had been laid on a rooming-house bed, Lincoln's "pulse began to fail; but his face even then was scarcely more haggard than those of the sorrowing group of statesmen and generals around him. His automatic moaning, which had continued through the night, ceased; a look of unspeakable peace came upon his worn features. At twenty-two minutes after seven he died."

Edwin Stanton, Democrat, high-priced railroad attorney who in Cincinnati once, in 1855, had rudely snubbed a gangly Springfield lawyer working on a case with him, but whom the generous-spirited Republican when president had nevertheless picked as the right man for the crucial post of secretary of war, a position that the incorruptible Stanton filled with distinction and with what grew into devotion to Lincoln himself: in the moments after the president quit breathing, it was the secretary of war, Hay tells us, who broke the silence. "Now," Stanton said, "he belongs to the ages." A clergyman present fell to his knees in fervent prayer, and Robert Lincoln went to fetch his mother, who, upon entering supported by her son, "cast herself with loud outcry on the dead body."

10. FROM WASHINGTON, D.C., TO SPRINGFIELD

He had been shot on Good Friday evening and died on Saturday morning. Lincoln's body was brought back to the White House; and, in a room upstairs, his skull was removed to allow for the autopsy (the misshapen lead Derringer bullet that had killed him recovered) and the body embalmed: blood drained, parts that would have hastened decay discarded, and the remains injected with chemicals that hardened them to something like stone. Easter came with its consolations and went, and Monday, and at dawn on Tuesday morning cannon boomed and church bells tolled anew. A great catafalque for displaying the martyred president had been built with haste and love in the East Room (the hammering a torture to Mrs. Lincoln upstairs); and all day Tuesday, the public was allowed to go in and file by, the line outside the White House a mile long, special trains having poured mourners into the city steadily over the past three days.

The rooms that those mourners entered were darkened, shrouded in black, mirrors and chandeliers covered with black cloth, black streamers hung along the walls. All day the file passed through, silent except for sobs of grief by the coffin: women and men, old and young, white and black, civilians and soldiers, the disabled on their crutches waiting, hobbling forward for a last look at their dead commander in chief.

No more than a second or two could be allowed for each passerby to gaze down at the immobile face paler and more statuelike than in life, as the line behind patiently, endlessly waited its turn. At 7:30 that evening the doors were closed. The funeral in the East Room began next day at noon. All of Washington's shops and places of business had shut, and the city's homes and buildings public and private were draped in black banners, black ribbons, black bunting. Flags were at half-staff. People wore black armbands, black hatbands. A *Lincoln Memorial* volume prepared soon after gives us those and other details fresh from the site, including who attended the funeral: cabinet members, senators, representatives, Supreme Court justices, generals, diplomats, the president's many friends, members of Mrs. Lincoln's family, although she herself remained too distraught to be present. Captain Robert Lincoln was there, at the foot of the coffin, with Major Hay nearby, beside Mr. Nicolay, back from his travels down South. We learn what clergymen led the earnest, lengthy prayers and precisely what words they uttered, and who gave the ample sermon, the very sentences he spoke, all closely printed in the *Memorial*, nearly eight small-font pages of the cleric's somber, perishable phrasings.

Navy Secretary and diarist Gideon Welles was there, and afterward Mr. Welles and Mr. Stanton rode together in the great procession—muffled drums measuredly beating—that accompanied the coffin up Pennsylvania Avenue, among immense crowds (Welles confirms) on either side, in a cortège the front of which already extended to the Capitol a mile and a half away before the carriages with the cabinet officers had even started to move. The *Memorial* tells us that the hearse, "drawn by six gray horses, each led by a groom," was followed by the "horse of the deceased, led by two grooms, caparisoned," with the president's riding boots reversed in the stirrups, followed by "the family of the deceased, relatives, private secretaries, and friends," followed by delegations from Illinois and Kentucky, followed by the current president Mr. Johnson and party, followed by members of the Cabinet. There, amid all the pomp, was where secretaries Welles and Stanton had been stationed, ahead of participants on foot and in carriages for a mile and more farther back. "The vacant holiday expression had given way to real grief," Welles notes of the surrounding masses on both sides of the avenue, "sorrow, trouble, and distress" on the faces of men and women, awe on the children's faces. But there were no truer mourners, he reports, "than the poor colored people who crowded the streets, joined the procession, and exhibited their woe, bewailing the loss of him whom they regarded as a benefactor and father." He adds a sentence that reveals his own intense impression of the day: "Seward, I am told, sat up in bed, and viewed the procession and hearse of the President, and I know his emotion."

Secretary of State Seward would survive the near-fatal bedroom assault, although disfigured for life from deep knife wounds down his cheek. And John Wilkes Booth would be caught after ten days in flight and a massive manhunt through Maryland woods into Virginia that finally pinned the assassin down, crippled, in a farmer's barn some seventy miles south of Washington. When Booth wouldn't come out, his pursuers set the barn on fire. Through a crack in the wall a soldier shot the armed killer at the barn door, in the back of the neck close to where Lincoln had been shot. Three hours later Booth died on the farmer's porch, whispering in pain, "Tell my mother . . . that I die for my country"—for the Confederacy. A military tribunal untenderly tried his accomplices, sentencing four of them, including one woman, to hang. The execution was carried out on July 7, 1865, others (judged less guilty, of the eight gathered in) having been put to various spans of years up to life at hard labor.

Well before then Lincoln's corpse reached Springfield and was in its receiving vault at Oak Ridge Cemetery, beside a smaller coffin for the president's son Willie. The journey to Illinois had consumed more than two weeks, delaying so that obsequies might be celebrated at cities along the way. Washington at the start had detained the martyr's body five days, providing an additional opportunity—through all of a drizzly, dreary Thursday—for the public to view for a last time, on the elaborate catafalque, their leader's earthly remains lying in state in the Capitol rotunda.

Finally, on Friday the 21st, a week after the murder, the funeral train set out for Baltimore. At the Washington depot that morning, a "few minutes before eight o'clock, Capt. Robert Lincoln, son of the President, accompanied by two relatives, arrived and took his seat in the cars. Messrs. Nicolay and Hay, the late President's private secretaries, arrived a few moments later and also took their places." The funeral train got under way soon after, engine bell tolling, its speed kept slow for safety but without any stops, to reach Baltimore two hours later. En route in "out-of-the-way places, little villages, or single farm-houses, people came out to the side of the track and watched, with heads reverently uncovered and faces full of genuine sadness." Indeed, "every five rods along the whole line were seen these mourning groups, some on foot and some in carriages, wearing badges of sorrow, and many evidently having come a long distance to pay this little tribute of respect, the only one in their power."

The journey must have reminded Major Hay (whom Secretary Stanton was to brevet as colonel within a month; hence, Colonel Hay from that time forward)—must have reminded him of the train trip four years earlier west to east, and for a similar purpose: to let as many people as possible see their president. Indeed, the itinerary of this current transit would follow the earlier, meandering, nearly two-thousand-mile route of the president-elect in reverse, with three exceptions: Pittsburgh and Cincinnati were to be omitted, and from Indianapolis the train would turn north to take in Chicago, before proceeding to its final destination. And as before, all along, crowds would be gathering beside the tracks beyond the train windows: in the countryside, at village depots, at towns, at stations in cities, as here in Baltimore at 10 A.M., dignitaries on hand in greeting: Governor Bradford, Lieutenant Governor Cox, General Berry, Hon. William B. Hill, secretary of state, and others of the Monument City's distinguished citizens.

Yet how different this journey! Instead of the red-white-and-blue bunting, the seas of cheering faces around each stopping place, the fireworks, the bonfires, the brass bands and loud parades, the enthusiasm, the joy—now all was somber, hushed, as the black-draped pilot engine made sure the tracks were clear ahead while the funeral train followed, Locomotive 238 pulling its seven cars, including the president's, all of them covered in black. When it halted at Baltimore, a procession began at 10:30 promptly to move from Camden Station—detachment of cavalry with buglers preceding, an artillery battery, infantry from the Eleventh Indiana Volunteers at Fort McHenry, the Guard of Honor rigid at present arms—all that ceremonial respect on display as the cortège advanced solemnly down Eutaw Street toward Calvert Street and the Exchange. There, on a canopied catafalque in the midst of elaborate floral arrangements, the lid of the president's coffin was opened and the people filed by, until "about half-past two o'clock, to the regret of thousands of our citizens, the coffin was closed and the face that was so dear to the nation was hidden from view, and, escorted by the guards of honor, the body was removed to the hearse."

Thus onward, to Harrisburg for further obsequies and viewing from nine to twelve that night; on to Philadelphia, reaching the Broad Street station at 4:30 the next afternoon ("It may be said that the entire route from Baltimore to Philadelphia was amid crowds of sorrowing people, for between villages and towns, all the way, farmers and their families assembled in fields and about houses, seriously and reverently gazing at the fleeting funeral *cortège*"); and onward, once there, in procession along the designated route through vast crowds to Independence Hall, for a viewing that lasted until one o'clock in the morning and resumed that morning at five; then on to Jersey City for viewing; to New York City, the remains displayed in City Hall and the procession the most elaborate in the metropolis up to then—rooftops, trees filled with people, every window crowded with people (living people, as surviving photographs a century and a half later freeze the blurry images in their corporeal reality to confirm), sashes removed from windows so that their view might be unobstructed—one window near Union Square, above the great dark procession seen passing below, containing Theodore Roosevelt, six-year-old Teedie with what may be his younger brother peering out, two little blurs, from an upstairs room in their wealthy grandfather's home.

On to Albany, to Buffalo, to Cleveland, to Columbus, to Indianapolis, to Chicago, the embalmer's art imperfect, so that the putty-like coloration had darkened and the presidential face turned grotesque toward the last; yet the crowds insisted on a glimpse of what was less and less recognizable, in Chicago pleading irresistibly that the coffin, which authorities had wanted to keep closed, be opened. April had turned into May, was three days into May before the remains of Abraham Lincoln reached Springfield, and the final elaborate procession was enacted: somber dignitaries, the military companies, the societies, the institutes, Knights Templars, Odd Fellows, Fenians, and always the multitudes, totaling hundreds of thousands by then, millions who had seen the train pass or gazed down upon those increasingly unrecognizable features, somberly, reverently, silently except for tearful sobs, minute guns firing, church bells pealing, dirges sounding, sermons intoned, amid the flags and black bunting and evergreen wreaths and the portraits of the Emancipator amid apt mottos hung on black-draped walls. And always the sadness.

Hay and Nicolay attended the final obsequies in the Illinois State House. But the two had traveled to Springfield on their own, having left the funeral train early, perhaps as early as Baltimore, to return to the White House, there to help with arranging the president's papers. Robert Lincoln was in charge of those now; and the secretaries were helping their friend put them in some kind of order—"Hay and I are still here arranging the papers of the office, which has kept us very busy," Nicolay wrote to his fiancée toward the end of April—get them into boxes, file them away somehow. Wearisome, sad work, in the forsaken upstairs emptiness of the White House, but not without satisfactions. Even that early, the secretaries were planning to write about their chief, their friendship with his son granting them access to material indispensable for doing so. For now, though, they had enough work in hand and new lives to launch, with Nicolay to wed Miss Bates back in Pittsfield in weeks ahead, his best man to be his friend John Hay, before the three set off for Europe together. Nicolay was to assume a fresh set of duties as consul in Paris—more of Secretary Seward's generosity—with Hay bound for his posting elsewhere in the same city, as secretary of the U.S. Legation.

"I think it will be a pleasant place for study and observation," the colonel had written a cousin in innocent hours of April 13, the day before the president was shot. "I shall no doubt enjoy it for a year or so—not very long, as I do not wish to exile myself in these important and interesting times." Colonel Hay was going away, he said, "only to fit myself for more serious work when I return."

But when he, and Nicolay, and Therena Bates—now Mrs. Nicolay—sailed together that July, with Hay's work in America done for the present, the colonel took along an invaluable cachet that would benefit him all his life, this young man of twenty-six (who would find so much to do with those years ahead) forever after made special for having once been close to Abraham Lincoln. No wonder Billy Herndon, Springfield attorney gathering information about his slain law partner, was eager to hear from Colonel Hay. And did finally, from Paris, September 5, 1866. "I am so constantly busy," Hay as *chargé d'affaires* answered the lawyer tardily, "that I have had no quiet day in which I [could] write you what you desired in your letter several months ago." What Attorney Herndon was after were intimate details, and Hay furnished them: that Lincoln's breakfast at the Soldiers' Home was "extremely frugal—an egg, a piece of toast coffee &c," and he would be up, dressed, done with breakfast, and on his way the three miles to Washington by 8 o'clock. In winter, at the White House, he didn't get up that early, not sleeping very well, although spending a good bit of time in bed. Ten o'clock was the official hour for the start of business, but the halls and anterooms were full long before then, "people anxious to get the first axe ground." The president wasn't methodical; "it was a four-years struggle on Nicolay's part and mine to get him to adopt some systematic rules." Whatever kept the public away from him the president resisted, "although they nearly annoyed the life out of him by unreasonable complaints & requests." Lunch for Mr. Lincoln was at noon, "a biscuit, a glass of milk in winter, some fruit or grapes in summer. He dined at fr. 5 to 6. & we went off to our dinner also." People, meanwhile, were crowding into the White House just about all day long.

Lincoln, it should be said, "was very abstemious—ate less than any one I know. Drank nothing but water—not from principle, but because he did not like wine or spirits." And he didn't read much: "Scarcely ever looked into a newspaper unless I called his attention to an article on some special subject." Nor was he modest. "It is absurd to call him a modest man. No great man was ever modest." And Lincoln *was* great. Hay ends his recollections with that judgment, he who had started with doubts about the gangly prairie lawyer back in Springfield ("I am beginning to respect him more than formerly," as of January 1861). By 1866, after living with his chief and working at his side through four intense, crisis-filled years, the knowledgeable, level-headed young colonel concludes his letter to Herndon with the flat assertion that "Lincoln, with all his foibles, is"—presumably because he freed the bondsman, put down rebellion, and preserved the example of the Republic for all the nations on earth—"the greatest character since Christ."

Mark Twain in July 1870. Photo by Matthew Brady. Courtesy of the Mark Twain Project, The Bancroft Library, University of California, Berkeley.

2

HAY AND MARK TWAIN: THE 1870S

11. LIVELIHOOD IN THE EAST

Mark Twain recalled years later—more than once and always fondly—that he met John Hay in 1867. If so, the meeting would have had to occur in New York City, which the Wild Humorist of the Pacific Slope (from San Francisco voyaging south to Central America, overland across Nicaragua, then north in the Atlantic) had reached by mid-January of that year: at 8 o'clock on Saturday morning the 12th had "stood in the biting air of the upper deck and sailed by the snow-covered, wintry looking residences on Staten Island—recognized Castle Garden—beheld the vast city spread out beyond, encircled with its palisade of masts, and adorned with its hundred steeples—saw the steam-tug and ferry-boats swarming through the floating ice, instinct with a frenzied energy, as we passed the river—and in a little while we were ashore and safe housed at the Metropolitan." The river was the Hudson, on the way to the East River, and the Metropolitan the local hotel where Californians liked to stay, where Mark Twain—or Samuel L. Clemens, as he would have signed the register—stayed for his first three weeks on this present occasion.

In the winter and spring of 1867, Clemens was thirty-one; Hay, off in Paris when the year began, was twenty-eight. They would have had to meet for the first time later than January and not after June, during which latter month both sailed in separate ships on different days for Europe, in Hay's case to Vienna until beyond the rest of the year, in the case of Clemens on a cruise that would return him to New York in November and change his life. But the humorist had much to do in New York City before setting off that summer. Already Mark Twain was known here in the East for an amusing sketch that newspapers far and wide had reprinted: "The Celebrated Jumping Frog of

Calaveras County." But not *well* known, as he was well known on the West Coast, the far-off West Coast, which back then you could reach from New York three ways. You could sail the 14,700 perilous miles around Cape Horn at the tip of South America. You could sail south far enough to cross overland at Panama or Nicaragua (as Clemens had just done in the opposite direction) and complete that shorter journey of five thousand miles on a different ship north to California. Or you could proceed on solid earth maybe part way by rail to the Mississippi and from there the two thousand miles overland—across the vast territories that Senator Douglas and Mr. Lincoln had argued about—in a wagon, on horseback, or by stagecoach to the far Pacific.

The Missouri-born Sam Clemens had gone West in a stagecoach six years ago, in 1861. That earlier June, near the start of the Civil War but before Bull Run turned it into a long-term conflict, he had served as second lieutenant in an irregular Confederate militia unit for no more than a couple of soggy weeks, long enough to lose a taste for warfare altogether, and in August had crossed the plains in a stagecoach to distant Nevada Territory, there to wait out the shooting back East. Sam meant to mine for silver out there, get rich, and in a few months when the war was over return to St. Louis and bestow the comforts of wealth on his widowed mother.

It didn't work out that way. The war didn't end as promptly as Clemens and a great many others had thought it would, and meanwhile he spent not four or five months but five and a half years in the West. As a prospector in his mid-twenties, the young man proved a bust, but in the late summer of 1862 he stumbled on a job that suited him better. He began writing for the *Territorial Enterprise* in Virginia City, a silver-mining town four years old and already boasting fifteen thousand people, perched in the foothills of the Sierra Nevada mountains close to the recently discovered Comstock Lode.

In those exuberant surroundings Clemens for the first time made use of the pen name "Mark Twain," signed to an article filed from nearby Carson City in late January 1863. During months ahead, spoofs, burlesques, tall tales, and much else that was pointed and amusing appeared over the odd *nom de plume*. The articles ran in the *Enterprise*, which exchanged newspapers to copy from and be copied by those in California, so that readers in San Francisco and Sacramento soon were looking forward to sketches over Mark Twain's distinctive name. "Everybody knows me," their author was able to boast well before the year was out to his folks back home, "& I fare like a prince wherever I go, be it on this side of the mountains or the other." And with his new pen name he was in time acknowledging a calling, "a 'call' to literature," as he described it, although literature "of a low order—*i.e.* humorous. It is nothing to be proud of, but it is my strongest suit." Long before this, Sam should have stopped meddling with silver mines and suchlike matters, "for which I was by nature unfitted & turned my attention to seriously scribbling to excite the *laughter* of God's creatures." Henceforth, he meant to content himself with doing just that as his way of earning a livelihood.

Some of his earlier scribbling had taken the form of travel letters. People before the war, in an agrarian society where the majority lived on farms or in towns and villages, liked reading about far-off places that most of them would never see for themselves. In 1853 Clemens had begun writing travel letters while venturing forth looking at the country firsthand, this restless, curious young typesetter who hadn't yet journeyed far from Hannibal, Missouri, the Mississippi River town where he grew up. In that year, at seventeen, he left Hannibal for good, taking a steamboat downriver the hundred miles to St. Louis, there setting type in a printing office long enough to get funds to travel east, to New York City, Philadelphia, and Washington. Just looking; just seeing what was to be seen: the Crystal Palace in Manhattan; the Liberty Bell and Franklin's grave and America's earliest cable suspension bridge in Philadelphia; the unfinished stump of the Washington Monument in the capital. People he met hoped the lad wasn't downhearted so far from home. "'Downhearted,' the devil! I haven't had a particle of such a feeling since I left Hannibal more than four months ago." And he found it easy to describe what he saw for readers of his brother Orion's newspaper back in Hannibal. Thus the footloose traveler was able to go where he chose and stay about as long as he wanted, setting type in printing offices for wages—at a simpler time when everybody got his news from newspapers, and just about every village could support a paper or two—as well as writing letters that his well-meaning brother printed and intended to pay him for, although somehow never getting around to it with any regularity.

Others would pay, though. On that three-weeks' stagecoach ride west in 1861, Clemens set out agreeing to write travel letters for a Keokuk, Iowa, newspaper; and in 1866, after his stint of close to two years at Virginia City's *Territorial Enterprise* (followed by some months freelancing in San Francisco—the popular "Jumping Frog" sketch came out of that later interlude), he persuaded the *Sacramento Union* to let him sail to the Sandwich Islands—Hawaii the largest of them—and write letters from an exotic locale that Californians were much interested in. He wrote his twenty-five letters, was paid $20 for each one, and had a grand time getting it done. The reporter had been dispatched to investigate the industry of the islands: sugar plantations, other exports, statistics. But the letters Mark Twain sent back provided much more than that, provided life and humor and voices and vivid verbal pictures (for he was a sharp observer and a fine mimic), so that on the mainland those new sketches by the "Jumping Frog" author were much talked of, with their singular, fresh style that gave information in such lively fashion. Late that summer of 1866 Clemens sailed back to San Francisco, toward augmented fame and an employer well satisfied—Missouri traveler born in the middle of America who had never ventured onto the ocean before this round trip over the Pacific now coming to an end. And he had loved being at sea, *loved* it, as he had thrived on the rigors of mule travel and rustic accommodations among the islands themselves. "Aug 13—San Francisco—Home again. No—*not* home again—in prison again—and all the wild sense of freedom gone. The city seems so cramped, & so dreary with toil & care & business anxiety."

He didn't plan to stay there long: meant to travel the world as Mark Twain writing his letters, would see and describe Japan, China—see it all. But first he must visit his folks back in St. Louis: mother, recently widowed sister, his niece Annie, and nephew Sam—none of whom he'd laid eyes on in six years. Visit with them, then back out to sea and over the globe at his leisure.

But before he could do any of that, opportunity pointed toward a different path he might follow. With his dry Missouri drawl, Clemens had spoken in public three or four times, at banquets and such, and appeared to have a knack for it. People liked listening to him. He had a popular subject, too: the Sandwich Islands, about which San Franciscans were curious. Lecturing, moreover, provided respectable entertainment in an era with far fewer decent amusements than our own. Why shouldn't he try his hand at it?

He did, at the Academy of Music, just after eight in the evening of October 2, 1866, before what turned out to be a delighted overflow audience, roaring with laughter and coming away not only highly entertained but also with knowledge enlarged. It was "one of the most interesting and amusing lectures ever given in this city," one newspaper assured the town the next morning; and suddenly, fortuitously, Clemens had found another way to make money: he could write his travel letters and could lecture about those travels, as he went on to do that same fall over California and into Nevada at such places as Grass Valley, and Red Dog, and You Bet, and Gold Hill.

But would western lectures with the raucous laughter they gave rise to play to more sedate, sophisticated audiences back East? Clemens boarded ship in December partly to find out, sailing from San Francisco south to Nicaragua, there disembarking to cross by mule train and lake boat, then reembarking at Greytown bound north for Manhattan, expenses covered by nine long letters back to the *Alta California* describing colorful personalities and tumultuous times on board: the horrendous storm that nearly swamped the vessel the first night out, the cholera that brought swift cruel death among passengers steaming north in the Atlantic: shipmates in fine health one day swaddled on the next and weighted and slid overboard. "The passengers are fearfully exercised, and with considerable reason, for we are about to have our fifth death in five days, and the sixth of the voyage." It was terrifying, the Wild Humorist of the Pacific Slope no more immune than others to the random fatal threat; yet at the end of the voyage, whatever Sam Clemens/Mark Twain was feeling on a bracing upper deck, his destination in sight as he glided through New York Harbor on that icy Saturday morning of January 12, 1867, he wouldn't be long ashore before he was eager to set sail again.

He remained on land nearly five months, increasingly restless while tending to a whirlwind of business. For employers at the *Alta* back in San Francisco he wrote the travel letters they were paying for, many describing New York City and the frenetic bustle of the place. Traffic below City Hall Park, for instance: "where drays, carriages, carts and pedestrians keep the great thoroughfare in a constant state of crowding, struggling, chaotic confusion." In the streets down there "the police are as thick as they are at headquarters in San Francisco at the changing of the evening watch. And how they work!—how they charge through the tangled vehicles, and order this one to go this way, another that way, and a third to stand still or back!—how they wade through mud and slush, piloting women safely through the fearful jam!" Fulton at Broadway was so bad they were building a pedestrian bridge to get people across. But despite all the crowds and the clamor, New York could be a "splendid desert—a domed and steepled solitude," Mark Twain warned his California readers, its anonymous atmosphere one that "will drive a man crazy, after a while, or kill him."

New York was a desert of solitude even for those restless souls, like Clemens himself, who had friends in town already. Cronies from the West had come east before him, a couple of whom he looked up early on. Frank Fuller was one, formerly acting governor of Utah Territory and lively Jack of many trades: licensed to practice law in Nevada, practitioner of dentistry in New Hampshire, agent, salesman building a fortune, and friend. Fuller wanted Mark Twain to lecture before New Yorkers, something the humorist was shy about doing so promptly. But western colleagues would take care of everything: book the hall, advertise, make sure the seats were filled. The Sandwich Islands would be his subject, and the hall they booked was spacious Cooper Union, in early May on an evening when—at its arrival—competition for spectators proved fierce: Japanese acrobats debuting in town that same night, Speaker Colfax lecturing at Irving Hall about his trip across the country, a popular Italian tragedienne giving her farewell performance. Clemens felt apprehensive, not even sure that his frontier humor would interest these refined easterners; they'll "call it coarse and possibly taboo it."

Meanwhile, another crony from out West was in town: Charles Henry Webb, formerly founder and editor (with Bret Harte) of the *Californian*, a San Francisco literary journal to which Mark Twain had contributed. Now Webb wanted to gather together various of his friend's sketches, including the "Jumping Frog," and see them published, get out a book of Mark Twain's articles this spring. All that was gratifying to a westerner trying to make his way in the East: the lecture forthcoming, the collection of sketches proposed, with Clemens keeping busy all the while scouring the city for subject matter for his letters to *Alta* readers, seventeen in all sent back from here on whatever caught his eye: "The Bewitching New Fashions," "Sunday Amusements," "The Dreadful Russian Bath," "The Great Masquerade" at the *Bal d'Opéra*, and—on March 2—a particularly intriguing development, unprecedented in America: a "Grand European Pleasure Trip" proposed. For his California readers Mark Twain described it in detail: prominent Brooklynites were getting up an excursion, "which promises a vast amount of enjoyment," so much so that the "passenger list is filling up pretty fast." The plan was to charter a steamer, have it equipped with uncrowded comfort, set sail this summer, and linger at various ports of call in the Mediterranean on the way to the Holy Land. "Isn't it a most attractive scheme? Five months of utter freedom from care and anxiety of every kind, and in company with a set of people who will go only to enjoy themselves, and will never mention a word about business during the whole voyage."

How Mark Twain envied them! How he longed to be on board! But for now he must pay that visit to St. Louis, to his family, writing travel letters along the way. "We took passage in the cars of the New Jersey Central at 8 P.M. of the 3d of March, and left port in the midst of a cheerful snow-storm," he wrote from St. Louis on the 15th, injecting himself into the reportage in a way that his readers (and editors) relished, in the course of a sentence that wound itself out as leisurely as the train ride and to about the length of the train itself:

> I call it cheerful because there *is* something exquisitely satisfactory in whistling along through a shrouded land, following blindly wherever the demon in the lead may take you, yet sensible that he knows the way, and will steer his unerring

course as faithfully as if it were noonday; sensible also that you are as safe there as anywhere, sitting with back against the bulkhead, and feet crossed on the next seat, and hat drawn down to shade the eyes from the lamp overhead—sitting thus by the comfortable fire, smoking placidly and dreaming of other times and other scenes, taking small heed of the storm without, yet scarcely conscious that it is snowing and is blowing drearily across the bleak moor as well, and that some people are out there suffering in it, and distressed, but that you ain't, that, on the contrary, you are perfectly happy, and tranquil, and satisfied, sitting thus, and smoking, and dreaming, and being timed and soothed by the clatter of the wheels—well, you know there *is* something unspeakably comfortable about it.

St. Louis when the traveler got there provided considerably less comfort. Clemens was moody with his family, and restless. So much had changed: political bitterness "still about as strong as it ever was" during the war, so that old friends "don't visit and don't hold any intercourse with each other." His own old friends had changed, or moved away, or died. He did lecture a couple of times to appreciative houses, and steamed upriver to lecture at towns he had known before the war: Hannibal, Quincy, Keokuk. But there, too, changes for the worse left him glum: "The railroads have badly crippled the trade" of the steamboats on the river, which "used to go crowded with passengers and freight all the time, but they have room and to spare now." And such river towns as Marion City, one that many of his California readers would know of "and be interested in learning its fate"; for those readers he quotes from his notes, scribbled with the site fresh in mind: "Half a dozen ruined frame houses just ready to cave into the river; a ruined frame church, with roof full of holes . . . Marion City used to be an important shipping point. The railroads killed it."

By mid-April he was glad to be back in New York, and before the month was over he could tell his readers about a book by Mark Twain due out May 1, no more than some of his earlier western newspaper pieces, but still: a book, a first book, which his California friend Webb had put together. *The Celebrated Jumping Frog and Other Sketches*, "$1.50 a copy. It will have a truly gorgeous gold frog on the back of it, and that frog alone will be worth the money." Something more his readers should know: "As per order of the ALTA, just received by telegraph, I have taken passage in the great pleasure excursion to Europe, the Exposition"—that is, the famous world's fair in Paris—"and the Holy Land, and will sail on the 8th of June. You could not have suited me better. The ship is the *Quaker City*, and she is being sumptuously fitted up."

Such, by this time, was the confidence his editors placed in Mark Twain's letters and the high satisfaction they felt in their author: the fare for the voyage a substantial $1,200, plus another $500 for time spent ashore at ports of call (totaling, say, $27,000 in our currency). Clemens had boldly suggested they pay his way, and obligingly the *Alta California*'s New York agent met him with check in hand on his return from St. Louis.

The lecture remained to be given, at Cooper Union no less, amazingly before a full house, so well had California friends here in Manhattan done their part. To be sure, many present held complimentary tickets, so profits were small, the speaker's take a mere $35 in the end. Nevertheless, on the evening of May 6, Mark Twain was standing where, seven years earlier, Abraham Lincoln had stood to give the speech that elevated an Illinois lawyer onto the national stage as a serious presidential contender. In his turn, this later westerner acquitted himself before judgmental eastern listeners about as creditably: "seldom," the *New York Times* wrote next morning, "has so large an audience been so uniformly pleased as the one that listened to Mark Twain's quaint remarks last evening." He let his California readers know about it, in a seventeenth letter in mid-May: "I had a first-rate success myself at the Cooper Institute the other night, but I am not going to say much about that, because you can get it out of the newspapers." Indeed, Mark Twain's Cooper Union lecture was widely reported on. "The Californians worked the thing up," Clemens continued, "and got about twenty-five hundred people in the house—which was well, because on my own merits I could not have accomplished it, perhaps. I lectured once in Brooklyn afterwards, and here again last night, and came out handsomely."

He was far from finished, though—more travel letters to write for the *Alta*, further preparations to be made for the excursion overseas, other outlets to try to interest in his writing (Greeley's *Tribune* for one), goodbyes to be said—but by June 8, Samuel L. Clemens was on board the *Quaker City*, unpacked and eager to steam forth. His agent, former acting governor Fuller, had his instructions: "Collect the ten cents a copy due me on all sales of my book ('The Jumping Frog & Other Sketches—by Mark Twain') from my publisher, C. H. Webb, from time to time, & remit all such moneys to my mother, Mrs. Jane Clemens, 1312 Chestnut street St. Louis, Mo." And as the *Quaker City* made ready to depart, Clemens wrote from on board to that Chestnut Street household as well (there would be, as it turned out, no money from sales of his book to send them). He lamented his recent wretched behavior in St. Louis toward all the family, proclaiming himself unworthy of the love that they nevertheless continued to give him unstintingly.

"You observe," in what he had just set down, self-reproachfully, apologetically, "that under a cheerful exterior I have got a spirit that is angry with me & gives me freely its contempt. I can get away from that at sea, & be tranquil & satisfied—and so, with my parting love & benediction for Orion & all of you, I say good bye & God bless you all—and welcome the wind that wafts a weary soul to the sunny lands of the Mediterranean!"

So he would be off before mid-June 1867. When he returned to New York in November, John Hay was long gone from there and back in Europe. Only briefly that year did Hay and Clemens's time in the city overlap, only for about a week in late February. Yet Mark Twain remembered and on several occasions repeated having met and become good friends with Hay in 1867, as, for example, while recollecting a scene where the two of them were together on a morning fourteen years later, in 1881, happily "chatting and laughing and carrying on almost like our earlier selves of '67"—until the front door opened, abruptly, intrusively, as prelude to an incident we'll revisit in its proper place.

12. HAY OVERSEAS

After lingering five and a half years out West, a shivery Sam Clemens had been gazing, on a morning in mid-January 1867, from the upper deck of the *San Francisco* over icy New York Harbor, while in France John Hay wound up affairs preparatory to coming home. Hay had left the White House soon after President Lincoln's death and ended by spending seventeen months in Paris, much of that time in a diplomatic post, although never with any intention of making a career of diplomacy. Paris was to serve the young man as a pleasant place for study and observation: "I shall no doubt enjoy it for a year or so," he predicted before setting out, "not very long, as I do not wish to exile myself in these important and interesting times." So, in the same January when, at the end of a voyage from San Francisco south, east, and north, Clemens had reached wintry New York, Hay was steaming west from Europe to land late that month at the same port, from which he proceeded directly via overnight train to Washington. Thus Clemens and Hay were not to meet quite so early as in those late days of January.

The diplomat had left Paris of his own volition. Hay's time overseas as secretary of legation had proved rewarding enough, and he had certainly been well qualified to fill the position that Secretary Seward provided him with. By the spring of 1865, under the tutelage of Abraham Lincoln during four years of crisis, what had been a novice of twenty-two progressed from apprentice to journeyman to master by twenty-six. Hay had discharged responsibilities in the White House—and as the president's emissary well beyond the White House—with aplomb and unfailing competence. He had worked hard, yet made the work look easy. He had moved among and won the confidence of many of the key players in the drama of the age. Stanton, Seward, Welles, Chase: good friends all, as were many others. Walt Whitman recalled that Hay "was very much liked by all grades of people in Washington." And why not? He was gregarious, socially adept, genial, and entertaining, even if a bit aloof from his office, as editor John Forney had observed at Gettysburg: never the backslapper, the pol. Forney marveled at the way Hay had "laughed through his term"; yet, for all the light touch, he had earned the confidence and trust of those he worked with. As for carrying such diplomatic skills overseas, he was in addition an able linguist: he learned German as a lad in Warsaw, Pittsfield, and Springfield; learned French at Brown and kept it up reading French literature. Moreover, never having seen Europe before sailing (with his German-born friend Nicolay and the new Mrs. Nicolay) in late June 1865 to assume his Paris duties, he brought with him, beyond solid grounding, an eagerness to encounter European culture face to face. For by then the young colonel was all but a match for so fabled a world, undaunted, a gentleman of quiet assurance, not readily intimidated, at his ease pretty much anywhere.

New Year's Day, 1866: at the Palace of the Tuileries, a formal reception for the Diplomatic Corps. Hay is about to be presented to the great Bonaparte's nephew, the erstwhile Louis Napoleon, now—after a coup d'état—His Imperial Majesty Napoleon III, by the Grace of God and the Will of the Nation Emperor of the French. In formal dress of—as he writes—more gold than broadcloth, a minor American diplomat from Warsaw, Illinois, waits his turn in line. His moment comes. Hay faces the emperor, smiles, bows, starts to move on. But he is detained: Napoleon III is staring—"a short stubby looking man, not nearly so tall as I," the object stared at recorded later—then in English poses a series of questions: "Are you arrived from Washington? Have you been previously engaged in Diplomacy? Were you present at the death of President Lincoln?" And isn't he young to be a *Co-lo-nel*? his interlocutor would wonder at their next meeting. "I answered his questions," Hay wrote afterward, "everybody looking with all their eyes to see what the great potentate had to occupy him talking to a light-weight Republican."

Despite the attention, the little emperor made a poor impression. Hay observed him at that later affair, "moving like a gouty crab: a man so wooden looking that you would expect his voice to come rasping out like a watchman's rattle." A complexion tallow colored, eyes "sleepily watchful—furtive, stealthy, rather ignoble: like servants looking out of dirty windows & saying 'nobody at home' and lying, as they said it." Perhaps so harsh a judgment of the despot was inevitable from one who had learned at Lincoln's side what a ruler should be, now facing a fusty little strongman whose coup d'état fifteen years before had, with a people's enthusiastic blessing, set aside the French republic to make way for the pomp of empire.

In the decade and a half since then, Napoleon III had rebuilt Paris: "a bright new spick and span city," Hay found on arrival, "with stretches a mile long of drab-colored stone palaces, all new and glistening, with avenues and boulevards with pavements like a bathroom floor." What the American had been looking for arose in part out of his reading (in French) *Les Misérables*: a city of the early nineteenth century still with the narrow, twisting streets of medieval Paris, "where they grow revolutions" and youth dreams of what "it must not talk about. But demolition has its teeth fastened there," Hay discovered, "and the great Boulevard St. Germain is steadily marching on, ripping, and crushing, and grinding to powder the oldest and most storied quarter, and evicting the wild and uncombed savagery of the Old City." Purposefully, of course: so that Young France could no longer throw up its makeshift barricades to topple regimes such as the present one, busily constructing the broad pavements and palaces of the Paris we know, that gorgeous City of Light. Hay, however, felt "the deepest interest" in the Old City and its vanishing "squalor and blackness," meaning to leave to American tourists "the beauty of the new dispensation."

Yet the secretary ended by choosing to live in the midst of the new dispensation, on the Right Bank near the *Arc de Triomphe*, not far from where he was working at the American Legation. The work, less demanding than what he had been used to in the White House, left him time to take advantage of cultural and social opportunities that imperial ambitions had provided: new parks such as the Bois de Boulogne and such older ones as the Luxembourg Gardens beautifully refurbished; the grand new *Opéra*, ornate cornerstone of the Second Empire; the theaters, museums, fine dining. Hay was growing *debonair*, a *bon vivant*, the better to guide worthy Americans, coming to him with their letters of introduction, through the sights and savory refreshments that the French capital offered so abundantly. And in such a setting Hay's muse had returned and was singing for him. He was writing again: a short story submitted to and accepted by *Harper's Monthly Magazine* back in New York, poetry. He was writing poetry: "*I stand at the break of day / In the*

Champs Elysées / The tremulous shafts of dawning / As they shoot o'er the Tuileries early / Strike Luxor's cold gray spire . . ." And—as at Brown and in Springfield and Washington—he was proving himself a favorite with the ladies, attending *salons, soirées,* a *bal* in the emperor's palace, returning to the Tuileries in "small clothes with knee-buckles and silk stockings, with coat and waistcoat, all black and cocked hat," to meet and unobtrusively gaze at the Empress Eugénie, ablaze in her diamonds and still beautiful at forty, although her face head on was less fine than in profile. Thus Hay wrote home to his family, this lucky cosmopolite's letters filled with the exuberance of a new, continental *joie de vivre,* as all the while he competently discharged his diplomatic duties. More than a year into them, we recall, in September 1866, Hay had to write Billy Herndon, Lincoln's Springfield law partner, apologizing for tardiness; in his chief's absence the acting *chargé d'affaires* had "had no quiet day in which I [could] write you what you desired in your letter several months ago."

The chief, John Bigelow (with whom his subordinate got along unfailingly well), was retiring and returning to America. All at once Hay's position appeared less attractive, a position he had held about as long as he chose to anyway. General Dix, Bigelow's replacement and an appointee of the current tenant in the White House, the Tennessee Copperhead Democrat Andrew Johnson, entertained views partial to the South with which the secretary of legation was unsympathetic. Accordingly, Hay began the process of winding down his exile, ready to return to those "important and interesting times" back home that he had regretted leaving when he first took on this European assignment.

Thus at the start of 1867, John Hay, back from France, landed in New York and proceeded on to Washington. He felt still at sea, he said, about what he wanted to do next. Not that he lacked for father figures to guide him: John Bigelow the latest one, the spirit of Lincoln as another that abided, for a third Hay's own father, whose advice the son valued and whom he had come home in part to see. Hay meant to get back to Illinois soon but went first to Washington, to call on William Seward, a fourth father figure and still secretary of state in the Johnson administration. The young colonel presented himself as a quiet petitioner, to a friend, one gentleman to another. (How Lincoln's former secretary had learned to loathe the massed, pushy office seekers begging in hallways for governmental favors! He would never be one of those.) Seward volunteered to do what he could. Would Colonel Hay be willing to serve as Mr. Seward's private secretary? Hay tactfully declined, lingering instead three weeks in Washington as he awaited further developments and visited with old, potentially helpful friends in former haunts, in homes and public settings where he had passed earlier, pleasant hours.

In late February he did venture to New York City, still in pursuit of a way to earn a living. The salary for the Paris interlude had been barely adequate; something a bit more remunerative was to be hoped for. The applicant went around to publishing houses in Manhattan: to Alfred Guernsey at *Harper's Monthly*, which had published "Shelby Cabell," the short story Hay had set in and sent over from Paris. Editor Guernsey would like to see more such stories, or articles of any kind from this author; but as for a life of President Lincoln, which Hay and Nicolay had resolved to write together, neither Mr. Guernsey nor anybody else in the New York publishing world was much interested in that. In the two years since the Emancipator's death, four hasty but apparently sufficient biographies of Lincoln had appeared to glut the market. "Nobody is keen for our book," Hay was thus obliged to report back to Nicolay, still in Paris at the consulate. "We will have to write it and publish it on our own hook some day, when we can."

Meanwhile, he must keep looking. But these would have been the precious few days during which Mark Twain met Hay, between February 23, when the latter arrived in New York, and March 3, when the two of them were gone from there. Hay set out for Chicago and Warsaw on the latter date, Clemens for St. Louis, comfortably sprawled across two seats in his railroad car near the stove's warmth, smoking and dreaming while a snowstorm raged beyond the windows. But for a week preceding their separate departures, both had been moving in the same small circle of New York journalists and literati. Hay had met Charles Webb, who was intent on publishing Clemens's newspaper sketches. Webb, or no doubt one or two others, could have managed the introductions. And once made, the meeting would all but inevitably have led to a couple of literary bachelors on either side of thirty getting along. Hay got along with people anyhow, but with the uncouth Clemens? Of course. Both loved to laugh and laughed with ease, and both had huge funds of anecdote to provoke laughter, stories each told superbly (at a time when entertainment was far rarer to come by, when people were reduced to gathering together and making their own entertainment). Clemens, in fact, was dazzled by Hay, and remained pretty much so for the rest of his life, even past the early 1880s— when their views of political matters sharply diverged—on into the 1890s and the new century. For now, though, late in these 1860s, the still raw Clemens, fresh from the print shops, saloons, police courts, and mining camps of the Far West, was all but awed by the accomplished Hay. For "in those earlier days," Mark Twain recalled thirty-seven years later, from Florence in 1904, John Hay "was a picture to look at, for beauty of feature, perfection of form and grace of carriage and movement. He had a charm about him of a sort quite unusual to my western ignorance and inexperience—a charm of manner, intonation, apparently native and unstudied elocution, and all that—the groundwork of it native, the ease of it, the polish of it, the winning naturalness of it, acquired in Europe." His new friend appeared, in short, "joyous and cordial, a most pleasant comrade."

And—with the Wild Humorist of the Pacific Slope engaged like Hay just then in promoting himself as a writer—the two westerners found matters of shared interest to talk about. In years immediately ahead they would extend their friendship. But for now, on March 3, 1867, Mark Twain was off to St. Louis, Hay to Chicago to meet with Robert Lincoln, recently admitted to the bar in Illinois and looking after his mother and his brother Tad, just shy of fourteen. Did Hay and Nicolay's understanding with the martyred president's son still hold? As for that, Bob would encourage any respectable book about his father, but he didn't mean to give up his keys to the vault where the Lincoln papers were stored. "He will keep them for the present," Hay reported back to Nicolay in Paris, "and still hopes for our assistance in classifying them." Reassured to that extent, Hay could proceed to Warsaw, where he found his mother well and his father at sixty without a gray hair on his head.

During the White House years and more recently, the son had sent from a meager salary what money he could spare to Dr. Hay to invest for him in a vineyard. Hay back East—with his Lincoln aura—had been offered a position as partner in a law firm and no doubt could have found work in publishing, but just now was hankering after Warsaw's agrarian simplicities: outdoors in the sun, doing fruitful labor with his hands. Once at home, he took "a deep interest in the destruction of caterpillars on my apple trees—in the planting of my own little orchard of 5 acres." Of late he was burdened, when reading for pleasure, with self-reproach over time misspent; but out in the fields, shoveling, planting, he felt free "from the sense of responsibility for the passing hour. I am doing work, substantial real work." And enjoying himself immensely, so that he began to calculate: his orchard and vineyard might yield him $500 a year; a few hundred more could be earned from lecturing and writing for the magazines. Costs were low in Warsaw. "It would be hard for me to imagine a pleasanter spring than I have passed," he wrote in his diary, each day ending in wholesome fatigue, good sleep, and a sense of honest work well done. So for a couple of months Hay thrived through that pastoral interlude among scenes of his childhood.

Until word reached him early in June from Washington. At $6,000 per annum (twice what he was paid to go to Paris), John Hay had been appointed to another diplomatic post, in Vienna. His command of German would serve him there as his French had served him formerly. Thus, at Secretary Seward's behest, he was called from Arcadia to pack once more, say his goodbyes, and catch a train bound East. He sailed from New York for Liverpool on June 29, Mark Twain having left the same port aboard America's first cruise ship three weeks earlier.

13. THE *QUAKER CITY*

The cruise that Sam Clemens had joined altered his already colorful life into something quite different. The voyage of the refitted, now swank paddle steamer finally got under way on June 10, 1867, sixty-five passengers on board: "tip-top people" embarked on a six-months' picnic, as Mark Twain described it beforehand, after a get-acquainted gathering on shore. Once at sea, however, the tip-top people proved far fewer than sixty-five, maybe six or eight, the rest older than Clemens had anticipated, and solemner, more sanctimonious, more hypocritical. Their presence in such force threatened to convert what should have been a pleasure cruise into, he said, a funeral procession without a corpse. Fortunately, it didn't take the humorist long to locate a handful of fun-loving folk: the smoking-room crowd all soon with their nicknames—Moult, the Cub, Jack, Dan—with three or four women passengers included among the number. Notably, Clemens soon formed a friendship with Mary Fairbanks of Cleveland, Ohio. "Mother," he and some of the boys took to calling her, even though Mrs. Fairbanks was only in her late thirties, seven years older than Clemens himself. But she did end by mothering the unpolished westerner, not only sewing on buttons and attending to his other sartorial requirements but also giving him guidance in matters of gentility, which he was in need of. And with an eye for lapses in taste, she read over the letters Mark Twain was writing for readers on shore: for the *Alta California* and for Greeley's *Tribune*, which paid better. Mrs. Fairbank's husband in Cleveland owned a newspaper, too, for which she herself was composing letters about the excursion; an early one reported to Ohio readers on her impressions of all the DDs and MDs among her fellow passengers, the "men of wisdom and men of wit"—those tip-top people—including one dinner table "from which is sure to come a peal of laughter, and all eyes are turned toward Mark Twain, whose face is perfectly mirth-provoking. Sitting lazily at the table, scarcely genteel in his appearance, there is something, I know not what, that interests and attracts. I saw to-day at dinner venerable divines and sage-looking men convulsed with laughter at his drolleries and quaint, odd manners."

Mrs. Fairbanks was to become Clemens's friend for a lifetime, as she set about gently refining his odd, quaint manners and that scarcely genteel appearance. Of course, given the cost of the voyage, the passenger list with its DDs and MDs would tend toward the elderly anyway, and the seriously affluent. Moreover, the genesis of the excursion—among the congregation at Henry Ward Beecher's famous Plymouth Church in Brooklyn—made it hardly surprising that many on board were pious, more interested (after their endless domino games) in prayer and the dinner hour than in dancing under the stars. But with his like-minded clique around him, Clemens soon saw to it that he was having a wonderful time afloat and ashore, as the ship put in at the Azores, at Gibraltar, at Tangiers, at Marseilles, the adventure by then well and zestfully under way.

From Marseilles, Mark and a few of his new chums set off by train for Paris to visit *L'exposition universelle*, the largest world's fair to that date. But the boys spent no more than two hours on the *Champ de Mars*, even in so brief a time less interested in exhibits than in the variegated people come together from around the world. Clemens did catch sight of Napoleon III (whose idea the fair was) elsewhere in Paris reviewing his troops, and was struck, as was John Hay earlier, by the little man's eyes: "half closed, and such a deep, crafty, scheming expression about them!" But what interested this traveler more was how the emperor, now surrounded "by shouting thousands, by military pomp, by the splendors of his capital city, and companioned by kings and princes," in earlier times had clung to his dreams through six years of prison and through exile in America and in England, where he "walked his weary beat a common policeman of London," all the while dreaming, "the butt of small wits, a mark for the pitiless ridicule of all the world"—dreaming and plotting until he got himself elected "President of France at last! a coup d'état, and surrounded by applauding armies, welcomed by the thunders of cannon, he mounts a throne and waves before an astounded world the sceptre of a mighty Empire!" To John Hay, whom ambition's lash had hardly touched as he awaited whatever chances life might bring along, Napoleon III was no more than a tinpot dictator who had destroyed the French Republic—thrown over a people's sovereignty that Mr. Lincoln had devoted his life elsewhere to perpetuating. By contrast, the ambitious Clemens, nurturing his own wild dreams, saw the French ruler reviewing troops at the Arch of Triumph as something rather more admirable: "the genius of Energy, Persistence, Enterprise."

That was the way of Mark Twain's letters to his *Alta* and *Tribune* readers: providing a goodly share of information about places visited and people encountered, all sharply observed but blended with the observer's often unorthodox reactions, expressed in always vigorous prose. In Milan, for instance, before Leonardo's badly damaged *Last Supper*: "The colors are dimmed with age; the countenances are scaled and marred, and nearly all expression is gone from them; the hair is a dead blur upon the wall." Yet admirers from far and wide come with their praise: Such grace of attitude! Such matchless coloring! What delicacy of touch! "What would you think of a man who stared in ecstacy upon a desert of stumps and said: 'Oh, my soul, my beating heart, what a noble forest is here!'" A guide without pretense or affectation, Mark visits Pompeii: "I always had an idea that you went down into Pompeii with torches, by the way of damp, dark stairways, just as you do in silver mines, and traversed gloomy tunnels with lava overhead." Not at all. "Fully one-half of the buried city, perhaps, is completely exhumed and thrown open freely to the light of day; and there stand the long rows of solidly-built brick houses (roofless) just as they stood eighteen hundred years ago, hot with the flaming sun." This cicerone gives us a tour of the place, vivid, evocative, each detail of interest: the bake shops, the broken pillars lying about, the streets rutted by ancient chariot wheels, mosaics still bright, one house that ladies are not allowed to visit, thresholds worn "with the passing feet of the Pompeiians of by-gone centuries." Rarely are the images less than remarkable; and little is left out, least of all the feeling of being there: "It was a quaint and curious pastime, wandering through this old silent city of the dead—lounging through utterly deserted streets where thousands and thousands of human beings once bought and sold, and walked and rode, and made the place resound with the noise and confusion of traffic and pleasure." In Constantinople, he discovers Santa Sophia to be "a colossal church, thirteen or fourteen hundred years old, and unsightly enough to be very, very much older. Its immense dome is said to be more wonderful than St. Peter's, but its dirt is much more wonderful than its dome." When people rave about Santa Sophia, he presumes they got their ecstasies "out of the guide-book (where every church is spoken of as being 'considered by good judges to be the most marvelous structure, in many respects, that the world has ever seen')." Or else they're "connoisseurs from the wilds of New Jersey who laboriously learn the difference between a fresco and a fire-plug and from that day forward feel privileged to void their critical bathos on painting, sculpture and architecture forever more."

His skepticism might have palled on readers, except that Mark Twain fore-stalls monotony by interspersing doubt with much playfulness and human interaction. As a tourist, he appears to be tireless, ever lively in his responses, always honest about what doesn't impress him as well as what does. For he finds plenty to admire and enjoy: the palatial Italian railroad stations, for instance, and the marvelous turnpikes. "When it is too dark to see any other object, one can still see the white turnpikes of France and Italy; and they are clean enough to eat from, without a table-cloth." As for the trains, "we have none like them. The cars slide as smoothly along as if they were on runners," at the end of their journeys pulling into great colonnaded depots of marble, ironwork, and glass.

He goes everywhere—evades quarantine to sneak ashore and see the Acrop-olis by moonlight, offers a shipboard salute of his own composition to the serf-freeing Czar of All the Russias, climbs (or is pushed and pulled up) a pyramid. At Beirut a group of eight disembarks from the *Quaker City* to cross the Valley of Lebanon on horseback bound for Holy Soil, three pious, souvenir-plundering shipboard pilgrims among them, with an Arab on a camel as their guard. In the heat of late summer they ride across those desert wastes. "Prop-erly, with the sorry relics we bestrode, it was a three days' journey to Damas-cus." But they had to do it in a forced march of two, "because our three pilgrims could not travel on the Sabbath day." Mark and the others "pleaded for the tired, ill-treated horses, and tried to show that their faithful service deserved kindness in return, and their hard lot compassion. But when did ever self-righteousness know the sentiment of pity? What were a few long hours added to the hardships of some over-taxed brutes when weighed against the peril of those human souls? It was not the most promising party to travel with and hope to gain a higher veneration for religion through the example of its devotees."

They did make it to Nazareth ("clinging like a whitewashed wasp's nest to the hill-side"), and Jerusalem ("So small! Why, it was no larger than an Amer-ican village of four thousand inhabitants, and no larger than an ordinary Syr-ian city of thirty thousand"), and Bethlehem (laden with "its troops of beggars and relic-peddlers"), and saw much else besides, there and elsewhere on three continents. And as he found means along the way, Mark Twain would send his letters back to New York and California; so that by the time the *Quaker City* finally returned to America and docked at the foot of Wall Street on Tuesday, November 19, 1867, readers at home had already become familiar with the early stages of the adventure through the first rollicking few of Mark Twain's fifty-seven letters to be published in the newspapers.

That same evening he wrote a fifty-eighth letter, for the *New York Herald*, a perhaps overly candid valedictory summing up the experience; and with that his task, like the voyage itself, was done. But in the days immediately ahead occurred what Mark Twain, looking back at the very end of his life, in February 1910, would regard as the turning point that had made him into what he would become. "When I returned to America," he recalled in the final article he ever published, "Circumstance was waiting on the pier—with the last link" of the several since childhood that had forged the chain that shaped his particular lifetime. "I was asked to write a book, and I did it, and called it *The Innocents Abroad*. Thus at last I became a member of the literary guild. That was forty-two years ago, and I have been a member ever since."

No longer a mere typesetter, or a journalist, or a writer of travel letters, but a full-fledged author. An old man's memory proved faulty, though. His fate had not met him on the pier exactly, but rather some days later in the form of a request from Elijah Bliss of the American Publishing Company in Hartford, Connecticut. "We are desirous," Bliss had written after preliminaries, "of obtaining from you a work of some kind, perhaps compiled from your letters from the East." The addressee's experience with his *The Jumping Frog & Other Sketches*—and not a dime to show for it—may have made Mark Twain leery of book publishing as a way to earn a living; but one sentence in Mr. Bliss's letter had got his attention. "We are perhaps the oldest subscription house in the country, and have never failed to give a book an immense circulation."

In genteel circles, subscription publishing had an aura faintly disreputable about it, aimed as it was at rural readers out of reach of bookstores. Publishers by subscription didn't need to advertise (and hence their books didn't generally get reviewed). Instead, the houses sent forth agents, drummers, who called on people remote from cities, in their homes in small towns, villages, and farms all over America. They called on them one by one with samples of forthcoming titles, taking deposits on books desired that would be printed, bound, and delivered only afterward. Yet whereas standard trade publishers in New York and Boston, whose products were in the bookstores and did get reviewed, would have a first printing of, say, five thousand copies, subscription publishers might well round up thirty thousand deposits from rural readers before even a single copy had been bound. Such readers, still abundant in an agrarian America that the new industrialism was only beginning to transform, constituted Mark Twain's kind of people, he told himself, far more than were the genteel sophisticates with access to bookstores in urban centers of the East. Still, in responding, Clemens wanted to be sure: Would Mr. Bliss please specify "what amount of money I might possibly make out of" such a book as was being proposed? His query addressed a matter, the humorist added, that "has a degree of importance for me which is almost beyond my own comprehension."

One way or another this erstwhile silver miner meant to get rich. Bliss was able to reassure him. The two met in Hartford, Clemens emerging from their talk elated. To his St. Louis family he wrote on January 24 about having just negotiated "a splendid contract for a Quaker City book of 5 or 600 large paper pages, with illustrations, the manuscript to be placed in the publishers' hands by the middle of July."

But, as usual, signing the contract proved the easy part. For one thing, the author soon learned that the *Alta California* people were planning to publish their own book of Mark Twain's letters, for which they held the copyright. That obliged Clemens once more to board ship out of New York ("I am so glad of an excuse to go to sea again") on March 11, 1868, bound for the Isthmus at Panama and on to far-off San Francisco. Face to face, the voyager persuaded his western employers to let him use the letters for his own project; but that left him still with much to do. He must replace opaque California references so as better to adapt the narrative to an eastern audience, and must provide bridges between the separate missives so that the story flowed smoothly through the many ports of call to the Holy Land and back. Moreover, although his audience would be primarily rural—villagers and farm families across middle America—the author was by no means ready to disregard the genteel of Baltimore, Philadelphia, New York, and Boston, gathering on evenings around their firesides to read new books aloud. To attract those families he must tone down the slang and irreverence, and soften whatever could give offense to delicate female sensibilities, a task Mother Fairbanks on shipboard had already guided him toward accomplishing.

Somehow it all got done, and nearly on time, so that while still in San Francisco Mark was able to write his preface, which clarified what the pages that followed were and were not. They are not, his three paragraphs explain, the record of a scientific expedition, and thus lack "that gravity, that profundity, and that impressive incomprehensibility which are so proper to works of that kind." What *The Innocents Abroad* was was merely an account of a pleasure trip; yet even so it had a purpose, "which is, to suggest to the reader how he would be likely to see Europe and the East if he looked at them with his own eyes instead of the eyes of those who travelled in those countries before him. I make small pretence," the author confessed, "of showing any one how he *ought* to look at objects of interest beyond the sea—other books do that, and therefore, even if I were competent to do it, there is no need."

So: not your conventional travel guide, but something different— informative enough, yet filled with high spirits and fun. His manuscript in hand, Clemens sailed back to New York, arriving near the end of July to proceed on to Hartford, where Bliss and his author gave it its finishing touches. Even so, the publisher's schedule imposed further delays. Finally, however, on August 15, 1869, appeared *The Innocents Abroad, or The New Pilgrims' Progress*.

And the book turned into a monumental success.

A glittering, astonishing success, in its first two years selling upward of seventy thousand copies, the author's share being 19¢ apiece. That is, from his handiwork Mark Twain earned some $13,300 without lifting a finger during those twenty-four months, at a time when a laborer working ten hours a day, six days a week took in under $500 a year, a skilled mechanic just over $800. And the book continued to sell. Indeed, it would remain—even after *Roughing It, The Gilded Age, Tom Sawyer, A Tramp Abroad, The Prince and the Pauper, Life on the Mississippi, Huckleberry Finn, A Connecticut Yankee in King Arthur's Court, Pudd'nhead Wilson, Joan of Arc,* and *Following the Equator*— even after those achievements, this earliest of his proper books, this *Innocents Abroad*, would remain throughout his lifetime the most popular of them all.

Moreover, almost from the first it became not just a popular but a critical success. Even though the book bore a subscription publisher's imprint, the august *Atlantic Monthly*, loftiest of American magazines at the time, stooped to notice it. Promptly and at generous length, in the issue of December 1869, the *Atlantic* reviewer commented not only on the humor in the book's plan—a six-hundred-page volume describing "a steamer-load of Americans going on a prolonged picnic to Europe and the Holy Land"—but also on the way Mr. Clemens had realized his intentions: "It is out of the bounty and abundance of his own nature that he is as amusing in the execution as in the conception of his work. And it is always good-humored humor, too, that he lavishes on his reader, and even in its impudence it is charming; we do not remember where it is indulged at the cost of the weak or helpless side, or where it is insolent, with all its sauciness and irreverence." The style, moreover, is freshly, wonderfully colloquial throughout: "As Mr. Clemens writes of his experiences, we imagine he would talk of them; and very amusing talk it would be: often not at all fine in matter or manner, but full of touches of humor—which if not delicate are nearly always easy—and having a base of excellent sense and good feeling." The author is already well known, under the pen name Mark Twain, "to the very large world of newspaper readers; and this book ought to secure him something better than the uncertain standing of a popular favorite. It is no business of ours to fix his rank among the humorists California has given us, but we think," Mr. Howells, the reviewer, concludes, "he is, in an entirely different way from all the others, quite worthy of the company of the best."

Singlehanded, *The Innocents Abroad* would elevate Mark Twain to a standing as one of the two or three most successful authors in the land. And all this while he was continuing his lecture tours in season. On such a tour that very December, in fact, in Boston, he dropped around to the *Atlantic* offices on Tremont Street to meet and thank its reviewer for so splendid, supportive, and detailed a notice. William Dean Howells turned out to be a year and a half Clemens's junior, and assistant to the great editor in chief of the *Atlantic*, James T. Fields. For his part, Howells never forgot that initial encounter with one who was fated to become among his closest friends: Clemens standing before the editor's desk in his sealskin coat with the fur side out, his "crest of dense red hair, and the wide sweep of his flaming mustache."

There in the flesh stood the grateful author, just turned thirty-four and hardly aware as yet of what fate and his efforts had bestowed upon him. For Mark Twain's *The Innocents Abroad* remains the best American book of travel ever written, still intensely alive and—perhaps even more impressive in a work of humor—still richly funny to us much different readers a century and a half further on.

14. POET AND JOURNALIST

John Hay knew William Dean Howells, had first sought him out as long ago as 1861, in Columbus, Ohio, during the train journey accompanying a new president-elect east from Springfield, Illinois. That was in an eventful February filled with bright bunting and cheering and handkerchief waving beside the railroad tracks and at every northern depot along the way, while rebels down South were proclaiming themselves the Confederate States of America. Hay as a young western poet, twenty-two years old, wanted to meet another such out of the West, for Howells a couple of years earlier had published jointly *Poems of Two Friends*, which Hay back in Warsaw read and enjoyed. But when he got to Columbus and made inquiries, the Ohio poet was absent; so all Hay could do was leave a message, get back on the train, and proceed East to take up his duties in the White House.

The industrious Howells had, in addition, been known to Hay, and to Nicolay, as the author of an earlier campaign biography of the then Republican nominee, Mr. Lincoln, which had been published in the late summer of 1860 and for which its author hoped (as did so many in those years of patronage before civil service) to be rewarded with a governmental post. Indeed, on June 10, 1861, young Howells was writing from Columbus, with "office-seeking impudence," to John Hay, now ensconced in the Executive Mansion, about his—Howells's—application for a consulship at Munich. The applicant had earlier submitted his qualifications, which "consisted of the usual certificates of good moral character and uncommon appropriateness for the place" (Howells did know German), the whole "couched in language so laudatory, that," he writes with winning modesty, "I could not more than glance at it." Yet no answer had been received, and no announcement that the Munich post had been filled. So "it has occurred to me (in the dismantled condition of my fortunes,) that possibly the President might yet name me for it, if I could be named to him." Thus this letter to Secretary Hay, "knowing that you see him, and trusting you will forgive the liberty I take with you." Howells closed his appeal to a stranger by mentioning the pleasure it would have given him "to have met you when you were in Columbus, and I hope that we may yet some day see each other—if only that I may have the opportunity of apologizing for the absurdity of this letter. Very respectfully."

Hay's reply was equally courteous, equally deft. He would preserve Howells' letter for its autograph of a poet out of the West whom he admired, and meanwhile had looked over the quite impressive application and remained hopeful about Mr. Howells's chances of gaining the Munich office. As it turned out, the Lincoln biographer's efforts were rewarded with a consulship in Venice, where young Howells spent the Civil War years in that agreeable setting, returning to America in 1865, by then a husband and father. He took an editorial position in New York City, which led to his moving soon to Boston and the *Atlantic Monthly*, behind a desk of which William Dean Howells at thirty-one was sitting when Mark Twain with his flaming mustache and dense red hair appeared before him late in 1868.

It was the same year during which John Hay's service in Vienna, begun in August 1867, ended. That second European posting had been no more meant as a long-term assignment than were Hay's earlier seventeen months in Paris. And really, there hadn't been much for the *chargé d'affaires ad interim* to do when he got to Vienna anyway. Hay was filling in until a permanent U.S. minister to the Austrian Empire could be confirmed back in Washington. The preceding minister, the eminent historian John Lothrop Motley, author of the three-volume *Rise of the Dutch Republic* (1856) and a four-volume *History of the United Netherlands* (1860–1867), had served with distinction in Vienna all during the Civil War, until differing with the State Department on an issue that led him to offer his resignation, never expecting it to be accepted. In Washington's political turbulence just then it was; and the distinguished Mr. Motley found himself in England out of a job, seething because he was now denied use of the Vienna archives in which he had been burrowing profitably for his study of the Thirty Years War. Hay on his way from New York stopped in London, where he made a courtesy call on Motley in mid-July 1867 and listened as the diplomat-historian "grew almost hysterical in his denunciation of the 'disgusting, nasty outrage' of his being turned out." But such were the wages of diplomacy; and Hay, in Vienna in his turn, didn't expect—or want—to last in Austria anything like that long.

Meanwhile, this acting *chargé d'affaires* perfected his German and enjoyed himself. Soon Hay was set up in a Viennese apartment "of three good rooms, kitchen and servant's room, for which I pay 1500 florins a year." He and Nicolay, over from Paris, managed a reunion; and afterward Hay traveled in Poland, to Warsaw and Krakow, "the quaintest and most entirely satisfactory town I ever saw." In November he was gone from Vienna again, for fifteen days seeing Budapest, Constantinople, and Corfu, an island at the latitude of New York but with late-autumn "roses in full bloom and oranges perfuming the air." Still, Hay was no Mark Twain when it came to the sea; "I hate the water worse than any cat. It will be hard to get me on the Mediterranean again."

On solid ground in December, he spent Christmas Eve with a hospitable Viennese family. "There was an enormous tree and presents by hundreds. The young ladies were pretty as ever and very easy and gay. I never saw better breeding than there is in the Haute Bourgeoisie of Vienna." He and Nicolay had talked of a trip up the Nile. "When do you think of starting? I shall try," wrote Hay to his friend, "to take a flight into Italy this winter—I should never have time to do it thoroughly, and then, if I can, next spring after I leave here, take a rapid run through Spain." Meanwhile, he had written to another friend, a State Department functionary in Paris, inviting him to come later and see Hay's vineyard out in Illinois, and "you will confess how much better and decenter is the life of a laboring man with honest content, than the vicious pleasures and hollow splendors of public service"—even as this same acting *chargé d'affaires* appeared quite at his ease enjoying Vienna's abundant pleasures and the splendors of Europe far and near.

In January early, in the new 1868, Hay's diary notes a dinner last night where the host—"a most amiable old gentleman"—led him off "and showed me his coffin and the skeletons of his friends, one of a woman, 'une bonne amie à moi,' whom he chucked under the chin and made the bony head wag and grin in the candlelight and the teeth rattle." Hay did get in his trip to Italy, for on March 23 he was back in Vienna at the end of it; and in late April was pausing to take stock. "I had no idea when I came abroad last summer that I should be here so long. I thought they would fix up the vacuum (abhorred of nature and office seekers) in a few months—so I came for a flyer, principally because I was a little ashamed of having been in Europe nearly two years and having seen nothing." The flyer turned out to have yielded an interesting, instructive interlude, with "very little work to do at the legation," so that by now Hay had seen about all he wanted of central Europe—all while drawing his salary "with startling punctuality" and, he noted, without burdening the home office with an overabundance of dispatches.

Thus, although ready to leave, of course he was glad he had come. And glad to find republicanism in the air, in Austria, in England, even in Bismarck's Prussia. "France still lies in her comatose slumber," this disciple of Lincoln lamented, "but she talks in her sleep and murmurs the Marseillaise. And God has made her ruler blind drunk," in order that Napoleon III's "antics may disgust the world with despotism. If ever," the American concluded, "in my green and salad days, I sometimes vaguely doubted, I am safe now. I am a Republican till I die. When we get to Heaven we can try a Monarchy, perhaps," under the King of Kings.

Here on earth, meanwhile, Mr. Motley's successor had been confirmed: Henry Watts of Pennsylvania, en route as U.S. minister to the Austrian Empire. With that, Hay submitted his resignation, and by mid-October 1868 he was in Liverpool bound for home. He had not ventured up the Nile or got to Spain as he wanted to, but was content after a fruitful year to be heading toward New York and on to his Warsaw family and vineyard.

And he would see Spain soon enough. Records of the months just ahead are somewhat scanty; but Hay was in Washington in this November 1868, visiting friends there and, in his words, quietly pursuing "a fat office." He had turned thirty, by no means well off and still not sure of what to do with his life. He did sell an article to Howells at the *Atlantic*: an account of the murder of the Mormon leader Joseph Smith by a Warsaw mob in 1844, when the article's author was a child of five in that Illinois village. Back home, he looked after his vineyards. To an appreciative audience in Buffalo he lectured in January on "The Progress of Democracy in Europe," pleased "at the absence of trepidation and duration of my voice," pleased too to have faced a large audience and given his speech without breaking down. The same lecture Hay delivered for a bit of profit in other western towns, including Warsaw. For a month he edited a Chicago newspaper at the urging of his friend Nicolay, returned from Paris with his wife and infant daughter to stay. And Hay was back in Washington in the spring, after a new president, Ulysses S. Grant, had been inaugurated, with political offices rapidly changing hands.

However the opportunity came about (his patron Mr. Seward having departed at the end of the Johnson administration), Hay was in New York that same summer, on July 10, 1869, at the Hotel Brunswick hours before sailing once more to Europe—he who had professed, cat-like, to hate the sea. This time the post the diplomat gained was in Madrid, as poorly paid secretary of legation, taking on duties like those from his Paris days. Assuredly he was qualified, and in the course of the year ahead would feel "glad I committed the folly of coming. I have seen a great deal and learned something. I speak the language," he wrote to Nicolay as early as October, "well enough to be understood and not well enough to be taken for a Spaniard." In fact, Spanish ways had absorbed him; so that, Howells having asked for more contributions to the *Atlantic*, Hay could send over informed, entertaining articles on Castile that the editor was pleased to publish. Even so, and as he had intended from the beginning, within the year he was writing, on May 1, 1870, to his superior, General Sickles, a letter of resignation, regretfully, because "my pecuniary circumstances compel me to sever the official relations which have been rendered so pleasant by your unfailing kindness and consideration."

Yet Hay lingered. A thorough if easygoing student, he had made the most of his time: observing, listening, learning the language, studying Spain's raucous politics up close, making influential Spanish friends. Still, "I have a curious year to look back upon," he wrote near its end, "more entirely out of the world than any since I came into it. There have been almost no Americans in Madrid and I have not been out of the city but once," to nearby Toledo, for "a few halcyon days favored by fate, weather, and other accessories, in that delicious old town." And yet he delayed, into the summer, to manage a couple of more outings beyond the Spanish capital before leaving for good.

Then, in early September 1870, he was in New York on his way to Illinois, dining momentously with Whitelaw Reid at the Union League Club. Hay had known Reid since White House days—like Howells a native of Ohio and back then the *Cincinnati Gazette*'s Washington correspondent, as well as a supporter of his fellow Ohioan Salmon P. Chase's aim to unseat Lincoln for the presidency in 1864. But any such opposition these six years later appeared far in the past. In the interval Reid had risen to be Horace Greeley's heir apparent at the *Tribune*, from which lofty journalistic height he was offering his friend Hay a position on the newspaper: that is, "if you were not a fellow of such diplomatically extravagant habits as to be beyond the reach of our modest salaries." The returning traveler promised to consider the offer, but first he must visit his family in Illinois. "I found Warsaw with a broad grin on its face at the lovely grape crop. My father made 1200 gallons of good wine, and even my shy little vineyard made its début with 240." Nevertheless, Hay ended by returning to New York, accepting Reid's proposal that fall of 1870, setting himself up in the Astor House, and going to work at the *Tribune* as an editorial writer for a comfortable $50 a week (something not far under $1,000 a week in present-day terms).

John Hay's new Manhattan address put him in a position to extend his literary acquaintances northward to Boston. Finally he met Howells up there—nearly a decade after he had made a vain effort to do so in Columbus, Ohio—and through Howells met James T. Fields, legendary publisher of Emerson, Longfellow, and Hawthorne. Like so many others, Mr. Fields was charmed by this suavely accomplished young visitor: "Come as often as you please to Boston," he wrote to Hay afterward. "Chaps the likes of you don't often stray this way"—and next time, this same chap was to be Mr. Fields's guest among the high literary notables of the Saturday Club. Moreover, Howells was continuing to run John Hay's articles from Spain in the *Atlantic Monthly*; the Boston publisher James Osgood would soon be making a book, *Castilian Days*, out of them.

Beyond all that, during these months something unexpected intervened to further a journalist's burgeoning career in letters. It didn't amount to real money, but it suddenly and definitely enlarged Hay's renown. In the *New York Tribune* of November 19, 1870, over the signature "J.H.," appeared a poem called "Little Breeches," seven stanzas of eight lines each mimicking the unlettered dialect of Illinois's Pike County, just south of the county where Warsaw was. To Nicolay again, in mid-December, Hay was writing of "that ridiculous rhyme Little Breeches of mine," which "has had a ridiculous run. It has been published in nearly the whole country press from here to the Rocky Mountains. As my initials are not known and they generally get worn off on the second print, I have not been disgraced by it." But J.H.'s identity couldn't stay hidden; and the fame that swelled up—although nothing like the solid, remunerative, and what would be enduring fame at just this time of Mark Twain's *The Innocents Abroad*—was remarkable nevertheless for a few lines of doggerel verse: the stir "Little Breeches" created, and the widespread celebrity it achieved for its author among readers of that epoch.

We like the lines less, perhaps, but people then were dealing with postwar changes in a new world forming: steamships, the telegraph, railroads, harvester combines, the Atlantic cable, massive accumulations of wealth that had grown out of textiles clothing the soldiers, out of beef feeding them; afterward a new world of western lands opening up and fortunes to be made by land speculators and makers of steel for rails; a world of cattle runs and mining and timber and graft; of cities swelling with odd-looking, odd-sounding immigrants; of industry and factory wages and labor unrest: a world in which the reassuring agrarian nostalgia of "Little Breeches" furnished a glimpse into a simpler past at a safe remove from present anxieties:

> I don't go much on religion,
> I never ain't had no show;
> But I've got a middlin' tight grip, sir,
> On the handful o' things I know.
> I don't pan out on the prophets
> And free-will, and that sort of thing,
> But I b'lieve in God and the angels,
> Ever sence one night last spring.

What had happened last spring was that the down-to-earth farmer addressing us had come into town with some turnips to sell, bringing his four-year-old Gabe along for the ride, a "chipper and sassy" young'un, "Always ready to swear and fight." On their way it began to snow, hard and ever harder. With his chores done, the farmer headed home, stopping a moment at Taggert's store for molasses, Gabe in the wagon outside in the gathering dusk. Out there something startled the horses, and they bolted. The farmer "heard one little squall" and, looking up, could only stare helplessly as "hell-to-split over the prairie Went team, Little Breeches, and all."

> Hell-to-split over the prairie!
> I was almost froze with skeer;
> But we rousted up some torches,
> And sarched for 'em far and near.
> At last we struck hosses and wagon,
> Snowed under a soft white mound,
> Upsot, dead beat, but of little Gabe
> No hide nor hair was found.

The men looked everywhere, until finally they had to give up. Then all the heartsick father could do was "flop down on my marrow-bones, Crotch-deep in the snow," and pray. The torches were burning low. In a sheepfold nearby was wood, which "me and Isrul Parr" went looking for. They found the sheepfold, and in it a shed for keeping lambs out of the cold. The two opened the shed door, and inside, among the warm, sleepy, white lambs, "thar sot Little Breeches," just as pert as ever you see.

> How did he git thar? Angels.
> He could never have walked in that storm;
> They jest scooped down and toted him
> To whar it was safe and warm.
> And I think that saving a little child,
> And fotching him to his own,
> Is a derned sight better business
> Than loafing around the Throne.

So ends the amazingly popular "Little Breeches" that John Hay dashed off and published in the *New York Tribune* in the late fall of 1870. In lines not quoted, a bit of humor to leaven the sentiment may lead us to like the poem hardly more: "And I'd larnt him to chaw terbacker," the farmer tells us of Gabe early on, "Jest to keep his milk-teeth white"; so that when the four-year-old is discovered unharmed toward the end, he chirps forth with, "I want a chaw of terbacker, And that's what's the matter of me."

Our own enlightened tastes aside, through the remainder of the nineteenth century and into the twentieth, the poem retained its popularity, long after the poet himself had lost all pleasure in it. By contrast, Hay continued to be pleased with a second Pike County ballad that he wrote, and which appeared in the semiweekly edition of the *Tribune* two months later, on January 6, 1871, to call forth an equally enthusiastic and long-lived response. "Jim Bludso, of the Prairie Belle" uses the same form—seven stanzas of eight lines each—and the same Pike County dialect to relate the heroic fate that a steamboat engineer met with on the Mississippi River:

> Wall, no! I can't tell whar he lives,
> Because he don't live, you see;
> Leastways, he's got out of the habit
> Of livin' like you and me.
> Whar have you been for the last three year
> That you haven't heard folks tell

How Jimmy Bludso passed in his checks
The night of the Prairie Belle?

Bludso wasn't what you'd call a good man—cussed, got in fights, had one wife in Natchez and another here in Pike—no better than a lot of the riverboat engineers; but you could count on Jim's word. The man's religion was his boat, and taking care of it, and not letting other boats pull ahead. But by now his *Prairie Belle* was "the oldest craft on the line," so it took on more than it could deal with when it got in a race with the *Movastar*. The *Belle* "she *wouldn't* be passed," though: tearing along, piling on wood for full steam, until finally the old boat gave way and burst into flames:

> There was runnin' and cussin', but Jim yelled out,
> Over all the infernal roar,
> "I'll hold her nozzle agin the bank
> Till the last galoot's ashore."

And he did:

> And, sure's you're born, they all got off
> Afore the smokestacks fell,—
> And Bludso's ghost went up alone
> In the smoke of the Prairie Belle.
>
> He weren't no saint,—but at jedgment
> I'd run my chance with Jim,
> 'Longside of some pious gentlemen
> That wouldn't shook hands with him.
> He seen his duty, a dead-sure thing,—
> And went for it thar and then;
> And Christ ain't a going to be too hard
> On a man that died for men.

Of course the pious—those of like mind with many of Mark Twain's pilgrims on the *Quaker City*—were incensed at holding up the brawling profane bigamist Bludso as a model, as they were offended by the image in "Little Breeches" of angels loafing around the Throne. But their sanctimonious condemnation of such heterodoxies only served to entice others to read and enjoy the two poems. Hay tried his hand at several more Pike County ballads, and the *Tribune* published those less successful efforts, to the number of six in all.

Yet one more he showed to his chief and friend Whitelaw Reid, who advised him not to let it see print. And with that, Hay's ascent into the ranks of then popular dialect balladeers plunged as suddenly as it had risen. Late in this year 1870, he was writing to Howells, "I will do no more songs," for his muse in that vein had abruptly deserted him; and when the eminent Richard Henry Stoddard approached him a few months afterward to include Hay's work in an anthology of American poetry, he politely but firmly declined. "I am no poet,—I make no claim whatever that way," the *Tribune* editor responded. "I have never written a rhyme which deserved to be printed,—still less to be gathered up and kept as specimens of literature. I can do some things as well as most men of my weight, but poems are not of them."

As for editing, Hay would prove himself able to edit with the best. Horace Greeley, still at the head of the *Tribune* and remembering his and Hay's dealings during the war as they tried in vain to negotiate peace with rebels at Niagara Falls, had been somewhat less keen than his assistant Reid to hire the fellow. But Mr. Greeley ended by declaring John Hay to be the best editorial writer the paper ever had. The new hire held that position for the next five years.

15. WEDDING IN ELMIRA

Mark Twain would muse in wonderment over Greeley and Hay. Clemens had connections to the *Tribune* himself, wrote *Quaker City* letters for the paper, and had been late in receiving a Hartford publisher's life-changing invitation to make a book of those letters because it was misdirected; Mr. Bliss's request should have been sent to Mark Twain in care of the *Tribune* office. So the humorist was at his ease in the corridors of the New York newspaper, even if, a couple of months after returning from their travels, he had enjoyed ruffling his more proper shipmate and good friend Mrs. Mary Fairbanks by informing her: "I am tired of writing wishy-washy squibs for the Tribune & have joined the Herald staff—2 impersonal letters a week. Mr. Bennett says I may have full swing, and say as many mean things as I please."

Mr. Bennett was the younger James Gordon Bennett, to the *New York Herald* what Greeley was to the *Tribune*. Clemens had been young himself back then, who in Italy in 1904, having reached a venerable sixty-eight, was musing with wonder about John Hay at that earlier time. Those thirty-some years later he recorded:

"John Hay was not afraid of Horace Greeley."

And, for emphasis, let the observation stand in a paragraph by itself; "it cannot be made too conspicuous. John Hay was the only man who served Horace Greeley on the Tribune of whom that can be said." Clemens goes on to bring the point up to his present, after the turn of the century: "In the past few years, since Hay has been occupying the post of Secretary of State with a succession of foreign difficulties on his hands such as have not fallen to the share of any previous occupant of that chair, perhaps, when we consider the magnitude of the matters involved, we have seen that courage of his youth is his possession still, and that he is not any more scarable by kings and emperors and their fleets and armies than he was by Horace Greeley."

As for the formidable Greeley, the humorist remembered having spoken to him only once. Mark would have glimpsed those unmistakable whisker-fringed features from time to time—was a guest with Hay, for instance, at Greeley's sixtieth birthday party; but the two met face to face, as it were, only the one time, "and then by accident." That was in the same year as the birthday party, in 1871, "in the (old) Tribune office. I climbed one or two flights of stairs and went to the wrong room." The visitor was looking for Colonel Hay and knew where his office was, but got careless. "I rapped lightly on the door, pushed it open and stepped in. There sat Mr. Greeley, busy writing, with his back toward me." The moment was awkward—"for he had the reputation of being pretty plain with strangers who interrupted his train of thought"—and the interview brief. "Before I could pull myself together and back out," Clemens tells us, "he whirled around and glared at me through his great spectacles and said—

'Well, what in hell do you want!'

'I was looking for a gentlem—'

'Don't keep them in stock—clear out!' "

"I could have made a very neat retort but didn't," the intruder adds, "for I was flurried and didn't think of it till I was down stairs."

A one-word retort: "Obviously"? In any case, testy Mr. Greeley's days on earth by then were few in number. The following year, at sixty-one, the editor leapt headlong into politics, easily persuaded to run for president of the United States as a Liberal Republican—the Democrats endorsed him as well—against the incumbent Grant. That fall Mr. Greeley waged a vigorous campaign to much ridicule; in the same year—1872—he was exposed (with other notables, including General McClellan) as a grasping dupe in a hoax wherein wildly overpriced land for sale out West had been deceptively seeded with diamonds; saw his unhappy marriage end with the death of his wife in October; lost the election decisively the following month; and—descending into madness—died on November 29, the only candidate for the presidency to die before the electoral votes were counted.

Clemens, meanwhile—no partisan of Greeley's—got on with his life, pointed in its new direction since publication, in mid-1869, of *The Innocents Abroad*. Elijah Bliss's invitation from the American Publishing Company had led directly to a journalist's becoming the most popular, arguably the most successful book author in America. But an equally consequential alteration in Sam Clemens's life had arisen out of the same *Quaker City* cruise that stirred Bliss's interest.

Among the passengers to the Holy Land back then, Mrs. Fairbanks of Cleveland had acquired two cubs to mother and instruct in the proprieties. One was the rough-edged westerner Mark Twain, in his early thirties. The other was an eighteen-year-old native of Elmira, New York, at his father's behest traveling alone in order to widen his horizons and sow at sea, decorously, whatever wild oats needed sowing. Charley Langdon and the humorist became friends. In port at Smyrna, Clemens was shown a miniature of Charley's older sister, Olivia, and said later that he fell in love with the image on the spot. When the *Quaker City* returned to New York in November, the Langdons were there to meet the voyagers; and Mark Twain was invited to dine with the family at the St. Nicholas Hotel. If he was uncharacteristically tongue-tied in Miss Langdon's presence, it was because (he later told her) he felt she was "a visiting *Spirit* from the upper air—a something to worship, reverently & at a distance." The evening ended nevertheless with another invitation, for their guest to visit the Langdons in Elmira. Seven months later, after returning from San Francisco—his manuscript of what would become *The Innocents Abroad* in the publisher's hands—he did so, for two weeks in August 1868, the two happiest weeks of his life up until then, in the midst of the rare hospitality and good humor that characterized that warm, cultured family.

With Olivia Langdon, twenty-two years old, Clemens fell deeply in love. Three times during the autumn he proposed to Charley's sister, before finally winning her consent. When Livy did give in, she did so ardently; yet her parents remained in doubt. They were charmed by Mr. Clemens, but knew so little of this westerner who had suddenly, exuberantly burst into their lives: this Wild Humorist of the Pacific Slope. Mrs. Fairbanks might help. The Langdons had befriended the Cleveland matron in gratitude for her kindness to their son aboard the *Quaker City*. On December 24, 1868, from Lansing, Michigan, in the midst of his seasonal lecture tour, Mark Twain wrote in ecstasy to "My dear good mother," to Mrs. Fairbanks, for Livy had read to him "your letter to Mrs. Langdon . . . & re-read & dwelt with particular delight upon the passage wherein you speak of placing full confidence in me—told her mother that that was just what *she* ought to do.—And I believe she does—& it is all owing to your cordial, whole-hearted endorsement of me, my loved & honored mother—& for that, & for your whole saving letter, I shall be always, *always* grateful to you."

Samuel Clemens and Olivia Langdon were married in Elmira, in the Langdons' parlor, on February 2, 1870, with Mrs. Fairbanks over from Cleveland, Mrs. Clemens up from St. Louis, and the bride's family all in attendance. Jervis Langdon—wealthy, self-made lumber and railroad magnate—gave his daughter away, and gave the bride and groom something else: a fine mansion to live in on Delaware Avenue in Buffalo, three hours from Elmira by train. In addition, Mr. Langdon ("the splendidest man in the *world!*" Clemens thought him) had made possible his son-in-law's purchase of a third ownership in the *Buffalo Express*, where the new husband was to pursue a career of editing and publishing. Langdon, philanthropist and a man of much kindness and humor, was, moreover, an abolitionist, whose convictions helped enlighten his son-in-law about the horrors of slavery, an institution the southerner in earlier years and during his brief time in a Confederate militia unit had taken unquestioningly for granted.

The newlyweds' Buffalo adventure began well. "She is the very most perfect gem of womankind that ever I saw in my life," the groom wrote to a friend from childhood days, of one who was even then "lying asleep upstairs in a bed that I sleep in every night, & *for four whole days she has been Mrs. Samuel L. Clemens.*" The bride was likewise prompt in writing to her mother: "We are as happy as two mortals can well be," and to her sister Susan in mid-April: "nothing seems able to mar our joy." Clemens as coproprietor of the *Express* even proposed that John Hay come to Buffalo and join him, and Hay in their exchange of letters appears to have found the idea attractive, although nothing finally came of what Mark insisted would have made his bliss complete.

Yet after so auspicious a beginning, the bliss was fated to be short-lived. The year in Buffalo turned disastrous. Not only did Clemens find the routine of newspaper work deadening. That August 1870, after a brief painful illness, his father-in-law, Jervis Langdon, sixty-one, succumbed to stomach cancer, a terrible shock to the many who loved him. Livy was heartbroken, and in her grief and her new pregnancy, was joined in Buffalo by a childhood friend, Emma Nye, come to help take care of her. But Miss Nye took sick herself, and that September died delirious on the premises. Livy's fragile first child, a boy named Langdon, was born prematurely in November. The mother was too weak to nurse him, and in February came down with the typhoid that had killed her friend. Her husband despaired. In March 1871, upon a slight improvement in Livy's health, the family moved—the new mother borne on a mattress—back to Elmira, Clemens's one-third ownership of the *Express* and their bridal home both sold at a loss.

And all that grim while, Mark Twain was trying to write a second, light-hearted book of six hundred pages, which Mr. Bliss back in Hartford was eager to publish. Its subject was to be the author's time out West, beginning with the colorful stagecoach journey of 1,500 miles from St. Joseph, Missouri, to Carson City, Nevada, that Sam took with his brother Orion in the summer of 1861. But did his publisher realize, the author cried out at the end of the Clemenses' Buffalo ordeal, "that *for seven weeks* I have not had my natural rest but have been a night-and-day sick nurse to my wife?" By now Mark might have hoped "that the vials of hellfire bottled up for my benefit must be about emptied.—By the living God I don't believe they ever will be emptied."

Still he plowed on, in the more congenial surroundings of Elmira, where Livy's health among family and friends improved, little Langdon appeared to be gaining strength, and this second book—taking shape under the formidable shadow of a first book's gigantic success—edged forward.

It would be about innocents at home, headed west across the American continent rather than eastward to Europe. Yet although only a decade in the past, how far away that no longer duplicatable ride to Nevada now seemed. The author himself was astounded. Back then, in 1861, he and his brother had sprawled on mail sacks in the cradle-like stagecoach that rocked them for twenty days steadily, gloriously westward, with the prairie spread out flat as far as you could see, window curtains snapping, the driver overhead calling out his cries to the horses, Sam puffing his pipe in contentment and scanning the horizon for the cloud of dust that would signal the brief speedy approach of the pony-express rider—all that gone, that romance of travel gone. So short a time ago, and how different now! At the start of the 1870s, Mark was writing about 1861, when "perhaps not more than ten men in America, all told, expected to live to see a railroad follow that route to the Pacific." It was scarcely believable: three weeks in transit then to cover what took a bit over four days now, in these early 1870s, gliding along on rails at an amazing thirty miles an hour in the comfort of a Pullman Hotel on wheels, a sleeping palace with a dining car a few steps forward, where—"in the sweet-scented, appetite-compelling air of the prairies"—waiters in spotless white provided mountain brook trout, antelope steak, and choice fruits and berries in silver service on snowy linen, along with bumpers of sparkling champagne to wash such delicacies down.

Railroads had made the tremendous difference, and the telegraph lines strung alongside, which had instantly rendered the romantic pony express obsolete. The same way the transcontinental railroad, completed in May 1869—prodigious engineering feat, for all the struggle and exploitation and corruption that went along with it—had made obsolete this cross-country stagecoach travel that is nowhere more vividly preserved than in chapters 2 through 21 of the book that Mark Twain was then laboring to finish. The draft of the whole done at last—the overland trip, the silver mining in Nevada, newspaper work during Virginia City's flush times, the desperadoes, San Francisco, the Chinese, as well as the Hawaiian adventure as a bonus—and with the author's family safely in the care of the Langdons, Clemens set off by train from Elmira in August 1871 to deliver his manuscript of *Roughing It* to Mr. Bliss in Hartford.

Hartford, Connecticut, was where Sam and Livy Clemens were soon to move, in October of this 1871, and live there, conveniently halfway between New York and Boston, for the next two decades. They proved to be supremely happy years in the main, in what was at the time the most affluent city by size in America, and America's most beautiful city, according to the widely traveled lecturer Mark Twain, who had seen his share of them. Livy had friends in Hartford, and Sam's publisher was there, insurance and banking along with the publishing industry accounting for Hartford's wealth. The parents of Livy's friend Alice Hooker were away, so they could rent the young marrieds and baby their comfortable home on the western edge of town, among spreading lawns and congenial neighbors in a distinctive community called Nook Farm. Hartford center lay eastward up Farmington Avenue no more than fifteen minutes off; and woods, a river, and meadows lay picturesquely to the west. In the Hookers' dwelling Sam and Livy would settle in for a year and a half, through months that brought them the anguish of little Langdon's death, that frail child's death from diphtheria before he was two years old. A grievous loss; but a second child had been born by then, three months earlier, in March 1872, a daughter, Susy, on whom the bereaved parents showered their love. And a month before that, in February, *Roughing It*, Mark Twain's second substantial book, was published and proceeded to sell, if not so well as its predecessor, well enough to add further splendor to its author's already effulgent reputation.

And through it all, Clemens was very much in love. Born in a two-room, shake-roof house in Florida, Missouri, this new husband meant to see that his heiress wife—reared surrounded by the comforts and culture of the Langdons' Elmira mansion—would lose nothing through having married him. He regularly marveled at his good fortune. As long ago as four weeks before his marriage, after spending seventeen months off and on in extended visits with the Langdons, he described at some length the wonder of it to Mrs. Fairbanks. "With my vile temper & variable moods," he wrote, "it seems an incomprehensible miracle that we two"—he and Livy—"have been right together in the same house half the time for a year & half, & yet have never had a cross word, or a lover's 'tiff,' or a pouting spell, or a misunderstanding, or the faintest shadow of a jealous suspicion. Now isn't that absolutely wonderful? Could I have had such an experience with any other girl on earth?" All the more amazing because Livy had been changing him. "She has stopped my drinking, entirely. She has cut down my smoking considerably. She has reduced my slang & my boisterousness a good deal. She has exterminated my habit of carrying my hands in my pantaloon pockets, & has otherwise civilized me & well nigh taught me to behave in company." Such reformations might have made a body "fractious & irritable, but bless you she has a way of instituting them that swindles one into the belief that she is doing him a favor instead of curtailing his freedom & doing him a fatal damage." Livy was, in short, "the best girl that ever lived," and he said it when the lunacy stage of love was behind him, and the angel Olivia had become a human being, even if one whose excellencies he could see more clearly than ever. "I used to say she was faultless (& said it with a suspicion that she had her proper share of faults, only I was too blind to see them,) but I am thoroughly in my right mind, now, & I do maintain in all seriousness, that I can find no fault in her."

His love for Livy would persist unshaken through thirty-four years—until he lost her to death—and in memory intensely thereafter. Yet Mark Twain's unconventionality, his wildness, his unexpected comic explosions as a grown man of western, childlike, plain-speaking frankness, would persist as well, and Livy would do no more to discourage such startlingly funny outbursts than to mildly, smilingly protest—"Oh, Youth!" (as she called him)—cherishing that vital side, also, of her husband's remarkable gifts. "I will be more reverential, if you want me to," he had promised Mrs. Fairbanks before his marriage, "though I tell you it don't jibe with my principles. There is a fascination about meddling with forbidden things." And about uttering that great source of the comic: the unexpected, the shocking ("Oh, Youth!") that often in his case hovered just barely on the proper side of Victorian decorum.

He remained youthfully wild to the end, his mind forever restless even as his heart stayed close to Livy. At the start of this year 1872, for example, Mark

Twain was out adding to the family's income by lecturing in Indiana, Ohio, West Virginia, Pennsylvania, and New York; and in mid-year, in August, the devoted husband set off alone on yet another voyage, to England, this time to lecture and explore over three months the possibility of writing a third subscription volume, about that country and its people and customs. Nothing came of the writing project, but the trip was revelatory nevertheless; for upon arrival, the author and lecturer was astounded to discover the extent of his popularity among these British. It soon became obvious that they had taken to his *Innocents Abroad* (as they would to his *Roughing It*) every bit as avidly as his fellow countrymen had. A single episode will serve to illustrate; in amazement and pride, he wrote of the September evening to Livy back home. In London's Guildhall, the visiting American in full formal attire had by invitation attended a quintessentially class-conscious, tradition-laden ceremony inaugurating the city's new lord mayor. Unrecognized, he took his assigned seat among the entitled guests, liveried servants all about. The name of each guest was being announced, an ongoing roll call, "a horde of great names, one after another," each one "received in respectful silence." Until one name was called, at the sound of which, Clemens writes to Livy, "there was such a storm of applause as you never heard." Mark Twain's name had been reached, and as he sat there the thunderous clapping persisted, "& they could not go on with the list. I was never so taken aback in my life," totally unprepared for it, for Clemens had "thought I was the humblest in that great titled assemblage—& behold, mine was the *only* name in the long list that called forth this splendid compliment."

It might have been enough to let him think he could undertake anything. Back in Hartford at Nook Farm that Christmas, with plans to bring his family to Britain to enjoy an extended stay in the spring, he and his wife and a couple of their several distinguished, affable, easygoing neighbors were dining together, the two gentlemen—Clemens and his friend from next door Charlie Warner—complaining of the deplorable quality of popular fiction just then. Livy Clemens and Susan Warner listened a while until moved to challenge their grumbling husbands. Then why don't you write something better? Neither one was a novelist: Clemens a writer mostly of imaginative nonfiction, Warner an essayist and editor of the *Hartford Courant*. But they accepted the dare that their wives had thrown down and confidently set to work. Just over three months later, in April 1873, with the Clemens family—husband, wife, two-year-old Susy, servants, and a friend as traveling companion for Livy—winding up preparations for that tour overseas, the collaborative writing effort was finished. The authors called their completed novel *The Gilded Age*.

16. JOHN HAY MARRIES

Gilt is a thin layer of gold applied over a baser metal such as brass or lead. An object fashioned from the cheaper stuff is thus made to look like the solid gold it isn't. The verb is *gild*, the adjective *gilded*. Shakespeare's *King John* (IV. ii. 11–16) tells us that "To gild refinèd gold, to paint the lily, to throw a perfume on the violet . . . is wasteful and ridiculous excess." On the other hand, the gold out of which we arose was pure, a mythical golden age in the distant past, a Garden of Eden from which humankind has fallen. Or perhaps such an age lies where the Enlightenment put it, golden in the future, toward the end of an ascent up which perfectible if often inept humanity struggles. Yet to some alive after the Civil War, the years in their present—with the new peace, and prosperity, and a progress convincingly on display at the great Centennial Exhibition in Philadelphia in 1876—may have looked like an authentic golden age, even as Mark Twain and Charles Dudley Warner's satirical novel (published near the very start of the period, in December 1873) suggested otherwise, its title implying that any such glitter was thin gilt in times that were leaden.

At a later period, in the 1920s, the authors' title was appropriated and applied to those same postwar decades in America in the second half of the nineteenth century, a Gilded Age of—among much else—rampant speculation (in particular, in railroads and land and town sites on that land), corruption (in governments federal, state, and municipal), fraud, graft, new wealth's gaudy ostentation (those mansions rising in Newport and along New York's Fifth Avenue), amid widespread hedonistic excess all but in sight of exploitation and squalor. The label, applied by the social theorist Lewis Mumford and the literary historian Van Wyck Brooks, has stuck: for convenience, the years from, say, the early 1870s to perhaps 1900 are now often referred to as the Gilded Age, although people living through the period—with the exception of Warner and the high-spirited, sardonic Mark Twain—held off applying the term to themselves.

About such matters as characterized America back then, John Hay as editorial writer at the *New York Tribune*, the most influential newspaper in the nation at the time, would have had opinions. But Hay had been hired for his knowledge of Europe, and was to articulate the *Tribune*'s position on such issues as the *Alabama* claims, wherein negotiations between Britain and the United States sought to determine what the former should pay as reparations for all the damage that Confederate vessels built in England during the Civil War had inflicted on American ships. Or Hay might editorially express the

Tribune's views on Spain and its possession Cuba, ninety miles off our southern coast and seething with insurrection. Inevitably, though, the new editor's interests widened, as did his services to his employer. He had not been hired as a reporter, yet Whitelaw Reid sent Hay west in October 1871 to cover the monumental catastrophe of the Chicago Fire that lay at the end of a thirty-eight-hour train ride, the editor-reporter reaching the still smoldering desolation two days after his thirty-third birthday. From there, despite severe limitations that the fire had imposed on his means of doing so, Hay sent back vivid accounts of the destruction, as well as interviews among the sufferers and bereaved, right down to Mrs. O'Leary's husband, Patrick, whose infamous cow, having allegedly kicked over a lit lantern that started it all, grazed placidly beyond the O'Learys' windows. Back in New York, Hay further widened the range of his work by writing art reviews, obituaries, and increasingly pointed criticism—scorpion-like, in contrast to the late Mr. Greeley's cudgels—of the corruption just under the gilt of President Grant's administration.

Delighted with such competent versatility, Whitelaw Reid soon raised his new editor's salary from the initial $50 a week to $65, regretting only that he couldn't go higher. Mark Twain might later grumble about it, recollecting that the young editorial writer had been "earning three or four times the salary he got, considering the high character of the work which came from his pen"; but those weekly $65 made John Hay one of the highest paid editorial writers in the country. And he was living well in Manhattan, dressing well (as he always did), and socializing in the various metropolitan clubs—the Century, the Lotos, the Knickerbocker—where he and his off-hours bosom companion Whitelaw Reid were welcome. For in the vacuum after Horace Greeley's death in November 1872, a struggle to take control of the *Tribune* had ended (through the clandestine support of the execrable Jay Gould) with Reid on top, and he would stay there as principal shareholder through the decades ahead, in 1875 moving the newspaper from its ramshackle five-story headquarters at the "Old Rookery" on Park Row to the far more imposing ten-story, brick-and-masonry, elevator-equipped, clocktower-crowned earliest of Manhattan's skyscrapers, at 154 Printing House Square, corner of Spruce and Nassau. The town paid attention. The two young bachelors, a year apart in age with Reid the elder—the one the poet and intimate of Lincoln, the other the publisher of the *Tribune*—were much noticed and their eligibility commented on.

By then, though, one of the two had found what would change his bachelor status. In Paris several years earlier, touring Americans had often called on John Hay at the Legation with their letters of introduction and hopes that the *au fait* secretary might help them dispose of their time in the French capital. Among such callers in the autumn of 1866 had been Andros Stone, president of the Cleveland Rolling Mill Company, with wife and daughters. Mr. Stone owned a home in New York City, and his nieces from Cleveland would later visit him there. The elder of the two, twenty-three years old, was named Clara, and John Hay met her in the Stones' parlor on Thirty-Seventh Street in early 1872.

Unlike Sam Clemens before him, the *Tribune* editor didn't fall promptly, fervently in love. Clara Stone returned to Cleveland, so he saw her only intermittently, when passing through that city on his way to and from his family's home in Illinois. Once, in August of the same year, he did encounter Clara by chance at a train station elsewhere in Ohio, after missing her in Cleveland on his way back from Warsaw via Buffalo to Manhattan. Later he told her of the impression she made on him then, in their brief time together in Painesville: "I could not help asking myself, 'What is the young lady to me that I should be so delighted to see her?' and then I thought she is very lovely and I like lovely girls—*voilà tout.*"

But it was more than that. Clara was ten years younger than Hay (as Olivia Langdon was ten years younger than Clemens) and, he judged, a "picture of fresh and beautiful life": calm, competent, not at all flashy, solid, a good Christian, with interests in literature but skilled at discharging the complexities of home management. And on his visits to Cleveland's Euclid Avenue, Hay had seen the remarkable home that Clara Stone lived in, and had met her younger sister, Flora, and her parents. Her father, Amasa Stone, was (like Clemens' father-in-law Jervis Langdon) self-made, by trade a New England carpenter, builder of churches and houses who, when scarcely out of his teens, had helped design and erect—in antebellum years when all such bridges were wooden—a truss-system railroad bridge of wood and stone that spanned the Connecticut River. The carpenter had branched out and prospered, in 1850 taking his skills and his young family to Cleveland, where he and his partners got into railroads: linking them, consolidating them, extending them well beyond bustling Cleveland—its population already upward of one hundred thousand—westward along Lake Erie and into Michigan, eastward into the newly discovered, soon booming oil fields of northwest Pennsylvania. Amasa Stone became president of the Lake Shore & Michigan Southern Railway, built Cleveland's great Union Depot, with his brother Andros formed the Cleveland Rolling Mill Company, invested in a woolen mill, more iron mills, a bridge manufacturing company. He designed railroad cars and built them, invested in banks and in Western Union, in Standard Oil, became a director of Standard Oil. And he erected a great brick mansion with turrets and Gothic windows, all rosewood and marble and hand-carved mahogany inside, "the finest, most complete and convenient residence west of the Hudson," the newspapers said, on Cleveland's beautiful elm-lined Euclid Avenue, with his wife and daughters and among neighbors who included Jeptha Wade, founder of that same Western Union that had revolutionized communications in the Gilded Age, and John D. Rockefeller, titan of Standard Oil.

Amasa Stone was, in short, a very rich man, himself a titan of industry. Jervis Langdon of Elmira, New York, had acquired his wealth through lumber, coal, and railroads, and at his death had left his three children—Susan, Olivia, and Charley—with funds sufficient to make them comfortable for life. Still, the Langdon wealth was hardly comparable to what Amasa Stone of Cleveland had gathered together by the 1870s. Like the Langdons, Mr. and Mrs. Stone had three children, theirs also a son and two daughters. But their son, Adelbert, while a student at Yale, drowned in the Connecticut River in 1865, leaving his surviving sisters as sole beneficiaries of the family fortune.

Nothing in John Hay's extant correspondence during his courtship—or during the years after their marriage when his life turned in a markedly different direction—suggests that his love for Miss Stone was based on anything less than devotion to Clara herself. "If there is any one reason why I loved you at first," he wrote to her, "it is because I respected you more than any other woman." Meanwhile, Hay's own professional prospects, already lofty, continued to rise. Around Christmastime in 1872 Reid raised his salary to $100 a week: "It is inadequate & late; but it may serve at least to mark the admiration every editor and owner feels for your writing and for you." And Hay's friend and former colleague John George Nicolay was settling his family in Washington, D.C., in order to assume the duties of marshal of the Supreme Court, an easeful employment that promised ample time for Nico to consult resources in the nearby Library of Congress. Perhaps Hay and his friend from Lincoln days might at last and seriously undertake the enormous, long-deferred task of putting together the life and times of the man whose memory they both revered.

Personally, too, the editor's prospects looked ever brighter. That winter Miss Stone came to New York for an extended stay with her Uncle Andros, an arrangement allowing her and Mr. Hay to see each other almost daily. Her suitor pursued his courtship with increasing ardor, and by early spring of that 1873 Clara was won over. "Ah think what you give," Hay exclaimed. "Beauty and goodness and youth, a rich and noble nature, candor and honor and affection, and in return you get only the worship of a soul which has no existence but in you." He loved her, he wrote after she had returned to Cleveland in April—"but I worship you also; you have come so strongly and bountifully to me that I can scarcely yet be at ease and contented in my happiness." That she had given him her heart "and lips and now your hand" was incredible. "If, like me, you had passed many years in the troubled current of the world, and met everywhere deceit and folly and sin, treachery and malice, then you would know how infinitely comforting it would be to meet one heart which is true and noble and kind, one which you could trust for time and for eternity. You lovely girl, if you had not cared for me, I should still have been grateful that I had known you. But to think that you love me, that you are to be mine forever! how can I be anything but humbly grateful?"

The sentiment sounded much in the mode of Sam Clemens's astonished gratitude that such a one as Olivia Langdon could love him, although the refined Hay, unlike the wild humorist, stood in no need of further polishing. He and Clara had agreed to keep their engagement secret for now, but by the late summer of 1873 he was sharing the news with close friends. With Nicolay, that he was engaged to be married to Miss Clara Stone: "She is a very estimable young person—large, handsome and good. I never found life worthwhile before." And with the then ailing bachelor Whitelaw Reid: "I wish I could see you in the same predicament. The fact of being in love, and seeing a good woman in love also, is a wonderfully awakening thing. I would not have died before this happened for a great deal of coin." Thus Hay could heartily urge his friend: "Get well, and then get engaged. Time flies."

He and Clara were married in the Stones' parlor on Euclid Avenue on February 4, 1874 (four years to the month, almost to the day, after Samuel L. Clemens had married his own heiress, on February 2, 1870, in the Langdons' parlor in Elmira, New York). The new Mr. and Mrs. Hay returned to the husband's rented bachelor quarters on East 25th Street in New York City and to John Hay's unsigned but much admired work at the *Tribune*. And as with the Clemenses' marriage, this one, too, began in bliss.

For the most part it continued that way. In time the couple rented a home on 42nd Street just off Fifth Avenue, where their first child, Helen, was born, on March 11, 1875. To Reid, March 15: "My wife says, when you come to the house, that you have got to hold the baby." But as the months passed, Clara felt homesick for Cleveland. Her father, who had learned to regard Hay in some respects as balm for the son he had lost, was acquiring in his late fifties the ailments of age. Accordingly, Hay had occasion to write to a friend from Spanish days: "my father-in-law wishes me to go into another line of business, which will bring me immediate wealth." Others noted the gentleman's prospects. Robert Todd Lincoln remarked to Nicolay about how Mr. Stone will someday bequeath to "J.H. and one other fellow"—whoever marries Clara's sister Flora—"from $6000000 to $8000000—which will make John to write with a first class gold pen." And by early June 1875, Hay, his New York life closed down, had taken his wife—that new mother—and baby and moved to Cleveland, to share with the Stones their magnificent home on Euclid Avenue.

Amasa Stone made the young people welcome. He gave to Hay—already possessed of a rare valuable share of the only one hundred shares of *Tribune* stock—two Lake Shore Railway bonds worth $10,000 (Mark Twain had earned what was thought to be a breathtaking $13,300 in two years of sales of *The Innocents Abroad*). And Mr. Stone gave yet more. He gave the young Hay family—as Mr. Langdon had given the newly married Clemenses—a home of their own, theirs on Euclid Avenue, to be built next door in the highest of styles: carved sandstone exterior, interiors done by New York's most sought-after decorators, woodwork hand-carved by the best of German craftsmen. Meanwhile, the labor that Stone put his son-in-law to seemed undemanding: "I do nothing," Hay told Nicolay, "but read and yawn. My work is merely the care of investments which are so safe that they require no care." Away from Manhattan's clamor and deadlines, the former journalist could look into the future with every likelihood that he and his friend from White House days might finally begin their Lincoln project in earnest.

The Hays' new home—all that could be desired in sumptuousness and comfort—was ready to move into in October 1876. A second child was born that November, a son named for Clara's brother, who had drowned eleven years before—Adelbert: Del they would call him. Of the baby's mother, Hay wrote, "We were not much known to each other when we were married. But I know her now and I never could have imagined so desirable a wife." Clara, too, was just where and with whom she wanted to be. So the Christmas season that year seemed particularly generous in its bestowal of blessings on the Amasa Stones and their Cleveland neighbors the Hays next door, even while disaster offered no hint of its proximity.

Snow was falling heavily on Friday, December 29, 1876, as Train Number 5, the luxurious *Pacific Express*, pulled out of the Erie, Pennsylvania, station, two locomotives and eleven cars bound for Chicago. At around 7:30 that night Number 5 with its crew and 159 passengers entered onto a bridge over Ohio's Ashtabula Creek that flowed seventy feet below. The first locomotive had reached the far side safely when the iron bridge gave way. The second locomotive derailed and, with all the cars it was towing, plunged to the bottom of the gorge. Ninety-two passengers died, some killed in the fall, some burned alive in the splintered, flaming railroad cars that capsized stoves inside had set on fire. The tremendous crash could be heard in adjacent Ashtabula, flames leaping high to locate the horror precisely. Townspeople rushed to the site, but in deep snow they had to cut their way down the overgrown banks to the riverbed, where they struggled to rescue survivors between the furnace heat of the still raging fire and the cold of that long winter night.

It was the worst train calamity in the United States up to then, and would remain so for another forty years. The line affected was the Lake Shore & Michigan Southern Railway; and the experimental iron truss bridge with its extravagant 154-foot span, which had given way under the weight of the snow and the Lake Shore train, had been designed and built to specifications insisted upon by Amasa Stone.

17. *THE GILDED AGE*

The Ashtabula Railroad Bridge might serve as an emblem of the Gilded Age, imposing from a distance but with defective underpinnings. In December 1873, three years to the month before the disaster, Mark Twain and Charles Dudley Warner had published their novel *The Gilded Age: A Tale of To-day*, which would furnish a name for the era. Mrs. Mary Fairbanks, by the way— Clemens's loyal fan—had read her *Quaker City* cub's new book at once but wasn't entirely pleased with it. The author knew why: she had read the whole novel. She shouldn't have done that, Clemens told her. She should have skipped Warner's part and read only what Mark Twain had written; and to help her do so, he cited the relevant chapters to reconsider: 1–11, 24–25, 27–28, 30, 32–34, 36–37, 42–43, 45, the first three or four pages of 49—also chapters 51–53, 57, 59–62, and portions of 35 and 56.

The advice was sound as a means of locating where most of the merit lies in *The Gilded Age*'s overabundant six hundred pages, composed to that length because purchasers of books by subscription were unlikely to pay for less. Rural patrons far from any bookstore gave salesmen invited into their parlors deposits only for forthcoming books of substance: fat books, reference books— family law, encyclopedic texts, household medicine. And if subscribers put down money for such a travel romp as *The Innocents Abroad*, even that must be hefty, to sit in its creditable girth on their bookshelves and, when opened, reveal pages copiously illustrated. Thus, *The Gilded Age* as a subscription publication was necessarily prolix, a loosely structured effort by two first-time novelists who had spent no more than a month assembling their thoughts and no more than two months writing all that prose. Clemens wrote the opening eleven chapters, turned the manuscript over to Warner to introduce his own plot in a dozen chapters, then got it back to resume in the next two—back and forth, with different characters in each and the plots no more than feebly intertwined.

Mark Twain was only being honest in what he wrote to Mrs. Fairbanks. Charles Dudley Warner's contribution contains the defective underpinnings of the enterprise: his plot of melodrama, clichés, and stereotypes, sluggishly propelled by a couple of bloodless protagonists. Mark Twain's portion may not be solid gold, but whatever in *The Gilded Age* retains value a century and a half later lies in the pages he wrote, which tell a mostly authentic story in vivid diction, with humor, a pulsating sense of Washington in the early 1870s, and a still pointed satire of, in part, the age's hypocrisy and greed.

Those vices soar to life through two vital inhabitants of Clemens's pages. Colonel Eschol Sellers, as an indomitably cheerful image of greed, evolved into one of nineteenth-century America's best-known fictional creations, both through the novel and through its creator's successful transposition of the character onto the stage. The actor John T. Raymond made a career out of playing Colonel Sellers more than a thousand times (as Joe Jefferson did for that other nineteenth-century staple of American drama, Rip Van Winkle). The Colonel thus became a type of his period that our own day may recognize: the buoyant schemer ready to speculate on just about anything, ever hopeful of making money off hogs or corn or mules or a snake-oil salve for sore eyes or a dreary little hamlet's potential to grow into a great metropolis. "There's millions in it!" the colonel would cry out exuberantly—and a few of his contemporaries did in fact make millions speculating, although Colonel Sellers never did, not the hopefully persistent, ever impoverished, ultimately endearing Colonel Sellers, who with Rip and Uncle Tom became a byword in his countrymen's late-century conversations.

And as Colonel Sellers embodies a part of Mark Twain's satire of postwar America's ubiquitous speculative greed, Senator Abner Dilworthy serves as the author's satirical exemplum of its hypocrisy. Inspired by a national scandal bubbling at the time the Hartford collaborators were writing their novel—it centered on the Kansas politician Samuel Pomeroy, charged with offering $4,000 to buy a state legislator's vote in order to get reelected to the U.S.

Senate—Mark Twain's fictional Dilworthy reeks equally of graft and sancti-
mony, the latter blatantly during visits to Sunday school classes where the
senator aspires to instruct little children in his facile pieties.

Clemens hadn't needed to venture as far as Kansas, however, for specimens
of corruption. Little more than a couple of easy hours by rail from Hartford,
New York City was awash in it. In this same 1873 when *The Gilded Age* was
written and published, William M. Tweed was being tried, in January, for
bribery and corruption in the New York courts, only to be acquitted but tried
again in November, convicted, and finally thrown into jail. Boss Tweed had
been running Tammany Hall and, effectively, New York City since 1866, in
those postwar years when widespread, inventive expansion of a newly peacetime America bred schemers galore. Tweed and his cronies did get things
done: found immigrants tenement rooms and jobs (in exchange for their
votes), finished building City Hall (though tardily and at exorbitant cost), and
developed Broadway and the Upper East and West Side, always raising money
along the way—by issuing watered bonds and through fraudulent contracts,
padded payrolls, elevated property taxes, and inflated rents—from which the
Tammany Ring grabbed its generous take off the top.

Bosses of political machines in other cities thrived through the Gilded Age
by similar means at the public's expense, as did politicians in offices both
state and federal. In fact, a huge political scandal—largest of a scandal-ridden
decade—had been uncovered at the federal level just the previous fall, of 1872,
one arising out of actions in the Lincoln administration, with the chartering of
the transcontinental railroad ten years earlier. By war's end, the Union Pacific
had begun laying rails westward from Council Bluffs, Iowa; but by then investors back East had seen enough of such construction to grow leery. Too many
roads were being built, including some that would never make back their
money: maybe roads such as this, the rails of which would span deserts and
mountains where cities weren't likely to rise up any time soon.

So private funding was proving hard to come by. But a fancy-sounding
company suggesting European wealth, Crédit Mobilier of America, was created to take on the responsibility of constructing this westbound transcontinental railroad. Congress had given the Union Pacific huge grants of public
land to convert into funds to get the road built; but the Crédit Mobilier's
charges to do the work were wildly inflated, billed to a Union Pacific whose
directors were also directors of the newly created construction company. In
effect, they were paying themselves; so that of the immense profits that such
overcharging produced, those same directors raked off a healthy percentage
for their own purposes, while using shares of the high-flying Crédit Mobilier

stock as gifts to congressmen who, when their federal legislation wasn't actively enabling the fraud, were being bribed to look the other way. Building the Union Pacific's part of the railroad across the West cost $50 million, but nearly half of that arose from overbilling, the excess diverted to the pockets of the directors, their cronies, and their co-conspirators in Congress. In the midst of the presidential campaign of 1872, the *New York Sun*, no friend of the incumbent, got its hands on means to expose the corruption: Grant's vice president Schuyler Colfax and fourteen federal legislators all were charged with being deeply implicated, enriching themselves at the people's expense. Soon Colfax's political career lay in ruins.

President Grant, however, running against the ill-fated Horace Greeley, survived the sensation to win reelection handily; nor did any of the several outrages that shook the capital during Grant's second term—the Whiskey Ring scandal and the gross malfeasance of *five* of the president's cabinet: specifically, his attorney general, his secretary of the treasury, his secretary of war, his secretary of the navy, and his secretary of the interior—do much to tarnish the general's reputation among his contemporaries. For instance, in all the millions of words Mark Twain wrote, he had almost nothing to say about Abraham Lincoln; yet he idolized Grant, exulted in his friendship with the general, spoke of him often and always glowingly, and would have voted for him any chance he got: our greatest leader since Washington, Clemens thought. What he saw, despite the scandals, was what the majority of his countrymen saw in the Union general: like Lincoln a humble man from hardscrabble beginnings, but of an open nature, modest, unassuming, who, until then having failed rather endearingly at much of what he undertook, stepped forth in wartime to save his embattled country. President Lincoln's enemies—throughout the South and among Democrats and Radical Republicans up north—lived on with a bitterness passed down to their children's children. Grant's wartime enemies mellowed—he had fought hard and won—as the North's views of the Confederate Lee mellowed; and if Grant's administration proved rife with scandals, none touched the general, who was regarded as personally incorruptible, a hero whose principal flaw was a tendency to be too loyal, too trusting. Thus Grant's tomb was elaborately dedicated in 1897; Lincoln's memorial had to wait until 1922.

As it happened, Mark Twain was out of the country during a crucial interval of Ulysses Grant's time in office. During the campaign in the autumn of 1872 when the Crédit Mobilier scandal erupted, Clemens was in England, having sailed from New York on August 21 to be surprised by, then revel in, his newfound English fame. He returned to America no earlier than November

25, well after the election. Back in Hartford, he and his neighbor Warner wrote their *Gilded Age*, and Clemens bought a handsome lot in Nook Farm to build a home on. Then he was off again, this time with his wife and year-old daughter Susy, in mid-May 1873—Livy's first time abroad—to enjoy travel, extended visits, and shopping through five months in England, Scotland, Ireland, and France. The family sailed for New York at the end of October; but once home, Clemens lingered only long enough to see wife and daughter settled, before boarding ship again for England, to secure the English copyright of *The Gilded Age*.

Initially, sales of the new work by Mark Twain and his friend proved gratifying. People were curious to read this *Tale of To-day*, a departure for the extraordinarily popular humorist-essayist-travel writer: collaborative fiction, a satirical novel set in the present. What would he do with such a subject? But sales didn't hold up, partly because of the work itself—put together in haste, with its two plots and two styles not always harmonizing—and partly because of the date of the book's publication: December 1873.

Three months earlier, on September 18, Jay Cooke & Company had declared bankruptcy. Cooke had been one of those speculators of the Gilded Age who did make millions, and millions, and more millions with his banking and investments, the latter principally in railroads. Just then the financier had been engaged in launching a second transcontinental railroad farther north, headed west out of Duluth, Minnesota, toward the Pacific at Puget Sound. But such an enterprise needed vast capital, for a long-term venture that would pay off far in the future, after towns had sprung up where mostly vacant land lay now. Investors shied away, and abruptly the great Jay Cooke & Company collapsed. The bankruptcy brought on financial panic. For ten days the stock market shut down. Banks failed. Businesses failed, thousands all over the country. Railroads failed, over fifty different lines within two months. Corporate profits shrank. Factories closed, throwing laborers out of work. Workers still employed saw their wages cut. The nation—and Europe—sank into a depression that persisted through most of the decade. The Panic of 1873, arising in large part from an overexpansion of railroad construction after the Civil War, brought on the most severe economic conditions (called at the time the Great Depression) that the United States had ever faced—or would face until nearly six decades later, when an even more resounding crash, in 1929, led dark years in the 1930s to appropriate the earlier designation as their own.

For all that, some people were able to ride out the hard times. Sam Clemens, born in a tiny frame house in the bleak frontier hamlet of Florida, Missouri, had arrived by early 1874 at an elevation seemingly above the vagaries of banks failing and businesses closing their doors. On the lot he had bought at fashionable Nook Farm, on Hartford's western edge, he was setting about, in that same winter and spring, to have a residence constructed that was worthy of his adored wife Livy. An esteemed architect and a noted interior decorator were hired, with Mrs. Clemens taking charge of details. The result was distinctive. "Many of the readers of *The Times*, doubtless, have had at least an external view of the structure, which already has acquired something beyond a local fame," one Hartford newspaper recorded on March 24; "and such persons, we think, will agree with us in the opinion that it is one of the oddest looking buildings in the State ever designed for a dwelling, if not in the whole country." Upon the completion of the residence, its owner—off with his family in Elmira during much of the construction—felt otherwise, and would continue to feel so through the nearly two decades the Clemenses lived there: moved to praise the "perfect taste" of the house's interior, the "delicious dream of harmonious color, & its all-pervading spirit of peace & serenity & deep contentment," as he wrote to his wife long after. "You did it all," he told Livy, "& it speaks of you & praises you eloquently & unceasingly. It is the loveliest home that ever was."

Today, beautifully restored on Hartford's Farmington Avenue, it is surely among the most memorable. And at the time some thought it the happiest, at

Nineteenth-century view of Mark Twain's Hartford home. Courtesy of Mark Train House and Museum, Hartford, Connecticut.

least through many of the years the Clemenses lived there. In Elmira that summer, in June 1874, Sam and Livy's second daughter, Clara, was born. They moved into their new Hartford home in October. Clara was turning seventeen when they left Hartford at last, filled with sadness at leaving, remembering so much joy: neighbors as close friends and their children always welcome, the parlor games, theatricals, ice skating on the Little River at dusk as lights in the great house came on, and the visitors from near and far. Several times William Dean Howells paid visits, and (according to Clara) "always brought sunshine and cheer into the house as no one else could. Everyone loved him and wanted him to stay a long time. His sense of humor and capacity to show it refreshed the hearts of all. To see him and Father enjoy a funny story or joke together was a complete show in itself. Both of them red in the face from laughing, with abundant gray hair straggling over their foreheads and restless feet that carried them away from their chairs and back again! I am sure no children ever laughed with more abandon."

It was a home, Katy Leary—the Clemenses' loyal maid to the end—reported, "that you would like more than anything else in the world. A happy, happy home—happiness budding all over—everybody always happy. Our life—it just rolled on like a smooth sea—wasn't a thing for eleven years"—she had come to them in 1880—"not a bit of sadness of any kind. There was always fun and excitement, especially when Mr. Clemens was around." Only, among such high and hospitable spirits it wasn't easy for an author to get work done. For that, Clemens and his family would spend their summers in Elmira, where Livy's sister Susan had built, on the hill behind Quarry Farm where they stayed, an octagonal study looking over the river valley and the distant hills. Mark Twain could retire up there in the morning—his family contentedly below—and spend his day in uninterrupted labor. There in the mid-1870s he was at work on something rather different: another novel but going back in time, before the Civil War and the industrial complexities that had followed with their crass materialism, back to a simpler agrarian world of the 1840s, in a village along the Mississippi River: a book for adults to recover their childhood from. He called it *The Adventures of Tom Sawyer*.

Livy and Howells both read the book in manuscript—Howells longed to be on that island with Tom, he said—but both told the author he had mistaken his audience. *Tom Sawyer* was for younger readers and should be marketed thus. Mark Twain complied. Initially, though, sales were disappointing, through no lack of interest but because the English edition had been pirated in Canada and sold cheaply across the border before Elijah Bliss could get his U.S. edition ready. The Hartford publisher may have been lukewarm about the product in any case: salesmen told him *Tom Sawyer* wasn't long enough, and was a novel besides; their subscription customers didn't generally buy short books or novels either. Thus the piracy of *Tom Sawyer* ended by costing its author money unearned, while adding to grudges he was building up against Bliss. Meanwhile, the new novel had to bide its time in hopes that sales might pick up later.

Nevertheless, that same summer of 1876 Mark Twain got busy on a sequel. The book just published was in the third person. The sequel would be in the first person, a disreputable chum of Tom's in their riverfront village speaking in his own dialect, as do the speakers in Hay's "Little Breeches" and "Jim Bludso." "You don't know about me without you have read a book by the name of 'The Adventures of Tom Sawyer,' but that ain't no matter," Huckleberry Finn begins his account from out of a vanished world. "That book was made by Mr. Mark Twain, and he told the truth, mainly. There was things which he stretched, but mainly he told the truth. That is nothing. I never seen anybody but lied, one time or another, without it was Aunt Polly, or the widow. . . ."

18. SUMMER 1877

The Ashtabula bridge disaster at the end of this same 1876 had led a committee of the Ohio legislature to summon executives of the Lake Shore & Michigan Southern Railway to appear before it promptly, in mid-January 1877, to explain. The railroad's chief engineer, Charles Collins, gave his testimony, the bulk of it technical, then went home and, on the following evening, shot himself fatally through the head. Amasa Stone, John Hay's father-in-law, founder and chief shareholder of the Lake Shore, seemed made of sterner stuff. His testimony flatly denied that defects in the bridge had caused the accident; a locomotive had simply derailed ("the bridge was carried down by the second locomotive in some way leaving the track"). Moreover, although Ohio law required that self-extinguishing stoves be installed in all railroad cars, the Lake Shore magnate contended that the stoves on his trains, though not in compliance, were safer than what the law stipulated—this despite the *Pacific Express*'s stoves overturning in the seventy-foot fall and bursting into wildly destructive flames ("I examined those stoves" of the self-extinguishing kind "and it was said they would not cause fire; my conclusion was that they were more dangerous than the ones we used—that there was no safety about them any more than any other stoves").

Regardless of such categorical assurances, Stone's Lake Shore Railway ended by paying damages of $500,000 (conservatively maybe $109 million in 2017 dollars), and Stone himself was roundly vilified through sermons, editorials, and pamphlets that found receptive audiences across a nation repelled by the Crédit Mobilier scandal along with other specimens of railroad wrongdoing in addition to profiteering: shoddy workmanship, favoritism, shameless indifference to worker safety and the public welfare. In such circumstances, it was agreed on Euclid Avenue that Mr. Stone, Mrs. Stone, and daughter Flora would enjoy a European vacation through the months ahead, leaving affairs at home in the by then competent hands of Stone's son-in-law, that quick business study John Hay.

Hay accordingly was looking after railroad matters through what turned into a frantic season in the summer of 1877. The year itself proved of high importance in American history. A presidential election the preceding November had left the nation through the following winter with an outcome still in doubt. Samuel Tilden, Democrat, reform governor of New York and enemy of corrupt Tammany Hall, had won the popular vote against Ohio's Republican governor Rutherford B. Hayes. But because three southern states submitted conflicting results—one electoral count derived from all white, thus Democratic polling; the other count, Republican, from polling places where African Americans managed to cast ballots—neither candidate had been awarded the disputed electoral vote. Was it to be President Tilden or President Hayes? Having lost the popular tally, Hayes presumed he had lost the election; but Tilden seemed oddly indifferent to results. His and Hayes's men appear to have come up with a backroom deal. The Democrats would concede, in exchange for Republican president Hayes's consenting to withdraw from the South federal troops down there since the Civil War.

The year 1877 thus marks the end of the North's strife-torn efforts to reconstruct what was the former Confederacy in a way that would lift newly emancipated slaves to the full citizenship promised them in the amended U.S. Constitution. But by then a majority in the North had had enough of Reconstruction anyway. The war was more than a decade behind them; yet the South was still, as Whitelaw Reid wrote in the *Tribune*, "crushed, wretched, busy displaying and bemoaning her wounds." A widespread opinion of northerners grown weary with it all, Reid included, was that we should put aside hard feelings and leave neighbors below the Mason Dixon Line (white neighbors, that is) to settle their domestic problems on their own. Reconciliation became the word (the "Word over all," in Whitman's poem), to be achieved by white northerners ceasing to meddle. Instead, they would extend their hands in friendship in order to grasp the white hands of their southern brothers in unity and peace.

But even as Reconstruction ended abruptly with the withdrawal of federal troops in the spring of 1877, that same summer a new conflict broke out, one that Colonel Hay would have to deal with directly. This different strife had nothing to do with slavery or Reconstruction; rather, it was about railroads.

Since the late 1830s, railroads had played an ever increasing part in American life, until by now, forty years later, you could ride from New York City all the way to the Pacific on rails. And railways had been driving industrialization; the nation's single largest corporation in 1877 was the Pennsylvania Railroad, employer of two hundred thousand workers. By then, the iron and steel web of roads was reaching toward just about everywhere, seventy-nine thousand miles of track with more to follow. So people could still make fortunes through having rails laid down; for the federal government, fully aware of the importance of such roads to the nation's prosperity, continued to give over large tracts of public land to help them spread. By 1890, when the rage for laying new tracks finally eased off, Congress had awarded 170 million acres of such land to eighty different companies, for railroads half of which never got built (thirty-eight million of those acres were eventually returned to public ownership unsold, with not a rail line to show for it).

Meanwhile, the Crédit Mobilier scandal of 1872 had taught the public a *political* lesson about corruption that involved railroads and congressmen intertwined for their mutual profit. In the following year the devastating Panic of 1873 taught another lesson, about how dependent the *economic* welfare of the nation was on the health of railroads. Overexpansion of rail lines led to financial collapse that fall, and panic, and long-lasting aftereffects. The railroads themselves were hit hard: less freight was shipped, fewer passengers boarded the cars, and, as profits shrank, workers who didn't get fired outright saw their wages cut. During the four years immediately after the Panic, railroads cut wages by 35 percent, on shifts lasting up to eighteen hours under sometimes dangerous working conditions, all while shareholders of their watered stock continued to receive plump dividends. Hard times for employees dragged on, until, in 1877, railroad wages were cut by an additional 10 percent as of June 1. With that, on July 16, at Camden Junction, Maryland, forty brakemen and firemen of the Baltimore & Ohio walked off in protest.

Such walk-offs had happened before, with a supportive crowd gathering and—here again as on earlier occasions—local police promptly dispersing the protesters. What happened next, though, was new to American life. On the following day railroad workers farther along the B & O line seized the depot at Martinsburg, West Virginia, preventing trains from moving in or out until wages were restored in full. Police arrested the leaders, but an angry crowd promptly freed them. That was new. And through days ahead, railroad workers in towns and cities all over the region—in Altoona, Harrisburg, Johnstown, Bethlehem—and even farther afield, as far away as Chicago, as Cleveland and St. Louis, struck in support of the original strikers. Not just railroad workers: miners, millhands, and dock workers struck. Trains were halted; freight couldn't move; travelers were obliged to change plans or give them up. And in Pittsburgh, on July 19, protests turned into a full-fledged riot. Police weren't able to handle the disruption, nor could the state militia. For the first time an American labor dispute had swelled into something far more serious than any mere local disturbance, and—again, for the first time—the army had to be sent in, on the corporate side. President Hayes, with his cabinet's concurrence, ordered 650 federal troops over from Philadelphia. When they reached Pittsburgh, the soldiers proceeded to fire into a raucous crowd, leaving twenty-five dead, many more wounded, on their way to occupying machine shops and the roundhouse.

With that, the infuriated strikers—sympathizers swelling their numbers— besieged the building the troops had taken possession of. Rioters set freight cars on fire and launched them into the roundhouse. Out of that now blazing structure soldiers fought their way and retreated, while the mob—maybe five thousand strong by then—got busy destroying railroad property. Some five hundred train cars and over a hundred locomotives were demolished, along with thirty-nine buildings set afire and reduced to rubble. "Pittsburgh Delivered Up to the Mercies of the Mob," the newspapers screamed, while mayhem spread all up and down the tracks, troops entering town after town to quell what had turned into an unprecedented, far-flung demonstration of working-class rage.

The propertied classes were appalled. John Hay in Cleveland, for one, watched events unfold with growing alarm. On the 24th, five days after the destruction in Pittsburgh, he reported to Amasa Stone overseas: "Since last week the country has been at the mercy of the mob, and on the whole the mob has behaved rather better than the country. The shameful truth is now clear, that the government is utterly helpless and powerless in the face of an unarmed rebellion of foreign workingmen, mostly Irish. There is nowhere any firm nucleus of authority—nothing to fall back on as a last resort. The Army has been destroyed by the dirty politicians, and the State militia is utterly inefficient. Any hour the mob chooses, it can destroy any city in the country— that is the simple truth."

One hears near panic in those phrasings. What would have come at once to Hay's mind—what loomed in the minds of others witnessing this breakdown in order, these insurrections here at home—was recent history in Europe; specifically, events that had grown out of that gouty little crab Napoleon III's earlier ambitions for glory. *La gloire*: to find it, the self-proclaimed French emperor had undertaken various foreign adventures, with England and the Ottoman Turks against Russia, by France alone against Italy, and against Austria, and finally very foolishly against Prussia, for Chancellor Bismarck's Prussia proved more than a match for the French. Shortly after the Franco-Prussian War began, in mid-August 1870, a large portion of Napoleon III's army was encircled and, at the Battle of Sedan on September 1, forced to surrender. The emperor himself was with his troops, taken as Bismarck's prisoner and promptly deposed by a provisional government back in Paris. Thus the Second Empire came to its inglorious end. The French would fight on under the new government, a republic—the third in France's history—but the effort was doomed. The Prussians laid siege to Paris, and by January 1871, the French capital had fallen. The war was effectively over less than six months after it started. A humiliated *Troisième République* was obliged to sue for peace.

What happened next in the confusions of France's collapse made America's propertied classes shudder and filled Europe's gentry with dread. In Paris, the workers seized power. National Guardsmen sent in to suppress the insurgency refused to fire on the people, turning weapons on their officers instead. For two months France's capital was ruled by workers' councils that set about ridding society of exploitation. No longer was a central government needed. Communes were to be established throughout the country, each run by a council that the masses would elect democratically. Workers ceased to be wage earners and became associates. Everyone was to be equal. Parochial schools would be secularized, capital punishment abolished. A committee of public safety was formed to see that the new order, which socialists and communists would have a say in shaping, was abided by and honored.

In noisy weeks ahead, Parisian emblems of the old order and the bourgeoisie were toppled. The pillar honoring Napoleon I in the Place Vendôme (a site Hay knew intimately) was pulled down and demolished; the Tuileries (the royal palace in Paris where the young diplomat Hay had been presented to Emperor Napoleon III and where he had gazed on the beautiful Empress Eugénie) was gutted in fire. Various churches were closed, their wealth appropriated for the people's benefit, monks and nuns arrested, some—an archbishop among them—put to death.

Of course such eruptions of working-class fury were not to be tolerated. On May 21, 1871, the provisional government of the Third Republic, temporarily at Versailles and supported by the rural, more conservative regions of France, sent an armed force into Paris and brutally crushed the Commune. In the bloody aftermath, French troops roamed the streets massacring communards. In a single bloody week, *une semaine sanglante* saw slaughter on both sides, and up to thirty thousand perished, as the National Assembly wrenched back power in the French capital from working-class usurpers and their extremist ideologues.

Repercussions of the brief Paris Commune were felt for years afterward and over far distances. Americans had comforted themselves that such an uprising could never happen here, in this land of opportunity, a meritocracy governed by laws and the ballot box, where (according to its founding document) everyone was equal already, and where wages, as compared with those in Europe, were high. But now, these six brief years later, here sat Hay writing to his father-in-law from Cleveland that the freight handlers "will not let the merchants have their goods, which are spoiling at the Depot." Clara and the children might have to be sent to safer surroundings. "The town," Hay wrote, "is full of thieves and tramps waiting and hoping for a riot, but not daring to begin it themselves. If there were any attempt to enforce the law, I believe the town would be in ashes in six hours. The mob is as yet good natured. A few shots fired by our militia company would ensure their own destruction and that of the city. A miserable state of things—which I hope will be ancient history before you read this letter."

Hay speaks of tramps: Cleveland was "full of thieves and tramps." Throughout the North the widespread disturbances, which had been ignited (the colonel like many others felt certain) by foreigners in our midst, fed on a new idling class of people: detritus from the Civil War, veterans, some not in their right minds, who during their enlistments had grown used to meals doled out and hours of loafing in camp, now returned from war to drift in such numbers as to become a public nuisance. They loitered in town squares or wandered from house to house begging for handouts. "Tramps" they were called, their numbers enlarged in hard times by the newly out-of-work. Newspapers of the 1870s were full of tramps' doings, implicating them in each of the numerous social disruptions of the time. As for the current troubles in Cleveland, those appeared to have calmed down by the 25th, a day after Hay had unburdened himself to Amasa Stone in the letter just quoted. Now he could add: "Things look more quiet to-day." (In fact, some five hundred Lake Shore workers had earlier walked off the job, although peacefully, without bitterness and with vows to drink no alcohol and damage no railroad property for as long as the unrest persisted.) "Passenger and mail trains will begin running as soon as possible, Mr. Couch says, and it is probable that the strike may end," Hay wrote, "by the surrender of the railroad companies to the demands of the strikers. This is disgraceful, but it is hard to say what else could be done. There is a mob in every city ready to join with the strikers, and get their pay in robbery, and there is no means of enforcing the law in case of a sudden attack on private property."

Blood had already flowed in Chicago, St. Louis, and other localities—hundreds of workers dead—although not in Cleveland. And in no instance did strikers initiate the violence. Moreover, only railroad property had been damaged or destroyed. Yet any such devastation was to be reprehended. Property owners by the very fact of their owning property embodied social value—of industry, discipline, responsibleness, thrift—just as those who owned nothing, tramps and other such riffraff, betrayed their shiftlessness and lack of initiative and foresight. In fact, civilization rested on property, an assertion that Hay and most of his literate contemporaries would have regarded as self-evident. Thus, mobs of the idle and uninvested, whom foreign intriguers (now Irish, somewhat later German, Italian, and Slavic) for their own ends could harangue into violence, were—by destroying property—striking at the foundations of civil society.

These present extensive riots ended only after the army dealt sternly with a few of them. Management meanwhile offered no concessions; Hay had been wrong about that (although the Lake Shore & Michigan Southern did grant its employees raises in the fall). Finding federal troops too much to contend with, the strikers simply gave up the fight and returned to work, early in August in the case of the last holdouts.

Yet the episode had been deeply unnerving. Lincoln believed in an America where a young man got to work with his good right arm apprenticing to a storekeeper or blacksmith or cooper, then earned his pay and put something aside until he was ready to set up shop on his own. In time he would do well enough to hire a helper or two, and that way would rise to a prosperity that provided his children with a better life, his helpers likely repeating the process. Examples abounded, some close at hand. Amasa Stone had begun as a carpenter, his wife was a seamstress; and now they lived in the grandest of mansions, vacationed in Europe, and would leave fortunes for their children. That was the American way, the American dream fulfilled.

Only, as broadly applied it was an agrarian dream, a Jeffersonian dream grown ever harder to come by. Hay, rising from modest beginnings in 1840s

Warsaw, Illinois, had for a short while labored in his vineyard before going to bed in weary contentment at night, and in that way fed an ardent faith in the Republican credo of respect for all honest work: for the artisan at his labors as well as for the magnate whose industry creates vast enterprises. One such enterprise fate had positioned Colonel Hay here in Cleveland to know up close, coming to understand its complex machinery and to admire the genius of the titan—his father-in-law—who had put it together. Perhaps with his Warsaw-bred values Hay stood too close to see clearly the larger changes that this new industrialism and its burgeoning corporations were wreaking on the lives of artisans: machines replacing skilled labor; work routinized, made repetitive; anonymous employers and accountants in distant board rooms arriving at fateful decisions; the tyranny of shareholders demanding their dividends and the crushing competition such demands engendered, rendering of less consequence a worker's welfare than his productivity and the company's profits. Local domestic labor, of weavers and tanners and coopers and subsistence farmers, was becoming ever less common; so that what Hay saw now and hadn't expected to—had rarely seen in the towns of his youth: in Warsaw, Pittsfield, and Springfield—were angry workers, quarrelsome and insolent workers, workers with accents that marked them as foreign, turned into mobs. What he did see was his government and his country behaving timidly, shamefully in the face of such insolence, along with "dirty politicians" currying the mob's favor—and vote—and themselves voting against building up the army while deploring the use of force, all their sympathies "with the laboring man," as he reported to Mr. Stone, "and none with the man whose enterprise and capital give him a living."

John Hay—poet, diplomat, journalist, resident of Cleveland's Euclid Avenue—had come to regard current affairs from the viewpoint of those possessed of such capitalist enterprise. Yet he would remain a Lincoln Republican all his days, and as such took seriously an obligation to participate in public life. How else was the mediocrity of politicians to be offset than by the informed and the educated agreeing to serve? Thus, after leaving the *New York Tribune* and moving to Cleveland, Hay had assumed an ever more active role in politics, supporting Republican candidates both nationally and at the state level with his pen, with his gifted voice in speeches before large crowds, and with his money. Ohio remained a crucial constituency; President Hayes was an Ohio man. And when Hayes's chief cabinet member, the distinguished William Evarts, in the late fall of 1879 sought out John Hay to fill a high vacancy, the colonel was persuaded to reenter public service, as assistant secretary of state, even though it meant leaving his family and moving to Washington for the duration.

Toward the end of November 1879, Hay took on his new duties. There were benefits. Washington was nearer the center of things than was Cleveland for all its wealth and bustle, and he knew Washington: its ways and many of its people. When Secretary Evarts was absent, Secretary Hay sat in for him. "Today was an important one in our history," he could write to Clara, with light irony, soon after his arrival. "I sat for the first time in Cabinet meeting, and took the place of highest rank in the room, at the President's right." Through one interval he served as Mr. Evarts's translator when the Frenchman Ferdinand de Lesseps, builder of the Suez Canal, came to Washington to discuss undertaking a similar project across the Isthmus of Panama. As always, Hay did his work well and seemingly without strain, earning the high regard of colleagues above, alongside, and below him. "His was one of those rare natures that win, without conscious effort, the deep and abiding affection of all who draw near," an associate of these same months recalled. They were months, before Lent, that included the social season in Washington; and Hay, who thrived in society, took full advantage, reconnecting with old friends and making new ones, some of whom he would remain close to for the rest of his life.

He was being of use while enjoying himself, yet he missed his family. Back in Cleveland, Clara gave birth to a third child, a daughter, Alice, in early January of the new year 1880. By July, still at his post, the assistant secretary of state noted, "My term is now one-half over, and I look forward to the 4th of March"—and the inauguration of a new president (Hayes having declined to seek a second term)—"with hungry anticipation. If my present mind holds, I will never again take an office—certainly not for years to come." He had just returned from a summer visit with his children in Cleveland—"they are three; two girls and a boy,—and there is nothing in this hot and dusty world which will compensate for the loss of their society." Hay did know himself well enough, however, to add that once home for a year he would be having "regrets of Washington and Europe." Even so, late in his present tenure, in December 1880, he declined an opportunity to remain that another Ohioan, the new president-elect James Garfield, offered him, in doing so feeling obliged to make clear: "I am not going back on Democracy. It is a good thing—the hope and salvation of the world." But having promised his family and Mr. Stone ("who at considerable inconvenience has taken care of my affairs") to come home on March 4, he intended to keep that promise.

19. "MY FRIENDSHIP WITH MR. HAY"

Mark Twain didn't think much of his friend John Hay's getting back into public life. There had been talk of Hay's running for Congress, about which

Clemens remarked to William Dean Howells: "The presence of such a man in politics is like a vase of attar of roses in a glue-factory—it can't extinguish the stink, but it modifies it." In that age of rampant bribery, the humorist opined that Americans lived under the best government money could buy. And "Reader," he wrote, "suppose you were an idiot. And suppose you were a member of Congress. But I repeat myself." The aversion dated to at least as early as the 1860s, when Mark Twain, journalist, had witnessed political shenanigans while covering the Nevada territorial legislature in Carson City. He gained more exposure after returning from the *Quaker City* cruise in late 1867 and acting briefly as secretary to Nevada's senator Bill Stewart in Washington. What the author gleaned from writing *The Gilded Age* in 1873 and from perusing newspapers all his life only strengthened his dislike of politics. As for the recent violence, in 1877, between workingmen and the owners of the nation's railroads that the army had to be sent in to put down, Clemens observed dryly to Mrs. Fairbanks that it was the sort of thing that happens when a government loses touch with the people it should be serving.

John Hay likewise had seen plenty of greed and hypocrisy in government, starting with pushy, fawning office-seekers in the anterooms of the White House; but to Hay, the prevalence of such aspirants provided all the more reason for good people to enter public life. That kind of obligation never weighed on Clemens, who in any case was seeing less of Hay than he once had. These days the primary axis of the author of *Tom Sawyer* followed along rail lines between Hartford, Connecticut, and Elmira, New York, whereas his friend the businessman and sometime federal functionary traveled now most often between Washington, D.C., and Cleveland, Ohio. Hay would be riding those very rails, for instance, if not precisely on March 4, 1881, as promised, then toward the end of March, on his way home to his family after completing fifteen months as assistant secretary of state in the outgoing Hayes administration.

Before leaving the capital the secretary had received important personal news from Whitelaw Reid, the *New York Tribune* editor (whose influential opinion on the 1877 strikes, by the way, jibed pretty well with that of Hay and most other property owners, that all such should be free to do with their property whatever they chose that the law allowed: if they owned a railway, say, to set the wages they'd pay—and be backed up by armed force as necessary—precisely the way a worker should be free to accept those wages or work someplace else). But just now, here in Washington on February 11, Hay was responding to Reid's personal news. "My heart is full of your happiness," he wrote. For the bachelor editor was finally getting married, at age forty-three, to a woman twenty years younger. "The best thing has happened to you which could happen," Hay assured his friend from his own experience as a married man, all the more confidently because he knew the bride-to-be. "You will have a good wife—good through and through—and I can tell you what that amounts to." And a very rich one besides (a point that Hay might have spoken to as well), for Whitelaw Reid's intended was Lizzy Mills, Darius Ogden Mills's daughter. Mills was just about the wealthiest man in a California rolling in wealth, what with its mining, railroad, and banking interests. Mills himself was in banking, retired since 1878 to New York City at age fifty-two to pursue philanthropy, leaving a summer home, Millbrae, of forty-four thousand square feet on six thousand acres near San Francisco, to return to at his pleasure.

Mr. Reid and Miss Mills were to be married in April 1881, after which they would enjoy a honeymoon of five months in Europe, before coming back and building a huge new home on Madison Avenue. Meanwhile, would John Hay take over the running of the *New York Tribune* in the editor's absence? That Reid would make the request says much about Hay's editorial gifts, six years having passed since the colonel sat at his desk at the *Tribune*; by now the great New York newspaper would have developed a number of plausible candidates to fill in for the absent editor in chief. But Hay was the one Whitelaw Reid wanted; so instead of proceeding from his year and a half in Washington to a deserved rest at home on Euclid Avenue, John Hay and his family moved in April to New York City, to take up residence in Reid's spacious Lexington Avenue quarters, during the groom and bride's nuptial travels overseas.

Hay performed admirably; just about everybody agreed on that. And it was during this New York interlude of five months that Mark Twain would later recall, from Italy in 1904, a mostly joyous reunion with his old friend in Reid's home on a Sunday morning in 1881:

Hay and I had been chatting and laughing and carrying-on almost like our earlier selves of '67, when the door opened and Mrs. Hay, gravely clad, gloved, bonneted, and just from church, and fragrant with the odors of Presbyterian sanctity, stood in it. We rose to our feet at once, of course,—rose through a swiftly falling temperature—a temperature which at the beginning was soft and summerlike, but which was turning our breath and all other damp things to frost crystals by the time we were erect—but we got no opportunity to say the pretty and polite thing and offer the homage due: the comely young matron forestalled us. She came forward smileless, with disapproval written all over her face, said most coldly, "Good morning Mr. Clemens," and passed on out.

There was an embarrassed pause—I may say a very embarrassed pause. If Hay was waiting for me to speak, it was a mistake; I couldn't think of a word. It was soon plain to me that the bottom had fallen out of his vocabulary, too. When I was able to walk I started toward the door, and Hay [he who, Clemens had assured us, was the only person in the entire *Tribune* office not afraid of Horace Greeley, and who as secretary of state in years yet ahead would prove equally unafraid of kings and emperors with their fleets and armies—Hay] now grown gray in a single night, so to speak, limped feebly at my side, making no moan, saying no word. At the door his ancient courtesy rose and bravely flickered for a moment, then went out. That is to say, he tried to ask me to call again, but at that point his ancient sincerity rose against the fiction and squelched it. Then he tried another remark, and that one he got through with. He said pathetically, and apologetically,

"She is very strict about Sunday."

Considering how differently Clemens and Hay regarded the railroad strike, among other matters, and how their views diverged further as the years advanced—Colonel Hay ever more deeply involved in political affairs—it speaks well for both that their friendship survived to the end. At John Hay's death in 1905, Mark Twain mourned with the nation "this loss which is irreparable. My friendship with Mr. Hay & my admiration of him endured 38 years without impairment." True, the two had emerged out of similar village surroundings at the river's edge. But young Hay by twelve was studying Greek, reading Virgil in Latin, and acquiring a speaking knowledge of German; he left Warsaw to pursue schooling at nearby Pittsfield Academy, from there to Illinois State University in Springfield, and from there at sixteen to Brown University in Providence, Rhode Island. Clemens's education, by contrast, was picked up informally, what he could gather working in print shops setting type, reading newspapers, and writing fillers and travel letters, the latter after he left Hannibal for good at seventeen and set about roaming.

Frequently, the young man in his travels bumped into rough types. Printers as a class were notoriously vagrant—their skills likely as much in need at the newspaper the next village over as where they were then—and often hard drinkers besides (Sam had taken an oath before his mother to avoid spirits, and abided by it during his earliest years away). By age twenty-one, his wanderings had put him in contact with a riverboat pilot willing to teach him to pilot steamboats along the Mississippi, the "one permanent ambition among my comrades in our village" where he had grown up. The skill was a hard one to master, guiding an awkward big craft up and down a river full of dangers to navigation constantly in flux; yet in 1859, at twenty-three, Samuel L. Clemens was awarded his coveted pilot's license. Again, life aboard steamboats and at the docks could be raw—brawling deckhands, sleazy gamblers, con men, prostitutes—yet Sam would have stayed, he said, at his lofty helm in that demanding, high-paying, and prestigious occupation for the rest of his days if it hadn't been that the Civil War shut down all civilian river traffic. Driven thus ashore, Clemens next joined a militia unit with his Hannibal pals to fight for the Confederacy; but the former printer and pilot lasted only a couple of weeks as a soldier before decamping for the West with his brother, clear out to Nevada Territory, where he tried to get rich mining for silver.

Years later, though, in 1874—after he had found a pen name out there and written his "Jumping Frog" tale, after he had come back East and sailed from New York to the Holy Land and made a wonderfully successful book out of the five-month adventure, after he had met the Langdons and married their daughter and moved to Hartford, after he had become perhaps the most successful author in America, living in a mansion and famous on two continents—Sam Clemens scavenging for something to write about proposed to Howells at the *Atlantic* that he revisit his time of piloting on the river, before war and the railroads and his settling on other ways to make a living had left the glory days of steamboat traffic far behind. Howells was enthusiastic.

Mark Twain's reminiscences, "Old Times on the Mississippi," appeared in serial form in the *Atlantic Monthly* from January to August 1875. They promptly elicited one notable response. "John Hay of his own free will & accord volunteers me a letter," the author wrote proudly to Howells, "which is so gratifying in its nature that I am obliged to copy it for you to read. I was born & reared at Hannibal, & John Hay at Warsaw, 40 miles higher up, on the river (one of the Keokuk packet ports)":

> Dear Clemens—I have just read with delight your article in the Atlantic. It is perfect—no more nor less. I don't see how you do it. I knew all that, every word of it—passed as much time on the levee as you ever did, knew the same crowd & saw the same scenes,—but I could not have remembered one word of it all. You have the two greatest gifts of the writer, memory & imagination. I congratulate you.

Thus saluted, the gratified author ended with: "Now isn't that outspoken & hearty, & just like that splendid John Hay? S.L.C."

Colonel Hay might well admire what his friend had retrieved from their shared past. Here, in a speech delivered late in life, is an effort of Hay's own to recover from childhood a similar recollection, one that leads up to the excitement stirred by a steamboat's briefly docking at Warsaw en route to far-off places:

> The years of my boyhood were passed on the banks of the Mississippi, and the great river was the scene of my early dreams. The boys of my day led an amphibious life in and near the waters in the summer time, and in the winter its dazzling ice bridge, of incomparable beauty and purity, was our favorite playground; while our imaginations were busy with the glamour and charm of the distant cities of the South, with their alluring French names and their legends of stirring adventure and pictures of perpetual summer. It [the South] was a land of faëry, alien to us in all but a sense of common ownership and patriotic pride. We built snow forts and called them the Alamo; we sang rude songs of the cane-brake and the cornfield, and the happiest days of the year to those of us who dwelt on the northern bluffs of the river were those that brought us, in the loud puffing and whistling steamers of olden time, to the Mecca of our rural fancies, the bright and busy metropolis of St. Louis.

Serviceable as it may be—and very much in the style of its era—Hay's public prose lacks that memorableness of a distinctive voice. Compare it with a similar passage early in "Old Times on the Mississippi," one that leads up to the identical concluding image. "After all these years," Mark Twain writes:

> I can picture that old time to myself now, just as it was then: the white town drowsing in the sunshine of a summer's morning; the streets empty, or pretty nearly so; one or two clerks in front of the Water Street stores, with their splint-bottomed chairs tilted back against the wall, chins on breasts, hats slouched over their faces, asleep—with shingle-shavings enough around to show what broke them down; a sow and a litter of pigs loafing along the sidewalk, doing a good business in water-melon rinds and seeds; two or three lonely little freight piles scattered about the "levee"; a pile of "skids" on the slope of the stone-paved wharf, and the fragrant town drunkard asleep in the shadow of them; two or three wood flats at the head of the wharf, but nobody to listen to the peaceful lapping of the wavelets against them; the great Mississippi, the majestic, the magnificent Mississippi, rolling its mile-wide tide along, shining in the sun; the dense forest away on the other side; the "point" above the town, and the "point" below, bounding the river-glimpse and turning it into a sort of sea, and withal a very still and brilliant and lonely one.

Dozy morning vividly on display, just before smoke belches above the trees and rouses an alert villager to bring the sleepy town to instant, excited life with his prodigious call: "S-t-e-a-m-boat a-comin'!"

Reviewing *The Innocents Abroad* when it appeared in 1869, young Mr. Howells of the *Atlantic* had observed: "As Mr. Clemens writes of his experiences, we imagine he would talk of them; and very amusing talk it would be." Exactly. One thing startling and welcome to genteel readers of the East was that western colloquial voice ("empty, or pretty nearly so"; "show what broke them down"; "doing a good business in water-melon rinds"; "away on the other side"), yet a voice that could be eloquent where appropriate, and always scrupulously accurate in its diction, always fresh, with lovely sentence cadences throughout. Perhaps the mid-twentieth-century critic Lionel Trilling made the point most forcefully in asserting that Mark Twain's style "is not less than definitive in American literature." The sentences that the author wrote, said Trilling, are "simple, direct, and fluent, maintaining the rhythm of the word-groups of speech and the intonations of the speaking voice." In fact, so prevalent has that particular stylist's way of expressing himself become that "almost every contemporary American writer who deals conscientiously with the problems and possibility of prose must feel, directly or indirectly, the influence of Mark Twain. He is," this penetrating observer of our literature and culture concludes, "the master of the style that escapes the fixity of the printed page, that sounds in our ears with the immediacy of the heard voice, the very voice of unpretentious truth."

Which would account for much about how the lecturer Mark Twain wrote except for the magic, the inimitable, all but instantly recognizable magic that no voice but his seems able to sound from the page, and he only fully in his supreme achievements: in large portions of this "Old Times on the Mississippi," for instance, and in *Adventures of Huckleberry Finn*, where a raft bearing two unlikely companions drifts down that same great moonlit river, between hostile banks a half mile off on either side.

20. MARK TWAIN'S MIDAS TOUCH

After "Old Times on the Mississippi" (1875), Mark Twain was reading proofs of *The Adventures of Tom Sawyer* in the summer of 1876, before getting to work on a sequel, *Adventures of Huckleberry Finn*, rendering its colloquial speech as magical dialect. But sixteen chapters into *Huck*, the author laid his manuscript aside, stumped as to how to proceed. A runaway slave and the ill-lettered son of the village drunk lounge on their raft on the nighttime current at three or four miles an hour down the Mississippi, having earlier drifted in flight through a heavy fog past Cairo, past the entrance of the Ohio River and the slave Jim's pathway to freedom. From that point on, the raft is carrying the two ever more deeply into slave-holding territory. How to rescue the white boy and the older black fugitive from such a geographical dilemma?

Clemens put the manuscript aside, and before long was setting out on a fifth trip to Europe, with his family and his closest Hartford friend, Rev. Joe Twichell of the Asylum Hill Congregational Church, intending to gather material for another travel book after *The Innocents Abroad* and *Roughing It*. The author saw Livy and the children settled comfortably overseas, then with Twichell proceeded for several note-taking weeks to explore portions of Germany, Switzerland, France, and northern Italy. *A Tramp Abroad* was the narrative result, published in 1880, the title echoing the first, massively successful book of travel by this same author, while drawing on the then newly widespread use of *tramp* as disreputable vagrant, with the additional meaning here of *hike*: the mild joke being that the two friends' mode of transport overseas turns out to be by just about every means—horse, mule, carriage, wagon, train, raft, steamboat, ferry boat—except on foot.

Back home, Clemens (always an omnivorous reader, that lover of English history—and of the diarist Samuel Pepys) next produced a different kind of novel, which greatly pleased his wife Livy and his daughter Susy, a novel set in sixteenth-century England and, as a *tour de force*, composed in the diction of the time: "forsooth," "eftsoons," "prithee," and so on. Mrs. Clemens and her daughter adored *The Prince and the Pauper*, in part because it wasn't a funny book; it was a serious entertainment aspiring to something higher than merely exciting the laughter of God's creatures (as Clemens himself had earlier defined his calling). Thus the new novel, published in 1881, was "unquestionably the best book he has ever written," in fourteen-year-old Susy's opinion, "full of lovely charming ideas, and oh the language! it is perfect, I think." Readers of our era have been less partial; nowadays *The Prince and the Pauper* is generally judged to be one of Mark Twain's feebler efforts, but he did have a lot of fun getting the archaic diction right, as he had played (in his love of words and wonderful gift of mimicry) with reproducing that earlier English for other purposes as well.

At Elmira back in the summer of 1876, when he was finishing *Tom Sawyer* and beginning *Huckleberry Finn*, Clemens in his high octagonal study wrote what in time would be privately printed as an eight-page pamphlet: "1601: Conversation as it was by the Social Fireside in the Time of the Tudors." Returned to Hartford, he took the manuscript along on one of his numerous strolls into the countryside with Joe Twichell, regaling his reverend friend by reading it aloud under the trees, the two of them both convulsed with laughter ("for between you and me the thing was dreadfully funny. I don't often write anything that I laugh at myself, but I can hardly think of that thing without laughing"). "1601" is represented as being "an extract from the diary of the Pepys of that day, the same being Queen Elizabeth's cup-bearer. He is supposed to be of ancient and noble lineage," an elderly gentleman who despises the sort of folk whom his Virgin Queen cavorts with sometimes: "the old man feels that his nobility is defiled by contact with Shakespeare, etc., and yet he has got to stay there till her Majesty chooses to dismiss him." What "1601" is as well is a demonstration of Clemens's love and mastery of language and his amused impatience with the hypocrisy of his own times, among genteel eastern values that this former Wild Humorist of the Pacific Coast, now a Hartford family man, continues to challenge in bursts of wildness. A brief sample:

I being her maites [majesty's] cup-bearer, had no choice but to remaine and beholde rank forgot, and ye high holde converse wh [with] ye low as uppon equal termes, a grete scandal did ye world heare thereof.

Then spake ye damned windmill, Sr Walter [Raleigh], of a people in ye uttermost parts of America, yt [that] capulate not until they be five and thirty yeres of age, ye women being eight and twenty, and do it then but once in seven yeres.

Ye Queene.—How doth that like my little Lady Helen? Shall we send thee thither and preserve thy belly?

Lady Helen.—Please your highnesses grace, mine old nurse hath told me there are more ways of serving God than by locking the thighs together; yet am I willing to serve him yt way too, sith [since] your highnesses grace hath set ye ensample.

Ye Queene.—God' wowndes [God's wounds—a mild oath] a good answer, childe.

[The elderly] Lady Alice.—Mayhap 'twill weaken when ye hair sprouts below ye navel.

Lady Helen.—Nay, it sprouted two yeres syne; I can scarce more than cover it with my hand now.

Ye Queene.—Hear Ye that, my little Beaumonte? Have ye not a little birde about ye that stirs at hearing tell of so sweete a neste?

[Young] Beaumonte.—'Tis not insensible, illustrious madam; but mousing owls and bats of low degree may not aspire to bliss so whelming and ecstatic as is found in ye downy nests of birdes of Paradise.

Ye Queene.—By ye gullet of God, 'tis a neat-turned compliment. With such a tongue as thine, lad, thou'lt spread the ivory thighs of many a willing maide in thy good time, an' thy cod-piece be as handy as thy speeche. . . .

Part of the humor here lies in the plausible imitation—in getting the late sixteenth-century diction about right—but also in the startling frankness with which those ancestors spoke, as contrasted with the more confined speech of Clemens's Victorian contemporaries on both sides of the Atlantic. For a while he and Twichell kept the joke to themselves, but in 1880 Clemens shared "1601" with his friend Howells, whom he had laughed with so often before, over so many matters, and who enjoyed this bit of Rabelaisian ribaldry well enough to recommend sending it on to John Hay, then in Washington.

Clemens did so, with the caution that Hay, having read it, send back the manuscript without making a copy. Hay from the State Department was thus soon in a position, on June 21, 1880, to approach another friend: "Dear Gunn: Are you in Cleveland for all this week? If you will say yes by return mail, I have a masterpiece to submit to your consideration which is only in my hands for a few days. Yours, very much worritted by the depravity of Christendom, Hay."

Three days later, having heard from his friend, Hay sent off a second note: "My dear Gunn: Here it is. It was written by Mark Twain in a serious effort to bring back our literature and philosophy to the sober and chaste Elizabethan standard. But the taste of the present day is too corrupt for anything so classic. He has not yet been able even to find a publisher." The diplomat was forwarding the treasure to Mr. Gunn "as one of the few lingering relics of that race of appreciative critics, who know a good thing when they see it. Read it with reverence and gratitude and send it back to me; for Mark is impatient to see once more his wandering offspring. Yours, Hay."

A third letter followed two weeks later. Washington, D.C., July 7, 1880: "My dear Gunn: I have your letter, and the proposition which you make to pull a few proofs of the masterpiece is highly attractive, and of course highly immoral. I cannot properly consent to it." Therefore: "Please send back the document as soon as you can, and if, in spite of my prohibition, you take these proofs, save me one. Very truly yours, John Hay."

A half-dozen printed copies were thus made: one for Gunn, one for Hay, and the rest for Clemens, who, having later been shown Hay's correspondence that led up to the printed version, awarded his friend consummate praise: "In the matter of humor," this foremost of humorists noted admiringly, "what an unsurpassable touch John Hay had!"

Subsequently, in 1882, Mark Twain besought a friend with a private printing press to prepare fifty handsome, mock-antiquated copies of the work that
the author might distribute to supplicants—"popes and kings and such people" in the United States and England. These many years later, of course, in
times more relaxed, "1601" is readily available; the internet turns up the complete text at once. But the insight that "1601" deals with—as to the way
conventions regarding what is acceptable language differ among generations—
continued to attract Clemens; so that a few years later, in chapter 4 of *A
Connecticut Yankee in King Arthur's Court* (1889), he was musing on the conversation of knights and ladies around the Round Table: "Many of the terms
used in the most matter-of-fact way by this great assemblage of the first ladies
and gentlemen of the land would have made a Comanche blush," Mark Twain
writes, and adds that if Sir Walter Scott—instead of creating conversations for
his medieval characters—had let them converse as they really did, we later
readers "should have had talk from Rebecca and Ivanhoe and the soft lady
Rowena which would embarrass a tramp in our day." Of course in his earlier
life Clemens had heard (and made free use of) the pungent Anglo-Saxonisms
of the frontier—of the riverboats and docksides and mining camps—until
Mrs. Fairbanks aboard the *Quaker City* in 1867 and Miss Langdon during
the following years, before and after she became Mrs. Clemens, helped him
differentiate such talk from the polish and sheen of eastern gentility. Prac-
titioners of the latter were to constitute an expanded readership for Mark
Twain's later writings, so it was well that he learned their lingo, partly through
association with such a dazzling specimen of gentility as was John Hay, met in
that same 1867 and possessed of his own high sheen through studying Greek
and Latin, attending Brown University, serving with Mr. Seward and others
in the Executive Mansion in Washington, and perfecting a cosmopolitan fluency as diplomat in three major European capitals.

To the more primitive world of his youth and young manhood, Sam Clemens would be returning now, in 1882. That spring, for the first time in fifteen
years, he would revisit Hannibal, his childhood home, and travel by steamboat
and railroad down the Mississippi as far as New Orleans, then back up clear
to St. Paul. Elijah Bliss had died two years earlier, Bliss of the American
Publishing Company, who had brought out all of Mark Twain's books right
through *A Tramp Abroad*, increasingly to the author's dissatisfaction. So at
Bliss's demise Mark Twain was free to acquire a new publisher, James Osgood
of Boston, whose list included John Hay's *Pike County Ballads* and *Castilian
Days*. Osgood's imprint was on *The Prince and the Pauper* as well; so even
though sales of that novel proved disappointing, the publisher was invited

along—he and a stenographer—on this current steamboat venture that would allow Mark Twain to recapture memories of an earlier era. For it was Clemens's plan to take the *Atlantic* articles that constituted "Old Times on the Mississippi" and double their size to form a subscription volume of six hundred pages. It would be called *Life on the Mississippi*, and James R. Osgood & Co. would bring it out in 1883.

But Osgood was a trade publisher, of books to be bought in bookstores. As such, he imperfectly understood the demands of subscription publishing, which required the recruiting of agents to go sell copies in advance on the basis of prospectuses pedaled from door to rural door. Accordingly, sales of *Life on the Mississippi*—like its predecessors ever since *Roughing It* (1872)—failed to meet Clemens's expectations. So for his next book he would forsake Osgood and set up a publishing house of his own, let his nephew-in-law run it, and name it after that same Charley Webster: Charles L. Webster & Co., Publishers. For one peripheral benefit of the month-long excursion back to St. Louis and down and up the Mississippi in 1882 had been to reawaken memories in all their vividness of Sam Clemens's Hannibal boyhood along the riverbank. Thus, back in Elmira he took up the manuscript of *Huckleberry Finn* again and, this time, finished it. And his own Charles L. Webster & Co. published it, just the way the demanding author wanted it published. We'll not bring the book out, he had said, until we have fifty thousand subscriptions signed up for it; and that's what they did. So that for the first time in fourteen years Mark Twain had a genuine money-making best seller on his hands; and in the rich wake of *Huckleberry Finn*, sales of *Tom Sawyer* picked up, too ("You don't know about me without you have read a book by the name of 'The Adventures of Tom Sawyer' . . . "). Soon *Huckleberry Finn* was banned as the veriest trash by the library committee of Concord, Massachusetts (Louisa May Alcott, although not a member, concurring in the library's judgment), a stiff-necked rejection that Clemens calculated would be worth another twenty-five thousand copies sold.

Suddenly so much seemed to be going his way. Lately the Hartford author had been in close touch with his hero, former President Ulysses S. Grant. Grant when he left the presidency in 1877 had embarked with his family on what developed into a triumphal two-year round-the-world tour, his popularity with his fellow citizens all the more exalted at his return. Many clamored for Grant to be reelected in 1880 to an unprecedented third term in the White House. (John Hay was not among them. Hay, unlike his friend Clemens, was no Grant enthusiast, had written editorials for the *Tribune* decrying the corruption of the Grant years, and had supported Horace Greeley's faltering

The Clemens family on the piazza of their Hartford home, May 1884.
From left: Clara, Samuel, Jean, Olivia, Susy. Courtesy of the Mark Twain Project,
The Bancroft Library, University of California, Berkeley.

candidacy that had aimed to replace the general in 1872.) Despite Hay's doubts, the Ohio-born Grant's name was entered at Chicago's Republican nominating convention in June 1880 as the favorite. The votes for him fell short, however, and at the thirty-sixth ballot, weary delegates settled on the dark-horse candidate James A. Garfield, also of Ohio, thus returning General Grant to private life for good.

By then the tanner's son had developed a taste for gracious living, so he joined the New York brokerage firm of Grant & Ward as a partner. The Grant referred to was Ulysses Grant Jr.—son Buck—and the Ward of Grant & Ward was Ferdinand Ward, the "Young Napoleon of Finance," another specimen of apparently boundless wealth in the Gilded Age. How could such a demonstrably able combination fail, all the less likely when the Grant of its title was soon presumed to be the renowned father? Yet it did; it crashed into bankruptcy in 1884, putting the swindler Ward in Sing Sing for six years and carrying virtually all of General Grant's money with it.

Abruptly impoverished, the general must make more, and at once, but by what means? At the *Century*'s urging, Grant would write for that magazine a personal account of the Civil War battles of Shiloh and the Wilderness. He proceeded to do so, with such surprising skill—for he had not fancied himself a writer—that the affiliated Century Publishing Company offered to pay their author what was judged a handsome sum if he would pursue to book length his personal memoirs from childhood to Appomattox.

Mark Twain got wind of the proposal, offered Grant far more generous terms to do the same work, stood by him when the general developed cancer of the throat and was forced to struggle in stoic agony day after day to conclude his two volumes, which not only were to provide for his family's financial support but also were destined to become a classic of American military history. The whole country, the whole English-speaking world watched, and read the daily bulletins that recounted a courageous, pain-filled effort to complete *Personal Memoirs of U.S. Grant*. The general did manage to finish it, a mere two weeks before his death in early July 1885. And Charles L. Webster & Co. published the volumes by subscription, to enormous success, so that in the following February Clemens was able to present the near-destitute widow Julia Grant with the largest single royalty check ever paid to an author or an author's heirs up to then: $250,000, with more—$400,000 in all—to come.

Yet even beyond that! In 1880, the year Elijah Bliss died, Clemens had been introduced to an engineer at Hartford's Pratt & Whitney plant, James W. Paige. Paige had invented a machine that set type, and Sam Clemens knew about typesetting, had lined up many an em by hand for newspapers in his day. What Paige's typesetter did, though, was set type mechanically, miraculously, far faster than any human being could, and didn't get tired, and didn't get drunk, and didn't go out on strike or fail to show up in the morning. With its nearly twenty thousand parts, the device was still being perfected, but Clemens knew enough to see its potential. Which was breathtaking; just about every newspaper office in the world would have to have Paige's typesetter once it was ready. Off and on through the mid-1880s Clemens in his notebooks calculated the high sums such sales and leases were bound to come to. Far beyond anything he could make writing books, the magical typesetter would bring in wealth like Rockefeller's, like Carnegie's.

The author had faith in his man Paige, and had the money to help such a poet in metal realize his glorious dream. From 1880 on, in full confidence of the millions in it, Clemens made available whatever funds were needed, in ever growing amounts, all the while marveling at—almost frightened by—his own good fortune; for, in fact (as he was heard to remark in the middle of the decade), whatever Mark Twain touched seemed to turn to gold.

Henry James in March 1890, as noted in his own hand. Courtesy of Houghton Library, Harvard University (MS Am 1094 (2246) f.33).

3

HAY AND HENRY JAMES: THE 1880s

21. APPRENTICESHIP OF AN AUTHOR

Henry James, thirty-two years old, met John Hay sometime before July 1875; for during that month and year he wrote the colonel a first letter that implies a previous meeting in company with Mrs. Hay, to whom the writer sends his kind regards. Perhaps William Dean Howells, good friend of both (Hay at the time better known as an author than James), introduced them. In any case, Henry James was looking for a job and hoped that Hay might help.

From Quincy Street in Cambridge, Massachusetts, the petitioner wrote that he had devised a plan to set himself up in Paris this fall and for a fee send back from there regular informative letters to a newspaper in America. "When I say a 'newspaper' I have an eye, of course, upon the *Tribune*"—and thus this appeal to Hay as the *New York Tribune*'s chief editorial writer. "There is apparently in the American public an essential appetite, & a standing demand, for information about all Parisian things"—an appetite that James was propos- ing to feed by means of three or four letters a month from the French capital "on a variety of topics—'social' matters, so called, manners, habits, people &c, books, pictures, the theatre, & those things which come up in talk about rural excursions & dips into the provinces." The writer goes on briefly to indicate his qualifications for undertaking such an assignment, qualifications that were unassailable. Indeed, the first three decades of Henry James's life leading up to this letter to Hay of July 21, 1875—a letter that would seem instrumental in James's realizing the aims of his fourth decade and the rest of his years on earth—had been extraordinary, arising out of a childhood utterly unlike Hay's, or Sam Clemens's, or Lincoln's, or Howells's, or just about any of his countrymen up to that time.

Henry James's paternal grandfather, dead eleven years when the grandson was born, had been a very wealthy man, the wealthiest citizen of Albany, New York. In a preindustrial world he had made his money the way agrarian wealth was often made back then, as a merchant, landowner, and banker money-lender. William James had come over from Ireland dirt poor at eighteen, in 1789, and had drifted to a job clerking in an Albany village store. Within six years he had set up his own store there, dealing in dry goods and farm products, and inside of a decade owned four more stores, a tobacco factory, and a store on John Street in New York City. By then Albany village, 135 miles up the Hudson River, had been designated the state capital and thus began to swell in size, all the more so after Fulton's *Clermont* steamed up the Hudson for the first time in 1807, to confirm that trade thereafter, no longer dependent on wind and sail, could move steadily in both directions between New York and Albany, upriver and down.

All during grandfather William James's maturity Albany grew, becoming the eastern terminus of the Erie Canal in 1825; and during that growth, land that the merchant bought increased in value, as did his dockside enterprises that provided goods for the New York market. When he died, in his early sixties in 1832, William James of Albany left behind not only ten surviving children by three wives but an inheritance sufficiently large that the fourth of his sons, the second by his third wife, a young man twenty-one years old at the time and destined to be the father of the novelist Henry James, received for his share a bequest of land yielding an income of $10,000 a year, a sum that by the most conservative calculations would amount in today's currency to twenty-five times that much. Approximately a quarter of a million dollars arriving every year from that moment on, so that Henry James Sr. (as the fortunate beneficiary would become) was spared worrying about working a day in his life for money. Instead he could muse—as was his bent—on social, moral, philosophical, and theological matters, and would write on such subjects and lecture on them, moving about and bringing with him what grew into his own large family.

This future father of the novelist had married in 1840 a well-to-do New York merchant's daughter, a happy marriage that lasted more than four decades. At the end, in 1882, Mary Robertson Walsh James died in January and her husband, grown listless and enervated at her loss, died that same December. In the interval of their years together, the remarkable James family was formed and grew up in privileged, cultured surroundings amid abundant wit and humor and among generally congenial, supportive parents and siblings, although as part of a household that shifted over distances at a father's whim as he searched for educational opportunities through the children's formative years.

There were five such James children in all, three of whom remain significant these hundred and seventy-some years further along. William was the oldest, born in early 1842, to live out his mature years as a psychologist, educator, and major American philosopher. Henry Jr., born in New York City in April 1843, was the second of the Jameses, a writer of novels, novellas, and literary criticism. Alice, the youngest of the five, died in her early forties, leaving behind a diary written and dictated during her final three years that has proved of much value for the light it sheds on a gifted woman's dealings with the limitations placed upon her sex in high Victorian times.

But it is on the second son, Henry James Jr., that the present consideration focuses. He was still an infant, only months old, when the intrepid family—father, mother, two very young children—set out from New York for a stay of two years in Europe, first in London, then in Paris. Indeed, the novelist Henry James's earliest recollection—he could not yet have been two when he took it in—was of what had to have been the pillar topped by Napoleon's statue in the Place Vendôme in Paris, the same that a communard mob pulled down twenty-eight years later in the aftermath of the Franco-Prussian War. Thus from very early on, the child had Paris in his blood.

In 1845 (and little Harry not yet three), the Jameses returned to America, this time to Albany—city of the father's birth and youth—where they took up residence near the late, wealthy William James of Albany's widow on North Pearl Street. In early 1846 they moved to Manhattan to be near the children's maternal grandmother just off Washington Square; but often during the next few years the family traveled back and forth between grandmothers paternal and maternal, Willy and Harry growing thoroughly familiar with both homes and with the overnight steamers that plied between the two cities. Meanwhile, Henry Sr. had bought a residence of his own in Manhattan, on Fourteenth Street near Sixth Avenue. There the Jameses lived for seven years, from 1848 to 1855, although they had not been settled four months before the father was writing to his friend Ralph Waldo Emerson that he had grown dissatisfied with American educational methods and was thinking of taking his family back to Europe for the children's sake.

By design, meanwhile, William's and young Henry's educations unfolded as varied and unconventional. Their father held strong, often radical views: opposed to the confining rigors of school or church either one, renouncing the Calvinist God he had grown up with in favor of an all-permeating Sweden-borgian God—indeed had written a book about that influential Scandinavian mystic: *The Secret of Swedenborg*, a secret that William Dean Howells after reading the book concluded Mr. James had kept very well. Howells could only marvel, in fact, that the author's interpretations, "which sentence by sentence were so brilliantly suggestive, had sometimes a collective opacity which the most resolute vision could not penetrate." The senior Henry James may be opaque as a writer, but he was the sweetest of men, filled with love for his wife, his children, humankind in general, and for a host of friends, among them many whose names endure: Emerson, Alcott, Thackeray, Washington Irving, Greeley, Thoreau, Margaret Fuller. And when the elder James lectured, it was noted how amiably he gave voice to what were often quite caustic opinions: against slavery, of course, in those antebellum years; but against property, too, and egotism, and most doctrines and dogmas, and whatever encroached on freedom.

Freed from any need of his own to earn a living, the father of five was able to advance his educational theories by moving his children from place to place along paths bewildering to us later pursuers: from Manhattan to England and France, to Albany, back to Manhattan, back to England, to France, to Switzerland; to New England at Newport; back to Switzerland, to Germany; back to Newport, to Boston, finally to Cambridge across the Charles River— the bulk of those moves in quest of a proper education for the four sons in the family, while the father continued to ponder and spread his airy convictions.

Out of such meanderings, in such company, was Henry James Jr.'s distinctive childhood fashioned. Daughter Alice would receive home schooling; and the boys got their share of that as well, in addition to stays of varying lengths in dame schools, academies, institutes, and colleges on two continents. A shaping part of young Harry's education did take place during the seven years the family lived on Fourteenth Street, when he was between five and twelve. In the very late years of the novelist's life, in his memoir *A Small Boy and Others* (1913), James recalled those times—bedimmed by the passage of six decades—with affection and what scholars have found to be astonishing accuracy. His pages evoke the living reality of a succession of tutors: Miss Bayou, Mrs. Daly, Miss Rogers, Miss Sedgwick, Mlle Delavigne, Mr. Richard Puling Jenks, and others alive and breathing in the 1850s, as well as of the theaters on Chambers Street and Park Place that Harry and his older brother Willy became addicted to by the time the younger was nine or ten, and of the freedom they felt and were allowed to indulge in wandering about those crowded, more innocent city blocks: roaming down to Barnum's Museum and the art galleries, gaping at storefronts, riding the horsecars up Sixth Avenue and back—as well as the long hours that this devouring reader spent in his father's library, poring over *Punch* and *The Illustrated London News* with such assiduity that when he arrived for a months-long stay in London in his early teens, the streets and sites he met with were already mostly familiar.

The family passed through London briefly in 1855, when Harry was twelve, on their way back to the Continent, via Paris to Geneva, in order to take advantage of the Swiss educational system. They reached their destination in August, but by October the disenchanted senior James had determined to move his brood back to England for the winter. By the early summer they were in Paris once more, the boys under the fruitful tutelage of Mlle Cusin, with a host of other instructors to take their turns: Mlle Danse, Amélie Fortin, Félicie Bonningue, tutors never forgotten, whose serial effort was to set the now adolescent Henry James along a path toward so complete a mastery of French that by his early thirties, back in Paris, he had become the entirely fluent, idiomatic, unaccented-French-speaking friend of Flaubert, Maupassant, and Daudet—and every bit as much at ease reading French authors as English or American.

Yet in this present 1858, after three years abroad, the family had returned to America by early summer, Harry fifteen by then and the Jameses settling in Newport—their first time in New England—a seaport town where the attraction was close friends of the father who had preceded them there. It proved a happy choice for the children, whose peripatetic rearing had obliged them to shape their society out of the family circle, each relishing the others' company throughout their travels. Now finally, for the first time, in Newport, young Willy and Harry could make friends of their own—beyond family, beyond the numerous uncles, aunts, and cousins who drifted in and out of their days— new acquaintances whose friendship would last through their lifetimes. And they could ride horseback, and fish, and go boating, and walk along the cliffs, and join young John La Farge in filling sketch books, and talk endlessly with "Sargy" Perry about literature.

But the father was restless again, and again got his family under way, in the autumn of 1859, back to Europe, to Switzerland, eventually to Bonn, where the children were refining their German in September 1860, when yet again Henry James Sr., giving in to his oldest son Willy's desire to resume the study of art under William Morris Hunt in Newport, dislodged the family for yet another voyage.

So the Jameses were settled once more on Kay Street in their Rhode Island village when rebel shells exploded over Fort Sumter in Charleston harbor on an early morning in April 1861. Three days later, on April 15—Harry James's eighteenth birthday—President Lincoln issued his call for seventy-five thousand volunteers, to which the northern states abundantly, enthusiastically responded. Two who volunteered to fight in the war were Henry James Sr.'s younger sons, Garth Wilkinson and Robertson, students in Frank Sanborn's experimental, coeducational, abolitionist school in Concord, Massachusetts. They were seventeen and sixteen when they enlisted, both serving with some distinction. Wilky was severely wounded as Robert Gould Shaw's adjutant in his black regiment's heroic, doomed charge up the battlements of Fort Wagner. Bob in uniform was somewhat ignominiously felled by sunstroke— but later, upon leading his troops in the retaking of Charleston, was promoted to captain. Wilky eventually recovered from his wounds sufficiently to go back into service, in a war that proved the high point of his and his younger brother's lives, for both were fated afterward to slide into frustrating, often unhappy shiftings about, Wilky's days troubled throughout by those war wounds, Bob's by anxiety, marital infidelity, and alcohol. The elder of the two died in Milwaukee at thirty-eight of Bright's Disease; the younger in his early sixties in the Concord where he had gone to school in his youth.

Of the older brothers, neither served in the Civil War. William, having studied art in Newport, shifted his interest to science (to his father's satisfaction) and entered the Lawrence Scientific School at Harvard, from where during more than a year of the conflict he was off with the zoologist/geologist Louis Agassiz on an expedition to Brazil and up the Amazon. Any wartime service that the violence-averse Henry Jr. might have contemplated gave way to an "obscure hurt" about which the sufferer remained enigmatic through his lifetime, an evasiveness that has provoked much speculation. The cause of the pain occurred in the autumn of 1861, during a fire in a Newport stable that young Harry was doing his part to put out. Somehow he got wedged in a fence angle to his detriment, agonizingly but in a manner that wasn't evident to others. Was it a testicular wound? More likely he damaged his back in some way; the Jameses had such a tendency. William suffered from back troubles in years ahead, and Bob did, and Alice did. Whatever it was, in Henry's case it was real enough—crippling when it did strike—although far from a continuous grievance. In its periods of dormancy the victim was able to ride horseback, and hike with friends in New Hampshire's White Mountains, and attend Harvard Law School briefly (as unprofitably as he had attended engineering school for a short time in Geneva), and write.

For Harry in his early twenties had begun to submit stories and book reviews to periodicals. Doubtless the name—Henry James Jr.—eased his entry into that world. His father had taken him as a child to meet Mr. Greeley at the old offices of the *Tribune*, to which the senior James contributed letters and articles, as he did to various other newspapers and magazines. So widely known was the elder namesake, in fact, that no editor need wonder who Henry James Jr. was. Thus in 1864, with the war still in progress, the son's first, highly melodramatic story appeared anonymously in the *Continental Monthly*: "A Tragedy of Error." And in the same year James at twenty-one began writing book criticism for the *North American Review*. In March 1865, the budding author published his first signed fiction, "The Story of a Year," in the prestigious *Atlantic Monthly* no less; and soon after young James started furnishing reviews and travel sketches to the newly founded *Nation*.

The war ended. The blockade of southern ports was lifted, and transatlantic passenger traffic resumed. In February 1869, Henry James Jr. sailed alone as one among the flood of postwar Americans bound for Europe. He was gone fifteen glorious months, in England meeting such notables as Darwin and George Eliot—then on to France and Switzerland, hiking over the Alps into Italy: Milan, Venice, Florence, Rome. In May 1870, Henry James returned home after much keen observing, with his horizons broadened and a first novel under way that would be serialized in the *Atlantic* from August to December of the following year. *Watch and Ward* it was called: apprentice work, but offering a promise of more effective prose to come.

And ahead lay another chance to get to Europe, accompanying his sister Alice and his Aunt Kate in May 1872. Harry remained with his beloved charges while they traveled through England, France, Switzerland, and Germany, at their side clear back to their ship that sailed from Liverpool in October. But their guide didn't return home with the other two travelers; James spent the rest of the fall in Paris, and December in Florence, and the new year into spring and summer delightedly in Rome, taking rooms, going for daily horseback rides to explore the Campagna, and thriving among the expatriate colony there.

And he was writing, and on his own at last was earning enough by his pen to support himself. Among much else, Henry James was writing a second novel, and had it just about finished when he sailed to America in early September 1874. *Roderick Hudson* this one was called, and it ran as a serial in the *Atlantic* the following year, starting in January. At the end of that same January James's first book was published: *The Passionate Pilgrim and Other Tales*. And a collection of his European travel writings, *Transatlantic Sketches*, appeared in April, with James Osgood publishing both titles and bringing forth *Roderick Hudson* in book form before the year was out.

By then the author had tried his hand at living for half a year in New York, but found it too expensive for what he could afford. So he moved back to his family's home, now on Quincy Street in Cambridge across from Boston, and from there on July 21 wrote to John Hay about a plan he had been mulling over that might serve to shape his future. The writer was hoping to become a *Tribune* correspondent in Paris, sending back letters from there that "would of course be welcome to whatever credit my signature might bestow upon them"—assuredly a signature the worth of which was on the rise. Its possessor closed his appeal to the newspaper editor with "kind regards to Mrs. Hay, & the best wishes for the prosperity of your summer. Yours very truly—HENRY JAMES JR."

22. JOURNALIST IN PARIS

A unique education had rendered Hay's petitioner as competently at ease in Europe as in the United States. In America the region Henry James knew was limited, far more so than Mark Twain's, for instance; but many an author is associated closely with one region: the Brontës with Yorkshire, Hawthorne with New England, Hardy with Wessex, Faulkner with the deep South, Mark himself (despite all his roaming) most tellingly with the Mississippi. Moreover, James's region was of a respectable extent and complexity: New York City, upper New York State, Newport, and Cambridge-Boston. Yet it was the comfort this same author, in his early thirties and his great career as a novelist only really getting under way, felt in Europe as well that set him apart. Gathered and retained from childhood, youth, and young manhood, that knowledge amounted to a firm grasp on the language, literature, geography, manners, customs, and culture of England, of France, and (a bit more tardily but hardly less firmly by now, in 1875) of Italy. And it was during these same months in the first half of 1875 that James had been settling on the country in which he might best pursue his distinctive talents.

For now, he had pretty well determined what the subject matter of his fiction would be. It would put to use what his education and temperament had given him such unusual insights into, precisely what his novel *Roderick Hudson*—currently appearing as a serial in the *Atlantic* and about to be published in book form at year's end—exhibited as its focus: a denizen of the New World coming into contact with the Old. In the present instance, a young bank employee in still semirural Northampton, Massachusetts, possesses an artistic gift that his provincial neighbors are ill equipped to appreciate. A wealthy connoisseur visiting the town comes upon a specimen of Roderick's sculptures and in his joyful excitement treats the untrained artist to an extended stay in Rome, where classical examples of the art abound and where a number of Hudson's countrymen are already set up as sculptors in a community amply able to encourage their efforts. What will happen when the immensely gifted though innocent American occupies a studio in a sophisticated, even jaded Old World city?

The theme abides. The pretty high school junior at the drugstore soda fountain catches the eye of a movie mogul passing through town and finds herself a starlet with a Hollywood contract. The rock band in Whitewater, Kansas, gets its lucky break. What will they make of it? For his part, Roderick dazzles the Romans with an initial specimen of his talent, attains a certain celebrity, neglects his sweetheart back home, falls desperately in love with a beautiful, rich cosmopolitan American expatriate, vainly pursues her, fritters away his gifts in distraction, and finally—in this early work by an author exposed to much nineteenth-century theatrical melodrama—ends a suicide.

True, the fates of a few of our own musicians, movie stars, and poets confirm the plausibility of so doleful an outcome; and, in any case, the international theme was assuredly of interest to James's early readers. As he mentioned in his letter to Hay: "There is apparently in the American public an essential appetite, & a standing demand, for information about all Parisian things." About European things in general: some of it pent up during the four recent wartime years when transatlantic travel had been cut off here at home. Some of the demand—the appetite—came from the wealth that the Civil War had bestowed on those who supplied uniforms and blankets for the troops, furnished munitions, provided steel for rails and armaments, produced the beef and beans. After peacetime arrived, possessors of that new wealth continued to prosper and were ready to travel. With the recent successful laying of the transatlantic cable, Europe felt closer, even as steamships were increasing in speed and commodiousness and comfort. Mark Twain was on board the *Quaker City*—America's first cruise ship—when it left New York bound for Gibraltar and the Holy Land in 1867; the wealthy Roosevelt family set sail with servants and trunks and eleven-year-old Teedie Roosevelt—future president—on board for a year of travel in Europe in May 1869 (the same year and month in which eastern and western sections of America's first transcontinental railroad met at Promontory Summit, Utah). In the new peace, wealth old and new, west and east, appeared restlessly on the move; so that in writing to Mr. Hay six years later, Henry James Jr. could allude to a widespread, still vigorous interest in Europe, and add: "I should come to the matter"—of the *Tribune* assignment he was seeking—"with a considerable familiarity with a good many points in French civilization, & should, I think, always feel pretty sure of my ground."

In other words, he would make a success of an overseas column that was certain to be popular with *Tribune* readers. Only, John Hay was no longer chief editorial writer for that newspaper by the time James's letter reached him. Hay had married and was a father and had moved to Cleveland by then, having laid aside his journalism career to grow rich as a businessman working for his father-in-law.

Still, the former editor remained a great favorite of his earlier employer at the *Tribune*, of Whitelaw Reid, whose trust would be demonstrated six years further on, when, at his own marriage, Reid turned over the reins of the newspaper to John Hay during the five months and longer that the publisher and his bride were enjoying their European honeymoon. Even now, and through those intervening six years, John Hay's occasional editorials, reviews, and suggestions sent from Cleveland were always welcome in the *Tribune*'s New York offices. As in this instance, when Hay relayed the substance of Henry James Jr.'s request east at once, with the recommendation that Reid act upon it favorably. *Transatlantic Sketches*, James's travel pieces for the *Nation* that Osgood had published in book form just this April, gave evidence of that author's perceptiveness and his masterful writing style. "I hope you will engage him," Hay wrote to his former boss and good friend. "He will write better letters than anybody—you know his wonderful style and keen observation of life and character." And you're even now paying a French correspondent, Hay went on, "$30 for a not very good letter" that has to be translated into English (Hay himself had done that chore while in the New York offices). "For, say, $20 or $25 James will write you a much better letter"—in English—"and sign his name to it"; and the American stood ready to start in mid-autumn. What Reid should do was let Houssaye, the Frenchman in Paris, "run on until James gets there and then discharge him" by means of a note "telling him how delighted you and the public have been with his letters, but that the labor of translation has been very difficult and now has become almost impossible through the removal from New York of the invaluable rooster who did it, etc., etc."

The logic proved persuasive, as Henry James was to learn under date of August 5, 1875. "Will you be so good," he responded gratefully to Hay, "as to let Mr. Reid know that I accept his offer of $20—gold, & that I expect to be able to write my first letter by about October 25th." Concerning remuneration, the new hire did feel obliged to add: "It is a smaller sum than I should myself have proposed, but being, as you say, good newspaper payment, I summon philosophy to my aid."

So James had his assignment to report from Paris, with a steady if modest income to help him get by overseas, one that he presumed his other writings would bolster. Thus on October 20, having bade his family goodbye and after a last breakfast with his friend and *Atlantic* editor William Dean Howells, the new *Tribune* correspondent boarded ship for Liverpool, Howells writing to Hay afterward that "Harry James is going abroad again not to return, I fancy, even for visits"—although the occasional visit did occur in time. Even so, Howells was right in effect: the American author, this early in his imposing career, was moving abroad for good.

James reached the French capital on November 11, 1875, and mailed off his first letter to the *Tribune*, "Paris Revisited," before a fortnight had passed. By then he was set up in a third-floor furnished apartment near the rue Rivoli, with the *Opéra*, the Louvre (where he and Willy had spent hours of their adolescence gazing at paintings), and the Place Vendôme—its central pillar restored—close at hand. And he found Paris looking beautiful, the wide boulevards of the late Napoleon III's imperial ambitions only fitfully scarred by evidence of the recent war, or the Prussian siege of the city, or the Commune that had briefly, bloodily followed four years previous to this glittering present.

And it was affordable. "When I reflect upon my last winter's disbursements in New York," James, once settled, wrote to his family back home, "it is remarkably cheap" in the French capital—one reason he had chosen France to move to. There were other reasons: James's fluent ease with French ways; the nourishment to be gained from the land of his literary idol Balzac; doubtless the increasingly unattractive materialism of the newly rich society back home that he had left; the creative independence Paris provided, out from under the roof of the family residence in still rural Cambridge, Massachusetts; and what it seemed Paris could furnish that his native country could not, focused as the latter was on practical efforts building and expanding a young nation and making of it a paying proposition. Thus America as yet lacked the culture that time and leisure alone provide, along with the traditions and institutions and customs that bestow on a place its distinctive picturesqueness and its sense of a human past. From those—of such abundance in the Old World, scarcer in the New—are spun, James thought, the threads out of which fiction writers weave their stories. But even beyond that, this particular American simply felt more at home among weathered building stones, place names rich with historic associations, the imposing evidences—some in ruins—of generations that have passed their lives on that same soil through centuries long gone. Young America lacked such atmosphere to the same degree. Moreover, Europe didn't seem alien to Henry James; it provided three of the four cultures that by great good fortune had entered his heart very early in a scarcely paralleled upbringing.

He remained in Paris a year, regularly mailing off his letters to the *Tribune*, with occasional trips into the French provinces and, briefly, only the one time, into Spain. In the summer of 1876 James sought from Mr. Reid a raise in pay, only to learn that his letters so far had not been quite of the kind that the newspaper wanted: not factual enough, not gossipy enough, not enough about recognizable people. They were full of atmosphere and eloquent writing, true, but more suitable to magazines such as the *Nation* perhaps, in which James's travel sketches had appeared to general satisfaction. In the future, could its Paris correspondent manage to write for the *Tribune* less in the manner of the essayist and more as a journalist?

James could not. A newsy, gossipy, personal letter was "doubtless the proper sort of thing for the *Tribune* to have," he replied in scarcely veiled annoyance. "But I can't produce it—I don't know how and I couldn't learn how." It would be rowing upstream, requiring much time and great pains. "If my letters have been 'too good,'" he told Mr. Reid, "I am honestly afraid that they are the poorest I can do, especially for the money! I had better, therefore, suspend them altogether. I have enjoyed writing them, however," he added tepidly, "and if the *Tribune* has not been the better for them I hope it has not been too much the worse."

So his career as a journalist came to an end, and James's stay in Paris ended as well, in December of this 1876, in favor of London. Over the fall he had grown impatient with French parochialism; Flaubert, for example, didn't know George Eliot's work, whereas George Eliot assuredly knew Flaubert's. James, of course, knew both, thoroughly, and preferred the society of others who did—which was one reason he crossed the Channel on December 10 without ever regretting the move, took rooms at 3 Bolton Street, Piccadilly, and lived at that London address for the next decade.

While still in France and needing the money, he had started another novel, *The American*, serialized in the *Atlantic Monthly* from May 1876 through twelve issues into the spring of the following year, those same months during which the author quit working part time as a journalist and moved his residence to England. "Is not 'The American' astonishing, even to us who always believed in him?" John Hay back home exclaimed admiringly to his friend Howells in February 1877, in the course of reading the installments as they emerged. This new novel did represent a marked advance over James's two earlier extended fictions, with its rounded portrait of Christopher Newman, self-made millionaire visiting France for the first time, with "his vast good-nature," in Howells's reading, "and his thorough good sense and right feeling." Newman is assured as well, and energetic of purpose as he seeks out an effete French aristocracy for his own generous uses: New World values confronting those of the Old. Vivid, unfailingly readable, and full of insight, *The American* stirred more discussion on both sides of the Atlantic than anything James had written up to that time. But in the following year appeared a novella even more talked about—so much so that the new work made the author's international reputation and remains the most popular fiction he ever wrote.

Daisy Miller: A Study may furnish current readers new to Henry James with their most attractive introduction to his world. An unblemished gem of a story, it exemplifies much of what was strikingly innovative about this fresh voice in western literature. We find ourselves on a beautiful summer day set down in the lovely garden of a Swiss hotel of the 1870s, on the shores of a blue lake with the Alps beyond. At a parapet overlooking the vista, a young American, twenty-seven years old, long a student at Geneva nearby and here to visit his aunt in residence at the hotel, is in conversation with a very pretty American guest to whom he has not been introduced. Talking with her, he grows "amused, perplexed, and decidedly charmed." Are all American girls as flirtatious as this? "Or was she also a designing, an audacious, an unscrupulous young person?" Assuredly Miss Miller is unsophisticated: in Europe, young unmarried ladies don't initiate conversations with gentlemen strangers. And now she is casually mentioning that she wants to see a nearby tourist site, but her mother won't go, and her younger brother won't go. Yes, Winterbourne has been there; and this new acquaintance offers to accompany the beautiful young woman the five miles or so to the Château of Chillon.

But before they can set out, he learns from his aunt, Mrs. Costello, that the Millers—those wealthy travelers from Schenectady on their first visit to Europe—are common, vulgar, the talk of the English speakers at the hotel, who are shocked by their brash behavior and eager to dissociate themselves from anybody who casts their countrymen in a bad light with the locals. She urges her nephew not to "meddle with little American girls that are uncultivated, as you call them. You have lived too long out of the country. You will be sure to make some great mistake."

Nevertheless, Winterbourne and his new friend do visit the castle and enjoy a pleasant time together. But why, toward the end of the excursion, is Miss Miller so vexed to learn that her escort will have to return to Geneva tomorrow?

"Oh, bother! I don't believe it!" And when he insists: "Well, Mr. Winterbourne, I think you're horrid!"

"Poor Winterbourne was fairly bewildered," we're told; "no young lady had as yet done him the honor to be so agitated by the announcement of his movements." Miss Miller teases him about an imaginary charmer tyrannizing him back in Geneva: "I suppose, if you stay another day, she'll come after you in the boat. Do wait over till Friday, and I will go down to the landing to see her arrive!" Winterbourne placates his young friend only by promising to call on her in Rome over the coming winter—an easy promise to make, as Mrs. Costello regularly winters in Rome, where her nephew has been planning to pay her a visit anyway.

In the months ahead he gets letters from that aunt. "Those people you were so devoted to last summer at Vevey have turned up here," she writes, and the young woman has become "very intimate with some third-rate Italians, with whom she rackets about in a way that makes much talk." When he reaches Rome, Winterbourne hears from Mrs. Costello that the girl "goes about alone with her foreigners. As to what happens further, you must apply elsewhere for information. She has picked up half a dozen of the regular Roman fortune-hunters, and she takes them about to people's houses." And where is the mother all this while? "I haven't the least idea. They are very dreadful people."

On several occasions in days ahead, Winterbourne encounters Miss Miller, who is friendly enough but always accompanied by a certain handsome young Mr. Giovanelli. Well, if that is how it is—yet neither Miss Miller nor Giovanelli appears impatient when her friend from the summer intrudes on their company. Winterbourne tries to warn the girl of her indiscretion. "Though you may be flirting, Mr. Giovanelli is not; he means something else." To which Daisy responds, "He isn't preaching, at any rate." And she tells her American acquaintance that she and Mr. Giovanelli "are very intimate friends." "Ah," Winterbourne murmurs, "if you are in love with each other, it is another affair."

Daisy's reaction to those words surprises him. She gets up, blushing, and answers sharply, "Mr. Giovanelli, at least, never says such very disagreeable things to me."

Winterbourne can't make it out. Later he learns that Daisy's mother thinks her daughter is engaged, but is she? He puts the question to her. "Since you have mentioned it," Daisy tells him, "I *am* engaged." And adds: "You don't believe it!" A pause. "Yes, I believe it," he says. "Oh, no you don't!" she cries. "Well, then—I am not!" And she leaves him to have tea with Mr. Giovanelli, which incidentally Mr. Winterbourne has never offered her. "I have offered you advice," he counters. And she, departing: "I prefer weak tea!"

Byron in a famous passage in *Manfred* celebrates the Colosseum by moonlight—the reason Winterbourne, in passing the great Roman ruin after dinner on a lovely spring evening a few nights later, steps aside for a moment to view the moonlit scene. Within, he comes upon a couple alone in the darker shadows. It is Giovanelli and Miss Miller. Suddenly "the riddle had become easy to read. She was a young lady whom a gentleman need no longer be at pains to respect." The American turns away, but Daisy has recognized him. "Why, it was Mr. Winterbourne! He saw me, and he cuts me!" She sounds not at all disconcerted. For his part, Winterbourne is furious at her companion for letting the girl linger in such a dangerous place, its air stagnant, miasmic. Every Italian knew to stay away from the Colosseum at night: breeding ground of Roman fever, of malaria, "bad air" such as that investing swamps and marshes, where are bred in fact the mosquitoes that only decades later would be identified as the true cause of the disease. Meanwhile, the young woman must be got away from here at once.

Nevertheless, within the next few days Daisy does develop the fever, and despite Mrs. Miller's diligent nursing dies of it, but not before charging her mother with her failing breath to tell Mr. Winterbourne that she never was engaged to the handsome Italian. In shock, Winterbourne doesn't at first understand the message, but later he realizes that he has done the girl an injustice, and remorsefully says as much to his aunt. What, precisely, does he mean? "She would have appreciated one's esteem," he tells her.

Mrs. Costello wonders whether that is "a modest way of saying that she would have reciprocated one's affection"? To which her nephew makes no further reply, although presently he concedes: "You were right in that remark that you made last summer. I was booked to make a mistake. I have lived too long in foreign parts."

23. BIG JOB WELL BEGUN

Such an abbreviated summary can only hint at the charm and subtlety of James's story. His settings—the Trois Couronnes Hotel in Vevey, its garden and view from the parapet at sunset; Rome in its nineteenth-century solidity and color—the social gatherings, the crowds strolling in the Pincio—are laid before us by means of telling detail, never too much, just enough that we may see them memorably and with entire confidence that the author knows what he's about. The characters—stiff, perplexed Winterbourne; dyspeptic, shy, ineffective Mrs. Miller; her petulant nine-year-old son; the dogmatic aunt, Mrs. Costello; the smiling, always deferential Giovanelli; Daisy herself, with her good heart and love of life—all those characters are fully realized, none superfluous, each speaking in his own individualized voice. The situation is of the present, real people behaving as people of that time in those circumstances would behave; with the result that James's novella seems to hold in amber certain days in the two distinctive places, with an assurance that leaves us feeling: this is how it would be if we could travel back there—recognizable, but all of a world fascinatingly different in dress, manners, customs, and modes of speaking.

Finally, the point of view, which gives *Daisy Miller* its unity, is not the omniscient author's, but rather Frederick Winterbourne's, limited much like our own. Only gradually, attentively, may we come at least partially to understand *our* world—much less Daisy's, which we are left to comprehend through what Winterbourne perceives only in part, imperfectly, as he ponders and misinterprets the girl's lively behavior until enlightened too late, to his regret, at the end of the story.

From London James had sent the novella to a Philadelphia magazine, which turned it down without comment. So the author gave it to Leslie Stephen, editor of London's *Cornhill* (and soon-to-be father of Virginia Woolf); the *Cornhill* serialized *Daisy Miller* in the issues of June and July 1878. Two American magazines promptly pirated the story in their July and August issues; so that by the time *Harper's* back home brought out an authorized pamphlet, in 1879, the novella had already been so widely read and talked about that the tardy copyrighted booklet provided its author with far fewer American sales than might have enriched him otherwise.

The chatter about *Daisy Miller*, meanwhile, provoked John Hay to protest, in an unsigned contribution to the *Atlantic* on Christmas Day, 1878. "To read the silly criticisms which have been printed," Hay began, "and the far sillier ones which are every day uttered in regard to Mr. James's *Daisy Miller* would almost convince us that we are as provincial as ever in our sensitiveness to foreign opinion." Readers have charged the author with being unpatriotic for living in London and daring to describe "an under-bred American family traveling in Europe. The fact," Hay writes, "that he has done so with a touch of marvelous delicacy and truth, that he has produced not so much a picture as a photograph, is held by many to be an aggravating circumstance." Yet those familiar with that author's writing—"(and I believe I have read every word he has printed)"—will recognize the novella's "straightforward simplicity and what I can only call *authenticity.*" Daisy's crimes, all of them, are merely conventional, with no intention "even to surprise, much less outrage, her censors." Hay insists that what the young woman does in Vevey and Rome wouldn't so much as be noticed in Schenectady. Here in America, in "every city of the nation young girls of good family, good breeding, and perfect innocence of heart and mind, receive their male acquaintances *en tête à tête,* and go to parties and concerts with them, unchaperoned." Not that Daisy was of that well-bred category; but her unsophisticated conduct "is without blemish, according to the rural American standard, and she knows no other." Moreover, any American gentleman who has spent time in Europe will recognize Miss Miller right off, having met her, Hay tells us, "under a dozen different names and forms. She went to dine with you one day at Sceaux, and climbed, with the fearless innocence of a bird, into the great chestnut-tree. She challenged you to take her to Schönbrunn, and amazed your Austrian acquaintances whom you met there, and who knew you were not married. At Naples, one evening—." But no need to pile on examples.

Incidentally, the point isn't that Winterbourne has missed out on the love of his life; for in the final sentence of *Daisy Miller* we learn that the gentleman returned to Geneva, from which city have come contradictory reports: that he is studying hard, and that he is attentive to "a very clever foreign lady." The point—a finer one—is that he must live with the knowledge that he has been unkind to a charming, good-hearted young compatriot, and has utterly failed to understand her. He has stayed away from America too long.

John Hay—former resident of Paris, Vienna, and Madrid; now of Cleveland—was himself pretty well re-Americanized by Christmas 1878, when he defended James's novella. Just two years earlier, after Christmas 1876, had occurred the horrific Ashtabula railroad disaster, the bridge designed by Hay's father-in-law giving way and plunging ninety-two passengers to their fiery deaths below. In early 1877, amid the outrage and contumely that followed, Amasa Stone appeared before a committee of the Ohio legislature to provide his defiant testimony, then left with his wife and younger daughter for an extended stay in Europe. In his absence his business affairs were put in the able hands of his son-in-law, who guided them through the turmoils of that violent summer of 1877, when Cleveland, like Pittsburgh, Chicago, Louisville, St. Louis, and other cities and towns of the Northeast and Midwest, was beset by the first widespread, far-reaching labor strife in American history. At the time, Hay's private correspondence to Amasa Stone overseas conveyed his anxious concern, but outwardly the colonel remained calm, and was able to surrender account books in good order when the Stones returned in the autumn to a Cleveland grown quiet.

Through all such interruptions—as well as many that preceded and followed—John Hay the businessman continued mindful of his obligations as historian. During the summer before, for instance, he had written to John George Nicolay, friend of the Lincoln years, about dreading and postponing the monumental task they had set themselves. "I went industriously to work last winter" of 1876, he wrote to Nico. "Got a fine start on my material and commenced putting it into shape"—had even written a few pages, until afflicted with double vision. The several doctors Hay consulted concurred that the patient should take it easy this summer and hope to get well by the fall. "That is the whole story," he explained in mid-June, "and I have never had the heart to write it before. I write now because I am greatly encouraged and begin to think I shall soon be all right again."

Hay's health did improve; then the following summer, of 1877—toward mid-August, as the railroad strife calmed down: "I think I can say now that I am started and can keep at work. If nothing happens adversely, we can have Lincoln inaugurated by the 4th of March, 1878. I have been very hard at work for a month or so, and sat down some weeks ago to writing," moving his earliest assigned portion of a long narrative up to 1830, Lincoln at age twenty-one. Health remained Hay's principal worry: "My old foe, the headache, is lying in wait for me, but I hope to get free." Yet, he confessed to Nicolay, progress was slow. "I write with great labor and difficulty—my imagination is all gone—a good riddance. I shall never write easily and fluently again."

In January 1878, Hay and his wife, Clara, traveled to Washington, principally to consult with Nicolay, by then possessed of the various Lincoln White House papers that Robert Todd Lincoln had kept under lock and key since soon after his father's murder. Since then, Robert Lincoln had moved with the inconsolable widow and his younger brother Tad to Chicago, where in time he completed his law studies, set up his practice, married, and fathered three children. By late 1868, the attorney's mother, still veiled and in deep mourning, had sailed with Tad for the less expensive cities and spas of Europe and remained there three years. During that time, and only after bitter, humiliating public debate, the Senate in Washington finally granted Mrs. Lincoln the pension that her few friends had been urging and that allowed her to return to Illinois.

Tad, however, on their Atlantic crossing home caught a cold, which developed into pleurisy and pneumonia. The young man died, age eighteen, in mid-July 1871, in Chicago, his mother in the hotel room at his side. Again, understandably, Mary was thrown into deep, prolonged grief. The widow's behavior became more erratic—voices from beyond the grave, her untidiness, her repeated purchases of multiple identical items charged and not needed (yet more gloves, curtains for a home she didn't live in)—to the extent that her last living son, Robert, felt obliged to seek a court order restraining his mother's liberty "for her benefit, and the safety of the community." As a result, for three months Mary was an unwilling inmate at a sanitarium in Batavia, forty miles west of Chicago, until fellow spiritualists secured her release. Clad in black to the end, Mary Todd Lincoln died in her early sixties at her sister's home in Springfield, in 1882. She and her surviving son Robert never fully reconciled.

Through all that domestic, very public scandal, John Hay's and John George Nicolay's friendship with Bob Lincoln remained intact. Hay, for instance, after returning from his visit to Washington and talks with his colleague there, was in touch with Lincoln from his Euclid Avenue home. The collaboration of the two former secretaries appeared to be proceeding well, he wrote, "and we now consider the big job well begun. It will take a long time yet, but we are in no hurry and I presume you are not." Incidentally, Navy Secretary Welles of President Lincoln's cabinet had just died. Does Bob think that Welles's son might let us make use of his diary?

Hay's own diary—that invaluable resource kept during the Civil War years—he had come upon among his papers just the other day, and wrote Nico about it in some excitement. But soon, in early April 1878, Hay had less agreeable news to report: "I am used up the Doctor says, and must lie off all summer." Should the patient go to Colorado for the prescribed rest? Or to Europe? Hay chose Europe. Leaving Clara for the first time since their wedding, he journeyed abroad with his brother ("my first friend and my best"), in what Hay described to Nicolay on his return as "the quietest summer of my life." Perhaps—although it hardly reads like a restful one, given wardrobe demands on ship and shore in that more formal age, the numerous trunks to hold them, servants to depend on, and the imperfect condition of European vehicular travel. "Spent a month or so in England, loafing in city and country; did not go to a single dinner party or Opera," the patient recalled; "then loafed through Holland and Belgium up the Rhine to Schlangen, where we stayed a month; then a little of northern Italy and Switzerland, then the Exposition and Scotland, and a week's sleepy rest at Windermere and home."

But Hay did dine out during his travels, in England in the spring, for instance, with Harry James—to find James in May 1878 the darling of London society. *Daisy Miller* appeared in the *Cornhill* in June and July, and the author's new novel *The Europeans* (set in New England) was running as a serial in *The Atlantic* the same year, a year in which Macmillan of London published a selection of James's critical writings: *French Poets and Novelists*. Indeed, Henry James had become much coveted as a dinner guest: cultured, impeccably well-mannered bachelor—notable besides—who over the winter ahead was to record having dined out by invitation 107 times, including visits to country manors, all the while gathering observations, anecdotes, and insights to inform his future work.

For James was working, every morning, diligently. Indeed, his output over these next few years was amazing, and of amazingly high quality. Soon he would begin work on what he saw as his "big" book, which would compare to his other books "as wine unto water," and which, once started, would take up his full attention. But before then he must clear his desk, of a remarkable and at the time controversial biography of Nathaniel Hawthorne, which he finished in 1879, and of a short novel for Howells that was done in 1880—one of his most attractive—set in the New York City of his childhood: *Washington Square* (which, with *Daisy Miller* and the later ghostly *Turn of the Screw*, constitutes perhaps the most accessible, most enticing of all the titles in James's massive corpus for readers to sample who may be approaching him for the first time).

Those works delivered, the author could now turn to what he saw as a major effort: "something on a larger scale than I have yet done," he wrote to Howells. In the spring of 1880, in a Florence hotel room, he began to write *The Portrait of a Lady*. The novel started its serial publication in England, in *Macmillan's* magazine, in October, in America in the *Atlantic* that November.

Hay, meanwhile, had returned from his European travels two years earlier with his health improved. Back in Cleveland in the fall of 1878 and into the following winter he worked on his and Nicolay's biography of Lincoln, and by March 1879 he could report to his co-author that he had written fifty thousand words on the project. But that same spring Hay's mother, now seventy-five, fell and broke her hip, so that the historian was obliged to spend three weeks in Warsaw, until she was up and in her rolling chair, and the family could return to their "comforting delusion" that their parents were immortal. That summer, however, found Hay—always generous with contributions to the Republican Party—again distracted, increasingly involved in Ohio politics; and in late fall (as earlier noted) he joined the administration of the then president, Rutherford Hayes of Ohio, as assistant secretary of state. Secretary Hay served in Washington for fifteen months until a new administration came in, in March 1881; then, from May to November, he filled in as acting editor of the *New York Tribune* until Whitelaw Reid returned from his honeymoon. In December back in Cleveland, before resuming his Lincoln project, John Hay took time to review Henry James's big new novel. Its serial run had ended, allowing *The Portrait of a Lady* to appear in book form that November. Hay's review, unsigned as was customary, ran in the *Tribune* on Christmas Day, 1881.

"No work printed in recent years," the reviewer announced right off, "on either side of the Atlantic or on either side the English Channel, surpasses this, in seriousness of intention, in easy scope and mastery of material, in sustained and spontaneous dignity and grace of style, in wit and epigram, and, on the whole, in clear conception and accurate delineation of character." During serialization James's new novel had been criticized for its title, because the heroine seemed the character in it least clearly revealed; yet, "after all," Hay maintains, "when we lay down the book, we cannot deny, if we are candid, that we know as much of the motives which induced her"—Miss Archer—"to refuse two gallant gentlemen and to marry a selfish and soulless scoundrel as we do of the impulses which lead our sisters and cousins to similar results." In fact, we know what Mr. James wants us to know about Isabel Archer, and precisely what we need to know. Hay's review is long, with extensive citations to illustrate what the novel achieves in characterization, description, and analysis, all those excellences guiding the reviewer toward his conclusion: "Of the importance of this volume there can be no question. It will certainly remain one of the notable books of the time"—a judgment the passing years have affirmed categorically. Henry James's *The Portrait of a Lady* stands among the greatest novels in the English language, the genius of its author—as the review in the *Tribune* concludes—"now, more than ever before, beyond question."

24. HAY WRITES A NOVEL

In months immediately ahead, during the winter and spring of 1882, John Hay wrote a novel himself. Like much else that the colonel attempted, he made it look easy; and the result turned into a best seller on both sides of the Atlantic. Not because of Hay's well-known name: both the magazine serialization and the book that followed appeared anonymously, an anonymity maintained beyond the author's lifetime. No more than a handful of people knew for sure who wrote it—although Mark Twain, acquainted with his friend's political leanings (so different from his own), made a shrewd guess to Mrs. Fairbanks: "*I* believe John Hay wrote it, but I don't know."

Hay called his novel *The Bread-Winners*. He set it in a city much like Cleveland, on a lake as Cleveland is on Lake Erie, thriving as Cleveland was thriving. Euclid Avenue, renamed Algonquin, appears in *The Bread-Winners*, where, in a lavishly tasteful home along that boulevard, lives Arthur Farnham, "one of those fortunate natures, who, however born, are always bred well, and come by prescription to most of the good things the world can give." However, through days immediately ahead, the much blessed Farnham will be obliged to deal with a civic crisis brought on by millworkers' discontent: "The labor unions have ordered a general strike," Captain Farnham learns from a friend; "they are holding meetings all over town to-night"—meetings that will soon shut down the mills, "putting anywhere from three thousand to ten thousand men on the streets." Among the strikers are "bad eggs"—not union men, but rather agitators from outside—come to stir up trouble by "going from place to place, haranguing the workmen," preaching so-called socialism, but what amounts really to "riot and plunder." As the strike advances, a knot of ne'er-do-wells heads for Algonquin Avenue, which, the ruffians have been encouraged to understand, is "heaped with riches wrung from the sweat of the poor. Clean out the abodes of blood guiltiness," the agitators cry, urging the rioters on.

One reads Hay's novel less perhaps for the style than the story; but we need hardly wonder at *The Bread-Winners*'s immediate popularity, which continued throughout the remainder of the nineteenth century and into the twentieth. It was translated into a number of foreign languages and by 1911 had gone through six editions (Hay's widow allowing the author's name to be revealed finally in 1907). Surely part of the explanation for that interest lies in the timeliness of the subject matter. Labor strife beset the 1880s as it had the 1870s, and would continue dramatically into the 1890s. Hay had lived through the disruptions in Cleveland in the violent summer of 1877; and even later, while he was writing his novel in this spring of 1882, the city around him underwent further alarms, as on May 11, when in Cleveland "the big blast furnace shut down, which sent 200 more men to join the thousands already walking about the streets. Those who were content with their wages, but were thrown out of work because of the closing of the mills, are working quietly to get the men to go back," a journalist on the scene reported, "but agents of the Amalgamated Association are working, on the other hand, to keep them solid on the demand that has been made."

Strikers sought not only a restoration of wages that owners had cut but an end to twelve-hour shifts around the clock and the institution of an eight-hour day. "All is going along quietly so far," the reporter on the scene informed his

New York readers, "and no disturbances have occurred anywhere as a result of the strike." Yet disturbances hovered, awaiting future developments (in June violence did erupt as strikers fought scabs) while Hay wrote on, he meantime filling his fictional strike with disturbances aplenty.

In Hay's novel, tramps and other such sullen disheveled types loiter about at street corners. The home on Algonquin Avenue next door to Captain Farnham's is suddenly, violently broken into for an "assessment," a widow and her beautiful nineteen-year-old daughter cowering in terror until a timely last-minute rescue. For Farnham has had the foresight (in the face of a craven mayor and a do-nothing police chief) to put an ad in yesterday's paper: "Veterans, Attention! All able-bodied veterans of the Army of the Potomac, and especially of the Third Army Corps, are requested to meet at seven this evening, at No.—Public Square"; that is, at the captain's office downtown, where a half-dozen Union veterans show up on schedule, eager to follow orders, as in chapter 14: "Captain Farnham Sees Active Service Again."

The novel is filled with action, and a substantial cast of characters beyond Farnham's next-door neighbors, Mrs. Belding (widow of the famous bridge builder Jairus Belding) and her lovely daughter Alice. Alice has just returned from finishing school in the East, her maturing beauty and grace quite bedazzling the captain. But another beautiful young woman has earlier entered Farnham's life, seeking help: Maud, upstart daughter of the worthy carpenter Saul Matchin, an artisan who aspires to nothing beyond doing his work well. Saul has in his house a young apprentice, Sam Sleeny, blond, blue-eyed, a good worker but a gawky lover, in love with Saul Matchin's daughter. Her high-school education, however, has filled pretty Maud with social ambitions, so she scorns Sleeny's awkward advances and instead is calling on Captain Farnham, in hopes that he will find her a genteel position in keeping with her desserts: in the town library or, possibly, as the captain's personal secretary.

Farnham needs no such assistance, but will see what he can do about the library. Their dealings climax in Maud's declaration of love for the captain, her near fainting at her boldness and his clutching her to keep her from falling, his kiss "on her red full lips parted in breathless eagerness" (a much-talked-about kiss among Hay's readers), her cry that he does love her then, his emphatic denial, and Maud's angry departure from the greenhouse, the fragrant setting of which has urged on the embrace. But jealous young Sleeny, the apprentice, working nearby, has witnessed a part of the ardent encounter, as has, by chance, Mrs. Belding next door. Dire consequences follow, which eventually involve a stealthy climb through the window of Farnham's study, a blow to the captain's head, a theft, a frame-up, a betrayal, a trial, an escape from prison, then vengeance and murder.

The murder victim is the novel's arch villain, the oleaginous Andrew Jackson Offitt, agitator and head of the Bread-Winners, a secret brotherhood made up of "the laziest and most incapable workmen in the town," whom Offitt is manipulating for his own purposes and profit. All ends well, however. The villain lies in a neck-broken heap on the Matchins' floor, the ill-gotten gains in his pockets retrieved and restored to Captain Farnham, who is recovering from the blow to his skull that young Sleeny, framed, had been sent to jail unjustly for delivering. Sleeny for his part has escaped from jail, disposed of Offitt the true criminal, been in effect exonerated, and won Maud's love. Workers have gone back to work at the mills, private property has been secured, and Farnham is successfully clearing the remaining low hurdle that stands between him and the lovely Alice next door as the novel ends.

The Bread-Winners offers pleasures yet—certainly to the antiquarian and social historian—as, for example, in its atmospheric description of the unwonted stillness a strike imposes on a city: shops closed, traffic thinned and slowed, the lively bustle of ordinary life subdued with the mills and foundries shut down, their fiery glare strangely absent from the night sky. Hay tells his story from the omniscient point of view, the author knowing all about everything and everyone; yet one feels—readers felt it at the time—that his view is hardly objective, but rather in favor of the rich, against the strikers, the discontented, the upstarts.

Like Mark Twain, this author had grown up on the Mississippi, in agrarian Warsaw, Illinois, where the workers Hay knew were likely apprentices—store clerks, cobblers, coopers, such carpenters as Sleeny—who dealt with their bosses directly. They weren't employees in sprawling factories under midlevel managers, with owners even farther off; that sort of workman in any abundance lay in the future. For his part, Hay (unlike Sam Clemens) had never been either apprentice or factory employee—when young had aspired to be a poet, had reluctantly studied law, had accompanied Lincoln as private secretary to Washington, from there had gone to Europe as diplomat, from there to New York to write editorials about foreign affairs and politics under his friend Whitelaw Reid, and from there to the capitalist haven of Cleveland's Euclid Avenue. What did he know about workers in the mills? Thus, when a certain Edward J. Shriver wrote to the *Century* while *The Bread-Winners* was running in its pages, in order to quarrel with the novel's assumption "that trades-unions are composed either of ignorant and lazy dupes, or of such wretches as Offitt," the anonymous author replied in the magazine defensively. What he had written was not about trade unions at all—Offitt was an agitator, not a union man—yet Mr. Shriver would know that "no important strike has ever been carried through without violence, and that no long strike has ever been ended without murder"; and that "only a few years have passed since we saw the streets of Pittsburgh devastated by murder, arson, and rapine, through a rising which agitators could originate but could not control." The anonymous author elaborated on his defense in a later, lengthier letter that the *Century* also printed: "I attempted," he wrote, "to describe certain types of moral perversion, which I have found among our working people, and I am denounced for not having filled my book with praises of the virtues which also abound among them." But that was not the novel's purpose, to praise what is unquestionably the "most intelligent and most prosperous laboring class in the world." Its purpose was simply "to give an absolutely truthful picture of certain phases of our social life which I had never seen in print."

The Bread-Winners is, indeed, among the earliest novels in American fiction to deal with that fresh subject. In years ahead strife between management and labor gave rise to other such novels, the more memorable among them taking the side of workers and their unions. Fiction by Frank Norris, Jack London, and Theodore Dreiser—all still read with interest—variously explore the exploitation of laborers around the turn of the century in a new capitalism rampant with unrestrained profit and greed. The very first paragraph of Hay's *Bread-Winners*, by contrast, introduces the handsome, well-bred Arthur Farnham, whose hands are approvingly described as having "the firm, hard symmetry which showed they had done no work," any more than John Hay had done manual labor since his young manhood pruning and harvesting his Warsaw vineyard. So complacently genteel a worldview took for granted that factories belonged to their owners. Workers were free to quit whenever they chose—give up their places to others ready to work on the terms provided; just as owners (Amasa Stone for one) were free to set those terms, in mills or factories that existed through the owners' initiative and know-how. A new industrial nation flooded with immigrants—and with foreign agitators of German tongue or broad Irish brogue to keep the unskilled stirred up—was one that Hay and many others were finding hard to adjust to. More decades of strife—and the new progressivism that a young President Roosevelt would help enact—were required to curb free enterprise's burgeoning excesses, which many had accepted as an inevitable part of the natural order.

The novel was finished by June 1882. It had been a trying winter and spring for John Hay, with workers walking off at the rolling mill and blast furnace and a strike at Western Union; plus his health problems—diphtheria in February and March, heart palpitations—and his hard push on the Lincoln project, forty chapters completed; plus, as well, this novel that had taken possession of him once he began it. Composed with the imagination and fluency that he had told Nico not long before had left him forever, *The Bread-Winners* was finished in maybe three months. Earlier, Hay and his wife had been planning an extended family vacation in Europe (Helen age seven, Del five, Alice two). Accordingly, in July they found themselves in England, where Mr. and Mrs. Hay—both thorough Anglophiles—left the children with their nurse on the south coast and set out to enjoy London at leisure before traveling and visiting extensively farther north.

In London Hay saw a good deal of Henry James, at one dinner seated contentedly between him and the poet Browning. And he saw Howells as well, to whom he showed *The Bread-Winners*. Although no longer at the *Atlantic*, the former editor liked Hay's novel well enough to recommend it to his successor there, Thomas Bailey Aldrich. Editor Aldrich consented, with little more than a glance, to serialize the work in the *Atlantic*'s pages, but only if the author put his name to it. That Hay declined to do, turning instead to Richard Watson Gilder, dynamic editor of *The Century Magazine* in New York, to whom he gave the novel while insisting on anonymity. Gilder agreed, paid $2,500 for the manuscript, and scheduled publication to begin in May 1883. As it happened, the serial was postponed to August, well after the Hays had returned to America, and it ran until January 1884, creating great interest, stirring many to wonder at the author's identity, and securing some twenty thousand new subscribers for the *Century*.

Meanwhile, the family had relished their long, elaborate European vacation. After retrieving the children and their nurse from Hastings, they journeyed leisurely to Paris, on to Cannes, to Italy for sunny weeks with Howells there, and back to Paris and further hours with Henry James. "I saw a good deal of John Hay, & C. King in Paris & got on beautifully with them both," James wrote to Howells from Bolton Street that November. "Hay is an excellent fellow, & King is a charmer."

Clarence King we'll hear more of later; but for now, Hay was feeling obliged to cut his vacation short. Amasa Stone in Cleveland had grown depressed, still smarting from the aftereffects of the Ashtabula Bridge disaster, brooding over bad investments, suffering from sleeplessness and indigestion, nerves all on edge, longing to turn his business affairs over to his son-in-law, who persisted in lingering overseas. In fact, Hay wanted to stay through the summer, in part to meet English dignitaries whose friendship might serve him in future. But Mr. Stone importuned. The Hays accordingly booked passage for May 10,

1883, Hay writing to Nico that "I am, I think, considerably better, though I have given up all hope of being twenty-one again"; and to Mr. Stone he wrote in order "once more to express my sympathy with your sufferings and my deep regret that your convalescence is so long delayed." This substitute son offered what consolation he could, ending his letter: "I rely on your strong constitution, your sober and moral life, the reserve of vitality you have about you, to wear out all your present troubles and to bring you to a healthy and happy condition again. You have so much to live for to enjoy the results of the good you have done and to continue your career of usefulness and honor."

Four months earlier than originally planned, the Hays arrived home—yet, even so, too late. In his sumptuous Euclid Avenue mansion, on Friday afternoon, May 11, 1883, the magnate Amasa Stone, among the wealthiest of Ohio's wealthy citizens, had taken a revolver into an upstairs bathroom, locked the door behind him, climbed into the tub, and put a bullet through his heart.

25. "THE ART OF FICTION"

From Hartford, Samuel Clemens wrote to his friend Howells on May 18, 1883, about having been "in Montreal three or four days ago, acquiring British copyright whilst my new book"—(Mark Twain's *Life on the Mississippi*)—"was being issued in London," when "that startling news came of the suicide of John Hay's father-in-law. And among the same telegrams was the news that Hay and his wife sailed from Liverpool just in time to escape hearing of the catastrophe." Thus—in days before wireless messaging—"these children are still enjoying themselves on the Atlantic, unaware of what is in store for them. How odd and strange and weird all this is. Apparently nothing pleases the Almighty like the picturesque."

Within the week Henry James, from Mt. Vernon Street in Boston, felt moved to write to his friend Hay "a few words, & I must venture to send your poor wife my friendliest remembrances. I thought of you when your ship came in the other day & of how much worse your disembarking would be than your voyage could have been, at its worst—thought of all this, & of you, with most tender interest and pity. Then I declined to think further, for it was bootless to follow you on your dreary, dreadful journey to Cleveland." James didn't know and "never had seen Mr. Stone, but I can imagine none the less the heaviness of his trouble & the darkness of that of poor Mrs. Stone. Please don't fail to say to Mrs. Hay that I particularly wish her—& perhaps may even allow myself to wish her mother as well—to know of my respectful sympathy."

After an additional few words in commiseration, the writer concluded: "It occurs to me that Mr. Stone's death may perhaps make Cleveland less your residence. Then why not Europe again? I sail on August 22nd. Believe me very faithfully yours—HENRY JAMES."

James had alluded with feeling to the darkness that the loss of loved ones brings with it. Twice recently he himself had journeyed to America and encountered a similar darkness: once after visiting his family for the first time in six years, at Christmas in 1881. From Cambridge in New England he had traveled to New York and on to Washington, where news of a sharp downturn in his mother's health brought him hurrying back, although not in time to reach her before her death, on January 29. By May 1882, James was back in London's Bolton Street (from where he ventured forth to greet Howells and the Hays on their separate arrivals in England that summer, and later to enjoy the company of the Hays and Clarence King in Paris in the fall). Then, for a second time, after yet another summons in December, James was sailing for America possessed of the sad news of his father's rapid decline; and again the son failed to arrive before Henry James Sr. died, on December 18, in Boston, on Mt. Vernon Street, where the family had moved after Mrs. James's death eleven months earlier.

On this second visit to the United States James remained until September 1883, in part as executor settling his father's estate and looking after his sister Alice, whom the recent family crises had newly afflicted with invalidism. Those obligations caused Henry to sail from New York later than expected, but he was back in London by early autumn and would remain abroad, resident in England, thereafter for twenty-one years, visiting America again not until 1904, for the next-to-last time.

For now, though, during the months immediately ahead, at London's Royal Institution on April 25, 1884, a public event occurred that moved Henry James to respond. There that evening the novelist Walter Besant delivered a lecture on "The Art of Fiction." Besant's own novels sold in the hundreds of thousands, his literary reputation among his contemporaries sufficiently elevated that those earlier readers might be surprised to learn how little remembered his name is now. What Mr. Besant was undertaking in his lecture was, in part, forcefully to assert—some decades before the development of motion pictures—the importance of the novel as an artistic form. Indeed, according to the speaker, novels are on a par with the greatest of all the arts, and the supreme novelists (he names Fielding, Scott, Dickens, Thackeray, and Victor Hugo) might properly rank with Raphael and Mozart as artists at the summit of creative achievement. The speaker is aware that many don't see it that way:

readers in general regard the novelist as "a person who tells stories, just as they used to regard the actor as a man who tumbled on the stage to make the audience laugh, and a musician as a man who fiddled to make the people dance." Indeed, some still consider fiction—storytelling—with affectionate contempt, feeling for the novelist what "the practical man feels for the dreamer, the strong man for the weak, the man who can do for the man who can only look on and talk." Anyone can write a novel, they say. The novelist isn't even relating historical truth; he or she is merely *telling a story*.

This present speaker was giving his lecture to correct that misconception. For the creating of fiction, Besant maintains, is "first and before all, a real Art": the oldest art, "because it was known and practised long before Painting and her sisters were in existence or even thought of"; the most religious art, "because in every age until the present the lives, exploits, and sufferings of gods, goddesses, saints, and heroes have been the favorite theme"; the most popular art, "because it requires neither culture, education, nor natural genius to understand and listen to a story"; the most moral art, "because the world has always been taught whatever little morality it possesses by way of story, fable, apologue, parable, and allegory"; the most influential art, "because it can be carried easily and everywhere, into regions where pictures are never seen and music is never heard"; the art most widely spread, "because in no race of men under the sun is it unknown"; and the art with the greatest power to teach, "because its lessons are most readily apprehended and understood."

Novels, moreover, are concerned with humanity, and accordingly (again, in that age before film) they uniquely let us see human beings in motion: "the real indestructible man beneath the rags and filth of a common castaway, and the possibilities of the meanest gutter-child that steals in the streets for its daily bread." Painting, for all its value, can't do that—can show us seascapes, still-lifes, portraits, but can't show us human actions and thoughts, motives, passions, hopes. Sculpture can't do it, being more about form than action. Music's abstractions can't do it. "Poetry alone is the rival of Fiction, and in this respect it takes a lower place, not because Poetry fails to teach and interpret, but because Fiction is, and must always be, more popular."

The novelist conjures up imaginary people in imaginary worlds, worlds "in which the shadows and shapes of men move about before our eyes as real as if they were actually living and speaking among us," worlds that we may summon "at our own sweet will, whenever we please to command them." And by means of those worlds, in nineteenth-century times, "the majority of reading mankind learn nearly all that they know of life and manners, of philosophy and art; even of science and religion."

Of course, to create such worlds successfully, one must have an aptitude, a gift; to do so superlatively well requires genius. But the aspiring novelist can be helped along, for there are rules, as there are in all art: in music rules of form and harmony, in painting of composition and perspective. "Rules will not make a man a novelist, any more than a knowledge of grammar makes a man know a language, or a knowledge of musical science makes a man able to play an instrument. Yet the Rules must be learned."

Besant's "The Art of Fiction" proceeds to enumerate and enlarge upon those rules. For one, train yourself to observe (most people don't really take in what's around them). Keep a notebook, of how people look, how they speak, of gestures, vivid incidentals. Observe closely, then learn to describe what you see. Select the few significant details that will evoke the sight sharply. Next—a cardinal rule—write about what you know and have experienced. And as you write, develop your style: attend closely to the shaping of every sentence you set down. Finally, of course, have a story to tell.

Those rules and Mr. Walter (later Sir Walter) Besant's lecture that conveyed them appeared that spring in a pamphlet, and it was the pamphlet that Henry James soon came upon—and that moved him shortly after to compose his own "The Art of Fiction." He begins with a diffidence not always a trait of this reviewer: "I should not have affixed so comprehensive a title to these few remarks, necessarily wanting in any completeness, upon a subject the full consideration of which would carry us far, did I not seem to discover a pretext for my temerity in the interesting pamphlet lately published under this name by Mr. Walter Besant." A fellow novelist thus welcomes Mr. Besant's contribution. According to James, art thrives on such discussions as the lecture encourages, as it does "upon experiment, upon curiosity, upon variety of attempt, upon the exchange of views and the comparison of standpoints." True, casual readers, who read mostly for amusement or information, may grow impatient with professional talk—about style and structure and similar technical matters. Such readers would agree that a novel ought to be "good," but would have their own ideas about what constitutes goodness in fiction. "One would say that being good means representing virtuous and aspiring characters, placed in prominent positions; another would say that it depends for a 'happy ending' on a distribution at the last of prizes, pensions, husbands, wives, babies, millions, appended paragraphs, and cheerful remarks. Another still would say that it means being full of incident and movement, so that we shall wish to jump ahead, to see who was the mysterious stranger, and if the stolen will was ever found, and shall not be distracted from this pleasure by any tiresome analysis or 'description.' But they might all agree that the 'artistic' idea"—the issue of aesthetics, the wrangling over technical matters—"would spoil some of their fun." And such analytical chatter might point as well toward a less than happy ending (or to no clear ending at all); for the ending of a novel "is, for many persons, like that of a good dinner, a course of dessert and ices; and the artist in fiction"—as distinct from the artless storyteller—"is regarded as a sort of meddlesome doctor who forbids agreeable aftertastes."

As for Mr. Besant's pamphlet, this greater (though considerably less popular) author largely concurs with it; the lecturer did well to broach so fruitful a subject. Moreover, the rules he provides for the aspiring novelist are expressed "in a manner with which it would certainly be unaccommodating to disagree. That the novelist must write from his experience; that his 'characters' must be real and such as might be met with in actual life; that 'a young lady brought up in a quiet country village should avoid descriptions of garrison life,' and 'a writer whose friends and personal experiences belong to the lower middle-class should carefully avoid introducing his characters into Society'; that one should enter one's notes in a commonplace book; that one's figures should be clear in outline; that making them clear by some trick of speech or of carriage is a bad method, and 'describing them at length' is a worse one; that English Fiction should have a 'conscious moral purpose'; that 'it is almost impossible to estimate too highly the value of careful workmanship—that is, 'of style'; that 'the most important point of all is the story'; that 'the story is everything'—these are principles with most of which it is surely impossible not to sympathize."

Nevertheless, James has his reservations, put forward with unwavering tact. "As I shall take the liberty of making but a single criticism of Mr. Besant, whose tone is so full of the love of his art, I may as well have done with it at once." The lecturer's rules are what have caused this fellow practitioner uneasiness. "They are suggestive, they are even inspiring, but they are not exact, though they are doubtless as much so as the case admits of." For the value of those rules—"so beautiful and so vague—is wholly in the meaning one attaches to them." Write from your own experience, Mr. Besant advises, and goes on to instruct the young lady writer in a country village what not to write about, and to caution a humbly placed writer not to introduce his characters into high society. That latter, James protests, "about the lower middle-class writer and his knowing his place, is perhaps rather chilling"; and anyway, "What kind of experience is intended, and where does it begin and end? Experience is never limited, and it is never complete"; it is rather a matter of sensibility: "The young lady living in a village has only to be a damsel upon whom nothing is lost to make it quite unfair (as it seems to me) to declare to her that she shall have nothing to say about the military."

Experience, after all, consists of impressions; and one person will need fewer impressions than another to make an experience out of them. "Therefore, if I should certainly say to a novice, 'Write from experience, and experience only,' I should feel that this was a rather tantalizing monition if I were not careful immediately to add, 'Try to be one of the people on whom nothing is lost!'" James himself was a close and careful observer all his life, highly practiced in selecting from those observations pertinent details to evoke what he had seen. He kept notes inveterately; and he could, moreover, make a great deal from the slightest hint. At a London dinner party, for instance, the actress Fanny Kemble told him about her brother's attentions to the daughter of a wealthy Cambridge University don. The young lady was homely; so her father concluded that her handsome suitor's motives must be mercenary (Miss Kemble herself, moved by sympathy, went to the girl and spoke against her brother privately). Yet the young woman had fallen deeply and obstinately in love. Whereupon the father thwarted the relationship by threatening—if his daughter persisted in her plans to marry Kemble's brother—to withhold the wealth she was due to inherit. At that news, the suitor revealed his true nature by absconding, the father proved he had been right all along, and the daughter's heart was broken. From so brief an anecdote (James declined to hear further details, which would only encumber the story he saw forming), he transferred the setting from England to New York City in the 1840s of his childhood, made the father a distinguished physician, and created the imperishable world of *Washington Square*.

That fully formed world, the entirety of which its author molded out of his imagination and the barest of hints, is palpably real. You believe unreservedly in Dr. Sloper, in Catherine, in Morris Townsend, in foolish Mrs. Penniman— believe what they say to each other, and how they say it, and how each responds, and what their motives are, and how they dress, and the furnishings and streetscapes they move among. Such an "air of reality (solidity of specification) seems to me," the creator of *Washington Square* writes in reference to Besant's lecture, "to be the supreme virtue of a novel—the merit in which all its other merits (including that conscious moral purpose of which Mr. Besant speaks) helplessly and submissively depend. If it be not there they are all as nothing, and if these be there they owe their effect to the success with which the author has produced the illusion of life."

Capturing reality thus becomes the novelist's "inspiration, his despair, his reward, his torment, his delight. It is here, in very truth, that he competes with life," James writes; "it is here that he competes with his brother, the painter, in his attempt to render the look of things, the look that conveys their meaning, to catch the color, the relief, the expression, the surface, the substance of the human spectacle." And to achieve that effect, Mr. Besant is quite correct in urging the taking of notes. The aspiring novelist, like the practiced one, "cannot possibly take too many, he cannot possibly take enough." Better still if the lecturer had told him or her what notes to take; but that skill, which no lecturer or pamphlet can teach, must become "the business of his life," the novelist's challenge and his or her constant striving to learn.

Elsewhere in his lecture, Mr. Besant speaks of different types of novels: of adventure, of character, of action—speaks of moral novels, of modern English novels. But for James, there are only two types of novels: "bad novels and good novels, as there are bad pictures and good pictures; but that is the only distinction in which I see any meaning, and I can as little imagine speaking of a novel of character as I can imagine speaking of a picture of character"—for paintings and novels both, as James understood them, are attempts to capture the air of reality. Nor is it needful in doing so to concern oneself (as Mr. Besant implies) with the separate parts of a novel: description, dialogue, plot (or action, or story). A novel isn't a machine made up of parts. Rather, it is "a living thing, all one and continuous, like every other organism, and in proportion as it lives will it be found, I think, that in each of the parts there is something of each of the other parts": the story revealing character, character determining the specific details of description, description substantiating the story. Nor, for James, is classifying novels into types very helpful. What is an adventure novel after all? What is an adventure? "It is an adventure—an immense one—for me to write this little article." Pick what you want for a subject, without regard to types. The novelist must be left free to develop whatever he or she chooses, high or low, noble or squalid. "We must grant the artist his subject, his idea, what the French call *le donnée*; our criticism is applied only to what he makes of it." The world of fiction embraces all humanity; and, as with other arts, novels thrive on experimentation. "The advantage, the luxury, as well as the torment and responsibility, of the novelist, is that there is no limit to what he may attempt." Of course if you as a reader don't care for his subject, leave his book alone. But the novelist may write on any human subject. What he or she does with it is all that matters. "The only obligation to which in advance we may hold a novel without incurring the accusation of being arbitrary, is that it be interesting."

And the only result that ultimately counts is whether a novel is good or bad: "the bad is swept, with all the daubed canvases and spoiled marble," James writes, "into some unvisited limbo or infinite rubbish-yard, beneath the back-windows of the world, and the good subsists and emits its light and stimulates our desire for perfection." Such a light back then, as far as human beings in motion were concerned, was effectively emitted only by novels. The theater (popular where available) provided somewhat of the same reportage: human behavior transmuted through art and projected more or less accurately. Narrative poetry did as well, with more or less success. In nonfiction, letters, diaries, journals, memoirs, and biographies (although often of people "greater" than ourselves, heroes and such), when assembled and published might coax us near to some sense of life as others have lived it. But only the novel does so consistently. That salient fact brought Henry James finally somewhere close to where Walter Besant started from: he ends by emphasizing for the aspiring novelist "the magnificence of the form that is open to him."

Nowadays things may look different. The novel may even be dying out—we regularly hear of its demise—as what formerly were shelves of books fill up with potted plants, display dishes, and DVDs; and the longing for stories gets appeased through the more readily apprehensible (if more passive) medium of film. But before film, think of those glorious names back then: Austen, Flaubert, Tolstoy—and what a miracle a novel appeared to be, and remains for some. The everlasting wonder of it: its portability, the richness of content captured within its pages, the shared pleasure as families gathered around their hearths to hear—as we this late can hear long-gone yet still recoverable voices in an actual person's imagination speaking out of worlds from the far past: what were then living articulations expressing what are now far-off griefs and joys and longings so like our own, those voices reaching us ever freshly and companionably from across the decades and centuries, voices from lips made immortal: Tom Jones's, Emma Woodhouse's, Wilkins Micawber's, Captain Ahab's, Madame Bovary's, Raskolnikov's, Isabel Archer's, all ready to speak again each time the worlds their novels comprise are taken in hand, in supreme instances standing ready to give expression once more to literary truths about those same griefs, joys, and longings every bit as valid as—and often more timeless than—the factual truths of history.

How is the miracle managed? Some few, like Walter Besant and Henry James, have striven to answer that question. For his part, Mark Twain—yet another nineteenth-century novelist—would list himself among the many who have little patience with such analytic inquiries. At this time, in 1884, Mark was working on *Huckleberry Finn*, which surely ranks among the supreme fictional achievements in American and world literature. Yet in the Jamesian sense, Clemens was hardly a novelist at all. Novels, in fact, didn't much interest the Missourian; for the most part, he didn't read them—he much preferred history, biography, and popular science. But how different those two towering giants were anyway: Sam Clemens of the rural South and West, out of poverty, self-taught in the frontier print shop, pilot house, and mining camp, plain-spoken skeptic whose singular clarity of expression was formed from journalists' prose and the lecture circuit, more performer than novelist, the plots of whose novels were frequently ill-shaped and episodic, but whose narrative voice was a thing of magic, all his own. Mark Twain, on the one hand, democrat often looking westward, brash and surprising and funny, his style deceptively simple and forthright, yet filled with feeling—and prodigious in its popularity. Henry James, by contrast, looking eastward, born in New York City and reared in affluence amid bookish surroundings from the start, urbane, patrician, steeped in European culture as in that of New York and New England, steeped from earliest awareness in genteel traditions and customs and manners that Sam Clemens would set about learning only after coming East in his maturity. And James's writing: observant, penetrating, wonderfully inventive and sensitive, but with a wit quieter than Mark Twain's—and a style increasingly caviare to the general, his achievement expressed in a manner increasingly subtle, convoluted, and qualified, so that Clemens (like others) wouldn't make the effort to read it. But then, the only novels Mark Twain could bear, he said, were the ones written by his friend William Dean Howells. For Howells by this present 1884 had become (in addition to his other impressive achievements as editor and literary critic) one of the premier American novelists, and the rare sort of novelist that Mark Twain professed to love. Howells's delightful *Indian Summer*, for instance, was appearing as a serial in 1885, and Clemens sat right down and read and praised the accomplishment: "you have done it with marvelous facility," he wrote from Elmira to his friend that July, "& you make all the motives & feelings perfectly clear without analyzing the guts out of them, the way George Eliot does. I can't stand George Eliot, & Hawthorne & those people; I see what they are at, a hundred years before they get to it, & they just tire me to death. And as for the Bostonians"— referring to Henry James's new novel that the *Century* was then serializing— "I would rather be damned to John Bunyan's heaven than read that."

26. CAPTURING REALITY, 1885

The heaven of Bunyan's *The Pilgrim's Progress* (1678) that Clemens hoped to avoid would put a golden crown on his head and set him to serving the

Holy One with continual praise and shouting and thanksgiving, while helping pass sentence upon the workers of iniquity, be they angels or men, with (Bunyan tells us) a say in judging each sinner as the enemy of both the Holy One and all such heavenly entrants as Clemens himself would prefer becoming, rather than read *The Bostonians*. That novel had been on James's mind while devising his response to Walter Besant's "The Art of Fiction"; it appeared in installments in the *Century* through much of 1885—the year when Howells's *Indian Summer* was serialized and Mark Twain's *Huckleberry Finn* was published—and was available in book form the following February.

James's latest work aimed at achieving something different from his earlier fiction. In one of the notebooks he kept throughout his adulthood, the author alludes to the difference: "The whole thing as local, as American, as possible, and as full of Boston; an attempt to show I *can* write an American story." What resulted was a tale of New England and New York in the mid-1870s, composed these few years later in London and filled with a "solidity of specification" that its author in responding to Besant had said provided the "air of reality" that was in general the "supreme virtue of the novel." Accordingly, *The Bostonians* records more details from daily life than had any of James's previous, "international" novels and novellas.

But then, each time he began a new novel, Henry James strove to write a different sort (there is, as he said, no limit to what the novelist may attempt), and he was a different kind of novelist anyway. Howells, the editor, fellow fiction writer, literary critic, and friend, had as early as 1882 set about defining the difference. In fact, in that same, earlier year William Dean Howells had published in the *Century* two quite remarkable essays, one in September, the other in November, one on Mark Twain, the other on Henry James, both essays brilliant in their prescient insights. The Mark Twain essay recognized, well before others did, that the Missouri humorist and by then author of, most recently, *Tom Sawyer* and *The Prince and the Pauper* was far more than merely a jokester. For one thing, he never looked for humor in the doings of the weak or vulnerable; "there is not an ungenerous line" in any of his books, "but always, on the contrary, a burning resentment of all manner of cruelty and wrong." Readers enjoying his work may miss its moralistic tendencies, but Howells insists that any who fail to take into account this author's indignation at wrongdoing and hatred of injustice will fall short of knowing the true Mark Twain. Additionally, astutely, the essayist reminds us that a mere humorist dates with the times he entertains, "as any one may see by turning back to what amused people in the last generation; that stuff is terrible." And like those earlier phunny phellows, "Mark Twain would pass with the conditions that have made him intelligible, if he were not an artist of uncommon power as well as a humorist," an artist who "portrays and interprets real types, not only with exquisite appreciation and sympathy, but with a force and truth of drawing that makes them permanent."

Truth for the ages—an assertion confirmed by Mark's continuing popularity through the many decades since (unlike, say, fellow humorists Petroleum V. Nasby or Artemus Ward, their fame long faded). That Howells was able to appreciate his friend's distinction so early may appear less surprising perhaps when we consider similarities in their backgrounds. Both—born a year and a half apart, Howells the younger—grew up in what was then, in the 1830s and 1840s, the West, the one in Missouri, the other in Ohio. Both Clemens and Howells as youngsters had forged ahead amid humble agrarian surroundings. Both were self-taught, gaining their love of language among newspapers in print shops, Clemens initially in his brother's, Howells in his father's. Both spent time on the river, Clemens on the Mississippi, Howells on a steamboat his uncle captained on the Ohio. And each when they met recognized in the other a similar sense of humor, as we've heard Clemens's daughter Clara recalling fondly, remembering the welcome that special visitor invariably received in their Hartford home: "To see him and Father enjoy a funny story or joke together was a complete show in itself."

A shared past would have encouraged Howells's appreciation of Mark Twain. That he appreciated the entirely different artistry of Henry James suggests the breadth of the man's experience and interests once he left Ohio. Like John Hay, Howells had hoped to be a poet. Moreover, he had sent poems out of Ohio to the newly founded *Atlantic* in Boston, where enough were accepted to encourage the young man to venture East in the summer of 1860 and meet his editorial benefactors. Soon he found himself dazzled at dinner at the Parker House in the company of the *Atlantic*'s editor, James Russell Lowell, and the publisher James T. Fields. Would young Howells like an introduction to Hawthorne? He emphatically would, and carried that introduction to Concord and a memorable visit with the author of *The Scarlet Letter*. And with Emerson. And with Thoreau. Back home in Columbus early in the following year, Howells (by then the author of a hasty campaign biography of Mr. Lincoln) was sorry to have missed out on a visit from a fellow poet over from Illinois, young John Hay traveling on the president-elect's train from Springfield to Washington. But Secretary Hay's call emboldened the aspirant a few months later to write to the White House in pursuit of a consular assignment in Munich. The outcome was a posting to Venice, so that Howells returned from there at the end of Mr. Lincoln's administration a cosmopolite, an author by then fluent in four foreign languages who was soon awarded the coveted position of assistant editor to the great James T. Fields at the *Atlantic Monthly*.

In that position he would encounter work submitted by young Henry James Jr.: "it was my fortune to read Mr. James's second contribution in manuscript," Howells tells us in his essay of 1882. " 'Would you take it?' asked my chief. 'Yes, and all the stories you can get from the writer.' One is much securer of one's judgment at twenty-nine than, say, at forty-five; but if this was a mistake of mine I am not yet old enough to regret it." The assistant editor had recognized at once a distinctive new voice in American fiction; "I admired, as we must in all that Mr. James has written, the finished workmanship in which there is no loss of vigor; the luminous and uncommon use of words, the originality of phrase, the whole clear and beautiful style." Other editors commended this fresh way of telling a story, so that from the start James proved successful in placing his work in the magazines. But readers of those magazines were, as Howells remembers, less partial to the novelty. James's fiction "was so strange, that, with rare exceptions, they had to 'learn to like' it." For one thing, this author's narrative voice was disinterested. Unlike Dickens and Thackeray, James merely presented, without judging; and his readers confused his impartial presentation of the various characters with his private opinion of them. "This confusion caused the tears of rage which bedewed our continent in behalf of the 'average American girl' supposed to be satirized in *Daisy Miller*, and prevented the perception of the fact that, so far as the average American girl was studied at all in *Daisy Miller*, her indestructible innocence, her invulnerable new-worldliness, had never been so delicately appreciated." Then too, Mr. James as author only glancingly addressed the unquenchable American penchant for humor: although he "portrays the humorous in character"—creates droll people enough—"he is decidedly not on humorous terms with his reader; he ignores rather than recognizes the fact that they are both in the joke." Thackeray and Dickens will nudge us toward the responses they want, providing authorial interpolations to guide us; but James in no way signals in his own voice that the characters he describes have anything ludicrous about them. On this point, Howells confesses "that I read him with a relief in the comparative immunity that he affords from the national facetiousness." For James is serious, and deals with serious matters. So the straight-out comical isn't a subject for his fiction, or the exotically fanciful, or the religio-historical, or the (ever popular) sentimental, or anything designed to hold the reader's interest by its rarity and scale. Rather, James seeks out the drama of the everyday, exploring motives of people undergoing challenges of daily life.

For he is less interested in retaining our attention through frenzy and tumult than in telling the truth about life as he and his readers live it.

The Bostonians, for example, nowhere depends for its appeal on the sensational. Early in its pages we do meet a handsome young woman of remarkable gifts, whose antecedents may be dubious—her father a fraudulent mesmerist and part-time faith healer. But Verena Tarrant's gifts are authentic, as displayed through lectures during which she holds her audiences enrapt to the final word, before releasing them to offer up their clamorous applause.

Miss Tarrant's subject is women's rights, according to James "the most salient and peculiar point in our social life" during these post–Civil War years. Since long before the war, Boston had been a center of reform, the seat of abolition that helped bring about the great conflict and shape its outcome. That outcome led directly to the Fourteenth Amendment (1868), ostensibly granting all citizens equal rights. No longer would a "person held to service or labor"—the Constitution's euphemism for a slave—be counted as three-fifths of a human being (as in the document itself, in order to appease the South by giving white southerners a larger representation in Congress than if blacks weren't counted at all). Now, with emancipation and the end of the war, every freedman had become a whole person, and a citizen able to vote. Whites down South resisted the change; but if the right to vote "is denied," the amendment reads, "to any of the *male* inhabitants"—white or black, of any state—"being twenty-one years of age, and citizens of the United States, or in any way abridged, except for participation in rebellion, or other crime, the basis of representation therein shall be reduced in the proportion which the number of such *male* citizens shall bear to the whole number of *male* citizens twenty-one years of age in such state."

My added emphasis alters the legal prose to make one word stand out; the term *male* had never intruded upon the Constitution before. Meanwhile, women had been agitating for *their* rights—themselves to vote, own property, attend universities, divorce—since before the war, most notably at Seneca Falls, New York, in 1848, where participants had rewritten the Constitution: "We hold these truths to be self-evident: that all men and women are created equal . . ." The raucous 1850s, however—with the decade's divisive Kansas-Nebraska Act, its Bleeding Kansas that followed, its appalling *Dred Scott* decision, its contentious issues that Mr. Lincoln and Judge Douglas debated—had directed the reform impulse away from women's rights to the rights of African Americans, their rights to pursue happiness and enjoy the fruits of their labor.

Freed slaves having apparently won those rights in the aftermath of Appomattox, some reformers who had worked to abolish slavery returned to agitating for an end to discrimination against women. Passing time has eroded the sharpness of James's specificities in a novel about Boston of 1875; but if we had been alive back then, we would have at once recognized the plausibility of his women's-rights lecturer Verena Tarrant. In 1872 a comely, fiery lecturer in her mid-thirties did actually run, illegally, defiantly, eloquently, for president of the United States on a liberal platform that promised women relief from their oppression (along with—among much else—labor reform and an income tax to redistribute wealth). Victoria Woodhull's father, by the way, was a shady character who put two of his teenage daughters to work as clairvoyants and faith healers, the older one Victoria, the younger one destined to become old Cornelius Vanderbilt's mistress, and the two together, gifted women both, founding a highly successful newspaper on Wall Street. James's readers of this tale of Boston, set three years after 1872, would be well acquainted with the colorful career of Victoria Woodhull, as they were with the success of Anna Dickinson, another popular lecturer of the age, with a following about as devoted as Mark Twain's. Accordingly, a female lecturer—figure commonplace in present-day America—would have struck the first readers of *The Bostonians* as by no means unlikely even in an age when women's roles were far more restricted than now.

The novel juxtaposes Miss Tarrant's views against those of Basil Ransom, of a distinguished Mississippi family that, like others in the South, had lost everything in the war. Formerly a Confederate officer, now an attorney, young Ransom has come north to recoup his fortunes. Physically, he makes a fine impression: handsome, tall, courtly. But his views on the so-called woman question are in every way opposed to those of Miss Tarrant. And again, if we were alive then, we would understand his views more readily than we do now, when they seem merely outrageous. For Ransom deplores "this fatuous agitation" for women's rights, in part because of its "pernicious effect" on women themselves, "on their manners, their person, their nature." He thus discusses his views with Miss Tarrant, with whom, despite her radicalism, he is falling in love. His dismissing of her lectures as fatuous is "very complimentary to me!" Verena breaks in lightly; but he charges on. "There are a thousand ways in which any woman, all women, married or single, may find occupation. They may find it in making society agreeable." And Verena: "Agreeable to men, of course." "To whom else, pray? Dear Miss Tarrant, what is most agreeable to women is to be agreeable to men! That is a truth as old as the human race."

What made Ransom's views more palatable to his age than they are to ours was the idealization of women throughout this later nineteenth century and into the twentieth, their being placed on very high pedestals. We've heard Sam

Clemens positioning Miss Langdon thus after their first meeting, where he viewed her as "a visiting *Spirit* from the upper air—a something to worship, reverently & at a distance"—an attitude never entirely absent from his and Livy's later married life. As did John Hay place his Clara on a pedestal. As did countless other Victorians in those transformative postwar years, in an America in flux as the nation expanded and immigrants poured in and fortunes were made at every turn, in land, oil, steel, beef, timber, mining, railroads— everywhere you looked fortunes made and lost and made again, and values flouted out there in the amoral marketplace, where men scrambled and clawed for the nation's peacetime prizes. But the home—the near-sacred home— sheltered moralities of an earlier time and passed those on, mothers (such was the ideal) nurturing their children in kindness and sympathy, in tenderness, generosity, honesty, and mutual helpfulness. In such crucial ways women made society agreeable, whereas without their influence life threatened to descend unchecked into ruthless competitiveness and dog eat dog.

At the start of *The Bostonians*, Basil Ransom brings his conservative, courtly doctrines up from the South via New York at the invitation of a distant cousin, Olive Chancellor, who is performing what she considers a familial duty. But almost as soon as he arrives in Boston, Olive takes a dislike to this visiting relative; for the wealthy Miss Chancellor is an ardent supporter of women's rights herself, and upon hearing Verena Tarrant lecture for the first time, on an occasion that the dutiful hostess has invited Mr. Ransom to attend with her—hearing Verena speak so forcefully, so movingly—Olive is enthralled, all but overwhelmed.

The novel at its core is a struggle between Olive Chancellor and Basil Ransom for the possession of Miss Tarrant's future. Olive persuades the beautiful lecturer to come stay with her, and in their days together she fills her protégée with "the history of feminine anguish. They perused that chapter perpetually and zealously, and they derived from it the purest part of their mission. Olive had pored over it so long, so earnestly, that she was now in complete possession of the subject." Thus she could demonstrate to Verena "how the exquisite weakness of women had never been their defence, but had only exposed them to sufferings more acute than masculine grossness can conceive. Their odious partner had trampled upon them from the beginning of time, and their tenderness, their abnegation, had been his opportunity. All the bullied wives, the stricken mothers, the dishonoured, deserted maidens who have lived on the earth and longed to leave it, passed and repassed before her eyes." And she led Verena to witness that sad, interminable procession, and extracted a pledge from her young friend that she would never marry.

Instead, the two women would live together in joy and furtherance of what they both believed in—Olive fulfilled through the eloquence that Verena possessed in such measure as to serve their shared cause gloriously.

Ransom for his part never hid his views that women were "infinitely tiresome when they declined to accept the lot which men had made for them. He had the most definite notions about their place in nature, in society, and was perfectly easy in his mind as to whether it excluded them from any proper homage." Of course they deserved homage. And respect—and the "chivalrous man paid that tax with alacrity. He admitted their rights; these consisted in a standing claim to the generosity and tenderness of the stronger race. The exercise of such feelings was full of advantage for both sexes, and they flowed most freely, of course, when women were gracious and grateful."

The novel—it is a long one, filled throughout with vivid subsidiary characters and palpable atmosphere—presents those two contrasting viewpoints on a contemporary issue with the dispassion that Howells had attributed to James's method in his essay of 1882. We are not privy to the author's own opinions, although led fully to comprehend what motivates Miss Chancellor and Mr. Ransom in theirs. And in the end, it is Ransom who prevails in the struggle. "I am to understand, then, as your last word," Verena says to Basil at a moment late in the story, "that you regard us as quite inferior?" To which he answers: "For public, civic uses, absolutely—perfectly weak and second-rate. I know of nothing more indicative of the muddled sentiment of the time than that any number of men should be found to pretend that they regard you in any other light. But privately, personally, it's another affair. In the realm of family life and the domestic affections—." "Don't say that," she interrupts; "it's only a phrase." "Well, it's a better one than any of yours," the southerner insists, always in kindly manner, pressing his suit.

And he wins her. In the concluding scene Ransom succeeds in persuading Verena to flee with him from the lecture hall and the audience impatiently awaiting the sound of her stirring voice. "Ah, now I am glad!" she says as the two reach the street, her public career abandoned. Yet we're told that the lovers' path forward will not be easy. Ransom has already assured Verena that she will be "poor, withdrawn from view, a partner of his struggle"; so that even this early and despite her professed gladness, the hood that obscures her features hides a face in tears. "It is to be feared," the novel's final sentence reads, "that with the union, so far from brilliant, into which she was about to enter, these were not the last she was destined to shed."

Such an ending leaves much unresolved. But as Howells suggests in his 1882 essay, what Henry James writes is sufficiently different as to raise a question of the satisfactions we should be looking for when we pick up a novel in the first place. "By example, at least," the critic clarifies, this author "teaches that it is the pursuit and not the end which should give us pleasure; for he often prefers to leave us to our own conjectures in regard to the fate of the people in whom he has interested us." In other words, "it is the character, not the fate, of his people which occupies him; when he has fully developed their character he leaves them to what destiny the reader pleases."

James's penetration in developing his characters is what compels our interest. By contrast, to the extent that *The Bread-Winners* still interests us at all, the characters as such in John Hay's anonymous novel interest us very little. From its opening page, Arthur Farnham appears as undiluted rectitude in motion, and the villainous Andrew Jackson Offitt remains a villain from his first appearance to his violent demise. All of Hay's characters (with maybe Maud as the single exception) are cardboard thin: Mrs. Belding, her beautiful daughter Alice, the befuddled Sleeny—all are there in service to the plot, the twists of which (both plausible and less so), in an American city of the 1870s, are what keep us turning the pages.

Hay does provide pleasures of setting—but Henry James does, too, in the latter's fresh descriptions of Boston in a horse-drawn age, of New York City, of a Cape Cod village. Along with other pleasures less evident in his friend Hay's novel—pleasures that so brief a treatment as this must slight, but that Howells has already suggested: "the finished workmanship in which there is no loss of vigor; the luminous and uncommon use of words, the originality of phrase, the whole clear and beautiful style." Yet it is James's handling of character that is distinctive, modern, un-Thackerayesque, un-Dickensian: the close analysis of characters' motives that Mark Twain insisted he couldn't stand (but how much of Clemens's goadings, about Hawthorne, George Eliot, and all those people who just tired him to death—how much of that is set down to tease his friend Howells, who adored each of the writers Clemens castigates?). It is fascinating, in any case: so many of the great novels of the nineteenth century are sociological, moving horizontally, geographically, among exterior events that we all agree matter. An anonymous donor bequeathes a young man a fortune. A couple wed. Someone of consequence dies and we attend the funeral. Yet here is Henry James composing a novel, on the *socio*logical theme of women's rights, that emphasizes his characters' *psych*ology, their private, interior promptings, moving vertically into their depths to account for what they do. "No other novelist, except George Eliot," Howells writes in his 1882 essay, "has dealt so largely in analysis of motive, has so fully explained and commented upon the springs of action in the persons of the drama, both before and after the facts." And he goes on, in a passage that raised shrieks of protest on both sides of the Atlantic, with savage retorts and belittling cartoons—towering statue of the late great William Makepeace Thackeray, author of *Vanity Fair* and *Henry Esmond*, six feet three in life, serenely godlike in death, beside whom pitiable little Howells, elevated on bound copies of the *Century*, hoists on his shoulders little, pitiful James, whose head even so reaches only to the far greater Thackeray's collarbone. "The art of fiction," wrote Howells in provoking such scorn, "has, in fact, become a finer art in our day than it was with Dickens and Thackeray. We could not suffer the confidential attitude of the latter now, nor the mannerism of the former"—all those musical cue notes provided in the authors' own voices—"any more than we could endure the prolixity of Richardson or the coarseness of Fielding. These great men are of the past—they and their methods and interests." What preoccupies the greatest writers of the present—and of the post-Freudian future in a coming, alienated age (Proust, Joyce?)—is "human nature much more in its wonted aspects," in its ordinary, customary behavior. Thus modern fiction declines to examine such motives of momentous public import as, say, why Booth shot Lincoln, or why the Founders when drawing up the Constitution felt moved to appease the South by grotesquely designating blacks as three-fifths humans, but rather "lighter but not really less vital motives. The moving accident is certainly not its trade; and it prefers to avoid all manner of dire catastrophes." Accordingly, the thematic climax of *The Bostonians* occurs quietly, during a man and a woman's private conversation on a bench in Central Park.

This new way of writing, according to Howells as of 1882, "finds its chief exemplar in Mr. James; it is he who is shaping and directing American fiction, at least." In closing his remarkable essay, a fellow author and critic admits that he himself likes a story that finishes by resolving the issues it raises; "but then also I like those which Mr. James seems not to finish. This is probably the position of most of his readers, who cannot very logically account for either preference. We can only make sure that we have here an annalist, or analyst, as we choose, who fascinates us from his first page to his last, whose narrative or whose comment may enter into any minuteness of detail without fatiguing us, and can only truly grieve us when it ceases."

27. NICOLAY AND HAY

From childhood on, William James—psychologist, philosopher, Harvard professor—critiqued his younger brother's doings. In this present 1885, for

A LITERARY COMBINATION.

*"A Literary Combination." Howells is asking, "Are you the tallest now, Mr. James?"
to which the other responds, "Be so uncommonly kind, Howells, as to let me down easy;
it may be we have both got to grow." From Life, February 22, 1883, p. 91.
Courtesy of the Boston Athenaeum.*

instance, after reading in the *Century* the first installment of *The Bostonians*, William in Massachusetts complained—in a letter that hasn't survived beyond the one sentence that the aggrieved Henry in London quotes in response— about the novel's characterization of a Miss Birdseye. "It is really a pretty bad business," the older brother had adjudged of Henry's creative effort; nor was he alone in seeing in James's bumbling, fictional spinster an actual person still alive, still esteemed as a woman who had devoted her life to reform. Of the living Elizabeth Peabody's two sisters, one had married Nathaniel Hawthorne, the other Horace Mann. Elizabeth herself, who never married, filled her own years with distinction by assisting in the 1830s at Bronson Alcott's Temple School in Boston and providing an indispensable firsthand account of that progressive experiment, by founding a bookstore that among much else promoted Hawthorne's early work, by hosting Margaret Fuller's celebrated Conversations there, by helping Fuller and Emerson edit *The Dial*, and by introducing kindergartens into American education. Yet though never doubting Miss Peabody's many merits, Henry James protested that his Miss Birdseye, like his other characters, was a composite; only the spectacles askew on her nose had been suggested by the figure of the venerable reformer. Still, he would be sorry for Miss Peabody's being under a misperception and, if his brother or anybody else found out she was, would write her an abject, respectful apology. For "I absolutely had no shadow of such an intention. I have not seen Miss Peabody for twenty years, I never had but the most casual observation of her, I didn't know whether she was alive or dead, and she was not in the smallest degree my starting point or example." That said, Miss Birdseye, although a minor character, "is, I think, the best figure in the book," Henry told his brother, and added that he regarded *The Bostonians* as "the best fiction I have written"—a not uncommon assertion from writers about their most recent effort—"and I expected you, if you said anything about it, would intimate that you thought as much—so that I find this charge on the subject of Miss P. a very cold douche indeed."

Another letter from William arrived lamenting the dawdling pace of his brother's narrative as encountered in later monthly installments. But the following spring, by May 1886, after the serial had completed its run and *The Bostonians* was available in book form, William had a change of heart. "I seize my pen the first leisure moment I have had for a week," he wrote to Henry eagerly, "to tell you that I have read *The Bostonians* in the full flamingness of its bulk, and consider it an exquisite production. My growling letter," he explained, "was written to you before the end of Book I had appeared." Now,

though, with the novel as a whole to consider without the month-long interruptions of its magazine installments, William could see excellences aplenty.
"There isn't a hair wrong in Verena," for instance; "you've made her neither
too little nor too much—but absolutely *liebenswürdig*," worthy of love, ador-
able. "It would have been so easy to spoil her picture by some little excess or
false note. Her moral situation, between Woman's rights and Ransom, is of
course deep, and her discovery of the truth on the Central Park day, etc.,
inimitably given." As for Basil Ransom, this same brother had happened while
in Washington recently to run into John Hay, who told him that Senator
Lamar, well qualified to judge, had remarked on how much he was enjoying
the portrayal of a fellow Mississippian in Henry James's new novel.

So authoritative an endorsement came from the notable Lucius Quintus
Cincinnatus Lamar II, before the war a member of the U.S. House of Representatives, author in December 1860 of Mississippi's Ordinance of Secession,
colonel in the Confederate Army, later Confederate minister to Russia and its
special envoy to England and France, and—after the war, having made his
peace with the Union and been granted its pardon—representative from Mississippi in the U.S. House once more, then in the Senate. Here in the mid-
1880s, Lamar was serving as secretary of the interior in the cabinet of the
Democrat Grover Cleveland, who, in 1888, would appoint Honorable Lucius
Q. C. Lamar to the U.S. Supreme Court. Also, that gentleman was one of the
few Mississippians Henry James had ever spoken with, and thus of necessity
an example when fashioning Basil Ransom, the one southerner in the novel
and, as such, a creative challenge that James of New York and London had
labored hard to get right.

Brother William's most recent letter, by the way, had gone on to assert that
readers "who crave more matter and less art" will likely be put off by the
subject and length of *The Bostonians*. "I can truly say, however, that as I have
lain on my back after dinner each day for ten days past reading it to myself, my
enjoyment has been complete." Descriptive passages had furnished particular
pleasure: "The way you have touched off the bits of American nature, Central
Park, the Cape, etc., is exquisitely true and call up just the feeling." William
thought to add: "Knowing you had done such a good thing makes the meekness of your reply to me last summer all the more wonderful"—his new tone
sure to salve any wounds festering in the brothers' complex relationship.

And Henry could take comfort in the news that L. Q. C. Lamar of Missis-
sippi found Basil Ransom credible. James's brother had learned of that from
Colonel Hay, who spoke with him on one of the colonel's several visits to
Washington from Cleveland. For Hay's co-author Nicolay lived in the federal

capital, and there kept under his charge Robert Todd Lincoln's dozens of boxes of White House documents. From those, the former secretaries were at last making solid progress on their long-projected history of the Lincoln years. So much progress that New York publishers, indifferent back in the late 1860s when John Hay first approached them, were now clamoring for the work. In New York this same spring of 1885, young Harper had told Hay that his publishing house was counting on it, had to have it; and—among numerous others—Gilder of the *Century* wanted the Lincoln, too. Accordingly, in July, that same Richard Watson Gilder journeyed to New Hampshire, to John Nicolay's cottage up there, and lingered two or three days reading 114 chapters straight through. The immersion led the *Century* to offer for serial and book rights $50,000, a temptation unprecedented (at the very least $1,250,000 now), well beyond the authors' resisting; so that a first installment, which Hay had composed about Lincoln's childhood and youth, was soon being scheduled to run in Gilder's magazine for November 1886.

The date lay nearly a year in the future; yet even that late, up to half the massive project remained to be written. Serials often began that way. For instance, early portions of Dickens's novels—each crowded with fresh characters acting out long, complicated plots—were in the hands of magazine readers before the author had worked through details of what to put in his late pages. Similarly with *The Bostonians*: the beginning of James's novel was in print in the *Century* while the later chapters were being composed—a practice that did at least allow that particular author to address his brother's earlier complaint. James was able to modify readers' first impression of Miss Birdseye ("a confused, entangled, inconsequent, discursive old woman," we are told near the start, "whose charity began at home and ended nowhere, whose credulity kept pace with it, and who knew less about her fellow creatures, if possible, after fifty years of humanity zeal, than on the day she had gone into the field to testify against the iniquity of most arrangements")—let James late in the novel qualify so barbed an impression with one more favorable. Toward the end of *The Bostonians*, a scene on Cape Cod relates Miss Birdseye's final moments before her gentle death, surrounded by admirers on a cottage porch at sunset. "You mustn't think," she murmurs at the last, "there's no progress because you don't see it all right off; that's what I wanted to say. It isn't till you have gone a long way that you can feel what's been done. That's what I see when I look back from here; I see that the community wasn't half waked up when I was young." The scene, among the most touching in the novel, provides a poignant tribute to the usefulness of one long, devoted life, here at its peaceful end among friends able to convey their gratitude and love.

So on occasion, for all its drawbacks, the earlier method of serial publication could provide a novelist with benefits, as it goaded him or her to get on with the job. But the pressure applied was formidable, installments already in print restricting the choices that fiction writers might make in devising what lay ahead. By contrast, Nicolay and Hay's nonfiction was free of that burden for the most part, time having disclosed the narrative shape—we know that Lincoln was shot—even as historical writing presented its own set of difficulties to fray authors' nerves.

Both Hay and Nicolay struggled with those challenges. One such inheres in every monumental task: just about every writer in the toils of a massive effort (the novelists Proust and Joyce, for two) must feel concern about living to finish it. As far back as the Civil War White House, Nicolay in his early thirties was away from his desk sometimes for weeks, recuperating out West; Hay's letters of the time worry about his co-worker's frailty. And as late as 1885, Nico is still struggling with eye troubles. Hay, too (as we've seen), suffered through much of his life from debilitating ailments, even as doctors on two continents found little specific to treat him for. The symptoms were real: headaches, colds, insomnia, heart palpitations, double vision, buzzing in the ears, inability to walk ten rods (the patient professed to feel fine otherwise) or get even that far without staggering as though drunk as a lord, although, he grumbled, without the hilarity or rum. Such complaints were generally attributed to nerves exacerbated by the faster pace of modern, industrializing life: noise, urban traffic, railroads. For Hay's ills, physicians most often prescribed rest, easy travel, and hot baths in watering places.

Thus ill health through recent years had imposed interruptions and postponements on the Lincoln project—as, with Hay, had editorializing, politics, and public service. But it was time to complete the drawn-out effort. "I am working like a Turk," the colonel wrote Nico from Cleveland in July 1885, specifying how much he had done on their common task since his last letter, then adding: "I am impelled by a fiend of hurry who yells in my ear, 'Finish! finish! and get it off your stomach!' If I could keep my present pace without breaking down we should be through easily in two years."

Their being in separate cities added its strain. The tasks had been apportioned between them, Nicolay generally preferring research on the Lincoln years and its politics, Hay the military and biographical sections. Material arrived from Washington. "Your package of documents is received," Hay reported of one such delivery, "and I regard it with dread and terror—like a magician contemplating a demon that he has raised and cannot lay. I will try to tackle it next week. I don't know where or how to begin—but will sail in anyhow." Near the end of the same year, 1885, he was writing to his friend: "I find *Murfreesboro* can be done concisely in less than a chapter. Are you doing Buell's *'Perryville'* Campaign? If not, I could sketch it in as an introduction to Murfreesboro and save that much space."

Because yet another worry—hardly unique with historians writing about the recent past—was an overabundance of material. Compression was called for, despite a most generous allotment of space in which to tell their story. The *Century* for its money would end by printing up to thirty-five double-columned pages of the *Lincoln* in every monthly issue through more than three years, from November 1886 to February 1890; and yet the magazine published only a third of the total. For the authors, surmounting all obstacles, did live to finish their project, which, once done, extended through a million and a half words into ten large volumes: *Abraham Lincoln: A History.* Ten volumes, with much left out even so. "I have been going over your schedule with some care in connection with the work I am doing," Hay wrote to his collaborator from Cleveland earlier in this same 1885, "and I can't help seeing a radical difference of view between us as to the extent of treatment to be given to each topic. For instance: You indicate as separate chapters, The President's War Council.—Stanton.—President's War Order.—President's Plan.—McClellan's Fiasco." But Hay had got all of that into a single chapter. "Again you have 'Manassas Evacuated' and 'To the Peninsula.' I shall make one short chapter of both." Looking ahead to Antietam and Burnside, the colonel planned to cover the ground in ten chapters, each of which he enumerated so that Nicolay might see—material that his collaborator off in Washington had allowed fifteen chapters for. "Now there is certainly matter enough to make 15 or 50 chapters of it, but I judge from my own weariness of the subject that no living man will read more than I am writing. We will be happy if they read as much."

Far off, meanwhile, Nicolay pushed on with his assigned portions. "There is Mexico and Diplomacy," Hay reminded him, "but until I have read what you have done I do not know how to tackle those. I had thought of doing Mexico and Maximilian in one—beginning with a long retrospect—but I have not the material here. I cannot begin in the middle of the Western Campaign without reading your articles on the earlier incidents."

That each was writing his sections independently made for yet another trial, the weightier because they had agreed that readers mustn't know which collaborator wrote what, the two having resolved to share credit and blame equally. Earlier, both had published books, Hay much the better known author—and the more sparkling stylist. Yet for this present task he was extinguishing the sparkle. The subject was grave, somber. And in any case, any heightened emotion or scolding invective would damage their presentation: "It would be taken to show that we were still in the gall and bitterness of twenty years ago." Nor should they allow themselves to turn into a couple of old dotards issuing a multivolume stump speech for the North or the Republican Party. Instead, "we ought to write the history of those times like two everlasting angels who know everything, judge everything, tell the truth about everything, and don't care a twang of their harps about one side or the other." With a single exception, fervently agreed on: "We are Lincoln men all through. But in other little matters, let us look at men as insects and not blame the black beetle because he is not a grasshopper."

One other point Hay mentions in passing: "we will not fall in with the present tone of blubbering sentiment," by which he meant this current sentimentalizing of the great conflict two decades after the cannon fell silent. All this about Reconciliation: Billy Yank and Johnny Reb clasping hands (white hands, of course) and returning captured flags at mellow reunions on grown-over battlefields. The Blue and the Gray—subscribing to Jeff Davis's formulation, in his memoir of 1881, of a war between the states, which posited two sovereign nations in gallant combat over the noble cause of states' rights. But that wasn't what the bloodletting was about. We Lincoln men were there; we know. We heard the Tycoon. The war was about a rebellion against the Union. "My paramount object in this struggle is to save the Union," Lincoln had written to Mr. Greeley in the midst of it; and precisely for that reason the president had refused to negotiate with southerners at Niagara Falls who purported to speak for a sovereign country, for the "Confederate States of America." No such entity existed—only insurgents rebelling against the Union; Hay himself, with Horace Greeley at the Falls in 1864, had delivered Lincoln's message to that effect. Now, with the war long past, the battlefields quiet, and the North—fed up with Reconstruction and weary of meddling in southern matters—having abandoned freed slaves down there to the unleashed fury of whites bent on restoring their prewar dominance, Nicolay and Hay must publish their work in order to remind Americans that the war that freed those slaves had been fought not over states' rights at all. The South had fought to preserve slavery; the North, to preserve the Union.

They must finish, in addition, so that their countrymen would know who Abraham Lincoln was. For soon after the assassination a spate of biographies had appeared—Raymond's (1865), Holland's, Arnold's, Carpenter's (all 1866)—treating the martyred president in near hagiographic terms. Out in

Springfield, meanwhile, Billy Herndon, Lincoln's law partner for sixteen years, who knew the man as a human being with human faults, had begun simultaneously, in the spring of 1865, to gather information about the townsman he had worked with and loved. Toward that end Herndon wrote former secretary John Hay to ask for intimate recollections of his chief; and young Hay, by then at the Legation in Paris, had responded. Herndon wrote to and called on many others, spent much time traveling over Illinois and into Indiana talking with people who had known Lincoln in his manhood and youth. What they told him, with what he knew from his own observations, the attorney summarized in a couple of startling lectures that disclosed a Lincoln quite different from the hagiographers': a far truer portrait, as he saw it, the real Lincoln. Herndon's notes—for he fell on hard times that left him unable to write his book—were bought and shaped into a ghostwritten tome (1872) under Ward Hill Lamon's name. That source shared with a wider audience what Herndon had uncovered about his partner's life, much of it previously unknown. Many details were commendable, entirely to Lincoln's credit. But some appeared as warts on the earlier, hallowed portrait: about his mother's alleged illegitimacy; about his disdain for his father; about the only true love affair of Lincoln's life, in New Salem, tragically cut short by Ann Rutledge's death at eighteen; about the subsequent grief that darkened the bereft lover's moods from then on, so strong at times as to verge on the suicidal; about his lack of conventional religious faith—"Mr. Lincoln was never a member of any church, nor did he believe in the divinity of Christ"—about the marriage he entered into later with the often appalling Mary Todd, and the embarrassments she caused him in the White House; about Lincoln's "overweening ambition, and the breathless eagerness with which he pursued the objects of it"—and his cool self-assurance (nothing humble about him except his beginnings) and the surprising fact that he read very little, although he did think a great deal, Herndon confirmed—more than most Americans—and never resorted to tricks or baseness in pursuit of what were invariably high purposes and policy.

With such contrasting revelations to confuse the public consciousness—warts-and-all challenging the hagiographic—Hay and Nicolay felt all the more compelled to get into print their own intimate knowledge of the Abraham Lincoln they had grown uniquely close to through four years of crisis. Behind what they set down lay a resource that no other biographer had access to: Lincoln's White House papers, eighteen thousand documents that were the property of the martyred president's one surviving son, Robert Todd Lincoln.

And Bob, a friend of theirs for a quarter of a century, would be allowed to see and approve every word of their manuscript, to delete or emend at his pleasure.

It turned out, judged by what survives of the manuscript, that Lincoln's son found little to cavil at, the little having to do with Hay's (quite accurate) depiction of Thomas Lincoln, Abraham's father. Bob felt sorry for his grandfather; might it not be better to ease up on a simple, illiterate farmer's shiftless indolence, thrust into notice only because his son had achieved so much? Hay made the changes, but it was good taste as much as censorship that moved him to do so. For like Robert Lincoln, the colonel valued taste highly. Thus, for example, Hay felt he had no business intruding on nuptial intimacies, so that Bob looking over the account of his mother and father's marriage met with nothing he needed to query.

Good taste led to all such (for us enfeebling) discretions. Yet within the bounds of taste, Hay and Nicolay would tell the truth. There was no reason not to. With their massive effort set to begin serialization in November, the colonel addressed Robert Lincoln in early January 1886. "Year after year of study has shown me more clearly than ever," Hay wrote, "how infinitely greater your father was than anybody about him, greater than ever we imagined while he lived. There is nothing to explain or apologize for from beginning to end. He is the one unapproachably great figure of a great epoch."

28. THE FIVE OF HEARTS

In that same January 1886, with pages and pages of their history yet to write, John Hay moved from Cleveland to Washington, partly to be near his collaborator, John George Nicolay. But he made the move more particularly in response to an even closer friendship, the closest of all Hay's many friendships over a gregarious lifetime. This one was with Henry Adams.

The two were born in the same year, 1838; Hay in Indiana, into a family of modest means, his father the village doctor. Eight months earlier, in mid-February, Adams had been born in Boston, into the most famous family in the United States. His great grandfather was John Adams, our second president; his grandfather was John Quincy Adams, the sixth president; and his father was Charles Francis Adams, gifted historian, legislator, and—all during the Civil War—Lincoln's very able minister to Great Britain. So young Henry entered life with every advantage, even his *maternal* grandfather one of Massachusetts's wealthiest citizens. The young man had gone to Harvard, graduated with distinction, embarked on the Grand Tour of Europe, studied to good purpose abroad, returned and was in the midst of the tumult in Washington during the secession winter of 1860-61 as private secretary to his father, who by then was representing Massachusetts in Congress. Thus through those turbulent times both Adams and Hay served as secretaries to public dignitaries, with Lincoln that spring designating Congressman Charles Francis Adams to be his minister in London. The next seven years, then, from 1861 to 1868, Adams's son Henry spent in England, as the ambassador's secretary.

During those years overseas, young Henry Adams grew informed in the intricacies of diplomacy, as did John Hay back in Washington. And like Hay, Adams wrote for the journals, serving as English correspondent for the *New York Times* and publishing substantial articles on an impressive range of subjects in such respected periodicals as the *North American Review*. At thirty, the young man returned home with his family at the end of his father's term as ambassador, its great achievement Minister Adams's having kept the English—a powerful majority of whom leaned toward the Confederacy—neutral throughout the war. The son by then was recognized as brilliant and able in his own right, invited two years later, in 1870, to become editor of the *North American Review* and to teach medieval history at Harvard.

Gifted and innovative in the classroom, Henry Adams—*Review* editor for six years—remained at Harvard for seven. In the course of those years the professor married Marian Hooper, daughter of a prominent Boston physician. Known as Clover, she was a young woman whom Henry James—his career as a fiction writer just getting started—had become acquainted with as well, in Cambridge in the late 1860s. An image from then preserves a glimpse of those people full of innocent life. One writes to another in February 1869: "I went to a delightful little party of Clover Hooper's, where I conversed for a long time with your friend Mr. Harry James . . ." And James himself, in September 1870, inquires of a correspondent: "Do you know Henry Adams?—Son of C.F.A. He has just been appointed professor of history in College, and is I believe a youth of genius and enthusiasm—or at least of talent and energy." In June 1872, that same Adams married Miss Hooper at her father's summer home north of Boston, and within a month the two embarked on a year-long honeymoon in England, Switzerland, Germany, Italy, and, by early December, in Egypt, there to partake of a three-month cruise along the Nile.

From Rome, Henry James writes to his brother William in April 1873: "In the way of old friends we have been having Henry Adams and his wife, back from Egypt and (last) from Naples, each with what the doctor pronounced the germs of typhus fever. But he dosed them and they mended and asked me to dinner." Their guest found his hosts pleasant and friendly, "and (as to A.)

improved. Mrs. Clover has had her wit clipped a little I think—but I suppose has expanded in the affections."

Her wit was what had drawn Henry Adams to Clover in the first place: that and her high intelligence, the freshness of her thought and expression, her sense of irony, her love of horseback riding, and her taste in furnishings (from their honeymoon travels the two brought back twenty-five wooden crates filled with such furnishings). Every Sunday morning as appropriate, abroad or at home, Clover wrote a letter to her father, to whom she was devoted. Those Dr. Hooper dated and scrupulously preserved, and their progress shows no such diminution of wit as James imagined. For example, like some others, Clover grew impatient reading *The Portrait of a Lady* (1881), with its tendency to analyze motives rather than get on with the plot. Harry James's next novel should be titled *Ann Eliza*, she wrote to her father; it wasn't so much that he bit off more than he could chew as that he chewed more than he bit off. She and her husband were living in Washington by then, Adams having resigned from Harvard, in 1877, and after four years of residence in Boston near his family—and close to Clover's father—moved to the federal capital. Ostensibly they went south so that Henry could consult government archives, preparing to undertake biographical and historical writing. The couple leased a home facing Lafayette Park opposite the White House, and soon felt at their ease: going on long walks and horseback rides together; making their domicile with its treasures of carpets, watercolors, and bric-a-brac inviting; and regularly entertaining interesting friends and acquaintances. Henry's historical studies meanwhile were prospering, to the extent that another trip to Europe was called for, to consult archives in London, Paris, Madrid, and Seville. Thus, in late May 1879, Mr. and Mrs. Adams sailed from New York bound for Liverpool.

By mid-June, they were settled in London, at 17 Half Moon Street, Henry James's Bolton Street flat no more than a block away. "The Henry Adamses are here—," the novelist wrote to a friend late in the month, "very pleasant, friendly, conversational, critical, ironical. They are to be here all summer and to go in the autumn to Spain; then to return here for the winter. Clover chatters rather less, and has more repose, but she is very nice, and I sat up with them till one o'clock this morning abusing the Britons."

During this months-long interlude, James saw the Adamses "launched very happily in London life. They are extremely friendly, pleasant and colloquial, and it is agreeable to have in London a couple of good American *confidents*." In Paris in September, the threesome reunited, together on Clover's birthday when she turned thirty-six (almost precisely five months after James had). She described the occasion for her father: "Mr. and Mrs. Jack Gardner, Mr. James, and we to dine in an open-air restaurant and then to the *cirque*, where Mademoiselle Jutan, an angelic blonde, filled our hearts with wonder and joy; then ices on the Boulevard in front of a café, and home at midnight." As late as September 1880, following upon their many evenings together, James writes from England: "I go in an hour to bid farewell to my friends the Henry Adamses, who after a year of London life are returning to their beloved Washington. One sees so many 'cultivated Americans' who prefer being abroad that it is a great refreshment to encounter two specimens of this class who find the charms of their native land so much greater than those of Europe." He did feel they were perhaps "rather too critical and invidious. I shall miss them much, though—we have had such inveterate discussions and comparing of notes. They have been much liked here."

And were liked back home, in Washington, and envied, and invitations to the Adamses' teas and dinners coveted as much on their return as before their leaving. Earlier, in February 1878, Mr. and Mrs. Hay—he in town to consult with Nicolay—had been welcomed into one such gathering on H Street, where only stimulating guests were met with, dullness the sole disqualifier. Clover's teas occurred daily at 5 o'clock, and the conversation among authors, artists, statesmen, their wives, and interesting passers-through was invariably lively and entertaining. Adams and Hay had met first, if briefly, maybe in the spring of 1861, assuredly by 1865, when the newly appointed Secretary Hay on his way to his duties at the Paris Legation paid a courtesy call on Minister Charles Francis Adams in London. Thirteen years later the younger gentlemen renewed their acquaintance, which soon became a fast friendship. But the Adamses were still overseas when Hay returned to Washington in late 1879 as assistant secretary of state in the Hayes administration; they were back no earlier than the fall of 1880, to settle again on H Street.

Thereafter, so close did the friendship become that the four of them and one other—that is, Henry Adams, Clover Adams, John Hay, Clara Hay, and Clarence King—informally formalized their special relationship as the Five of Hearts. Hay ordered from Tiffany's enameled pins that the five might wear at reunions, and had stationery made with a small Five of Hearts imprinted on it. To her pleasure, he designated Clover first of the Hearts, the heart in the five-card's upper-left corner. And King had a heart-shaped tea set made for their use when they came together. Clarence King was a prepossessing, eloquent explorer, mountaineer, geologist, and head of the just-founded U.S. Geological Survey, whom the others in that mostly brilliant group of five considered the most brilliant among them. But he was flighty as well, unreliable.

After successfully exploring and surveying out West (it was King who exposed the fraudulence of the Colorado diamond field that Greeley, McClellan, and other gullibles including young Hay had invested in in the early 1870s), he would go on applying his gifts to seeking a fortune from mining ventures in Mexico, an aspiration that kept the charming, much loved, but elusive King on the move, often in Europe trying to rustle up investors and thus depriving the other four Hearts of his company.

From this point forward, however, John Hay and Henry Adams stayed in virtually constant touch with each other, each the other's closest friend for the remainder of their days. The abundant letters they exchanged attest to the richness and rewards of their friendship. Each could be entirely himself with the other, even though they differed on crucial matters: Adams a Democrat, Hay the most ardent of Republicans; Adams at this stage of his life reform-minded, Hay by now wary of anything that bred agitators or jostled the status quo. Both, though, shared a reverence for the great English historians Gibbon and Macaulay; and as Hay under their influence was engaged with Nicolay in writing a multivolume chronicle of Lincoln and his times, so Henry Adams—having edited the papers of Albert Gallatin, Jefferson's secretary of the treasury, and written a biography of him, and one of the eccentric congressman John Randolph of Roanoke—was launching a monumental effort toward what would become, he thought, a three-volume study of the United States in the administrations of Jefferson and Madison, from 1801 to 1817. In the event, the undertaking at its completion in 1891 came to nine volumes, an achievement that readers best qualified to judge have valued as the greatest single work of history ever written by an American.

Over an earlier Christmas, Henry James had been visiting his family in New England for the first time in six years, after which he paid an initial visit to Washington, in January 1882. By then, John Hay was back in Cleveland, his services in the state department ended, as was his stint replacing the honeymooning Whitelaw Reid in the editor's chair at the *Tribune*. So James didn't see Hay; but the novelist spent much time with Henry and Clover Adams on that occasion, benefiting from their salon that gave them a wide acquaintance with interesting figures—"I have seen a good many people, chiefly under the influence of the Adamses and find the social arrangements and the tone of conversation very easy and genial"—until the novelist was summoned urgently back to Cambridge, tardily as it turned out, not reaching his family's Quincy Street home until shortly after his mother died.

And it was in the following year, in the fall of 1883, that Henry Adams grew alarmed at a developer's plans to erect a six-story apartment building on a lot adjacent to his own rented house on H Street. With Mr. Stone's recent demise, was there anything keeping Hay in Cleveland? The two friends talked about it. Adams was well off certainly, and his wife had her own income; but neither could approach such affluence as the Hays now possessed. By December, four of the Hearts had bought the next-door lot for an extravagant $75,000, a third of that the Adamses' smaller portion, their home to be built for only the two of them; with $50,000 as the Hay family's larger share—a grander home to be erected on the corner, at H Street and 16th. They hired Adams's friend and Harvard classmate H. H. Richardson, architect (among much else of note) of Trinity Church in Boston's Copley Square and of Sever Hall at Harvard, to draw up plans. In March 1884, Richardson brought drawings to Washington for his clients to inspect. Both the Hays and the Adamses were delighted, Clover as much as the others; and work on the two houses got under way.

All went well, although more slowly than either client wanted, and at higher cost, through 1884 and into the spring of 1885. But off in Boston Dr. Hooper, Clover's father, had fallen ill. In March, the daughter went north to nurse him, her beloved parent and confidant, who at the death of his wife in her mid-thirties, when the child was five, had retired from his practice to devote full time to rearing Clover and her two siblings left behind. Dr. Hooper had relished this daughter's budding wit, and her intellect, and her independence, and encouraged her to develop that clear, delightful mind that Henry Adams fell in love with. Now in Boston, the emotionally delicate daughter was helping to nurse her father in what proved to be his final illness, Adams visiting Cambridge twice and writing to her regularly through the ordeal.

Robert Hooper died in mid-April. Thereupon Clover, utterly stricken, fell into a deep depression. Nothing could bring her out of it, through spring into summer, on into fall, through November, into December. Two years earlier, Henry had encouraged his wife's interest in photography, a popular hobby then as now, but then with its clumsy array of equipment: bulky camera, tripod, heavy plates, trays, chemicals. Clover proved adept at the craft, mounting and labeling her work in albums. But that ceased, and nothing else seemed able to lift her from her grief. At some point, despondent, she wrote her sister Ellen a note (found among Adams's papers years later, after his death) in which she spoke of Henry's being "more patient and loving than words can express." Clover would have it understood: her husband was not to be blamed—"beyond all words tenderer and better than all of you even." But she wrote also, pitifully: "If I had one single point of character or goodness, I would stand on that and grow back to life."

On a Sunday morning in December, with no longer any use in filling such mornings writing to her father—

But what drove her to it: his death, which left her adrift? Her family's propensity toward melancholia? Earlier suicides among her brilliant, emotionally unstable relatives?—her aunt crazy as a coot, Henry's brother Charles had exclaimed. Her very real problems with the Adams family, who never much cared for her (part of why the couple went south), or she for them? Her husband's increasing distraction with the history he was writing? Their inability to have the children both would have welcomed? What drove her to it on a Sunday morning, Henry having stepped out briefly to consult with a dentist about an aching tooth? That was the moment Clover Adams seized, ingesting potassium cyanide used in developing her photographs. When her husband returned, he found her body upstairs, lifeless on a rug before the fire.

Clover Adams killed herself on December 6, 1885. Three days later, John Hay, who adored her, wrote from New York to his dear friend, the grieving widower: "I can neither talk to you nor keep silent. The darkness in which you walk has its shadow for me also. You and your wife were more to me than any other two. I came to Washington because you were there. And now the goodly fellowship is broken up forever. . . ."

Here the writer must have paused, dismayed before an array of worn-out phrases that the world's griefs have called forth. "I cannot," he went on, "force on a man like you the commonplaces of condolence. In the presence of a sorrow like yours, it is little for your friends to say they love you and sympathize with you—but it is all anybody can say. Everything else is mere words." One hears echoes of the tenderness, delicacy, and restraint in an earlier such letter, charged with comforting a mother of five sons reportedly killed in battle. "Is it any consolation," Hay in this present, shared anguish continues, "to remember her as she was? that bright intrepid spirit, that keen fine intellect, that lofty scorn of all that was mean, that social charm which made your house such a one as Washington never knew before, and made hundreds of people love her as much as they admired her. No, that makes it all so much harder to bear."

He would do anything to help. Adams responded: "Nothing you can do will affect the fact that I am alone in the world at a time in life when too young to die and too old to take up existence afresh; but after the first feeling of desperation is over, there will be much that you can do to make my struggle easier. I am going to keep straight on, just as we planned it together"—Henry, Clover, John, Clara—"and unless I break in health, I shall recover strength and courage before long. If you want to help me, hurry on your house, and get into it. With you to fall back on, I shall have one more support."

The bereaved Adams kept straight on, moving into his own new home toward the end of the month when his wife died. From Cleveland, Hay moved into his—unfinished, adjacent to his friend's—the following month, on January 26, 1886. Clara with the Hays' four children joined her husband in Washington a week later.

29. ELEVATING LINCOLN

Through forty-one years the two red-brick residences loomed on their choice site in the federal capital, Hay's rounded roof extending over Adams's more compact but equally solid home adjoining, directly across from Lafayette Park. On the far side of the park was the White House, where each evening a window alight upstairs marked the room that Hay and Nicolay had shared during four years of civil war. This close to where his career began, Colonel Hay when he chose could reflect on the substantial distance he had come in the quarter century since. Luck had played its part, of course, that and Hay's personableness. Luckily his uncle's Springfield law office was next to Mr. Lincoln's at a time when the neighboring attorney won the Republican presidential nomination. And Uncle Milton was fond of his nephew, and Nicolay was, and Mr. Lincoln was, and Mr. Seward, and later Whitelaw Reid. Both luck and personableness figured in Hay's meeting, loving, and winning the love of the wealthy Clara Stone. During her father's final tortured weeks, the bridge-building magnate had fretted about bad investments, yet the fortune that Amasa Stone left his two daughters in the spring of 1883 proved enormous, maybe as large as $20,000,000 (conservatively $500,000,000 now)—a sum so well managed during the remainder of Hay's life as to have grown considerably by the time of his own death, two decades on.

Such growth owed little to the Hays' economies. They were lavish in spending: on extensive travels, on Clara's shopping sprees in Europe, on Hay's art and antique purchases, on his political generosities and those to such friends as the improvident Clarence King, on the two houses built for the Hays, with another to follow. For after moving to Washington, the family kept the mansion in Cleveland staffed, so that Clara and the children might return at their pleasure to visit the widowed Mrs. Stone; Hay himself generally managed two or three weeks there each fall, duck shooting with his Cleveland friends. Meanwhile, this new home, its entrance at 800 Sixteenth Street, appeared so sturdily constructed as to defy time's roughest batterings (actually, the domiciles side by side were demolished in 1927, well after the death of Hay and

Adams both, to make way for the Hay-Adams Hotel, which prospers elegantly on the same site still). But then: the new granite-and-sandstone, brick-faced exterior, the turrets, gables, huge chimneys, the Hays' great deep Romanesque archway entrance. And inside, twelve thousand square feet of spaciousness; the entire third floor for servants; the basement for kitchen, laundry, and furnace room; and in the two floors between, the handcrafted mahogany of the grand entrance hall and staircase—wide enough for ten people to walk abreast on—the coffered ceiling in gold leaf, the jewel of a marble and onyx parlor, the superbly proportioned dining room, over the entrance to the library medallions expressly executed for Hay of—with their flattered cooperation— William Dean Howells and Henry James. And inside the library a portrait of James at twenty-one by his Newport friend from adolescence, John La Farge. Modern plumbing throughout, of course; and upstairs the five large bedrooms, each room up and down with its elaborate fireplace. "I have forgotten the name of the hall fireplace," Hay wrote to his elder daughter years later, she well married by then and building a home of her own. But it was "a pink tinge, you remember. In the library the fireplace is yellow, and the hearth is a red dish porphyry. The name they called it, I think, was 'Boisé d'Orient.'" And in the capacious dining room was the most beautiful of all the many beautiful fireplaces, of emerald-green marble that "looks like *under* the sea," a guest wrote to her hostess playfully, so that when attending parties "we'll all have to dress like mermaids with funny tails."

Adams's house, its entrance around the corner at 1603 H Street, was rather less opulent, although equally substantial, designed, as was Hay's, by the American architect who—except for Louis Sullivan and Frank Lloyd Wright—proved without peer in the late nineteenth century and (although Richardson died in 1886, at forty-seven) on into the twentieth. For now, though, Adams would remain only a short while in his Richardson home. During that time, he commissioned his friend Augustus Saint-Gaudens to execute in bronze an allegorical figure of—as it turned out—a hooded woman seated (was she Grief, or Peace?), which became the haunting memorial at Clover's gravesite in Rock Creek Park, where Adams and his wife used to ride. And the widower traveled. In June 1886, with the artist La Farge as companion, Adams set off for Japan, not returning until October. In years immediately ahead he traveled to Cuba for a first visit and, with a longtime English friend, took an extended, circular trip over the Far West (1888). Back home, Henry Adams pushed forward his history, keeping at it sometimes ten hours a day. In 1889, Charles Scribner's Sons published the first two volumes of the

John Hay's Washington mansion, 800 Sixteenth Street. Henry Adams lived adjacent, at 1603 H Street, the street at the left of the picture, which runs alongside Lafayette Park and the White House opposite. Courtesy of the Library of Congress.

History of the United States during the Administrations of Thomas Jefferson and James Madison. Four more volumes would appear in 1890, with the final three volumes in 1891. Thus Hay's neighbor kept straight on through his grief, surviving by means of supportive friends, hard work, and travel, setting out at the completion of his labors in August 1890 for yet another year and a half of voyaging, La Farge again as his traveling companion, this time in the South Seas.

Through much of the same period, between 1886 and 1890, Hay and Nicolay would be working hard as well, completing and reading proof of their own impressive effort: *Abraham Lincoln: A History*. There were setbacks, one of them grievous. Just weeks before Clover's shocking death late in 1885,

Nicolay's wife, Therena—the fiancée who had waited for him in Pittsfield all during the Civil War, saving his faithful, informative letters from the war-tense capital, afterward his helpmeet in all he did, including her crucial assistance with this history that he and Hay were writing—Therena Bates Nicolay suddenly took ill and died, in November.

But the collaborators kept on—work, in fact, the grieving Nico's best anodyne—so that four years later, late in December 1889, Hay was able to write to Robert Lincoln: "It has occurred to me that you might like to get to the end of the Magazine publication of our book, without waiting a month, so I send you this last instalment. They are putting the book into type as fast as we can revise and read the proof, but it is an enormous job, and will require several months to complete it." Still, the end was in sight. "The publishers think best to have the whole book ready before they begin to publish—they will then put out the volumes rather rapidly, two at a time. There will be ten volumes. It will be dedicated to you."

Within a few weeks, at the start of the new year 1890, Hay was moved to complain good-humoredly to his friend Howells about having to work "so like a dray-horse of late that I have seen nothing, heard nothing, read nothing; our proof-reading is half-over. You know nothing of proof-reading," he chided that prolific author of both critical and creative prose, whose eminently attractive novels had continued to appear all this while: *The Rise of Silas Lapham* in 1885, *Indian Summer* in 1886, *A Hazard of New Fortunes* in 1889; "with you," Hay wrote, "it is the perusal of a charming author, no more—with us it is reading an old story, musty and dry, and jumping up every instant to consult volumes still mustier, to see if we have volume and page right in the margin—and the dull story right in the text. I am aweary of it."

Tired though he was, those 4,790 pages making up the ten volumes were by now nearly all filled, the serialization in the *Century* of only a third of the whole, which had begun more than three years earlier, winding down at last with the fortieth installment this very February. Half a year on, on July 8, 1890, Hay could write to Nicolay from the Knickerbocker Club in New York: "They have just put the last page in my hands, twenty minutes before my train starts for Cleveland." Only two things were left to do: "shorten p. 348 two words and lengthen the last page a line or two. P. 348 can be shortened by striking out 'calmer nor' in the first line." But this practiced editor couldn't "on the spur of the moment invent a sentence or two to lengthen the last page. I will see what I can do when I get to Cleveland." Accordingly, from the Cleveland station some hours later, a telegram went off to Washington: "To fix last page I can introduce on page 350 what Sherman says: General Grant, after having met the ruler of every civilized country on earth, said Lincoln impressed him as the greatest intellectual force with which he had ever come in contact."

The words were added, the final chapter thus filled out, and the joint task of more than fifteen years was done.

Howells reviewed the volumes early and prominently, in the pages of *Harper's Monthly*, as not only "the most important work yet accomplished in American history," but as "one of the noblest achievements of literary art." Gilder was likewise delighted with Nicolay and Hay's work (and what it did for the *Century*'s subscription list), as well as with how it raised the stature of Abraham Lincoln. Lincoln's son had already—in 1888, during the serialization—written Hay: "Many people speak to me & confirm my own opinion of it as a work in every way excellent—not only sustaining but elevating my father's place in History. I shall never cease to be glad that the places you & Nicolay held near him & in his confidence were filled by you & not by others." Indeed, *Abraham Lincoln: A History*, by John George Nicolay and John Hay, shuffled the ranking of American presidents from that time forward, the, in effect, one-term country lawyer from Illinois—"greater than ever we imagined while he lived"—hoisted above the then all but venerated two-term war-winning President Grant, and two-term President Jackson, and all the other predecessors save one, the first, President Washington, of whom Lincoln would soon be acknowledged a peer. Hay noted the shift while writing to Nicolay under the anniversary date April 15, 1889, having the evening before attended Walt Whitman's lecture on the martyred president in New York City: "The *Tribune* this morning, speaking of the lecture, calls Lincoln 'this country's greatest President'—without qualification." In years ahead, the judgment would be ever more widely accepted, its genesis largely to be found—more than in any other source—within the popular serialization then appearing before the 250,000 readers of the *Century*, and in Hay and Nicolay's soon-to-be-published ten volumes, those providing not only firsthand knowledge but also unique access to White House papers over space ample enough to present the evidence of Lincoln's greatness fully, authoritatively, and unanswerably.

Not that *Abraham Lincoln: A History* escaped criticism, then and later. From the first, its very amplitude was quarreled with: the digressions, the slavish transcribing of overlong documents, the rehashed battle scenes, those 395 pages relating the South's moves toward secession during which Lincoln hardly appears. Yet Hay protested privately that, long as it was, their *Lincoln* was a *tour de force* of compression. "In nine cases out of ten the people who criticize it blame us for having treated too briefly this, that, or the other subject, in which they are specially interested." Herndon, for one, was livid about all that the collaborators omitted, concerning Lincoln's shiftless father, his mother, his marriage, his religious views, his ambition, about Ann Rutledge. That crucial, early love affair Hay dealt with in no more than an uninformative sentence or two: at New Salem, young Lincoln "had become much attached to a young girl named Ann Rutledge, the daughter of one of the proprietors of the Rutledge place. She died in her girlhood, and though there does not seem to have been any engagement between them, he was profoundly affected by her death." Herndon's personal knowledge confirmed that Mr. Lincoln was "sad, gloomy, and melancholic," but not because (as Hay suggested) people enduring the spare hard life of the frontier all tended that way, but rather because of one particular individual's "organism, his make-up and his constitution." That, and "the untimely death of Ann Rutledge," this former law partner insisted, "and his unfortunate marriage to Miss Mary Todd, and the hell that came of it," were the true causes of Lincoln's melancholy.

Of his late friend's marriage and the hell that Herndon found there, about all one learns from Nicolay and Hay is that "on the 4th of November, 1842, a marriage license was issued to Lincoln, and on the same day he was married to Miss Mary Todd, the ceremony being performed by the Rev. Charles Dresser," and that four sons were born of the marriage, only one of whom, the eldest, survived to maturity. Herndon guessed that it was that lone survivor, dedicatee of the massive work, who bore responsibility for the collaborators' excessive discretion throughout its pages. They were "afraid of Bob; he gives them materials and they in their turn play *hush*." The result of such *hush*—despite passages of eloquence, force, and feeling, particularly in pages recounting what Nicolay and Hay had witnessed firsthand in Springfield and Washington—is too often a pervasive stylistic blandness, as, for example, when, about Lincoln, we're assured that "It is as useless as it would be indelicate to seek to penetrate in detail the incidents and special causes which produced in his mind this darkness as of the valley of the shadow of death. There was probably nothing worth recording in them," and, anyway, Hay tells us, "It is enough for us to know that a great trouble came upon him, and that he bore it nobly after his kind."

Such evasions were in part in deference to Victorian values and to the colonel's own sense of good taste, in part to a suppression of striking verbal effects that would have distinguished one collaborator from the other, in part to an avoidance of subjective feeling that would have belied the posture of these authors as everlasting angels above the fray, who cared not a twang of their harps for one side or the other. All that said, the work struck its early (and with equal force its later) readers as aggressively biased toward the northern side. Which charge the baffled Nicolay addressed privately, to Gilder: "We deny that it is partizanship to use the multiplication table, revere the Decalogue, or obey the Constitution of the United States. When logic, morals and law all unite to condemn the secession and rebellion of 1861, he will be a rash critic to pronounce censure upon anyone who helped put down that rebellion, or who ventures truthfully to record its incidents." Describing traitorous behavior for what it is was hardly partisanship, however much such a record might go against the tide of reconciliation then sweeping the land.

Of course there are faults in a work so vast, perhaps most notably in that generic, stately prose that the collaborators affected as appropriate to their somber subject matter (all in sharp contrast to the taut, vivid, concrete style that Hay's friend Henry Adams obliges us with in his own extended, nine-volume historical study of Jefferson and Madison's earlier years in the White House). Hay and Nicolay's blander prose evokes, moreover, a Lincoln too often tepid. "Seldom do we see him vent his anger," the scholar Michael Burlingame has observed, or "succumb to depression, tell bawdy stories, reject his father, cruelly ridicule his opponents, toss off a clever pun, suffer domestic misery in a woe-filled marriage, or scramble for political preferment." Never, we might venture to say, do Hay and Nicolay recount such behavior. Lincoln "becomes an insufferably respectable paragon of bourgeois virtues," Professor Burlingame summarizes, and adds: "No attempt is made to analyze or illuminate his inner life."

But an analysis of Lincoln's inner life would appear more a twentieth-century expectation than a nineteenth. Rather than analyze, Hay and Nicolay as everlasting angels pass judgment omnisciently from above—on McClellan, Chase, Stanton, and the southerners—the way Dickens and Thackeray do in their novels. Hawthorne, ahead of his time, may analyze his characters; George Eliot may. In those pre-Freudian days, Henry James very notably analyzed his. But James was innovative; in Howells's opinion he led the way. Are we fair, then, in faulting Nicolay and Hay for failing to illuminate Lincoln's inner life, given their lack of the means, the knowledge, or the desire to do so?

Despite its flaws, *Abraham Lincoln: A History* remained for more than half a century—until precisely twenty-one years after Robert Lincoln's death on July 26, 1926—the one indispensable source of Lincolniana. Only on a summer minute after midnight in 1947, at the Library of Congress, was the vault containing our sixteenth president's White House papers ceremoniously opened to general study at last. Before then, what was known of those vital papers was in Nicolay and Hay. And though no one now would read their ten volumes from first page to last (if more than ten or twenty people ever did), the mammoth work of those collaborators of the 1880s, considered selectively, still offers rewards, as in its description of Springfield in the 1830s and of Washington in the secession winter, in its elegant eviscerations of McClellan and Stonewall Jackson, in its vivid accounts of Gettysburg and of Vicksburg's fall, and—among much else—in its clamor, fear, and grief echoing outward from a shot fired inside Ford's Theatre on a damp April evening in 1865.

30. JAMES AND THE THEATER

Both Hay and Nicolay had worked hard completing their *Lincoln*, particularly from, say, 1885 to 1890. But in following Hay through the same years, what may strike us is the amount of leisure the colonel also found time for. Even as early as 1878, seven years before the earlier of the dates just mentioned, we recall that Hay on doctor's advice set aside preparatory work on *Lincoln* in order to travel to England and the Continent for several months of needed rest, prescribed to cure his nervous prostration. In London on that curative journey he dined with Henry James. Again, in the summer of 1882, Hay and his family were back on the Continent and in England, again spending time socially with James, there and yet again in Paris, returning to Cleveland no earlier than May 1883. That September, he and Nicolay vacationed in the Rocky Mountains. In May 1884, at Clarence King's urging, Hay was in London, where he hosted a breakfast for King, Henry James, James Russell Lowell, and one or two others, before returning home in mid-June. In 1885, as we've seen, he finally got down to serious work on *Lincoln*; but—having moved into a new home in January 1886—he escaped the humidity and heat of Washington that summer by traveling to New Hampshire, to look for land for sale that might serve as the site for a family retreat. In 1887 the Hays were again in London for the jubilee celebration of Queen Victoria's half century on the throne, dining with James before traveling through Wales and Scotland, returning home in September. In 1888, in May, Hay bought land overlooking Lake Sunapee in New Hampshire, then spent the summer with his family in sight of Pikes Peak in Colorado, a vacation that the four children loved, but that the father ("under par," as he noted, not for the first time) would have preferred to be spending in England. Where—having set in motion the construction of The Fells, the Hays' new summer home on Sunapee—he was yet again, in 1889, making his customary rounds through Scotland, Wales, and back to London.

So that by 1890, the friendship between John Hay and Henry James, nourished during such frequent visits, was fully shaped. An exchange of letters that year suggests the informality of their relations by then. June 5, 1890, from 800 Sixteenth Street, Washington: "My dear James, I send you by post today a little book of verses—all I have ever written, or shall write—my farewell to Parnassus. It is one of a little edition I have had specially printed for my good friends and lovers." This very afternoon, Hay continues, he was drinking tea "with one of the most charming women in America, Mrs. Cabot Lodge, and you were spoken of, as often happens when two or three of the right sort are gathered together. I bragged of my acquaintance with you and Mrs. Lodge said 'Give him my regards, if he has not forgotten me—and tell him how much I like *The Tragic Muse*.' And thereupon said things about you which made me pale with envy." Clarence King has sent word, by the way, that he "is coming to Washington to see me this month & then will sail for England. It is my private opinion that he will do neither—but I tell you that you may at least enjoy as much of the anticipation as you have credulity for." Another mutual friend, Henry Adams, "whose History is regarded by Cognoscenti as the best thing of our time, is going to the South Sea Islands next month." The writer and Nicolay meanwhile "have about a month more of work" on their *Lincoln*—"we are now finishing the 9th Volume; there will be ten." Mrs. Hay has taken the children and gone to Cleveland, with the mercury in Washington at 94°. "I wish you were here to enlighten me on lots of things. What a surprise we got in the fiançailles of Stanley and Miss Dorothy Tennant. You, who are a deep student of the female heart under civilized environment— could explain it to me. But with my unassisted human reason, it is a dark matter." Oh, and Larkin Mead, artist (and Howells's brother-in-law), "has sent me a replica of his medallion of you and bids me send it to you, with his love. Where shall I send it?" To your London address, or "would you rather have it in the Boston Museum? Or shall I give it to Congress or Mrs. Lodge— 'if you remember her'? Yours faithfully . . . P.S. : Was it 'The Tragic Muse' ms. you were going to give me? or the next one? I told you how to send it; simply let Steven 4 Trafalgar Square have it & he will do the packing and shipping. Don't forget it."

Henry M. Stanley was the brawny Welsh-born (and low-born) American journalist, adventurer, and African explorer; Miss Tennant was the high-born English artist Dorothy Tennant, whom James knew as "a most charming creature." "Oh, dear old Stan," she had assured him earlier, "that will never come to anything." Contradictory news concerning Miss Tennant's marital intentions was now reaching James away from London, in Bavaria, where, in answering on June 23, he told Hay his letter had been like sunshine breaking through the local torrential rains. "You always make me homesick for Washington," James went on, in the course of a reply of some length, chattily at its ease. As for Mrs. Lodge, "Please assure her of my vivid & grateful remembrance—she once kindly gave me to dine." And if Adams hadn't yet started for the South Seas, "give him my love & tell him that if he wants savage islands he can't do better than come back to the British." As for Clarence King, "I would stay a season in London for *him*"—this veteran of society's demands having left London specifically to *avoid* the season, with an excess of them behind him by now. Hay's verses will be delightful to find "when I return to London"; meanwhile "I have directed the ponderous *Muse* upon you. The kindest remembrances to Mrs. Hay. Ever, my dear Hay, very faithfully yours HENRY JAMES."

In that relaxed manner the friendship of those two entered this new decade, a decade distinctive enough to have acquired more than one designation: the Gay Nineties—*gay* in the older sense of "abounding in social pleasures," much as the 1920s would become known as the Jazz Age, and for similar lighthearted reasons. Again, the terms *mauve decade* and *fin de siècle*—"end of century"—came to be applied to these specific ten years before the nineteenth century turned into the twentieth. Its ostentations and frivolities led the decade to be regarded, as well, as capstone to the Gilded Age, the post–Civil War period in American history that derives its name from the novel Mark Twain wrote collaboratively with Charles Dudley Warner as far back as 1873. *The Gilded Age*, particularly Clemens's sharper-toned half of that novel, is satirical, exposing the greed of times awash in profiteering and political corruption. The humorist—this warm-hearted satirist—would continue using laughter and ridicule to expose vice on into the 1880s, most notably in *Adventures of Huckleberry Finn* (1885). We recall that Clemens set up his own publishing firm, Charles L. Webster & Company, to bring out that new novel precisely as he wanted it, and with great success. The success was enlarged substantially by his securing the rights to publish General Grant's *Personal Memoirs*, an even more remunerative triumph than *Huck*, enough almost to frighten Mark Twain, for whom it appeared that whatever he touched in those heady days turned to gold.

"Mamma and I have both been very much troubled of late," Clemens's precocious and much-loved thirteen-year-old daughter Susy noted on February 12, 1886, "because papa, since he has been publishing Gen. Grant's book, has seemed to forget his own books and work entirely, and the other evening as papa and I were promonading up and down the library he told me that he didn't expect to write but one more book, and then he was ready to give up work altogether, die or do anything, he said that he had written more than he had ever expected to." In the event, Mark Twain did write more, quite a bit more, much of it of a satirical nature, with laughter present but the mood increasingly dark, as in *A Connecticut Yankee in King Arthur's Court* (1889). Yet the truth was that this complex man, so alert to his times' excesses— mansions risen along Fifth Avenue, elaborately ornate "cottages" at Newport, private parlor cars, yachts and ocean liners, endless extravagant parties, fortunes spent that were made while ravaging the West: timber clear-cutting, land-grabs for mineral wealth—hankered, as he had ever since an impoverished childhood, after wealth himself: had traveled first-class even when he couldn't afford it, had earned wealth, married wealth, and of late (while Livy and Susy worried) had been reaching out for a fortune even greater than what the hugely successful American author already possessed, or than this recent founder of one of America's major publishing houses appeared poised to earn from abundant new business that Grant's *Memoirs* was urging on Charles L. Webster & Company.

Even beyond that: ahead glittered profits from sales of James W. Paige's typesetting machine. Clemens knew about typesetting, had spent many hours in his youth setting stickfuls of type; but Paige's amazing machine set type far faster than the ablest human fingers ever could, with fewer errors and those few more easily corrected. "I reckon," Mark wrote complacently, "it will take about a hundred thousand machines to supply the world, & I judge the world has got to buy them—it can't well be helped." By 1890 the Hartford humorist had seen what those moving parts of Paige's compositor could do—uncanny, all but alive, could even justify right-hand margins, align right margins as straight as those on the left, and without human help! Only a few months more, while the poet in steel wrought his magical instrument to perfection, with Clemens continuing to calculate profits far beyond what the writing of books could ever provide, future profits that justified his present directing of royalties from those same books, loans from his wife's inheritance, earnings from his publishing house into helping Paige put the finishing touches on the stupendous invention that printers worldwide would soon be obliged to have. Only a little more tinkering before profits began pouring in.

Henry James, his patience much tried by the end of the 1880s, had been looking around for some way to put weight on what he considered his own scrawny income. In that regard, *The Bostonians* back in 1885 had been a disaster. While it was still appearing as a serial in the *Century*, in October, its author shared with his brother William fears that this new novel "will be, as a finished work"—in book form—"a fiasco, as not a word, echo or comment on the serial (save your remarks) have come to me (since the row about the first number) from any quarter whatever. The deathly silence seems to indicate that it has fallen flat. I hoped much of it, and shall be disappointed—have got no money for it, hoped for a little glory." The initial row was, of course, over Miss Birdseye's resemblance to the living reformer Elizabeth Peabody; after that settled down, the novel received almost no formal notice at all in America, a novel that is acknowledged a masterpiece now, and one that, according to F. R. Leavis, "could have been written only by James." Leavis, the influential twentieth-century English literary critic, goes on in his vigorous way to declare *The Bostonians* so good that it makes "the imputed classical status of all but a few of the admired works of Victorian fiction look silly." Yet the rare reader who read it at its first appearance didn't care for James's picture of Boston or reform, didn't care as much as before for James's writing in any case. "The worst thing in our time about American taste," John Hay had remarked to his friend Howells as far back as 1882, "is the way it treats James. I believe he would not be read in America at all if it were not for his European vogue. If he lived in Chicago he could write what he likes, but because he finds London more agreeable, he is the prey of all the patriotisms. Of all vices I hold patriotism the worst when it meddles with matters of taste."

James never expected his fiction to have mass appeal; yet one writes what one must. And this author's aspiration was scrupulously to tell the truth, to observe and understand life as lived in his lifetime, to the extent that his own experience permitted, and transmute that perceived truth into art. That may have worked for a while, but tastes change. As the 1880s advanced, the market that American magazines provided for stories by the exile Henry James shrank. He went on writing and sending off stories as wonderful as "The Aspern Papers" (1888), but with fewer rewards than formerly, markedly fewer than in the days of *Daisy Miller*, which had let him savor his one brief taste of commercial success.

Besides stories, he continued with his novels, although those, too, suffered a decline in sales: *The Princess Casamassima* (another long novel, like *The Bostonians*, published, amazingly, in the same year, which, again, is far more highly regarded now than in 1886), *The Reverberator* (1888), *The Tragic Muse* (1890), the novel Mrs. Cabot Lodge was currently enjoying. Indeed, among Hay's "right sort," Henry James had his devotees: Mrs. Lodge, Hay himself as one of the earliest. Constance Fenimore Woolson was another enthusiast of all James's writing—from Cleveland, a friend of Hay's, grand-niece of James Fenimore Cooper, aunt of Hay's brother-in-law Samuel Mather, iron-ore magnate married to Clara Hay's sister Flora. Miss Woolson was a novelist and short-story writer herself, and an increasingly popular one, whose work Henry James reviewed respectfully in a collection of critical essays published during these years as *Partial Portraits* (1888). And she was but one among others who adored the work of Henry James, all of it, Woolson to the extent that she hunted up and became personal friends with the author, and they spent time together in the 1880s and on into the early 1890s. Still, the number of such adherents, however intense and loyal, was not large—was small enough, in fact, to cause this novelist, who had passed on most of what he inherited from his father's estate to his brother Wilky's family and for the care of his invalid sister Alice, nervously to look about for a more lucrative way to augment what lately seemed to him very modest gleanings.

He turned to the theater. James had always loved plays, since he was nine or ten attending New York playhouses with his brother William down on Chambers Street and Park Place. In Paris he early grew attached to the Théâtre Français, "going every night, or almost," and—when social engagements permitted—he went to theaters in London's West End with the regularity of devoted moviegoers today. Moreover, like our own novelists who write screenplays, James with his well-instructed eye tried his hand at writing plays for the stage, reveling in the challenges. Mark Twain wrote plays, by the way; Howells did too, both of them persistently in the 1880s and 1890s, with some success. By no means was Henry James alone in that ambition.

Edward Compton of the Compton Comedy Company approached the respected author to write a play that his troupe might perform. Compton suggested that James dramatize *The American*, his novel of 1877. To do so, the novelist-playwright planned to "extract the simplest, strongest, baldest, most rudimentary, at once most humorous and most touching play" out of that early, nuanced prose fiction. He would reduce the number of characters, would drastically tighten the action, would utterly change the ending of what is in part a love story, which in the novel concludes (logically, but perhaps not altogether satisfyingly) with the beautiful aristocratic young widow retiring to a convent rather than marry the hero. James's play ends differently, when the widow defies her family: "CLAIRE. Urbain! (*The* MARQUIS *stops, surprised, as with a challenge, and* CLAIRE *goes on speaking out loud and clear.*) You can carry our mother as well some remarkable news of her *daughter*—the news that I've determined—and (*looking about to the others*) I'm glad you should all *hear* it!—to become Mr. Newman's *wife*!

"NEWMAN. (*Springing to her, and as he folds her in his arms.*) That's *just* what I wanted to *see*!"—as the curtain falls, on an ending that may have obscured its implausibility by providing what would bring the audience pleasure.

In April 1890, James told a friend of having "written a big (and awfully good) four-act play, by which I hope to make my fortune." Having started so well, "I mean to follow it up with others." With that, he went off to Italy and from there to Bavaria, where Hay's letter of June caught up with him, then was back in London before the end of summer to help Compton and his touring company through rehearsals in whatever way he could. He was tremendously excited. Reluctantly the playwright submitted to cuts in his text, eagerly followed the company into the provinces, coached actors on delivering their lines, helped the handsome Englishman Edward Compton, playing the lead, convey Newman's American inflections by speaking "a little from the nose" and drawing out the vowels: *lawng* for long, *wauhnt* for want.

They opened in Southport, a resort suburb of Liverpool, at the Winter Gardens Theatre, on January 3, 1891. James had arrived on New Year's Day, in time for the dress rehearsal. The hours of waiting dragged by. "I *am* at present in a state of abject, lonely fear," he wrote to William on the day of the opening, "too nervous," he said, "to write more—and yet it's only 3 o'clock and I've got to wait till 8." Evening finally came, and attendance was impressive, carriages assembled as before a performance in London or in Milan at the opera, even the poorest of the 1,500 seats taken, the audience "select as well as numerous."

Compton as manager and star had arranged for his author to watch from back stage, in a seat behind the curtain. The actors were tense, but the play went off well, with no miscues, no fluffed lines, no scenery collapsing. Then it was over, and (as the late Leon Edel, superbly knowledgeable biographer, writes), "For the first time in his already long career as an artist Henry James heard his work applauded." The actors were taking their bows. Cries of "Author! Author!" arose from the audience; and from on stage Edward Compton approached the wings, reaching out for James's hand. Then Henry James found himself standing in the glare of the footlights bedazzled, gazing blindly (as he later wrote to a friend) into the great obscure horseshoe of seats that was making "agreeable sounds from a kind of gas-flaring indistinguishable dimness and the gratified Compton publicly pressed one's hand and one felt that, really, as far as Southport could testify to the circumstance, the stake was won. Of course it's only Southport—but," this dazed, ecstatic playwright admitted, "I have larger hopes."

Theodore Roosevelt as police commissioner of New York City, mid-1890s. Courtesy of Houghton Library, Harvard University (Roosevelt 560.22-001).

4

HAY AND THEODORE ROOSEVELT: THE 1890s

31. A COMMONPLACE CHILDHOOD?

Theodore Roosevelt met John Hay on a squally night in September 1870, when the future president (then "Teedie" to his family) was eleven years old. Teedie's father, also Theodore Roosevelt, had known young Hay since the early months of the Civil War, having met him in Washington where the elder Roosevelt had gone to confer with President Lincoln. These nine years later, he ran into Lincoln's former secretary again, back from serving as a diplomat in Paris, Vienna, and Madrid, on his way to Warsaw, Illinois, but stopping off in New York to confer with Whitelaw Reid about writing editorials for Greeley's *Tribune*. On bringing his friend home, Roosevelt Sr. addressed his wife: "Mittie, I want to present to you a young man who in the future, I believe, will make his name well-known in the United States. This is Mr. John Hay, and I wish the children to shake hands with him." Which they did, each in his well-mannered way. Young Master Theodore Roosevelt and Mr. John Hay, the boy's senior by precisely twenty years and nineteen days, would remember that handshake for the rest of their eventful lives.

Years later, Teedie, grown to adulthood—the pet name long since discarded—insisted to Richard Watson Gilder that there had been nothing interesting about his early years; "they were absolutely commonplace. It was not until I was sixteen that I began to show prowess, or even ordinary capacity." But sixteen would take the record to late 1874, leaving out far too much that had helped form Teedie into the Colonel Roosevelt, Governor Roosevelt, President Theodore Roosevelt that he became. In fact, those early days were anything but commonplace—were extraordinary, and with little about them that was devoid of interest.

Come to that, is any childhood commonplace? Lincoln thought his was—"the short and simple annals of the Poor"—but history thinks otherwise. As for Roosevelt's first sixteen years, those, admittedly, could hardly have contrasted more sharply with his log-cabin predecessor's, the Great Emancipator whom our twenty-sixth chief executive would idolize above all others who came before him. The two—our twenty-sixth and our sixteenth—were born a considerable distance apart in time, place, and circumstances. The Lincoln-Douglas debates had just ended, the last of the seven at Alton, Illinois, on October 15, 1858—with Lincoln forty-nine years old—when, less than two weeks later, on the 27th of the same month but far from any such rural setting, Theodore Roosevelt Jr. was born in comfortable surroundings at 28 East 20th Street, New York City.

The infant came to consciousness in the midst of a distinguished family. For one thing, the well-off Roosevelts were among the oldest families on Manhattan Island, their presence dating back more than two hundred years to when the settlement was still Nieuw Amsterdam. A pig farmer from Holland, Klaes Martenszen van Rosenvelt, had settled on the island in 1649. Seven generations later, van Rosenvelt's progeny were still there, for the most part respectable farmers and merchants over all that long interval. One descendant did set up a glass-importing firm that made a lot of money in a burgeoning city much in need of windowpanes; and the most recent Roosevelt, little Teedie, would come to know that gentleman as his grandfather, out of whose upstairs window near Union Square the same little boy and his younger brother were in time to peer down on President Lincoln's funeral cortège as it passed in full solemnity along Broadway below.

The child having grown to maturity, even after meeting hundreds and thousands of people, would regard his father—friend of Secretary Hay and youngest of the grandfather's five children, all sons—as "the best man I ever knew": brimming with health and energy, handsome, fearless, powerful, yet gentle and compassionate. "He would not tolerate in us children"—four in all, two boys and two girls—"selfishness or cruelty, idleness, cowardice, or untruthfulness." Roosevelt Sr.'s aversions are worth pausing over, because each one sank deep into the son's nature. *Selfishness*: the father from early on was tirelessly, selflessly philanthropic, and on a large scale, his efforts benefiting in concrete ways not only the general public but also the poor, the sick, and the crippled. Such a man would eschew *cruelty* to man or beast. *Idleness*: with his optimism and energy, the father was one who made every hour count, in his business affairs, his philanthropies, and exuberantly in his social life and domestic recreations. Get action, he urged his children, his own days and ways demonstrating what that meant. Don't sit around. Find things to do. Keep busy with outdoor activities, with gratifying curiosity, with being of use. *Cowardice*: his worshipful children, who presumed their father was afraid of nothing, witnessed his fearlessness on more than one recorded occasion. *Untruthfulness*: he was honest, and expected honesty in others, assuredly in his children. Always tell the truth. Moreover, "He made us understand that the same standard of clean living was demanded for the boys as for the girls; that what was wrong in a woman could not be right in a man. With great love and patience, and the most understanding sympathy and consideration, he combined insistence on discipline. He never physically punished me but once"—after Teedie bit sister Anna's arm—"but he was the only man of whom I was ever really afraid. I do not mean that it was a wrong fear, for he was entirely just, and we children adored him."

From such a father the boy learned values of industry and discipline and enjoyment of life—learned those lessons well. Teedie's mother, for her part, stirred the child's imaginative side. She was a southerner, reared on a plantation in Georgia; and although Roosevelt Sr. ("Thee"—they all had pet names) was an abolitionist and a strong Union man, their marriage was close and happy, even as the mother (Martha—"Mittie"—judged one of the most beautiful women in New York City) remained an unreconstructed southerner to the end of her days. A fine storyteller and mimic, she would regale her children with tales of life on the plantation, of its rituals: the balls, the hunts for bear and wildcats, the picturesque ways of the slaves (always "servants"), of duels and ghostly doings and disappearances at sea, all the stuff of romance that became a rich part of Teedie's youth and of Theodore Jr.'s maturity.

The boy had been born a normal, active infant, but before age four he was stricken with an illness that dominated his childhood, afflicting him intermittently with the gravest consequences. There was nothing commonplace about the asthma that seized little Teedie, often in the middle of the night, generally (although no one took note of it) on or just before Sundays, choking off his breath, terrifying the entire family. "I was a sickly and timid boy," this son explained in recalling his father's kindness throughout. "He not only took great and untiring care of me—some of my earliest remembrances are of nights when he would walk up and down with me for an hour at a time in his arms when I was a wretched mite suffering acutely with asthma—but he also most wisely refused to coddle me, and made me feel that I must force myself to hold my own with other boys and prepare to do the rough work of the world. I cannot say that he ever put it into words, but he certainly gave me the feeling that I was always to be both decent and manly, and that if I were manly nobody would laugh at my being decent."

The children all had ailments. Anna ("Bamie"), the eldest, four years older than Teedie, suffered from curvature of the spine, condemned to wear a heavy, painful brace through years of her childhood. Elliott ("Ellie"), fourteen months younger than Teedie, suffered in his adolescence and afterward from acute headaches, fainting spells, and periodic, crippling seizures. Corinne ("Conie"), a year and seven months younger than Elliott, like the older of her two brothers was afflicted with asthma, although she less acutely. Partly for the fresh air, presumed a tonic for that affliction, the children spent much of their childhood outdoors, their father renting summer homes variously along the Hudson, in New Jersey, and on Long Island, where the youngsters exulted in staying through the warm months for as long as the seasons let them. And Teedie, of that self-described commonplace childhood, at a very young age became a devotee of zoology, assembling zoos of small creatures—mice, moles, spiders, crayfish—and studying them closely, filling notebooks with detailed sketches and observations. His knowledge grew formidable. Then, at a moment not before he had reached ten or eleven, he realized he wasn't seeing what his playmates saw. He spoke of it to his father, and only that late was fitted with spectacles, so that all at once—imagine such a crucial delay!—the full range of the world opened up for him. For the first time myopic Teedie saw distances, saw the tops of trees, saw distant birds. He became fascinated with birds, studied them systematically, tirelessly, sketched them, filled notebooks with birds, knew their habits and learned the Latin names that designated their genus and species.

He (of the commonplace childhood) grew adept at taxidermy; and his parents in their wisdom indulged him in the stench and mess of it, as long as he was employed enjoyably and with intellectual benefit. The whole family loved Teedie, and admired him: his sisters, his younger brother, his mother and father. The little boy's acute sufferings—propped up all night in order to breathe, being hustled off in his father's carriage at speeds that might force air into his choked lungs, home remedies anxiously applied of black coffee, brandy, a cigar, back rubs, hot towels on the little heaving chest: all that had focused the family's attention on Teedie from early on. And—a curiosity of asthma—once an attack, however severe, had passed, the victim on the following day, even after sleepless nights, was able to resume his active life with vigor and pluck.

His father, impressed by such pluck and by the boy's intellect, took him aside. Teedie was approaching his twelfth birthday, a professional examination having found him to be precociously bright but "by no means robust." You have, Roosevelt Sr. cautioned him, "the mind but you have not the body, and without the help of the body the mind cannot go as far as it should. You must *make* your body. It is hard drudgery to make one's body, but I know you will do it." According to his mother, who was there, Theodore Jr. clenched his teeth behind the characteristic half-grin and vowed, "I'll make my body."

With the discipline and diligence that the young scientist was already demonstrating, he set about doing so. A gymnasium was installed on a piazza upstairs in the Twentieth-Street home. Years later Teedie's sister Corinne recalled watching her brother perform the monotonous body-building exercises that the horizontal bars and other contraptions offered out there. To her amazement he kept at it, in effect, for just about the rest of his life: most vigorously hiking, horseback riding, rowing, wrestling, doing judo, fighting with singlesticks, boxing on into the White House. For now, though, he was starting with the parallel bars, patiently, faithfully, relentlessly, hour after hour. And with the barbells. And with the punching bag.

In addition, at the time that the eleven-year-old met and shook hands with John Hay, he and his family had not been back long from a most thorough, industrious, and by no means commonplace tour of Europe that had extended through an entire year, from their landing in Liverpool on May 21, 1869, to their sailing from Liverpool for home on May 14, 1870. For each day of the trip young Teedie (eleven years old!) kept an ample, observant diary, kept it accurately, too, recording what the family did, what they saw (to the extent that his tentative spelling allowed him to), whom they met, how he felt. And though he sometimes felt miserable—headaches, toothaches, upset stomach, severe asthma attacks—and though he wasn't spared homesickness, he noticed and recorded an enormous amount all over Europe, the family by the end having stayed in over eighty hotels and traveled several thousand miles in every conceivable conveyance, dutifully seeing just about all that children should see in England, France, Switzerland, Italy, Germany, and back for more weeks in Paris and London.

Two years later, another such trip: this one, like the first, planned by Teedie's father, much of it to the dry air of Egypt for the sake of the asthma—two glorious months ascending the Nile and back: the antiquities, the myriad birds, young Theodore hunting and bagging some two hundred of them, ashore each morning and off on donkey back with his spectacles and shotgun, each afternoon under the awning on deck at his taxidermy—and later through the new Suez Canal, and into the dry air of the Holy Land. Later still, along the Danube, and the youngsters' five months in Dresden, adding up to another full year and more abroad: itinerary to work out, the staggering logistics, lodgings to arrange, the multitude of trunks to pack and keep track of, the servants accompanying, treasures bought to send home; and this time Teedie reveled in it all, a crucial part of his education from the departure in October 1872 to the return to New York in early November 1873.

During the two years between those grand adventures, grandfather Cornelius Roosevelt had died, bequeathing large inheritances to his sons. Theodore Roosevelt Sr. was now a very rich man, so that his family returned not to the Twentieth Street brownstone but to a much larger home, a mansion rising uptown and filled with luxuries at 6 West Fifty-Seventh Street, near Central Park. All this as economic panic raged through the land. Yet none of the hardships of the Panic of 1873 appear to have affected the Roosevelts (any more than they did the Clemenses, erecting their own new home in Hartford at about the same time); so that for young Theodore, as Teedie had grown into becoming—grown taller, filling out somewhat at fifteen—a different life was beginning.

Here, then, we might pause, toward the end of 1873, a year short of the verbal line that the adult Theodore Roosevelt drew as having divided his childhood and youth in two. Everything in the earlier years he recalled as "absolutely commonplace," for only at *sixteen* (he assured Richard Watson Gilder), only after late eighteen seventy-*four*, did the young man begin to show "prowess, or even ordinary capacity."

32. TRAGEDIES AND CONSEQUENCES

That same lad at *four*teen along the shores of the Nile: "In a walk in the Afternoon I observed five small waders viz: Gotanus Hypoloucus and ochropus, Gallinago media & gallinula, and Charidrins minor. These and Rhyncca Lengalensis are the only small waders I know of that inhabit Egypt"—this entry of January 4, 1873, not atypical; nor is it set down to impress anyone, merely for the young ornithologist's information in a journal kept during the exhilarations of his family's second tour overseas.

The unpredictability of their afflictions—Theodore's asthma, Elliott's fainting—was part of why the boys were homeschooled from the start; both Bamie and Corinne were similarly instructed (as young affluent women often were—as were Alice James and the Clemens girls). Some of it, to be sure, reflected the social level at which the Roosevelts moved, along the upper crust, so that the children's playmates, for instance, were usually cousins, abundant among the families of Roosevelt Sr.'s four brothers. Corinne had a little friend, Edith Carow, admitted early into the select circle, the girls the same age, the Carows living nearby, the father a longtime, improvident friend of Mr. Roosevelt's. So Edith was part of their group; but the rest of their playmates were most often other Roosevelts, and their classrooms were at home, amid tutors and the family.

Now, however, Theodore Jr. was aspiring to go to Harvard, and had begun studying to pass the entrance exams. Arthur Cutler had been hired to help him; and for two years (in the midst of which, presumably, the boy's life stopped being commonplace), preparations went diligently forward, the candidate strong in history, geography, science, and modern languages, weak in classical languages and math. Cutler marveled at the young man's industry, and years later could still look back with awe at a pupil who "never seemed to know what idleness was. Every leisure moment would find the last novel, some English classic, or some abstruse book on Natural History in his hand." Thus, by late July 1876, Theodore Jr. could share his joy with his sister Bamie: "Is it not splendid about my examinations? I passed well on all the eight subjects I tried."

The young scholar entered Harvard that fall, graduating in the class of 1880. He was drawn to the college for its science program, with every intention of pursuing the biology for which he had already shown such aptitude. But Harvard stressed laboratory work; the active young Roosevelt's love of the outdoors led him to prefer work in the field. Thus during his college years his devotion to the natural sciences waned (although remaining as a strong interest throughout his life). For now, however, he grew increasingly preoccupied with *political* science instead.

His father had led the way. Theodore Roosevelt Sr. became involved in civil-service reform, a heated issue at a time of widespread corruption at all levels of government. Rather than the present patronage system (whoever won an election won its spoils, present officeholders replaced by the victor's partisan cronies or others with money or favors to trade for a place on the public payroll), a movement was afoot to award such offices on merit alone, after tests to determine candidates' fitness for positions that, once bestowed, would be retained through changing administrations. Theodore Roosevelt Sr., a most respected figure, was President Hayes's reform choice for collector of the Port of New York, to be charged with dispensing vast numbers of political plums. The man's known integrity insured their fair distribution. The Senate had to confirm the appointment, however; and Senator Roscoe Conkling, boss of the New York State Republican political machine, had a say in the matter.

The powerful senator blocked the president's choice, leaving his own man in place to accommodate whatever cronies Conkling's machine might send along.

The period was a time of great stress in Roosevelt Sr.'s life. He loathed Conkling, loathed the grubbiness of politics, which at present appeared to affect him physically—this hearty, active gentleman who before now had seldom been ill, seldom seemed to tire. What felled him was diagnosed as peritonitis. His older son off at Harvard grew alarmed. Then the father felt better; the family spent Christmas of 1877 together, and life appeared to resume its normal tenor, until early in the new year, when the illness burst out in force, with excruciating stomach cramps bringing on great howling groans. Young Theodore was sent for; Elliott at home witnessed the suffering, caused by a rapidly growing, strangulating tumor in the bowel. Theodore Roosevelt Sr., forty-six years old, died in agony on February 9, 1878, hours before his elder son, informed late in order not to intrude on his studies, could get home from Cambridge.

But what a life the gentleman had led in those few years, and what an example he set. How much joy he found in existence, and how much good he had done. He helped establish the Children's Aid Society to benefit the city's many homeless children, and every Sunday evening appeared at their Newsboys' Lodging House to eat with them and call each youngster by name. In 1866 he helped start the New York Orthopedic Dispensary and Hospital to treat children suffering from spinal deformations (as did his own beloved Bamie). With other wealthy New Yorkers he founded the Metropolitan Museum of Art; and the charter of the American Museum of Natural History was approved in the Roosevelts' parlor on Twentieth Street, its imposing edifice on Central Park West rising under his watchful eye. Alas, and most uncharacteristically, illness kept this beloved civic personage from attending the inaugural ceremonies of the structure that owed so much to his efforts—illness as a preamble to the cancer that ended the philanthropist's life so early, so cruelly, in February 1878.

The sudden loss devastated the entire family, of course, the older son most grievously. But Theodore Jr. maintained a stoic composure in public, keeping his sorrow to himself. Only through a private journal does the agony of those dark months pour forth: sharp, recurring memory stabs, of "when I kissed the dear dead face and realized that he would never again on this earth speak to me or greet me with his loving smile"; of "the first clod dropping on the coffin holding the one I loved dearest on earth"—thus through spring, into summer, into fall, even that late: "oh, how my heart pains me when I think that I never was able to do anything for him in his last illness!" What finally carried the mourner through such anguish were his bottling his feelings up in himself, his applying himself to hard work at college, and his determining to make himself worthy of such a parent if he could. For the loss had filled young Theodore with self-reproach: "I often feel badly that such a wonderful man as Father should have had a son of so little worth as I am"; again, "How little use I am, or ever shall be in the world"; again, "I realize more and more every day that I am as much inferior to Father morally and mentally as physically"; again, "How I wish I could ever do something to keep up his name!"

Time dealt with that last, Roosevelt applying himself in ways that endowed his and his father's shared name with a worldwide, lasting renown—of Theodore Roosevelt the son, however, eclipsing the more local, perishable fame of the father, New York City's earlier nineteenth-century benefactor.

Theodore Jr. was a sophomore at Harvard when his father died. In the fall of his junior year he fell in love. His beloved was a Boston Brahmin, Alice Lee, related to a classmate and friend who had introduced them and who bore the name Saltonstall, honored in Massachusetts since colonial times. Alice herself, seventeen and lovely, was of the best stock, a fact that the Roosevelts, authentic Knickerbockers, were by no means indifferent to. Young Theodore's friends at Harvard, for instance, were select rather than extensive; and he reveled in his election to the Porcellian, most exclusive of Harvard's social clubs (and in the White House was pleased when his daughter, grown to marriageable age, became engaged to a Porc). Meanwhile, the young Miss Lee of whom he was enamored was assuredly of the proper social class. With the vigor he brought to all his undertakings, Theodore courted Alice for more than a year before finally wearing down her resistance. In May 1880 the two became engaged. "How she, so pure and sweet and beautiful can think of marrying me I can not understand," he marveled in his diary, "but I praise and thank God it is so."

In June, Roosevelt graduated from Harvard *magna cum laude*, Phi Beta Kappa. Later that summer, he and his brother Elliott set out West for six weeks on a bachelor's last fling, a hunting trip together as far as Minnesota, Elliott having proven himself an excellent shot down in Texas, where he had gone to improve his health. Returning from their joint hunt, Theodore hurried to a reunion with his sweetheart in Chestnut Hill: "I cannot take my eyes off her; she is so pure and holy that it seems almost a profanation to touch her, no matter how gently and tenderly; and yet when we are alone I cannot bear her to be a minute out of my arms." In October, on the twenty-seventh, at the

Universalist Church in Brookline, Massachusetts, he and Alice Hathaway Lee were married. It was his twenty-second birthday,

Moving into the Roosevelt mansion in New York City, the newlyweds were soon caught up in a social whirl for which the bride was eminently well prepared. She and her mother-in-law got along splendidly, Mittie being one of the city's social leaders. Teas, receptions, banquets, soirées, balls, Monday night operas, parties at Delmonico's: an event to attend every day; and the groom proved as adept as his bride in carrying out the rituals—the proper fork, the dancing, when and how to bow. Joyously the two went off to Europe for five months in the spring of 1881, Theodore still slight of build but in such glorious health that he climbed the Matterhorn. Returned home, he found much else to keep him busy: a manuscript begun in his senior year at Harvard on the naval war of 1812; law school at Columbia; new social and domestic pleasures; and his perpetual reading (Roosevelt read with extraordinary rapidity—two or three pages a minute—and with utter concentration, often a couple of books a night, with astonishing recall). In October, young Mr. and Mrs. Roosevelt moved into their own cozy dwelling on Forty-Fifth Street. And the young man got into politics.

It wasn't what people of his social class normally did. Politics in the main was for tavern keepers, horsecar conductors, Irishmen. "We felt that his own father would not have liked it," a cousin explained, "and would have been fearful of the outcome. The Roosevelt circle as a whole had a profound distrust of public life." Which meant simply, Theodore reasoned, "that the people I knew did not belong to the governing class, and that the other people did— and that I intended to be one of the governing class; and if they proved too hard-bit for me I supposed I would have to quit, but that I certainly would not quit until I had made the effort and found out whether I really was too weak to hold my own in the rough and tumble."

That fall, canvassing for votes, the candidate persuaded his Fourth Congressional District to elect him comfortably to the New York Assembly. Thereupon, this youngest member—at twenty-three—ever to sit in the state legislative body put aside his law studies and, as 1882 began, undertook the duties of a one-year term in Albany.

In this new arena Roosevelt—in his own words—"rose like a rocket." For all his youth, no one could intimidate him. Nobody frightened him. He was his father's son, had feared only one man in his lifetime, that same father, now dead, whom he had loved above all others. In addition, young Roosevelt was utterly self-assured: much loved by all his family from earliest days, serenely confident of his abilities, uncowed by his elders—by professors at Harvard, by

legislators in this great hall of the capitol, or by any other figures of authority—
and indifferent to making enemies (anyone of strong character, he said, makes
enemies). The pols would have to take him as he was: a rich, Harvard-
educated dandy to the point of foppishness, his assertive high-pitched voice,
his explosive falsetto laugh, the glasses, the loquaciousness, the self-righteous
moralizing that sometimes edged into prudishness.

And from the start he loved it all: conflict day after day, each day filled with
excitement and a sense of his being of use. And the dandy, the snob, the
socialite found he could work with all sorts of people: "with bankers and
bricklayers, with merchants and mechanics, with lawyers, farmers, day-
laborers, saloon-keepers, clergymen, and prize-fighters." And with reporters:
instinctively Roosevelt sensed how to provide the press with good copy.
Nobody's creature, entirely his own man, he would speak his mind and fight
for what he believed in; and journalists loved it. He skipped the freshman part
of sitting back diffidently observing; from the first his upper-class voice rang
out in that daunting legislative hall, a whirlwind of energy everywhere at once,
demanding to be heard. In his first year he took on an eminent judge who he
was convinced was corrupt. So tellingly did the young man make his case for
impeaching state supreme court justice Theodoric R. Westlake that it required
the political machine's every effort to spare the judge's complicit hide. Meanwhile, Roosevelt had made his name thus early as a crusader: principled,
incorruptible, unafraid, fighting for the people against a squalid alliance of big
business, venal politicians, and a corrupt judicial bench.

He won a second term, for 1883, handily; and even that early, young as he
was, his Republican colleagues chose him as their minority leader. And then
a third term, by more votes than any other candidate. With his party restored
to power by a large majority in 1884, the young leader was chosen speaker.
Weekdays Speaker Roosevelt was engaged with municipal-reform measures in
the state capital, weekends in New York City with his wife, well advanced in
her first pregnancy. The work was exhilarating, his prospects brilliant, Alice
(now back in the Roosevelt mansion as her time approached) doted on by her
mother-in-law, and Bamie, and Elliott, and Corinne.

On February 12, 1884, the father-to-be in Albany received a telegram: his
wife had given birth to a healthy baby girl. Legislators gathered around with
congratulations. Hours later a second telegram arrived. The mother was doing
poorly; he should return home at once. But the weather was foul. In the
densest of fogs the five-hour train trip between Albany and New York City
slowed to a crawl. Finally Roosevelt arrived at Fifty-Seventh Street to learn
that his mother, the beautiful Mittie, ill earlier with what was thought to be no

more than a bad cold, was dying of acute typhoid fever. On the floor above, Roosevelt's wife Alice lay deathly ill as well.

He hurried to his wife's side. In the advanced stages of Bright's Disease—kidney failure—she hardly knew him. He held her in his arms until called downstairs. There, at three in the morning of Valentine's Day, Roosevelt saw his mother die. He returned to his wife's bedside and cradled her for hours. She died at two that same afternoon.

Such a simultaneous double tragedy, from unrelated illnesses, in peacetime, is simply beyond imagining. The bereaved son-husband-father reacted singularly to so singular an event. "The light has gone out of my life," he scrawled in his diary and drew an X across the awful day. Dazed, stunned, he avoided the baby. The funeral was on Saturday, February 16, in the Fifth Avenue Presbyterian Church: two hearses out front, two rosewood caskets at the altar, a mother dead at forty-eight, a wife at twenty-two. "There is nothing left for me," the survivor wrote two days later, "except to try to so live as not to dishonor the memory of those I loved who have gone before me." Bamie would be given Baby Lee to rear. At the older sister's urging the new father signed a contract that allowed construction to begin on a home on Long Island, at Oyster Bay, planned earlier and meant for his wife and their future children.

Three days after the funeral, Theodore Roosevelt resumed his seat in the capitol at Albany. "I think I should go mad if I were not employed." He worked obsessively, bill after bill introduced and fought for, with not a word about his grief. People dared not pity him. He worked at legislating; and (having written two short, touching memorials of his young wife, one in his diary, the other printed for family and a few intimate friends) he silently, with equal intensity, sought to extirpate Alice Lee from memory. He was never heard to utter her name again. Baby Lee would grow up as Alice Roosevelt and entwine her life with her father's, yet could write after his death that he never once spoke to her of her mother. His *Autobiography* (1913) doesn't mention Alice Lee, not even to record the bare fact of their marriage. Nor are there more than two or three sentences about his own mother in the whole of the volume. What grief Roosevelt bore—harrowing as it was at the start—he kept to himself for the rest of his days.

He had declined a fourth term in the legislature; but as a delegate-at-large he did attend the convention in Chicago in early June 1884 that chose the Republican presidential nominee. There, he and the Massachusetts delegate Henry Cabot Lodge worked together against the party favorite, the charismatic

James G. Blaine, a presidential contender twice before but tainted by revelations of corruption that the candidate was never able adequately to explain away. Blaine won the nomination anyhow, on the fourth ballot, to the disgust of many in his own party, who subsequently deserted (Mark Twain among them) as Mugwumps, to vote for the Democrat, New York's reform governor Grover Cleveland.

Would another reform-minded New York politician bolt from the Grand Old Party and cast his vote with the Democrats? Roosevelt hesitated. He felt his political life was ended in any case. At the convention in June he had fought against the nominee Blaine and thus had little to hope for from a Republican victory in November, even less from a Democratic one. Indeed, it would be five years before this erstwhile assemblyman held a position of public trust again; and it was only then, in 1889, that his life intersected, for the first time since childhood, with John Hay's. By then, five eventful years in private life had brought about great changes in the fate of the orphaned widower who had declined to serve a fourth term in the lower house of the New York legislature.

On June 9, 1884, the Republican Presidential Nominating Convention in Chicago having concluded its work, Roosevelt boarded a train headed farther west, toward Little Missouri, Dakota Territory. The previous fall, in October, he had been out there—this inveterate hunter—on a ten-day bison-hunting expedition in palmy weeks before the recent February birth of his child and the dreadful, simultaneous loss of his wife and mother. The bison were vanishing from Dakota Territory; Roosevelt had wanted to hunt a buffalo before they were all gone, and he did so. And while he was there he invested some of the money inherited from his father in the cattle-ranching business. With the bison gone, grazing land would open up to beef cattle; Roosevelt was by no means alone in seeing the commercial opportunities of such a development.

During the years immediately ahead—his public life in abeyance—the life of private citizen Theodore Roosevelt altered drastically in three ways. The West provided the setting for the first of the alterations. He would invest $80,000 in a ranching enterprise and lose much of it, more than half his head of cattle perishing in the terrible winter of 1886–87, a natural disaster beyond anybody's reckoning. But the financial loss aside, that couple of western years furnished him with incalculable gains. He had taken his griefs out there in June 1884 and worked through them, a solitary horseman roving over the prairie landscape and amid the buttes and canyons of the Badlands until the loneliness, the silence worked their magic. Very early Roosevelt came to love this land: its wildlife, its birds, the people. A stranger at first with his custom-made cowboy duds and his four eyes and eastern ways, the dude soon won admiration and wide respect through his energy, stamina, and a zest for living the life the ranchers lived and doing the work they did. His neck thickened; he grew barrel-chested, rode in the saddle for up to thirteen continuous hours a day, enjoyed it all, complained about nothing.

Biographers, justly drawn to so colorful a story as was unfolding, have written whole books on Roosevelt's time out West, a story well and (even when sounding like a tall tale) truthfully told by the principal himself. That Roosevelt was moved to relate the story in his own words points to the second of the three great changes that his five years out of public life brought about. Having lost what amounted to a fortune in the cattle-ranching business, the somewhat chastened cowboy looked elsewhere for ways to earn a living. A president of the other party sat in the White House, and New York's governor and legislature were also Democratic. So the former Republican assemblyman must turn to something other than politics for a livelihood. He would become, he said, a literary feller. Already he had demonstrated an aptitude for writing: the project begun in his senior year at Harvard—a study of the naval war of 1812—he had gone on to finish during the first couple of years after graduation. The work was published in 1882, an astonishing achievement by a busy young man of twenty-three, a book dealing with nautical, highly technical matters that (for all its dry terminology) has remained the definitive account of an arcane subject ever since. So well esteemed was *The Naval War of 1812* by Theodore Roosevelt that, soon after publication, a copy was ordered placed on every vessel in the U.S. Navy. Now the author would turn to writing much else, and for popular consumption: not only magazine articles that made his name familiar nationally as a man of letters, but also a second book, in 1885, *Hunting Trips of a Ranchman* (dedicated "To that Keenest of Sportsmen and Truest of Friends, My Brother, Elliott Roosevelt"), in which the author vividly evokes the western world that he had come to know and love.

There was a need for whatever earnings might arise from such writing. They would play their part in the third great change that befell Theodore Roosevelt during these five mostly private years. On a trip from out West back East in the fall of 1885, he met, coming out of Bamie's home, Edith Carow, Corinne's little childhood friend now a young woman of twenty-four. Edith and Theodore had grown close as children: picnics together, his rowing her around the inlets of Oyster Bay, the eleven-year-old on his first trip to Europe breaking into tears of homesickness when his mother chanced to come upon a picture of little Edith back in New York. In their teens, before Teedie went off to Harvard, the two were effectively sweethearts, until a rupture of some sort occurred in a summer house that his diary speaks of their entering, after which, abruptly, further mention of Edith Carow ceases. Now they met again, renewed their friendship, renewed their love. Edith and her widowed, straitened mother and sister were moving to England for economy's sake. Before she left, she and Theodore became betrothed, keeping their engagement secret. Roosevelt, meanwhile, had succumbed to the temptation of running for mayor of New York City, one of two liberals in a three-man race. As expected, he lost (but had a bully time anyway). Afterward, leaving little Alice with her grandparents—the Lees, in Boston—he and his sister Bamie sailed together late in 1886 for England. There Edith Carow and Theodore Roosevelt were wed, at the start of a marriage that turned out to be filled with love and domestic happiness lasting through the bridegroom's lifetime.

The newlyweds honeymooned in Europe (while, far beyond their ken, the terrible winter of 1886–87 raged over the Plains back home), then returned to Sagamore Hill, the home at Oyster Bay, three-year-old Alice coming to live with them. The child was joined by a half-brother, Edith and Theodore's first child, Theodore Jr.—Ted—in September 1887. Roosevelt, his cattle days pretty much behind him, resumed his writing: two biographies, a book of essays, another book on ranch life, and a scholarly work in progress that would result in the ambitious multivolumed *Winning of the West*.

Incidentally, in that earlier autumn of 1884, when Roosevelt had hesitated about bolting the party rather than vote for its chosen nominee, he ended up throwing in his lot with Blaine the Republican after all, even campaigning back East for the tainted candidate. Nevertheless, Democrat Grover Cleveland won the election with Mugwumps' help, the help of Republicans unwilling to vote for a party candidate of fine mind but questionable morality. Now President Cleveland was completing his first term, the Democrats ready to nominate him for a second four years. Republicans for their part turned to Benjamin Harrison, ex-senator from Indiana, dull, but of unsoiled reputation. Roosevelt, who thrived on campaigning, campaigned for Harrison as well, colorless though he was. The tally on election night was close. Cleveland, who won the popular vote, was denied his home state of New York's crucial electoral votes through Tammany Hall's intervening to defeat their reform-minded fellow Democrat. The Republican Harrison thus ascended to the White House. Roosevelt, loyal Republican who four years earlier had stayed with the party that others were leaving, now saw his name put forth for a place in the new administration. Eager to return to politics, the literary feller seized what opportunity had offered and, in May 1889, took his seat as one of three civil service commissioners in Washington. He would remain at that post for the next six years.

33. HAY DISCONTENTED

The new position had its drawbacks. Roosevelt's salary wasn't much—$3,500 a year—particularly for a gentleman with a growing family, a large drafty house to maintain at Oyster Bay, the lease of a Washington home to arrange for, and the subtraction from his assets of up to $50,000 lost from bad investments and natural disasters out West. Moreover, his duties promised to make him few friends, and those few only among the reform-minded Mugwumps, whom Roosevelt scorned for their disloyalty to his party. For their part, loyal Republicans—like the Democrats—hardly wished this new commissioner well in his reform efforts, content as they were with a status quo that offered them substantial benefits putting supporters on the public payroll.

Still, civil-service reform had been his father's cause late in life, and Roosevelt Jr. had himself earlier fought in the New York Assembly to clean out rot that went along with Tammany's dispensing of political jobbery. Moreover, a dramatic event since his father's death had thrust civil-service reform into wide public favor. Sixteen years after President Lincoln breathed his last in a crowded bedroom across from Ford's Theatre, another president was murdered—and just three years after Roosevelt Sr.'s death from natural causes in February 1878. The philanthropist had died unable to contribute to reforming the corrupt patronage system, frustrated by Senator Roscoe Conkling, who had moved to keep his own man—Chester A. Arthur, a thorough machine politician—in the post of collector of the Port of New York, there to pass out political favors the way Senator Conkling wanted them distributed. As early as July 1881, however, only four months after a new president had been inaugurated, a disgruntled office seeker mortally wounded James A. Garfield in a Washington railway station; President Garfield died of his ill-treated wounds eleven weeks later.

The vice president who succeeded him in the White House was the same Chester A. Arthur who had been Conkling's man as collector of the Port of New York. But once in his new high office, the natty and amiable Arthur (whom Henry James met and dined with in Washington and pronounced a gentleman) behaved more independently as president than he ever had as machine pol. His predecessor had been assassinated by an unbalanced office seeker denied the job he felt was owed him for imaginary services rendered.

That set the public clamoring for reform. In 1883, Senator Pendleton of Ohio and others got a bill passed that President Arthur signed most willingly. The Pendleton Act created a civil service commission to oversee appointments to designated federal offices only after open examinations and on the basis of merit alone. These six years later, in the spring of 1889, it was that commission of three that Theodore Roosevelt was joining in Washington and soon would be leading.

The post had its drawbacks, but there were advantages as well. Not only was the reform it was charged with implementing—of replacing cronies with qualified public servants—dear to the present incumbent's heart, as it had been to his father's. Roosevelt loved a fight in a good cause anyhow, and civil-service reform promised plenty of fighting, because whatever success came his way would be at the expense of politicians deprived of public offices they were now, in effect, bestowing on the highest bidders. Well, let them grumble about what he was up to; Roosevelt at a still youthful thirty would relish taking them on. Meanwhile, his new assignment put him in Washington—another advantage—no longer the oversized village of prewar times, when sovereignty resided mostly in the states, but an established metropolis of some two hundred thousand permanent residents attracting influential people from all over America, all over the world. The Union's antebellum sovereignty, which the separate states shared, had given way to a strong central government set up in the course of waging a civil war that created a Nation. What had been the United *States* plural—*are*—before the war were thus transformed into the *United* States singular, *its* federal capital altered accordingly, with wide, gaslit, tree-lined boulevards and vistas of granite and marble that the center of a great national power merited.

Amid its new culture and diversions, significant people were to be encountered, no company more select than among the chosen few who gathered regularly for breakfast in Henry Adams's home facing Lafayette Square and the White House. To this coveted society Roosevelt gained prompt access. Henry Adams as professor at Harvard back in the 1870s had for a graduate student Henry Cabot Lodge, holder of one of the first Ph.D.s ever earned in America, under the professor's direction, in history. And Lodge since then had become Theodore Roosevelt's closest friend. The friendship, in some ways an unlikely one, had been forged shortly before and during the Republican nominating convention in Chicago in 1884, where Lodge and Roosevelt together fought to deny James G. Blaine the presidential nomination. It was an unlikely friendship because Lodge wasn't very likable: a Boston Brahmin of cold demeanor and superior airs, condescending when he bothered to notice you at all, indifferent to whether you liked him or not. But Lodge was brilliant, genuinely erudite (more so than the warmer, far more personable Roosevelt), a historian, biographer, and current member of the House of Representatives from Massachusetts. It had been Lodge who urged the new Harrison administration to reward Theodore Roosevelt's loyalty to the party; it was Lodge who brought the Roosevelts into Henry Adams's company; and it was in Lodge's home that Roosevelt took a room, after Mrs. Roosevelt (expecting her second child in the fall) returned to Oyster Bay and Sagamore Hill.

In the spring of 1890, toward the end of the Washington social season, Henry Adams noted with uncommon cheerfulness: "Our little set of Hays, Camerons, Lodges, and Roosevelts never was so intimate or friendly as now, and for the first time in my life I find myself among a set of friends so closely connected as to see each other every day, and even two or three times a day, yet surrounded by so many outside influences and pressures that they are never stagnant or dull." The pressures included Adams himself overseeing publication of the nine volumes of his great work on Jefferson and Madison, Hay about done with his and Nicolay's *Abraham Lincoln: A History*, Lodge's two-volume biography of George Washington published just last year, and Roosevelt's first two (of four) volumes of his *The Winning of the West*, published in 1889 as well.

The Camerons whom Adams mentions as partners in their breakfast pleasures were Mr. and Mrs. Donald Cameron, he the son of Lincoln's first, corrupt secretary of war, who was replaced by the incorruptible Edwin Stanton. The recently deceased Simon Cameron was a political power in Pennsylvania, and his son, now in his mid-fifties, had served for many years as senator from that state. But it wasn't the wealthy, dour, poker-playing, bourbon-drinking Don Cameron who enlivened gatherings at breakfast (what we would call brunch) at 1608 H Street. It was Cameron's much younger, second wife, Elizabeth, "Lizzie," not yet thirty, who brought such charming liveliness to the proceedings. Clara Hay was welcome in the group as well. Mrs. Hay was, after all, one of the original Five of Hearts, although Clover Adams (who had been fond of Clara) confided to her father that that particular Heart never had much to say, her husband—superb conversationalist—being able to talk for two. The group valued Edith Roosevelt highly as well, by this spring of 1890 back in Washington (now the mother of two boys) with her husband and children in a rented home. And the wife of the aloof representative from Massachusetts, Theodore Roosevelt's best friend Henry Cabot Lodge, was an additional bright star of the company.

Mrs. Cabot Lodge, "Nannie"—it may be remembered—would be drinking tea with John Hay a little later this year, on June 6, Clara Hay having taken the children and returned to Cleveland, as her husband will write to his friend Henry James from next door around the corner in his mansion at 800 Sixteenth Street. Hay's tea during a 94° afternoon not far in the future was, he told James, with "one of the most charming women in America," to whom "I bragged of my acquaintance with you and Mrs. Lodge said 'Give him my regards, if he has not forgotten me—and tell him how much I like *The Tragic Muse*.'"

If Mrs. Lodge was one of the most charming women in America, Mrs. Cameron was surely the other, at least in the opinion of John Hay and Henry Adams. The widower Adams, in fact, was in love with Lizzie Cameron, with Elizabeth Sherman Cameron, in a well-documented, though properly late Victorian way. And for a while at least, just around this time, John Hay, doting husband and devoted father of four, was in love with Nannie Lodge.

For all that, by his own testimony Hay appears to have been—through the weeks and months of these late 1880s turning into a new decade of the 1890s—pretty steadily dispirited. One may wonder why, given the causes he had for self-satisfaction. The massive work with Nicolay, *Abraham Lincoln: A History*, volumes commercially successful and critically esteemed, appeared in 1890, the great effort finished at last and highly commended. That same summer Hay watched from nearby Newbury as his new, handsome retreat began to take shape above the shores of New Hampshire's Lake Sunapee, with Clara and the children thoroughly enjoying the pastoral recreations it provided. Hay himself, through his scintillant letters, maintained a wide correspondence with some of the most interesting figures of the time. His gold-plated financial affairs were being reliably managed in Cleveland. He traveled regularly, always in style, to Europe as to another home—this product of Salem, Indiana, and Warsaw, Illinois—and in America he stood high in Republican councils, although preferring to work behind the scenes. In 1888, for instance, at the Republican convention in Chicago that nominated Benjamin Harrison, Hay was actively if quietly involved, laboring on behalf of candidate Senator John Sherman of Ohio (brother of General William Tecumseh Sherman and uncle of Hay's and Adams's Washington friend Lizzie Sherman Cameron). Sherman came in second in the balloting, which was disappointing; but Hay kept his involvement up by sending a generous check to the winning Harrison campaign (without thinking much of Harrison himself), and meanwhile he had made a warmer friend of Sherman's campaign manager Mark Hanna, Cleveland industrialist and soon-to-be mentor of another Ohio politician with a future, Major William McKinley.

Why was Hay discontented, then, and over so long a period? Finishing a massive project can leave one feeling that way, the preoccupation of many years suddenly ended, that book closed. His good friend and next-door neighbor Adams was setting off in August 1890 to be gone a year and longer exploring the South Seas. The artist John La Farge would go with him, but Hay longed to go himself, and was having to deal not only with his dear friend Adams's extended absence and the breakfast gatherings adjourned but also with a realization that he would probably never see the Far West himself, the West Coast, the Pacific. His place for now was here at the Fells, in New Hampshire, with his wife and children at Sunapee.

Hay's health continued intermittently troublesome. In late April 1891 he sailed alone for England, his yearlong infatuation with Nannie Lodge at an end. Arriving in London with a bad cold picked up on shipboard, he didn't get much help from doctors. "I do not believe it pays, at my time of life," he wrote home to Clara, "to travel alone and I shall never do it again." Yet he kept busy, visiting art galleries and auction houses, calling on Robert Lincoln—Harrison's minister to England—and hosting a dinner at the Bristol Hotel for Henry James, Bret Harte, and Elizabeth Cameron and party: her daughter Martha, stepdaughter Rachel, and Harriet Blaine, recently arrived in London.

The doctors did advise Hay to take his cold out of the foggy city. He went to Paris and stayed with Whitelaw Reid, Harrison's minister to France. And as he wrote to Clara, somewhat disingenuously, in Paris he ran into "the Cameron clan." Lizzie was more forthright, in late May writing to Adams during his travels in the South Seas: "John Hay and I have had a real Parisian spree. I hope you are jealous. Please don't tell him I told you, but we dined in a *cabinet particulier*"—private dining room for two in an elegant Parisian restaurant—"and went in a lover loge to a ballet. I actually felt wicked and improper. He did, too, for he felt obliged to follow up the precedent and to tell me how much he loved me."

Soon Hay returned to London, collapsing there with what he thought was a heart attack but what the doctors diagnosed as indigestion. Lizzie arrived a few days later. "He told me yesterday," she wrote to Adams, "that he felt that this was the last year of his life." Yet Hay was well enough to accompany Mrs. Cameron to the Dulwich Picture Gallery and to take her to a pantomime featuring the love-smitten Pierrot. "When I think," she wrote Adams teasingly, "of how freely I am seeing him, and that it might be you—! It *will* be you soon." For the enthralled Adams was starting the seventeen-thousand-mile voyage to rendezvous with Mrs. Cameron in Paris. "We are having a desperate affair," she encouraged him in his resolve, "so hurry up. Something must break it up before we return to Washington. It was that night in Paris that did the mischief."

Henry Adams reached France from the South Seas and Australia in October of this 1891. By then Hay was long back in the States. As for any "affair" between him and Mrs. Cameron, Adams had responded complacently: "Fascinate John Hay by all means." In fact, "The more you please others, the more you delight me." Yet after a year of separation and considerable epistolary ardor (Lizzie: "To think that you are coming, are on your way! That I shall see you, shall take you home. I can scarce realize it tho' I walk on air in consequence." Adams: "I am grateful as though I were a ten-year-old boy whom you had smiled at, and put in rapture of joy at being noticed."), when the close friends came together at last for their two weeks in Paris, the longed-for interval proved unsatisfactory for both. Lizzie appeared always surrounded by others, always busy with other commitments. Adams fretted over it, trying to understand. "I would give you gladly as many opal and diamond necklaces as Mr. Cameron would let you wear," he assured her, "if I could only for once look clear down to the bottom of your mind and understand the whole of it."

Hay would have occasion to make much the same lament. He had come back to America in July and was with Clara and the children at Sunapee by early August. Lizzie and Adams had their unsatisfactory reunion in Paris that October. Clara returned to Cleveland, Hay was in Washington, and Adams remained in Europe until February. Thus Hay was hosting a couple of dinner parties in Washington in late fall with Lizzie among the guests, others present including the Blaines, the Lodges, and the Roosevelts, as Mrs. Cameron reported in the series of extraordinary letters she and Adams exchanged for three and a half decades. Meanwhile, a new year 1892 was beginning the Washington social season: diplomatic receptions, debutante balls. And yet it wasn't the same. Like Adams in Paris, Hay in the federal capital was finding Mrs. Cameron always surrounded by others. Presumably in late January he wrote a note to Lizzie, undated, unaddressed, unsigned, delivered by hand. Why does he mind all these people around her? He didn't mind them in Paris or London, any more than a devout worshipper minds being in a crowded church. "I give it up. I will not try to comprehend you. Still less can I criticize you. I shall never know you well enough to do either." But he did go on to muse on Mrs. Cameron's way with men, how—when Lizzie not long before had left the group—all the men broke into cries of admiration, taken with her ability by means of some divine gift to "assume to each one of them the form, the eyes, and voice of his ideal." More specifically: "A form of perfect grace and majesty, a face radiant with a beauty so gloriously vital that it refreshes and stimulates every heart that comes within its influence; a voice, a laughter so pure and so musical that it carries gladness in every vibration of the air. You sweet comrade, you dear and splendid friend, who is worthy to be *your* friend and comrade? I am humbled to the ground before you."

Hay's note contains considerably more ("My proud goddess, my glorious beauty, my grand, sweet woman, I want to shut my eyes to everything about you here, and adore you as I did at Dulwich, as I did on the terrace by the Thames. Why is it different now?")—but one pauses in wonderment. What sort of creature was this Elizabeth Sherman Cameron? Photographs and oil portraits hardly tell us. Anders Zorn's painting of her seems inadequate to the praise she excited; she didn't care for it herself. But it was in her expression, her smile, her voice, her manner, her carriage: all that is absent from the surviving silent, static visual evidence. Her family had urged her at twenty to marry the smitten widower twenty-two years her senior, father of five grown children, the eldest of whom was older than Lizzie. Mr. Cameron was very wealthy, very proud to have such a beauty for his wife, and possessed of a will no match for hers. Early on she had made it clear to her husband, as she told Adams, that he was to keep his jealousy to himself: "I must talk to whomever I pleased whenever I pleased." Meanwhile, there were rules to the game she was playing. In her public attitudes she was a delight to behold, widely read, highly intelligent, in love with being admired—subject to the rules—and able to rein in both Adams and Hay when they broke those rules (as presumably Adams transgressed in the Paris fortnight and Hay did, too, with this present overardent note; thereafter he was limited as to the number of times he might write to her). Still, she retained both their loves for the rest of their lives. Hay would die in 1905, Adams in 1918, Lizzie in 1944, well into her eighties, secure in the love of two brilliant—Adams perhaps the most brilliant American of his time—highly capable men to the last.

And what of Clara? All the while that Hay, always discreet (one of the rules), was enraptured with Lizzie Cameron, he continued writing devoted letters to Clara Hay. "When I think of the seventeen years you have been with me, the happiness and content of the heart you have given me, I am filled with a wondering and grateful sense of my great good fortune. In the whole world there was no other woman who could have made me so happy and I found just the one." This to Clara back in the States, from London at the end of May 1891, with Hay and Elizabeth Cameron there together alone through much of the month that followed.

Elizabeth Sherman Cameron. Courtesy of the Library of Congress.

How can we know even those who are living and breathing around us, let alone those from that foreign country of the past? Photographs and an Anders Zorn portrait of Clara herself strive to make Mrs. Hay into a handsome woman like Elizabeth Cameron; but not even her husband in courtship days saw his beloved quite that way. Her regular features in youth were attractive, but she was large-boned and grew stouter as the years advanced. Still, away from her, Hay wrote often of wanting to be back in her arms, to kiss and caress her. He loved his wife, loved his children, loved being with them (even though his health seemed to suffer when he was). Moreover, his despondencies through these same years never registered on those who knew him only socially, who saw only the fortunate, famous husband and father, excellent listener, teller of apt, memorable anecdotes, genial dinner guest and frequent, attentive host. None but his most intimate friends, such as Henry Adams, were privy to an ongoing gloom; and even Adams was denied knowledge of his friend's true feelings for Lizzie Cameron.

One all but despairs: how can we hope to know people, really know them, then or now? "I give it up. I will not try to comprehend you." "If I could only for once look clear down to the bottom of your mind and understand the whole of it."

34. THE USES OF WEALTH

Clara was Hay's bulwark, of course. "She is a very estimable young person, large, handsome, and good," he had written to Nico near the start, in August 1873, announcing his engagement to Miss Stone. "I never found life worth while before." Later, in 1881, her goodness was perhaps too formidably on display when, returning from church on a Sunday, she found her husband in ungodly hilarity with Mark Twain, which occasioned a brief, icy greeting that hastened the guest's departure, Hay at his side sheepishly murmuring that Mrs. Hay was very strict about Sunday. Generally, though, she had been reared in a mansion full of servants on Cleveland's grand Euclid Avenue to behave in a manner appropriate to her station, reserved by nature yet trained in the best of finishing schools, well read in literature, stylishly and immaculately turned out, at ease meeting social demands, and the Hay family's placidly reliable disciplinarian. Hay himself was entirely indulgent with his daughters, as both Helen and Alice when grown recalled affectionately—and with Clarence, the late-born of the four. Only Del, their second child, was a disappointment: fat, dull, and lazy, his father groused to Henry Adams. Meanwhile, Del's mother was spoken well of by all their many friends. Henry James, who saw the Hays together on numerous occasions, never failed to send his regards to Mrs. Hay; the caustic Clover Adams was fond of her, quiet though Clara remained; Mrs. Cameron went out of her way to note how fine Mrs. Hay looked and how well she entertained, at least at the Fells. For Clara thrived living the life that the wife of John Hay lived: the dining, the furnishing of homes, the attending church on Sundays, bringing her cultivated taste in fashion and art to shopping and traveling, quite comfortable accommodating her husband's peripatetic ways. Indeed, they both came equally to love England and travels on the Continent, as content with paying regular visits to Sir John and Lady Clarke in Scotland, to Sir Robert Cunliffe in North Wales (two baronets, longtime friends of Henry Adams) as they were with lingering in London's galleries, antique shops, and social settings.

Clara's inherited wealth made such a life possible. Without her, what might Hay have done with himself? A successful editorial writer for a major New

York newspaper when they met, the colonel as a quick study would be good at almost anything he undertook: poet, former presidential secretary, former diplomat, former essayist, former assistant secretary of state, businessman, lecturer, historian; yet he had seemed to drift from one thing to another. Thus he owed the Stones much, including eight years of tutelage in Cleveland under the shrewd eye of Clara's industrialist father, which led Hay to become an able custodian of money himself. During those years Clara presented her husband with a family and gave his life direction. Although he had never been improvident and at their meeting had resources of his own from the *Tribune*, her situation provided wealth beyond anything Hay could have imagined back in Illinois. And she trusted him to make use of it, as her father had trusted Hay with the management of the Stone enterprises, urging him to hurry back from Europe to resume charge of them and before his death designating Hay coexecutor (with Clara's sister's husband, Samuel Mather) of the vast estate that that same self-inflicted death left for Amasa Stone's two daughters.

Mather, a Cleveland native, had inherited industrial wealth as well, his father the founder of the Cleveland Iron Mining Company. Mather's wealth, in fact, when combined with Flora Stone's, sufficed to make him extremely rich. So it was natural that Samuel Mather would be approached in early 1893 by his friend Mark Hanna to come to the aid of William McKinley, erstwhile member of the House of Representatives, now governor of Ohio, who had been thrown abruptly into deep financial trouble. A Mr. Walker of Youngstown had helped McKinley in earlier years. Thus, when appealed to, the latter had returned the favor, signing a note for Robert Walker, and again signing, and yet again, in what were assumed to be extensions of the same loan. But each signature endorsed a new note and fresh indebtedness. In this precarious year over which the Panic of 1893 loomed, Walker's tin-can factory went bankrupt. All at once McKinley learned that he owed not the few thousand that he thought he was vouching for but a total beyond $100,000. Samuel Mather pledged $5,000 right off to help, and got in touch with his brother-in-law seeking further support for the governor.

But Hay, ahead of the game, had already sent a check directly to McKinley as soon as he learned of the Major's plight, intimating that more would follow. Pullman, Armour, Frick, and others fell in line, allowing McKinley's well wishers to deal smoothly with a situation that had threatened the governor's hopes of being reelected later this year—not to mention any chance at the presidency three years on. In a vote of sympathy in hard times, Governor McKinley won reelection overwhelmingly that fall to a second two-year term; yet in all the excitement he would not forget that Colonel Hay had been among the very first to come forward. "I have no words with which to adequately thank you," he wrote to the colonel, expressing his deep sense of appreciation and obligation. "How can I ever repay you & other dear friends?"

To such satisfactory uses might wealth be put. Again, a few months later, the Hays as a family were able to set out on a leisurely sojourn abroad for more than a year, in fact sailing with servants and luggage just a few days after the New York Stock Exchange crashed on June 27; the Panic of 1893 couldn't shake the Hays' rock-solid holdings. Thus they were comfortably in Europe in the autumn when news from Henry Adams reached them of the distressing plight of their friend Clarence King.

Adams and Hay both thought the world of King, had from the beginning of the friendship some fifteen years earlier: a brilliant man, witty, generous, a gifted writer and speaker, yet a man of action as well as words, handsome, brawny, and of exquisite taste. King was a geologist, a mountaineer, an explorer, first director of the U.S. Geological Survey, quite irresistible to women, and yet a man's man for all that. His company was uniformly delightful, if increasingly hard to come by. Except for rare visits of a day or two, Clarence King always seemed to be somewhere else: in Mexico, in London, in the Far West pursuing mining ventures or rustling up investors in new mines, any one of which might make him wealthy, even while he lived as though rich already.

King did have a quirk, which his close friends knew about: a taste in women that preferred the more primitive among them anthropologically to the more refined. He had, for example, confessed to Adams that "to kiss a woman and feel teeth through her thin lips paralizes me for a week." What Adams and Hay didn't know—what no one knew—was that in the late 1880s King had met a former slave named Ada Copeland, now a domestic servant thirty-seven years old, and in September 1888, after convincing her that he with his pale skin and blue eyes was an African American Pullman porter named James Todd, had married her. King had a mother all this while in Newport, with various other relatives dependent upon him, and from whom he kept his secret. But his expenses were abruptly increased, as a newly married husband and wife named Todd set themselves up in Brooklyn, and Ada a year later gave birth to a first child. Very little survives of their relationship as it unfolded, but some letters do, from James Todd to Ada: "I thank God that even if I am forced to travel and labor far away from you [I] have the daily comfort of remembering that far away in the east there is a dear brown woman who loves me and whom I love beyond the power of words to describe."

The man's financial affairs, meanwhile, were in shambles. In the late 1880s King had begun borrowing considerable sums from both Hay and Adams, always in the form of loans, using the art he owned as collateral. Now, in the present 1893, Ada Copeland Todd was giving birth to a fourth child, even as financial panic raged over America to catastrophic effect. King learned, for instance, in mid-summer that the National Bank of El Paso, which he had founded and bought shares in heavily, had been forced to close its doors for good. His money was gone. Through days ahead, King came undone, hair grown shaggy, beard ragged, clothes unkempt, until by the end of October he had fallen among those derelicts we overhear muttering in public places. Accordingly, on a late October Sunday at the Lion House in Central Park, a tramp's agitation and rage grew loud enough to create a disturbance. The police were called. The offender gave his name as Clarence King, his address as the Union League Club. He was arrested for disorderly conduct and soon committed to the Bloomingdale Asylum for the Insane in Harlem Heights. There he remained for the next two months.

The Hays were in Paris when Adams's incomplete, uncomprehending news of King's misfortunes reached them. "It would seem incredible to anyone but you," Hay responded, yet "King has not written me a letter for a year and has never given me the least hint of his affairs except that they were desperate. I have sent him money and securities sufficient, I hoped, to clear him, but have never been informed that he received them, much less what he made of them. I am as much worried over him as if he were my child, but I do not know what to do to help him, in face of his obstinate silence." On the scene, Adams was planning immediate aid through a trip with King to Cuba as soon as they let the inmate out, presumably in January. That gave some comfort. Jolly him up and get him to come to Washington afterward, Hay wrote. "Now that his affairs have gone to everlasting smash we can set him up in a bijou of a house"—a further example of the uses to which apparently endless wealth may be put.

More of that wealth was allowing Del to attend Westminster School in Dobbs Ferry preparing for Yale, while his sister Alice and younger brother Clarence, now nine, were with tutors outside Paris perfecting their French. Mr. and Mrs. Hay and Helen, meanwhile, could proceed in the chill of this new year 1894 southward to warmer weather in southern France and Italy, so that those three were in Rome in late January when Hay read in the newspaper of the death of Constance Fenimore Woolson.

Miss Woolson (as noted earlier) was another of Hay's friends, from a well-to-do family in Cleveland, an aunt of Hay's brother-in-law Samuel Mather and a popular novelist and short story writer. She was considerably more popular than—to name one author—Henry James, although Miss Woolson was among James's most devoted readers. Born in New England in 1840 (making her three years older than the novelist she so admired), she had moved with her family to Cleveland while still very young and remained there twenty years, traveling with her father back East and vacationing at the Woolsons' cottage in northern Michigan, where some of her memorable short stories are set. Her father died when she was nineteen. She, her mother, and a sister then moved to St. Augustine, and from there Fenimore (as Henry James would learn to call her) traveled widely through the South. Her stories by then were being published in the best American magazines. Her mother died in 1879. Unmarried, possessed of sufficient means, Miss Woolson then moved to Europe, where she lived in one hotel or pension after another for the rest of her life.

She kept mostly to herself, preferring it that way. Her writing absorbed her (as his absorbed James). She was given to long walks to keep healthy, and to rowing when she could. As the years advanced she became ever more deaf, which added to her isolation. But she had not been long in Europe before she met James, and the two became friends. He admired her work as from one on whom nothing is lost, envied her sales, and wrote sensitively and quite favorably about her achievement.

In fact, during the 1880s James and Miss Woolson were often together, in England, in Paris, in Geneva, in Italy, discreetly, a bachelor and spinster conforming with the proprieties of the age. Perhaps Miss Woolson entertained thoughts of marriage to the great novelist; assuredly James basked in her admiration. Thus he was keenly distressed while writing to John Hay from London toward the end of January 1894: "Your telegram, & Nevin's share in it, last night, lifted a terrible weight off my spirit, and I can scarcely express to you the comfort I take in the knowledge that you are in Rome and that poor Miss Carter, with her burden of dreadful exertion and responsibility, has been able to look to your sympathy and cooperation."

Miss Carter was Miss Woolson's cousin, summoned urgently from Munich; Robert Jenkins Nevin was rector of St. Paul's American Church in Rome. James had meant to be on his way south by then himself, bought his ticket at Cook's yesterday with plans to arrive in Rome at six Tuesday morning, "in order, simply, to stand that day, by that most unhappy woman's grave." But returning home he had come upon an item from Venice in a local newspaper, "which gave me the first shocking knowledge of *what* it was that had happened. Before the horror and pity of it I have utterly collapsed."

For the report asserted that Constance Fenimore Woolson, age fifty-three, had not fallen from a window of her Venetian quarters in the small, cold hours of January 24, but had jumped, committed suicide. "Miss Woolson was so valued and close a friend of mine and had been so for so many years that I feel an intense nearness of participation in every circumstance of her tragic end & in every detail of the sequel." But the *image* of those last sad, lonely moments—"a woman," James reflected in his letter to Hay, "so little formed for positive happiness that half one's affection for her was, in its essence, a kind of anxiety." Still, he had never dreamed of such an end as this. Yet to what extent was James himself, the remote Henry James, to blame for it? "I can't *think* of Venice for the present—nor of any other inevitable vain contacts in Rome (apart from the immense satisfaction of seeing you & your wife); for the moment there is nothing of value for me to *do*." He must stay here. But would Hay be so good as to see that flowers with James's name attached were laid beside the grave? For upon first learning the news, Hay as friend of the deceased had at once wired the American legation in Venice offering to cover all expenses transporting the remains to Rome for burial in the Protestant Cemetery, close to Shelley's grave and Keats's—"the blest Roman cemetery that she positively *desired*—I mean in her extreme love of it," James noted in his letter. Hay had seen to that, and had located a plot in the crowded grave-yard, and had written to his brother-in-law, the deceased's nephew Samuel Mather, of matters attended to, and a little later to Henry Adams: "We buried poor Constance Woolson last Wednesday," January 31, the Hays in attendance with the American minister, Mr. Potter, a Richard Greenough, and two unknown Englishwomen—the deceased, in Hay's summation, "a thoroughly good and most unhappy woman with a great talent bedevilled by disordered nerves. She did much good and no harm in her life, and had not as much happiness as a convict."

An event searing James with so vivid an image, of a dear, admired friend alone, desperate—"the horror and pity of it"!—deaf in the winter cold of foreign quarters (had she been suffering as well the ache of unrequited love?), was to be followed just one year further on by the ineffaceable recollection of yet another most painful evening. *The Tragic Muse*, which Mrs. Cabot Lodge enjoyed, had proved no more popular with the general reading public than had its two predecessors: *The Princess Casamassima* and *The Bostonians*, works on which Henry James had labored hard and placed high hopes, hopes three times disappointed as each in turn was largely ignored. Seeking income elsewhere, the novelist had returned to his passion for the theater, prospering at Southport, near Liverpool, in early 1891, and as a budding playwright found himself at the final curtain led before the footlights to receive hearty applause from an audience well pleased at the premiere of his *The American*, which went on to earn further acclaim in the provinces and to enjoy a creditable run of two months in fashionable London.

During these years in the early 1890s, James continued writing short stories, but he was working hard and hopefully as well on crafting plays to adorn the English stage. In the summer of 1893, for instance, he wrote a play for the matinée idol and theater manager George Alexander to star in. Accordingly, in December 1894, Henry James's first full-length originally plotted drama, *Guy Domville*, went into rehearsal, scheduled to open at London's St. James's Theatre on January 5.

Opening night proved to be very grand, the playwright's many friends of taste turning out in full evening regalia to fill the theater stalls. The pit and gallery were full as well, but with a less elegantly clothed clientele, less interested in Henry James—many wouldn't have known who he was—than in watching anything the popular "Alick" starred in. What George Alexander was starring in this evening would be rather a change from his usual fare. He was playing a handsome, young, French Roman Catholic about to forsake substantial worldly blessings in order to become a priest. The time is 1780, with the situation complicated by Guy Domville's abruptly learning that he is the last of the Domvilles and thus has a duty to return to the secular world, marry, and beget heirs who will carry on the distinguished name.

The issue would interest James—celibate life dedicated to an ideal (of religion, of art) that compels forsaking the distracting rewards of marriage and parenthood. No doubt the issue was of some interest to bejeweled ladies and polished gentlemen in the stalls, although less so perhaps to those humbler folk in the pit and the gallery. Anticipating as much, the playwright "had gone down on all fours to make simple & obvious à la partie of the meanest intelligence" his *Guy Domville*, as he explained to "Beloved John Hay" (thus his responding salutation), who wrote commiserating over what happened that opening night. "The subject of my little play demanded that I shd. put Catholics en scène, & the British public won't stand Papists. I thrust them back into the last century & toned them down with the mellowest old-world atmosphere of amiability & grace, of an ingenious & human little story—but it was no go." Toward the end Alexander as Guy—having arranged that his intended marry a worthy secular suitor while he himself withdraws into the cleric's celibate world after all—begins a moving, poignant farewell: "I'm the last, my lord, of the Domvilles . . . ," at which a voice from the gallery yells rudely down, "It's a bloody good thing y'are."

Rather more than a no-go, the play was a disaster, made unambiguously so by the jeering, booing, and catcalling that accompanied the descent of the final curtain. Elegant attendees in the stalls did their best to overwhelm the ruckus from the gallery by rising and applauding with prolonged vigor, shouting out "Author! Author!" George Alexander, appalled star and manager, accordingly staggered to the wings and sought out the bewildered Henry James, who from high nervousness had avoided the play entirely until just before that final curtain fell. Amid all the uproar Alexander for whatever reason led James onto the stage, where the playwright needed time to make out that a portion of the audience was hooting his play in derision. He stood stunned, frozen in place while the outcry continued, the stalls persisting in their frantic support, clapping with determination, calling out their approval. And though the play would run for five more weeks, and though it brought down on James "a flood of letters from known & unknown," as he wrote to Hay, "some 25 times more copious than all the 25 years of my mere literary modesty had done," and though "many who went to see it at all appear to have gone 3 or 4 times," for one horrible, prolonged moment—was it three minutes? five?—he had stood frozen before the footlights, only dimly discerning the fervent multitude, only gradually realizing that the uproar from out of the dimness expressed not simply unrestrained delight but, apparently in even greater measure, outrage and rejection. It was a very public humiliation, which Henry James came to regard as "one of the most detestable incidents of my life." What the gentleman had hoped for was merely to make a little money by giving pleasure; but after this, he couldn't "*afford* to write plays," he told another correspondent. "I have written 6 in all, and have made no money to speak of by any. I must do immediate work that pays. These are the wretched tragic facts"—his overwrought diction, two months after *Guy Domville* had closed, conveying how the pain and heartbreak lingered.

35. DEGRADATION AND REFORM

Three years earlier, in May 1892, Theodore Roosevelt at his post as civil service commissioner in Washington was reporting to a close English friend, then absent, formerly one of the happy few regulars at their H Street breakfasts. "Henry Adams is exactly the same as ever; we dine with him tomorrow night. John Hay," the letter goes on, "still has for his idols James G. Blaine and Henry James Jr—a combination which indicates a wide range of appreciation." Not that Roosevelt cared for Blaine or James either one. With Cabot

Lodge, the New Yorker had worked hard back in 1884 to deny the Plumed Knight the Republican nomination for president. Blaine won it anyway (although not the election); and Roosevelt, good party man, went so far as to campaign for his summertime opponent in the fall. According to the *New York Times* (October 19, 1884), he was doing just that before the Brooklyn Young Republican Club by attacking Mugwumps, Republicans who on moral grounds refused to vote for their party's candidate and were voting for the Democrat Cleveland instead. "Plenty of men were willing to complain of the evils of our system of politics," the *Times* reported Roosevelt as saying, "but were not willing to lift a finger to remedy them. Mr. Roosevelt said that his hearers had read to their sorrow the works of Henry James. He bore the same relation to other literary men that a poodle did to other dogs. The poodle had his hair combed and was somewhat ornamental, but never useful." Rather like the Mugwumps, who "were possessed of refinement and culture to see what was wrong, but possessed none of the robuster virtues that would enable them to come out and do the right."

A decade later Roosevelt's opinion of James hadn't risen. Theodore enjoyed discussing literature with his correspondents, among them Brander Matthews, professor of English and drama at Columbia. "By the way, have you seen that London *Yellow Book*?" the commissioner inquired of the professor in June 1894. "I think it represents the last stage of degradation. What a miserable little snob Henry James is. His polished, pointless, uninteresting stories about the upper social classes of England make one blush to think that he was once an American."

Having written much else besides, James did often write about English manor houses and drawing rooms and what went on inside them. It was a subject he knew very well. Sir Walter Scott wrote about Scotland; Dickens wrote about London; Hardy wrote about the English West Country: authors tend to write about what they know. The story in the first issue of a new quarterly, *The Yellow Book*, that had set Roosevelt off was James's "The Death of the Lion," which does indeed contain a manor house, but presents its denizens in an unflattering light, meanwhile concerning itself with much else beyond their shabby doings. Somewhat as in *Guy Domville*, written about the same time, "The Death of the Lion" addresses the need for the serious artist to dedicate himself to his work amid distractions that must be resisted. It deplores, as well, the tendency of the times, those same 1890s, to glorify— "lionize"—celebrity for its own sake, without any real understanding of or interest in the work achieved by the "lion" of the moment. The story considers the hypocrisy of society and the dangers society's attentions pose to the dedicated artist, as well as the corruptions of the media—the dailies and weeklies—in their scramble for gossip, for personality to write about, with little interest in the work that has brought the personality into notice. "The Death of the Lion," in other words, has much to say to readers of our own era, and says it in James's distinctive, penetrating manner, a story with autobiographical undertones but rendered with a uniformly light touch and not a jot of self-pity.

Some of all that, Roosevelt at his reading pace of a couple of pages a minute may have missed. After spending a few hours with the novelist a decade further on, he would modify his opinion; but for now there was little about the cogitative bachelor Henry James in his early fifties in England that would appeal to the younger (at thirty-six), ever active, politically minded, intensely patriotic, devoted husband and father of five—with one more to follow—who was Theodore Roosevelt, civil-service commissioner in Washington, D.C., in June 1894.

For one thing, the expatriate James's virtues were hardly robust, hardly the manly, outdoor variety that Roosevelt's life extolled. And the latter was bound to scorn a willful choice by any American, literary or otherwise, to live his life outside the United States. As a fellow writer, Roosevelt knew the challenges of authorship; he had already written and published extensively and would write more. His subjects, however—nature-focused, or historical, or biographical, or scientific, or polemical, or political, or public-spirited—differed from James's. Yet his wide reading, research, and accumulated knowledge confirmed Roosevelt's conviction that the United States was the greatest country in the history of the world, and that the American whom the continent was fashioning was a new breed of human, at his best resourceful, inventive, democratic, and self-reliant as none before had been. Having lived and labored among such people out West—the ranch hand, the cowboy—he had found them laconic, uncomplaining, and sturdily independent, men who looked you in the eye. And Daniel Boone's Kentucky frontiersmen, shaped by the rigors of the life they led: Roosevelt had read much about them, had gathered together their actual, often ill-lettered documents, and from those had been composing his *The Winning of the West*. The world had not before seen such men, molded by the frontier as they pushed ever westward, ever farther from clerical superstitions, feudal remnants, and hierarchical vestiges of the aristocratic Old World that Mr. James appeared so entranced by.

Civilizations rise and fall. Having read his ancient history, Roosevelt could sound out the drumbeat of mankind's westward march: Mesopotamia, Egypt, Greece, Rome, Spain, the British Isles, one after the other. Now America, greatest of all civilizations thus far. This omnivore read widely in natural history as well. Darwin's *On the Origin of Species* appeared the year after he was born, a volume Roosevelt studied closely in his youth and returned to often. At Harvard (besides studying anatomy under Henry James's brother William), he absorbed current thinking on anthropology and race—Lamarck, cranial sizes—while continuing to read natural and social sciences on his own. He subscribed wholeheartedly to evolutionary thinking: that not only flora and fauna evolve, but races, religions, and cultures do, the latter moving out of the primitive into the savage, the barbarian, on to the civilized, and from there to decadence and decline. As for that last stage, *The Yellow Book* provided a current example of decadence, and hence Roosevelt deplored it, as he deplored the overcivilized snob Henry James, pursuing in its pages his effete triflings with English drawing-room life.

Over these same years, nearer home, the commissioner had been wrestling with his own heart-wrenching specimen of decline. His brother Elliott, best friend from childhood, hunting companion of their bachelorhood, best man at Theodore and Alice Lee's wedding—the handsome, charming, much loved Elliott to whom *Hunting Trips of a Ranchman* was admiringly dedicated—had turned as an adult into little more than a full-time socialite. In late 1883 Elliott married another such, the beautiful Anna Hall of New York City, with whom he had three children. He dabbled in banking, played some polo, attended the races, but mostly he seemed to party, always charming, at the piano regaling the company with comic songs. Meanwhile, an earlier habit of Elliott's had grown into full-fledged alcoholism. His irregular behavior got into the papers: the sanitarium in Austria; a well-known political brother's trip to Paris for the sake of Elliott's children, to protect trust funds from further depredations; probationary plans set up; a relative providing work of a sort in Virginia for a year's trial at sobriety before Elliott would be allowed to rejoin his family. In late 1892, Mrs. Elliott Roosevelt, the beautiful Anna, age twenty-nine, readying a New York home to receive him, came down with diphtheria, to which she succumbed. The widower appeared inconsolable, although not long after was observed back at his light-hearted, bibulous partying. A servant of Anna's, Katy Mann, had come forward with charges that Anna's husband was her infant's father; Theodore had the matter investigated, then settled on a lump sum in trust for the child. Elliott, drunk, crashed his carriage into a lamppost, his formerly handsome face all puffy from drink and deep cuts and bruises. Living with a mistress on the Upper West Side, one evening he leapt from a window, yet somehow survived. Not long after, in the midst of delirium tremens, Elliott was gripped by a seizure on his apartment stairs and died a dismal death, on August 14, 1894. He was thirty-four. His mistress, Mrs. Evans, could not have mourned him more deeply had he been a model consort; and his oldest child, his daughter Eleanor, then nine, carried with her through the rest of her life memories of horseback rides with her loving father, of the tender letters he wrote to her, of rare visits of a day or two that he was permitted to spend at home. Eleanor's future years included marriage to a distant cousin, more than a decade as First Lady of the United States, service as ambassador to the United Nations, and—toward the end—the public's generally endorsed opinion that she was the most admired American woman of the twentieth century.

Her Uncle Theodore, who while in the White House gave his favorite niece away at her wedding to the Columbia law-student groom, Franklin Roosevelt, had never been a drinker himself, was drunk—more or less—only once, at his initiation into the Porcellian Club at Harvard. From then on Roosevelt took no more than the very occasional glass of wine or claret. Meanwhile, he had done what he could for his brother, until reaching a point where he gave it up. Nothing more would help. At news of Elliott's death, about all this surviving brother could manage was: "Well, it is over now; it is fortunate it is over and we need only think of his bright youth."

He got on with his work. Theodore Roosevelt knew plenty of ways to keep busy (Don't be idle, his father had taught): family, exercise, hunting, writing, reading, his many friends, his public duties. He had assumed the responsibilities of civil-service commissioner in May 1889, and by that June was already actively investigating patronage abuses as far away as Milwaukee. The thousands of post offices all over America provided ample opportunities for dispensing employment, with abundant occasions for fraud, graft, and nepotism. The Milwaukee postmaster Roosevelt was after was a Democrat, but the new commissioner felt no hesitation in going after Republican transgressors as well. In this same June he took on no less a figure than the Postmaster General of the United States, the wealthy John Wanamaker of Philadelphia, esteemed Republican department-store owner who had given generously to President Harrison's campaign. Of course the commissioner at his ill-paying post wouldn't win friends either Republican or Democratic that way; but his job was to enforce the law—the Pendleton Act—and he meant to do it. Meanwhile, he and Edith were both enjoying Washington, dining out or in with guests five or six nights a week: fascinating guests—diplomats, artists, authors, scientists, statesmen. Thus he pushed cheerfully forward, not caring much about criticism or about Harrison either—the little runt of a president, as he dubbed him privately—meaning to discharge his duty even-handedly for two or three years at least, before returning to writing full time at Sagamore Hill.

For this present position was a dead-end toward any political rewards at the national level. President Harrison, meanwhile, gave his commissioner little of his time, but did leave him to pursue corruptions regardless of party, until the election of 1892 denied a second term to the Republican incumbent (against whom it was charged that anyone who shook Harrison's flaccid hand became a Democrat). Grover Cleveland regained the White House; but, to Roosevelt's surprise, the Democrat asked his predecessor's commissioner to stay on, complimenting a young Republican politician's integrity while confirming that the civil-service post was independent of party favoritism.

Roosevelt did agree to remain, without planning to do so for long. Too long a service with the Democrats might cast doubts on the New Yorker's party loyalty. Thus in 1895, when a reform mayor, a Republican, offered him the chance, at better pay, to clean up New York City's notoriously corrupt police department, Theodore took on the challenge with zeal. He did regret leaving Washington and his friends at the seat of federal power; but Edith and the children could now return home to Oyster Bay, no more than fifteen miles from this new posting in metropolitan government.

It was a very public assignment, much watched by the press, and Roosevelt made the most of it. He promptly got rid of two shady, longtime figures high in the police department who were presumed to have been ensconced immovably amid their many corruptions. The new commissioner took to strolling the beats at 2 A.M., accompanied by a couple of brawny policemen and a reporter or two, in order to catch patrolmen—when found at all—sleeping on duty or drinking in late-night pubs. The newspapers loved it. They loved less well, although assuredly reported, Roosevelt's shutting down the city's beer halls and taverns on Sundays. Sunday was the workingman's one day off, the one day for the many working Germans in the city to relax in their biergartens, the Irish in their taverns; but Commissioner Roosevelt hadn't been hired to enable the public's leisure. He was there to clean up the department and enforce the law. The Sabbath-closing ordinance, largely disregarded before, was on the books. Change the law; but until then, the taverns would stay shut on Sundays, to New Yorkers' disbelief and their loud, persistent, indignant protests.

On balance, though, Roosevelt of ever expanding renown was getting things done, and people admired him for that. The press could hardly keep up with him, and the thirstiest townsfolk had to concede that the young reformer was incorruptible, courageous, and tireless—even joyful—in his willingness to take on offenders.

And with all that, busy as he was, New York City's police commissioner found time during the next presidential election cycle to campaign yet again for his party. He had done so for Blaine in 1884, for Harrison in 1888, for Harrison a second time in 1892. And, on Thursday, October 15, 1896, he was back, addressing the American Republican College League in Chicago's vast Coliseum. Robert Todd Lincoln presided, in a hall filled with loyalists who, when Roosevelt was introduced, cheered the police commissioner to the rafters for two full minutes before letting him begin. He took out after the Democratic presidential nominee, William Jennings Bryan, new on the political scene but already the object of more scorn from this speaker than the likes of a Henry James could ever call forth. "Bryan's dominant note," Roosevelt told his fifteen thousand listeners, "is hysteria. Instead of government of the people, for the people and by the people, which we now have, Mr. Bryan would substitute a government of the mob, by the demagogue for the shiftless, the disorderly and the semi-criminal." The Democrats, he cried, were "fit representatives of those forces which simmer beneath the surface of every civilized community and which, if they could break out, would destroy property and civilization." Given a chance, he went on, the present Democratic nominee would replace the government of Lincoln and Washington with "a red government of lawlessness and dishonesty as phantastic and vicious as the Paris Commune itself."

A specimen of political rhetoric in the 1890s. It all made for "immense fun," the business of "our quadrennial Presidential riot," as Theodore described it to the same English friend, Cecil Spring Rice, to whom he had written about John Hay's two idols, Blaine and James. Springy overseas (best man at Theodore and Edith's wedding) would relish reading of America's "interesting and exciting, but somewhat exhausting, pastime. I always genuinely enjoy it and act as target and marksman alternately with immense zest, but," Roosevelt admitted, "it is a trifle wearing."

36. "YOU MIGHT DO WORSE THAN SELECT ME"

The Democrats in 1896 had nominated William Jennings Bryan of Nebraska for president. The Republicans chose William McKinley of Ohio, with bimetallism emerging as the principal issue for the two camps to wrangle over. The U.S. Constitution decrees, in Article 1, Section 10, that "No state shall . . . make anything but gold and silver coin a tender in payment of debts"; *bimetallism* in the 1890s denoted a movement to reestablish *both* metals, gold *and* silver, as legal tender in the United States. So bloodless a term applied to a currency squabble nevertheless brought with it plenty of agony and outrage. Capitalists, people of property, decried any departure from the established gold standard; representatives of the laboring classes—mill hands, factory workers, farmers—wanted silver as well as gold legal, thus inflating money by increasing its supply. For in those hard times surrounding the Panic of 1893—of falling prices in grains, of wages cut and workers laid off and strikes erupting violently (at Homestead in 1892, at Pullman in 1894)—many laboring people struggled with debt; $500 repaid in silver would likely require less to come by than what had been borrowed several years earlier in gold. Of course creditors wanted to be repaid in coin of full value. Thus, Commissioner Roosevelt the other day at Chicago's Coliseum could charge that Mr. Bryan "champions that system of dishonesty which would steal from the creditors of the nation half of what they have saved."

Bryan, for his part, felt that he was championing the voiceless, the downtrodden, those left behind in an industrial age of wealth gathered into the hands of the few, in part by means of combinations never before seen in America. *Trusts* was a new word in the economic lexicon: Rockefeller's Standard Oil Trust of 1882, the beef trust that followed, the sugar trust, the tobacco trust—companies previously in competition with each other merged into cooperating entities. In a campaign different from earlier ones, young Bryan—the Boy Orator of the Platte was thirty-six—railed against such massive new combinations and against the monopoly and favoritism they bred. Railroads (a convenience that had permitted the far-flung trusts to form in the first place) allowed this Democrat to scurry around the country eighteen thousand miles in the fall of 1896, delivering some six hundred speeches—"begging for the Presidency as a tramp might beg for a pie," John Hay grumbled to Reid. Previous presidential nominees had behaved more decorously, affecting a diffident demeanor until the public's voice summoned them irresistibly to serve. Thus Major McKinley, like his predecessors but unlike the scampering Democrat Bryan, remained throughout the canvass sedately at home, emerging on his front porch to greet the deluge of supporters who Republican railroad magnates made sure had passes to travel in festive mood among roistering groups to Canton, Ohio, to behold their nominee in person.

Hay was reluctant to brave such crowds, but he, too, came at last by invitation to Canton. "I spent yesterday with the Majah," he reported to Adams in late October, the campaign nearing its end. "I had been dreading it for a month, thinking it would be like talking in a boiler factory"—marching bands, cheering mobs, McKinley's front yard on North Market Street packed with partisans. But the candidate in person "met me at the station, gave me meat & took me upstairs and talked for two hours as calmly & serenely as if we were summer boarders in Bethlehem, at a loss for means to kill time. I was more struck than ever with his mask. It is a genuine Italian ecclesiastical face of the XVth Century."

What they talked about we're left to surmise. McKinley's face, by the way, though maybe an unrevealing mask, was a handsome one: cleft chin, strong jaw, clean-shaven at a time when facial hair remained much in fashion, as it had been in the White House uninterruptedly since Lincoln's beard, and would continue after McKinley left that edifice right up to clean-shaven Woodrow Wilson in 1913. For after all the present campaign commotion, the sedentary Republican governor did win his race for the White House comfortably, and not in small part through the generous monetary support of such property owners as John Hay. Hence the compliment paid to Colonel Hay of being met by the nominee himself at the Canton railroad station.

The two liked each other, in their reserved way, and had gotten to know each other well in the years since 1893 and Colonel Hay's prompt forwarding of a check for $1,000 to help Governor McKinley out of his financial jam concerning loans of over $100,000 naively countersigned while the governor's friend Mr. Walker of Youngstown was still solvent. Since then Hay had contributed regularly to furthering McKinley's political ambitions. In August 1896, for instance, after furnishing another of several such contributions, the colonel promised to send along an additional $1,000 each month until the November vote that would end the campaign. And he gave speeches on McKinley's behalf, and wrote letters of support to the newspapers, and helped Mark Hanna with fund-raising, all (he insisted) with no strings attached, with no expectation of a *quid pro quo*, simply because, despite their differences, Hay had come to admire McKinley, who, in any case, would never have taken money from someone who expected a favor in return. To Hay, Governor McKinley appeared of presidential stature, a man of principle and character, somewhat dull perhaps but immune to bribery, still living in the modest, two-story frame house he had occupied in Canton since his days as an attorney there. Hardly an intellectual and by no means a flashy conversationalist, he was nevertheless amiable, astute, and one distinguished—in Hay's words—by "great moral earnestness." A deep voice served the major well when addressing the public, and he was an attentive listener, as well as industrious, kindly, and compassionate. Moreover, he would be his own man in the White House; Hay felt sure of that. No one was going to lead the major around.

So they became friends and closer ones in the years ahead, a friendship that remained on an honorific-plus-last-name basis to the end, yet no less deep for that. Soon after the election results were in, Commissioner Roosevelt wrote to Hay from New York: "We are at sea here as to whether you are going to be Secretary of State or Ambassador to England." The thought had occurred to others as well. Why not? It was an open secret by then that the colonel was eager to reenter public life, long persuaded that democracy depended on the willingness of intelligent and experienced citizens to serve. And he had much to recommend him. The aura of the great Lincoln surrounded Hay all his adult life, ineradicably as private secretary during the Emancipator's lifetime but more recently, since the publication of the ten volumes of *Abraham Lincoln: A History*, as—with Nicolay—the foremost living authority on the Republican idol. Moreover, several times Lincoln had entrusted young Hay as his personal envoy on delicate missions of diplomacy; and subsequently, after his chief's murder, the younger man ably occupied diplomatic posts in Paris, Vienna, Madrid, and later in Washington, where he had filled the responsible position of assistant secretary of state in President Hayes's administration. Besides, Colonel Hay was widely traveled in Britain, had many friends there— including figures prominent in government—where his appointment to high office in the new McKinley administration would be much approved of.

The president-elect was left in no doubt about Hay's willingness to serve as ambassador to the Court of St. James. In early January 1897—the campaign over, the vote in, the victor chosen—Hay drafted a letter about the pending appointment: "I do not think," he addressed McKinley, "it is altogether selfishness and vanity which has brought me to think that perhaps you might do worse than select me." For the following reasons: "1. My appointment would please a good many people & so far as I know would offend nobody." 2. Hay with his health and at his age (nearing sixty) didn't mean to hold the office long, thus putting it "at your disposal in some critical time when it might serve a useful purpose. 3. As I have no claim on the place, and as it is really above my merits and deservings, I think I would be more grateful than anyone else would be, and would do as much to show my gratitude." His case might have been argued more forcefully; but, though restrained, Hay did add that whoever was sent should be chosen promptly; he knew enough of London (where he and Mrs. Hay had spent last summer, yet again) to know that already it would be "difficult to find a suitable house for an Embassy."

Inauguration Day was March 4, 1897, and McKinley made the appointment before the month was out, the Senate confirming it in short order; so that Ambassador Hay and his family were able to get under way from New

York aboard the *St. Paul* bound for Southampton as early as April 14. The London *Times* was but one of many newspapers, overseas and here at home, that applauded the choice. "Colonel Hay," wrote George Smalley, American correspondent for the *Times*, "is a diplomatist by natural gifts and training, with the tact, sagacity, quick perceptions, solid basis of knowledge and high capacity essential to success." But in the Hay household, what excitement, what agitation must the decision have set off: all the elaborate and necessarily hasty preparations—the shopping, the clothes, the deciding what to bring (including the family silver); for Ambassador Hay meant to represent his nation in high style. One thinks of Mrs. Lincoln, with her extravagant wardrobe so that no one in Washington would find occasion to look down on her coming from the rustic West. All rusticity had long been bred out of the urbane Hay family, of course; but they would leave nothing for England to complain of, nothing wanting in diplomatic bearing, in polished manners, or in knowledge of courtly etiquette when Colonel Hay led the embassy of the United States of America. Toward that end, the family brought with it two carriages—a brougham and a landau, both newly monogrammed—and five horses, along with the great number of necessary steamer trunks as well as servants to tend them. Daughter Helen, now twenty-two, accompanied her parents, as did Hay's best friend Henry Adams (thus three of the Five of Hearts en route), Adams whose own father had departed thirty-six years earlier on the same mission to England, charged with the heavy task of keeping the United Kingdom neutral during the American Civil War then erupting.

Among the many delighted with Hay's appointment was Henry James, in London. "This is tremendous and delicious," James wrote to his friend when first learning of it (by means of a premature announcement in the papers, as it turned out), "and my emotion overflows." Hay as ambassador made "the plot of existence thicken more delightfully—even across the hiatus of the Atlantic—than anything I can manage on paper this morning, at least until I have embraced you. I long for the hour when I shall come as near as I dare to laying hands with that intent on your inviolable ambassadorial person. You change the whole prospect—you light it up in a manner more festive than any sight I supposed still reserved for these aged eyes." Accordingly, Henry James presented himself at Southampton when the *St. Paul*, bearing the new ambassador and his family, docked on April 21. Warm greetings among old friends were exchanged in happy confusion, prepared remarks were delivered to the press, and luggage was retrieved for the train ride to London and the arrival later that day at 5 Carlton House Terrace. There the Hays had rented an earl's grand residence, its entrance on ultra-fashionable Pall Mall, windows in back looking over the Horse Guards Parade and St. James Park. Of course the mansion was well furnished throughout, with a staff in place that included chef, butler, kitchen maids, house maids, and footmen, and a bedroom and sitting room on the third floor for Helen. It was all quite lavish. "The scale of expenditure on which he has established his household and the gorgeousness of his entourage cause even the English people to gape," Hearst's *New York Journal* reported, perhaps with some exaggeration as regarded immediate English neighbors, each very wealthy, many titled on so exclusive an avenue and virtually born blasé.

For seventeen months Hay served as American ambassador to Britain, an office he filled irreproachably. On earlier occasions he, his wife, and Helen had been presented to the queen; now, bearing his credentials, Hay was standing again in full dress before Her Majesty, and Mrs. Hay was granted her own audience, and husband and wife concurred that the seventy-seven-year-old monarch was unpretentiously gracious and no more intimidating than your grandmother. Later Victoria would remark that of all the American ambassadors she had known (and the list was long, through sixty years, extending back to 1837), Mr. Hay she found most interesting. The Hays' diplomatic socializing was of course extensive, even though the ambassador declined invitations by the score. There were speeches to deliver, a task at which John Hay by this time was expert, as when he spoke in Westminster Abbey to general approval at the unveiling of a bust to Sir Walter Scott. He wrote official dispatches that the president in Washington read with interest and pleasure, so well connected, well informed, adept, and fluent had this practiced author of such documents become since being introduced to the genre in long-ago Civil War years.

These months may have constituted the happiest seventeen in Hay's life. Back in the United States, meanwhile, Theodore Roosevelt had taken steps to improve his own professional satisfactions. For the commissioner had grown frustrated with his work in New York City, having reformed a cumbersome police bureaucracy as far as he felt he was likely to. His friend Hay was amused, accordingly, before his own trip by invitation last fall, to learn of Teddy's making the same pilgrimage with Cabot Lodge to Canton to confer with the Republican presidential nominee. And Lodge, now (since 1893) a senator from Massachusetts, would late last year and into this new year 1897 be lobbying the president-elect on Roosevelt's behalf, angling for his good friend's return to Washington.

Thus during the same April when the Hay family sailed for England, the Roosevelts moved from New York back to the federal capital, Theodore to assume the duties of assistant secretary of the navy in the McKinley administration. Though the president had been reluctant ("I am afraid he is too pugnacious"), the appointee appeared well qualified for his position, having written authoritatively on naval history, and since then having his views confirmed, in *The Influence of Sea Power Upon History, 1660–1783* (1890), by Captain Alfred Thayer Mahan, instructor at the new Naval War College in Newport, regarding the critical importance of naval power for asserting a nation's greatness. It was at the Naval War College, in fact, in early June, within two months of his having assumed his new duties, that Assistant Secretary of the Navy Roosevelt delivered a speech expressing those views, which he and Captain Mahan shared, for a vastly stronger navy—many more battleships, cruisers, and torpedo boats, of course at considerable expense but worth every penny—as all the while America went on pursuing its Gilded Age material blessings in times of peace.

Roosevelt began his address by quoting General Washington: "To be prepared for war is the most effectual means to promote peace." And to illustrate the point: "in the only contest which we have had with a European power since the Revolution, the War of 1812," the speaker observed, "the struggle and all its attendant disasters were due solely to the fact that we were not prepared to face, and were not ready instantly to resent, an attack upon our honor and interest; while the glorious triumphs at sea which redeemed that war were due to the few preparations which we had actually made." Much would be urged—by the Czar of All the Russias, by Andrew Carnegie and others—on behalf of disarmament and arbitration. Disarmament would be insane; a nation doesn't lay down its weapons on the mere promise that others will do so. As for arbitration: "Arbitration is an excellent thing," Roosevelt conceded, "but ultimately those who wish to see the country at peace with foreign nations will be wise if they place reliance upon a first-class fleet of first-class battleships rather than on any arbitration which the wit of man can devise." America at peace is a prosperous nation; yet "a really great people, proud and high-spirited, would face all the disasters of war rather than purchase that base prosperity which is bought at the price of national honor. All the great masterful races have been fighting races, and the minute that a race loses the hard fighting virtues, then, no matter what else it may retain, no matter how skilled in commerce and finance, in science or art, it has lost its proud right to stand as the equal of the best."

Thus Secretary Roosevelt early on, on June 2, 1897, publicly advocated for the power invested in his new office. Across the Atlantic two months later almost precisely to the day, Ambassador John Hay in England was expressing privately feelings of more tender purport. Mrs. Hay and Helen were sailing back to America for a visit with Clara's widowed mother, Mrs. Stone, in Cleveland, not to return until the fall. Their ship was still within sight of the British coast when Hay responded to an invitation from Elizabeth Cameron to pay her a visit over the Channel in France. "Twenty times," he wrote, "I have made up my alleged mind to drop everything & go—but then comes a lucid interval and I see that 'Desertion' never looks pretty in a court martial. I cannot leave this blessed island."

But the ambassador wrote on, to let Lizzie know that he remembered their time together here in London and that he missed her. "You are beautiful, and clever, and splendid, and charming and fascinating and lovely. But you are, more than all, sweet. It is a keen, living sweetness that lifts you up above all others in charm; that makes the sight of you, the sound of your voice, the touch of you, so full of delight. One can never have enough of you, never. It is because you are so sweet, because the memory of you is so entrancing, that I find a dozen spots in this grimy town like Paradise. The vivid beauty of your face the day we came back from Kensington shines out even now in the mist & fog and gloom and makes the whole town throb with pleasure. . . ."

And to Clara the same day: "I have a few minutes before breakfast," Ambassador Hay wrote, "and cannot put them to a better use than writing to you."

37. CUBA, 1898

Early in the Civil War, in Washington, John Hay had met Theodore Roosevelt's father, Hay just turned twenty-three, Roosevelt Sr. thirty. On trips there the New Yorker stayed at the Willard Hotel, where Hay and Nicolay often went for supper. "I obtained a room at Willard's," Thee wrote to his wife, Mittie, during one such visit, November 7, 1861, "dressed myself and called upon Hay, explained my object in a few words and was immediately shown into the next room where the President sat." The object referred to was the formation of a so-called Allotment Commission, through which Roosevelt Sr. and a couple of friends could serve the Union by benefiting soldiers' families, whom war was depriving of their primary breadwinners. The philanthropist had already been lobbying Congress for the same purpose: he proposed calling on regiments in the various camps in order to urge soldiers to set aside a part of their meager pay to send home, to families who would get no pecuniary relief from their hardship otherwise. Lincoln listened to the proposal, read the relevant documents, and endorsed the request; so that thereafter Theodore Roosevelt Sr. spent many long, arduous months of the war away from his own home, riding in all weathers, at all hours, by all means but often on horseback, from camp to camp. "I stood out there in the dark night," he wrote to his wife of one such solicitation, "surrounded by the men with one candle showing glimpses of their faces, the tents all around us in the woods. One man putting down $5 a month said, 'My old woman has always been good to me and if you please change it to $10.00.' In a minute half a dozen others followed his example and doubled theirs." By such patient persuasion was a philanthropy rendered that finally yielded several millions of dollars to benefit dependents, Roosevelt and his friends covering upper New York state as others extended the effort into neighboring regions. Of course the New Yorker accepted no pay for his labors, which were typically selfless and of aid to the innocent, as well as of humane benefit to the Union.

But it was not as though Theodore Roosevelt Sr. bore arms in the Union's fight. For his wife's sake, for the sake of that unreconstructed southerner Martha Bulloch from Roswell, Georgia, whose three brothers were serving with the Confederate forces, Thee never wore the Union blue or lifted a weapon against the enemy. Rather, he (like many others) paid a substitute to do his fighting for him, a decision that his daughters said he regretted for the rest of his life. His older son, Teedie, no more than three at the time, regretted it as well when he came of age—found in it the only flaw in the behavior of an otherwise faultless and adored father.

Did that account for Theodore Roosevelt Jr.'s bellicosity in his adulthood? At Theodore Sr.'s death the son lamented: "How I wish I could ever do something to keep up his name!"—or to atone for his dereliction when the Union was threatened? Or was it the boy's feeble childhood, stricken with asthma and easily bullied, that made this younger Roosevelt so aggressive until and after the feebleness was overcome? He came to feel that combat taught the most crucial of all virtues, *manliness*, the absence of which, in nations and individuals both, was a defect that no other virtue could redeem. Thus in his western years, out in Dakota Territory in 1886, the fiery ranchman, age twenty-seven, was keen on avenging a border incident against far-off Mexico by leading a bunch of cowboys south into combat: "as utterly reckless a set of desperadoes as ever sat in the saddle," although in the event their services weren't needed. Five years later, a mob killed two American sailors in Valparaiso, after which President Harrison accepted the Chilean government's apology, to Roosevelt's disgust. According to John Hay, Teddy hissed "through clenched teeth that we are dishonest. For two nickels he would declare war himself, shut up the Civil Service Commission, and wage it sole." Again, in 1895, the Monroe Doctrine having involved his country in a dispute between Venezuela and British Guiana, Roosevelt confided to his friend Lodge: "I do hope there will not be any back down among our people. Let the fight"—with Great Britain—"come if it must. I don't care whether our sea coast cities are bombarded or not; we would take Canada."

I don't care whether our sea coast cities are bombarded or not. And all this while there was another hotspot that the new assistant secretary of the navy had been keeping his eye on. He wanted Spain out of Cuba.

In the eighteenth century, Spaniards had possessed the largest empire in the world, much of it in the Western Hemisphere—in South America, Central America, and over huge areas of North America through our present West and up the Pacific coast to Alaska, as well as all of Texas, Louisiana, Florida, and out into the Caribbean. By the end of the following century those New World holdings had shriveled to a mere two islands: Puerto Rico and Cuba. Some ninety miles off the southeastern tip of the United States, Cuba by then had been under Spanish domination for four hundred years, and by no means always benignly. Americans had long presumed that the island would fall into their hands in time. In the 1840s, President Polk of Tennessee quietly offered Spain the then colossal sum of $100,000,000 to purchase it, assuming that Cuba would become a state of the Union; a decade later, in mid-September 1858, Senator Douglas, debating Lincoln at Jonesboro, Illinois, was interrupted with terrific applause when he gave an assurance in passing that America would be acquiring Cuba soon. But Spain was not selling, to presidents Polk or Pierce or Buchanan or anyone else. So southerners, who had wanted the island to extend their prospering slave economy (and for the additional power that Cuba's two senators and various representatives would give them in Congress), lost interest in the acquisition after the Civil War, as all the while miseries of Cubans under Spanish rule intensified.

Agents of the distant government in Madrid grew ever more corrupt, arbitrary, and tyrannical, driving insurgents to fight for independence and a Cuban republic, *Cuba Libre*. Officially the United States remained neutral, right up to this last decade of the nineteenth century, by which time Spain had installed more than one hundred thousand troops on the island to keep subjects in line. It had as well, in 1896, sent over a new military governor, General Valeriano Weyler, to take matters even more firmly in hand. Weyler's troops found it hard to distinguish the innocent peasantry from rebels, who by now were resorting to guerrilla tactics (burning crops, blowing up railroad tracks, firing hit-and-run at isolated groups of soldiers). Thus Weyler emptied towns in order to segregate the peasants within fortified camps, *reconcentrados*—forerunners of internment and concentration camps of the following century.

Those soon became overcrowded, filthy, and fever-ridden. Travelers through Cuba brought word north of horrors inflicted on a miserable populace. A Cuban junta in exile elaborated on atrocities that "Butcher" Weyler was reported to have perpetrated, and that Hearst's mass-circulation *New York Journal* and Pulitzer's *World* competed in publicizing as a stunningly successful means of selling their newspapers.

"During the year preceding the outbreak of the Spanish War"—for war was coming—"I was Assistant Secretary of the Navy," Theodore Roosevelt wrote shortly after the conflict ended. "While my party was in opposition, I had preached, with all the fervor and zeal I possessed, our duty to intervene in Cuba, and to take this opportunity of driving the Spaniard from the Western World. Now that my party had come to power"—with McKinley's inauguration—"I felt it incumbent on me, by word and deed, to do all I could to secure the carrying out of the policy in which I so heartily believed; and"—Roosevelt adds revealingly—"from the beginning I had determined that, if a war came, somehow or other, I was going to the front."

But neither Spain nor President McKinley wanted war, the major having had his fill of it at Antietam, with the corpses piled high. Madrid offered gestures of conciliation: released political prisoners, talked about Cuban autonomy, alleviated conditions in the fortified camps, closed some down. But on February 15, 1898, during a courtesy visit of a few weeks in Havana, while lying peacefully at anchor in the harbor at 9:40 on a quiet evening, the U.S. battleship *Maine* abruptly, horrendously exploded, killing some 260 Americans on board. These many years later, examiners of the surviving evidence generally agree that the explosion was most likely caused by a coal fire aboard igniting stored ammunition; yet in the midst of the rabid war fever of 1898 an inquiry, hastily convened, concluded differently: the cause was external. Spaniards were blamed. They protested, condoled, denied that the harbor contained any mines. Yet the whipped-up fury of public opinion— "Remember the *Maine*! To Hell with Spain!"—proved overwhelming. On April 25, Congress declared war.

At once Theodore Roosevelt applied for an army commission and, on the day he received it, May 6, he resigned from the navy department and set about gathering together an army force to lead into battle. Volunteers rushed to the call in numbers exceeding places available by twenty to one. The lucky few chosen mustered in a field outside San Antonio, with Lieutenant Colonel Roosevelt in his new Brooks Brothers uniform as deputy commander of this First U.S. Volunteer Cavalry, under his close friend Colonel Leonard Wood. A couple of weeks followed of drilling and training these "Rough Riders,"

Roosevelt in his element at last, engrossed, strict but fair, knowing the name of each man under his command, treating all equally: Harvard men, Yale men, policemen, cowpunchers, ranch hands, Westerners, Indians, each stirred by patriotism and a thirst for adventure. He and Colonel Wood got the men to Tampa, to the staging area for invading Cuba, and, in the midst of twenty-five thousand other recruits and massive confusion, their leader pushed till he saw his own five hundred aboard troopships and finally under way.

The war itself didn't amount to much, hardly three months before Spain sued for peace, although of course no one knew that at the start. And it was the navy more than the army that brought peace about. Before resigning his naval post, the assistant secretary, in the absence of vacationing Navy secretary Long, had ordered Commodore Dewey in Hong Kong to move at once, the instant war was declared, on the Spanish in Manila Bay. Thus, on May 1, Dewey was able to surprise and destroy the Spanish Pacific squadron at anchor (ten paltry, outmoded vessels) without losing a single American life, an exhilarating victory with which to begin hostilities. And Spain's rather more formidable Caribbean fleet lay bottled up in a harbor in Cuba, at Santiago, until daring finally, in early July, to venture forth against American naval vessels to its own destruction before it could reach the open sea.

The U.S. Army, by contrast, was beset with problems throughout: rancid beef for the troops, wool uniforms furnished them to wear in sweltering heat, not enough wagons, not enough feed for horses and mules. Yet Roosevelt did get his Rough Riders into battle against the Spaniard and acquitted himself brilliantly, a veritable hero conspicuously mounted ahead on his pony Texas while his men behind awaited orders on foot (another army foul-up, steaming from Tampa with room on board only for officers' horses, the cavalry's mounts left back on shore). It was July 1, 1898—"the great day of my life"—the men crouching at the base of a hill in the smoke of battle as their colonel (Roosevelt had been breveted full colonel on the battlefield) galloped ahead toward the enemy on the hill adjacent, reconnoitering. He stood out an easy target, yet that lone horseman appeared utterly unafraid. War correspondent Edward Marshall of the *New York Journal*, observing, called him "the most magnificent soldier I have ever seen." In full view of the Spaniard, the colonel sped up the slope of the next hill over, halting at a barbed-wire fence not forty feet from the summit. Leaping down, he turned his horse loose and shouted to his men to come on. Under heavy fire they plunged forward across an open field, their colonel in the lead, up toward Spanish soldiers in entrenchments at the top. Through the bloody moments ahead, losses among the Rough Riders were three times those of the enemy, but it was the Spaniard who yielded. The crest was taken. Santiago lay exposed below.

The assault formed the army's single dramatic victory of the war, well covered by reporters and photographers accompanying the troops. And it was hardly over before Roosevelt and his men were raring for more: they wanted to take Havana, invade Puerto Rico, invade Spain. But the fighting was about done. Santiago fell ten days later, and Spain sued for peace on August 12.

Meanwhile, as summer days advanced, tropic fever more deadly than either side's weaponry bore down on the colonel's men. With nothing left here for his troops to do, Colonel Roosevelt had them ordered out and up to a more salubrious climate, to New York and a restorative camp at Montauk, at the eastern tip of Long Island. Once there, he found horses at last for his cavalry to ride, and photographers came out from New York City to get pictures of these Rough Riders showing off their equestrian skills, and reporters wrote stories back of the shameful inadequacy of the encampment provided such heroes, and Colonel Roosevelt's family arrived from Oyster Bay, and President McKinley paid a call on the Rough Riders and their heroic colonel—now America's most famous soldier, his popularity immensely enhanced, his future prospects golden; already there was talk of running Theodore Roosevelt for governor of New York State.

The fame spread overseas. A message dated July 27, 1898, arrived for Colonel Roosevelt from London, from America's ambassador to the Court of St. James: "I am afraid I am the last of your friends to congratulate you on the brilliant campaign which now seems drawing to a close, and in which you have gained so much experience and glory. When the war began I was like the rest," Ambassador Hay confessed, "I deplored [your leaving] your place in the Navy where you were so useful and so acceptable. But I knew it was idle to preach to a young man. You obeyed your own daemon, and I imagine we older fellows will all have to confess that you were in the right." Indubitably: Roosevelt's crowded hours on San Juan and Kettle hills transformed his future. "You have written your name on several pages of your country's history," Hay assured him meanwhile, "and they are all honorable to you and comfortable to your friends."

One more paragraph the diplomat added, four early words of which have adhered to Hay like burrs—usually quoted out of a context that reads in its entirety:

It has been a splendid little war; begun with the highest motives, carried on with magnificent intelligence and spirit, favored by that Fortune which favors the brave. It is now to be concluded, I hope, with that fine good nature, which is, after all, the distinguishing trait of the American character.

The "little" does sound condescending, even callous, from a gentleman far from Cuban trenches that had recently contained dead bodies in the blue and white uniforms of the Spanish regular army, he by whom they were vanquished bearing witness to his Rough Riders' sharpshooting: "most of the fallen had little holes in their heads from which their brains were oozing." But in little wars as in big, the dead are no less dead; and, as Hay wrote, this *was* a little war, of two or three months duration. And the "splendid"?—from one who had himself seen troops horribly mangled after Bull Run at the start of a big war, a murderous conflict that lasted four heartrending years ("the wounded, bereft of arms, of legs," Lincoln's secretary had noted at the time, "eyes put out, flesh wounds in the face and body, and uniforms crimsoned with blood"):—the ambassador's literal "splendid" these thirty-eight years later alludes, perhaps, less to the Cuban conflict itself than to the high motives with which this Spanish-American War was undertaken—disinterestedly to liberate an island people from tyranny; to the Fortune-favored spirit with which the war was fought, at Manila Bay, off Santiago, and on San Juan Heights; and to the promise, of the Teller Amendment passed in Congress before its commencement, that the United States was entering the conflict without thought or intention of gaining territory.

During those same exciting summer weeks in 1898, while newly commissioned Lieutenant Colonel Roosevelt was forming soldiers out of raw recruits in San Antonio, getting them to Tampa and ashore in Cuba, leading them on July 1 up Kettle Hill to close in combat with Spaniards entrenched at the summit, John Hay in London pursued his not disagreeable duties as American ambassador: writing his handwritten dispatches on British views of current events to his president back home, attending to the numerous social demands and ceremonial obligations, keeping older diplomatic friendships in good repair while cultivating new ones, and at dinner on more than one occasion seated at the right of the queen (a favorite with her, in fact, as far as so elevated a personage was permitted to show favor).

That same June, the J. Donald Camerons arrived in England to lay claim to a massive old manor house that they had rented in Kent, near Dover. Don Cameron was along with his wife, Lizzie, and their daughter Martha (in whom the father appeared to take only passing interest, already possessed as he was of five grown daughters by a first marriage, the eldest of them three years older than was this second wife). Henry Adams was of the company, and—the way

John Hay with friends and members of his family at Surrenden Dering, Kent, in August 1898. Private collection.

Lizzie liked it and Don perhaps less so—various other friends would be coming and going at Surrenden Dering as summer days flowed on. There they found gardens, a deer park, and pleasure grounds of beauty and wide extent spreading out from a house—according to Adams, about as big as Versailles—that was set on a rise and with a history reaching back to the fifteenth century (fire destroyed most of the sprawling structure in 1952). Yet even with Camerons nearby, Hay couldn't get away from diplomatic duties at Westminster; so he and his family came down only in August, when for a time the mansion served as a summer embassy.

A photograph shows a group of guests gathered on steps before Surrenden Dering that summer of 1898. Neither Lizzie nor Clara is among them, but Lizzie's daughter Martha is, age twelve then and seated on the lowest step beside Hay's daughter Alice, who is eighteen. Helen Hay, now twenty-three, sits on the step behind her sister. On the same step at Helen's right are three others, including her younger brother Clarence, thirteen, knickered knees drawn up beside his father. And there sits John Milton Hay in his sixtieth year, dressed as are all the males, young and older, in impeccable coat, high-necked collar, and neckware, as the four females on what was a warm August day are amply bloused to the neck, white sleeves to their wrists, skirts to their ankles. Hay's son Del, a graduate of Yale by then and working with his father at the Embassy in London, stands besuited at the farthest right, near Henry Adams, erect in profile on the steps gazing down at the others. The host, Don Cameron, stands behind them all, nearest the entrance door.

The faces are mostly serious (doubtless the longer exposure discouraged smiling) and none is detailed, although you can make out Hay's fastidiously shaped and trimmed mustache and Vandyke, as well as the flawless grooming generally that the age expected of a certain class, both male and female. Perpetually amazing: once all were flesh, occupied space on the planet, cast shadows—these few of the very people we've been considering verified thus as historical, words quoted theirs that they wrote down or said for others to attend to and record. The camera has preserved a moment in lives at Surrenden Dering, manor house in Kent, from which, after the photographer was done, the guests relaxed in their places, or returned inside, or stepped onto the lawns, their hour ticking its minutes away precisely as ours does now, while those evanescent figures were standing or sitting at the solid entrance of a mansion long since vanished.

The Camerons weren't getting along, although too well bred to make their differences public. Don had withdrawn from politics, rented out their house at Lafayette Square, and would move back to his estate in Harrisburg. Although divorce was out of the question, Lizzie had no wish to return to Pennsylvania, disliked boring Harrisburg, would live in Europe instead, where she could see and entertain her many friends. One such invited here during these summer weeks was Henry James, who the year before had leased Lamb House, in Rye, in which to live out the rest of his days, alternating with briefer stays in London. Like others, James came over to visit. And it was here in Pluckley parish, near Rye and Dover, at Surrenden Dering, that John Hay, on the evening of August 14, was brought a cablegram from America:

IT GIVES ME EXCEPTIONAL PLEASURE TO TENDER TO YOU THE OFFICE OF SECRETARY OF STATE, VICE DAY, WHO WILL RESIGN TO TAKE SERVICE ON THE PARIS COMMISSION, TO NEGOTIATE PEACE. IT IS IMPORTANT THAT YOU SHOULD ASSUME DUTIES HERE NOT LATER THAN THE FIRST OF SEPTEMBER. CABLE ANSWER.

WILLIAM MCKINLEY.

38. THE BENEFICENT WORK OF THE WORLD

To his president's unexpected summons, Hay wrote two replies. The poetical side of his nature ("I loafe and invite my soul," another poet—and Hay's earlier friend—the late Walt Whitman had sung) sought ease, uncertain health urging a preference for leisure throughout the younger man's life; just now, for instance, he was suffering from kidney problems, so wouldn't be able to get back to Washington by the first of September in any case. Yet he sent the second cable, accepting what was offered, his friends at Surrenden Dering telling him he had to. "It was impossible," the ambassador realized, "after the President had been so generous, to pick and choose, and say, 'I will have this and not that.'" As he had often done in the past, Hay honored the other side of his nature by taking on a demanding public duty, although to his brother-in-law, Sam Mather, he confessed to a sense of inadequacy before the particular tasks that this duty entailed: "I feel as if I had been drawn into a match with Corbett"—Gentleman Jim Corbett, recent heavyweight champion—"and the day was drawing on, and all my hope was to be knocked out by an early blow which would not kill me."

At any rate, Hay's tenure at the Court of St. James had been a shining success—all the more reason to regret its ending abruptly. "If it is possible," the *Times* of London—not conspicuously pro-American—editorialized about Hay's leaving, "to speak of any envoy from one country to another as ideal, the word may be used of Mr. Hay. He knew England, and before he had been in this country a year England came to know him and to like and respect him." Indeed, Hay's major achievement as ambassador—there was wide agreement on this—was to improve relations between the two great English-speaking nations. No one person could likely have brought about such a change; the historical moment would have had to help. But as recently as three years earlier those relations were very tense, enough to make Police Commissioner Roosevelt hope our people wouldn't back down; nor did he care if Great Britain bombed our coastal cities, because we would take Canada. President Cleveland's message to Congress that December of 1895 had pronounced it the duty of the United States "to resist by every means in its power as a willful aggression upon its rights and interests" any British effort to exercise jurisdiction over territory that the United States considered Venezuelan. The issue concerned what was the proper border between our South American neighbor and British Guiana alongside; and the public heard the president's formulation of that issue as threatening war if Britain, in trying to settle it, violated the Monroe Doctrine.

In the event, the disputed boundary was submitted to arbitration, and the crisis passed. But what a difference in mutual regard these few years later! Ambassador Hay himself, addressing a distinguished audience at the Lord Mayor's Easter dinner in London last April, had alluded to "a friendship that I am sure the vast majority of both peoples hope and trust is to be eternal." No mere expediency had brought the United States and the United Kingdom together. "All of us who think," the ambassador had said, "cannot but see that there is a sanction like that of religion which binds us to a sort of partnership in the beneficent work of the world. Whether we will it or not, we are associated in that work by the very nature of things, and no man and no group of men can prevent it. We are bound by a tie which we did not forge and which we cannot break; we are joint ministers of the same sacred mission of liberty and progress, charged with duties which we cannot evade by the imposition of irresistible hands."

The conviction stated publicly last April—of a sacred mission that the United States and the United Kingdom with their common language held jointly: "a sort of partnership" to do "the beneficent work of the world"— Colonel Hay brought with him five months later to Washington. There, on September 30, he took up his new responsibilities as secretary of state. His immediate predecessor in that office, briefly, had been Judge William R. Day of Canton, Ohio, McKinley's longtime close friend and legal advisor, now head of the U.S. commission meeting with Spanish counterparts to negotiate specific terms concerning the peace treaty that would officially end the Spanish-American War. The negotiators deliberated into December, during the course of their talks obliged to deal with a matter that few had thought much about before the war began: what to do with a sizable Spanish possession on the other side of the globe.

Was it "the beneficent work of the world" to become involved in the fate of the Philippines? As with Cuba, so with that far-off archipelago of eight million people: Spain had ruled over both for centuries. In both, those native to the islands generally loathed the Spaniard and wished him gone. Nevertheless, Judge Day of the peace commission in Paris thought that—the war having been fought over Cuba and Puerto Rico—we should give the Philippines back to Spain. President McKinley for his part admitted that before war broke out, he couldn't have found the Philippines on a map within two thousand miles; yet during the conflict, he came to feel that we should at least keep one island of the seven thousand as a coaling station, where our merchant ships could replenish fuel and supplies on their way to and from China. Colonel Roosevelt, campaigning this fall for governor of New York State, was certain we should take the entire archipelago under our protection, administering it ulti-mately for the benefit of the Filipinos, to whom we would return their cluster of islands much improved, whenever (maybe a century from now) the evolving natives were able to govern themselves.

Really, what were the alternatives? Like so many others, Anglo-Saxons— British and American—of the 1890s were (though the word didn't exist until the 1930s) profoundly *racist*. And many among them, including Hay and Roosevelt, thought in Darwinian terms, of races evolving as does all animate nature. Thus, patently, some races were more advanced than others. Cauca-sians were most advanced, more specifically the very Anglo-Saxons who had developed such essentials of high civilization as representative government, habeas corpus, trial by jury, freedom of assembly and of religion and of the press. Liberty and progress: these were the gifts that an American protectorate might offer the benighted Philippine people. And what alternative would serve the world better? Return the archipelago to Spain for further exploitation and misrule? Turn the Philippines over to the natives, who would be at one anoth-er's throats before our departing ships had dropped below the horizon? Or leave the islands a prey to the Germans or Japanese?

That last, if the United States abandoned Filipinos to their fate, loomed as something more than a possibility. It was altogether probable that the Japanese or some European power, most likely the Germans, would move to take pos-session of the archipelago. Back in late 1884, Germany's chancellor Bismarck had invited Europe's industrial powers to a conference in Berlin, where they proceeded to carve up Africa among themselves: Britain, France, Belgium, Portugal, Spain, Italy, and Germany appropriating large swatches of the Dark Continent as colonies or protectorates. That arrogance was a product of the times, of improved transportation—iron ships, iron rails, iron horses—and of industrialism, racism, and missionary zeal: of the outward expansion of factor-ies, having produced more goods than their countries could absorb, seeking markets and raw materials; of racism, which viewed indigenous peoples of Africa, of Manchuria, of Australia, and elsewhere as inferior to the white races of Europe (and a cheap labor force); and of a missionary impulse that led Europeans to regard their intrusions as something beyond mere commercial grabs for markets, rather as a means of advancing civilization worldwide. Not just from Europe. From Japan as well. From Russia. And from America, which, in July 1898—as fighting in the Spanish-American War wound down—acceded to the entreaty of white settlers in the Republic of Hawaii by officially designating those islands a U.S. territory.

All this while, European powers continued to expand, some now in search of "spheres of influence," a more seemly term, perhaps, than "colonies": France in Indochina, Russia in Manchuria, Japan coveting Korea. In that setting, over this fall of 1898, the mild-mannered McKinley at prayer became persuaded that the entire Philippine archipelago must be ours, in order to enact a "benevolent assimilation" that would give the brown people out there hospitals, schools, roads, the English language, the Protestant religion, and all the many blessings of democracy. Secretary Hay instructed the peace negotiators accordingly. Madrid protested but was in no position to bargain; they acceded perforce, and we agreed to pay $20,000,000 for what was arguably no longer Spain's to sell.

So this was the stirring, grasping, complex world that confronted John Hay in his new duties in Washington. And it was the particular historical moment that accounts in part for a friendlier relationship arising between the United States and the United Kingdom. Britain, involved like the other powers in grabbing for lands in Africa and China, welcomed our friendship as counterweight to its new, militant rivalry with Germany. The kaiser, who had read Mahan's *Influence of Sea Power*, was building battleships and cruisers to overtake Great Britain as mistress of the seas, convinced that navies were the essential military force of these global times (as many in the century fast approaching would conclude that air power was). Such fleets required coaling stations, a fact that Americans, now possessed of Hawaii and the Philippines, had learned as well.

But Filipinos regarded their archipelago as already an independent republic in the making, the natives engaged since 1896 in driving out Spain from all but Manila when the Spanish-American War erupted. Commodore Dewey destroyed Spain's Pacific squadron, and Filipinos helped American forces take the capital, expecting as a reward that their republic would be recognized at war's end. Instead, they got a U.S. military occupation, although with assurances of independence at some future date. Early in the following year, on February 2, 1899, insurgents clashed violently with U.S. forces (who saw their adversaries as "niggers," "gugus," and the like). A protracted, bloody, merciless war between natives and foreign occupiers followed. Four years and seventy thousand American troops were needed finally to put it down.

That was a military problem, but with diplomatic ramifications that Secretary Hay, new at his job, would have to deal with. At the same time, European powers and Japan were threatening to carve up the huge, feeble, very rich Chinese empire the way Africa had been carved up not long before. In 1895, Japan went to war with China, which in six brief, humiliating months was forced to sue for peace. The victor imposed a sphere of influence on Korea and took Formosa (Taiwan) outright. Long before then, foreigners had gained access to certain Chinese trading ports—Canton first, then Shanghai, Hong Kong, and others. After Japan's revealing victory, Germany from its port of Tsingtao spread its sphere of influence deep into Shantung province, Russia into the Liao-tung Peninsula, Britain at Kowloon and along the Yangtze River, and France farther south, on the Luichow Peninsula. China's obvious military weakness had emboldened them all.

Attending to advice he sought out, moving shrewdly day by day, Hay dealt through 1899 with the threatened dismemberment of the Chinese Empire in a way that was to bring his nation much credit and him sudden fame as a statesman-diplomat of international standing. The United States wouldn't join the carrion rush on China by tearing off a sphere of influence of its own, yet as a new industrial power it craved a share in the massive wealth of the China trade. The secretary's solution, patiently arrived at over months of endeavor, was the securing of assent one by one from powers already possessed of such spheres that they would acquiesce in each other's claims, that they would not discriminate against any other power's trading in their spheres, and that they would continue to respect the integrity of the Chinese Empire—wouldn't carve out a chunk of it for themselves. Each nation agreed to abide by those terms if all the others would. Hay waited, then—receiving no emphatic demur—abruptly declared that all had assented. John Hay's "Open Door Policy" went into effect: French traders could trade without discrimination in Britain's sphere of influence, German traders in Russia's, and America—with no territorial ambitions at all—could trade with each of the treaty cities at no disadvantage, while the wobbly Chinese Empire remained intact.

The policy seemed to affirm the purity of American motives in the Philippines, for we would appear to have no more long-term craving for a Pacific archipelago than, demonstrably, for a piece of mainland China. Yet war raged on in the islands, as Filipinos fighting earlier to rid their land of the Spanish overlord now fought bitterly against the American intruder. Very much as Cuban insurgents had fought against the Spanish tyrant. Much as Boers—descendants of Dutch in South Africa—were fighting this same fall of 1899 against the invading British, who, lured by gold and Cecil Rhodes's imperial ambitions, were intent on establishing dominance on the Dark Continent "from the Cape to Cairo." And soon, in China, much as native Chinese were rising suddenly against Foreign Devils, to murder and burn and drive the lot of them out.

These were the Glorious and Harmonious Fists, a secret society whom Westerners called "Boxers" because of the peculiar martial arts they practiced. In the summer of 1900, the native combatants burst forth against Western missionaries and Chinese who had converted to Christianity, slaughtering thousands of the latter, setting fires, tearing up the railroad between Tientsin and Peking, China's capital. In June the Boxers laid siege to the British embassy there (that is, in modern Beijing), where foreigners had sought refuge, "the entire city in the possession of a rioting, murdering mob, with no visible effort being made by the Government in any way to restrain it." Those anxious words are Edwin Conger's, America's man on the spot, in a hurried cable to Hay in June. Then silence. For weeks, no word could be got into or out of the tormented region. Through July the rampage tore on. Boxers had murdered the German minister and killed a Japanese diplomat. Nine hundred foreigners were trapped in the legation. Virtually all Christian religious missions in the capital had been burned to the ground. News continued sketchy, but what unconfirmed bits filtered through back home were terrifying. Relatives and friends waited helplessly, in suspense and fear. In mid-July, a British newspaper reported that everybody holed up in the embassy had been murdered. St. Paul's cathedral in London planned a memorial service.

Could the trapped Americans still be alive? Hay on the other side of the globe found a way circuitously to send a message to Conger in cipher: "Communicate tidings bearer." Would it even get through? An answer arrived, also in cipher: "For one month we have been besieged in British Legation under continued shot and shell from Chinese troops. Quick relief only can prevent general massacre." But was the message authentic? One more exchange of cables: provide bearer with middle name of Minister Conger's wife. The correct answer came back: Alta. They were alive.

From the Philippines, U.S. soldiers had arrived with orders to work in concert with other nations but make no alliances. The combined forces secured Tientsin, and a contingent nearly twenty thousand strong from America, Japan, and various European powers advanced the eighty miles toward Peking. On August 14, 1900, they burst into the capital to relieve the haggard, overjoyed inmates at the Legation. Of the nine hundred, sixty-six had perished during the siege; the rest were saved.

Hay had retired to the Fells on Lake Sunapee by then, leaving the department in the able, trusted hands of his subordinates. The strain had exhausted the secretary, not well in any case, suffering from backaches and problems with (as he said) his hydraulics. Yet for delivering the captives from the Legation, for avoiding an extension of warfare in China, for preventing a dismemberment of the Chinese Empire, and for securing to the United States all the advantages of the China trade without any entangling alliances with European or Asiatic powers, Hay was being hailed as a world diplomat, a statesman who achieved his ends through principle, high morality, conciliation, and patience, all in the interest of peace. Secretary Hay returned to Washington in early October, overwhelmed with plaudits from around the globe.

And in that same month, Mark Twain finally came home to stay. The same Western world so full of praise now for Secretary of State John Hay had been made aware, over the decade of the 1890s just ended, of the remarkable vicissitudes in the life of Samuel L. Clemens, so that its sympathy and admiration were fully awakened on the humorist's behalf, and all the newspapers reported the arrival at the New York piers at ten Monday evening, October 15, 1900, of the S.S. *Minnehaha*, bringing Mark Twain and his family home. "Mr. Clemens never looked better, was in a splendid humor, and greeted his friends with the most affectionate cordiality." Reporters clustered around with their questions; and Mark Twain, an old newspaperman himself, obliged.

The scene on the docks was jubilant, for a gentleman who had suffered through just about every extreme of emotional turmoil during the preceding ten years. Generally, the public was aware of Clemens's trials, but now was no time to ask about that. "They gave you the courtesy of the port, didn't they?" a bystander called out. And Mark answered in his characteristic slow Missouri drawl: "Yes, I wrote to Secretary Gage"—Lyman Gage, McKinley's secretary of the treasury—"telling him that my baggage was on a 16,000-ton ship, which was quite large enough to accommodate all I had, which, while it consisted of a good many things, was not good enough to pay duty on, yet too good to throw away. I accordingly suggested that he write the customs people to let it in, as I thought they would be more likely to take his word than mine."

A reporter asked the celebrity to tell them what he had been up to over so extended an absence from his native land. "Now, that's a long story," Mark answered, "but I suppose I must give you something, even if it is in a condensed form." He and his family had left for France, for Aix-les-Bains, in June 1891, intending to stay for a few months, but found living expenses more reasonable overseas. Thus, after a time, they moved on to Berlin, to the Riviera, to the baths near Frankfurt, then through much of 1892 in Florence, where the author wrote most of his *Joan of Arc* and *Pudd'nhead Wilson*. In the spring of 1895, Clemens, his wife, and his daughter Clara had started from England on a year-long lecture tour that circled the globe, across the northern United States, to Australia, India, South Africa, and finally back to England. There he lingered another year: "I was lecturing, reading, or working hard in other ways, writing magazine stories and doing other literary work." Then to Switzerland, on to Vienna for an extended stay, then back to England, to Sweden, and again to England, before arriving finally in New York City this October evening in 1900.

And "everybody's glad you're back," reporters assured him, "which you know of course." Among much else, they wanted his views on the Philippines. Would he talk about that? The beloved writer and sage—has any other American in our entire history been more widely loved?—answered them candidly. On that world-encircling lecture tour, "I left these shores at Vancouver," he said, "a red-hot imperialist. I wanted the American eagle to go screaming into the Pacific. It seemed tiresome and tame for it to content itself with the Rockies. Why not spread it's wings over the Philippines, I asked myself? And I thought it would be a real good thing to do": to make Filipinos, after their suffering under tyranny for three centuries, as free as ourselves.

But since then Mark had traveled the world and read the newspapers, "and I have read carefully the treaty of Paris, and I have seen that we do not intend to free but to subjugate the people of the Philippines. We have gone there to conquer, not to redeem," even though it should have been both our pleasure and our duty to free those people and let them handle their domestic affairs in their own way. "And so," this returning exile told the reporters forthrightly, "I am an anti-imperialist. I am opposed to having the eagle put its talons on any other land."

39. FAMILY GRIEFS

At the beginning of the 1890s, the Clemenses in Hartford had appeared to be among America's most fortunate families: husband living in a gorgeous mansion with a loving, much loved wife and three attractive daughters—highly successful author possessed of a worldwide following, adored lecturer, shrewdly prospering businessman, founder of a leading American publishing house, investor in a wonderful new typesetter soon to be indispensable in just about every printing office on the globe. Yet a year later, in June 1891, the family closed up their over-expensive home—said goodbye to servants, to friends, to pets, and, "tear-blinded," daughter Clara, then just shy of seventeen, remembered forty years later, "passed, for the last time, through the front door and away to unknown lands."

Misled by success, Charles L. Webster & Co., Publisher, had overextended itself, taken on more projects than it could ever discharge. From Europe in the four years ahead, Clemens crossed the Atlantic fourteen times in an effort to straighten out his tangled affairs—nor could he have muddled through except for a fortuitous encounter with a great fan of Mark Twain's who happened to be a titan at the apex of Standard Oil. Henry Huttleston Rogers took Clemens's financial woes in hand and patiently worked through them as a labor of love. Charles L. Webster & Co. would have to declare bankruptcy; and although not legally liable for his publishing company's indebtedness, Mark Twain must pay off its creditors, all $90,000 owed to them (over $2 million now), for the humorist's reputation was worth more than money. Hence, the world lecture tour, and the book that resulted, *Following the Equator* (1897), proceeds from which ventures (along with Rogers's investments of any excess) did succeed in satisfying everyone to whom the bankrupt publishing house was indebted.

Newspaper readers took admiring note. Rogers had looked, as well, into the Paige-typesetter affair and confirmed—to Clemens's relief—that the invention was all its inventor said it was. At last a specimen was actually put to work in the pressrooms of the *Chicago Times-Herald*. But once set to the daily grind, the complicated machine kept breaking down. It was "most interesting, most fascinating," Rogers reported, "but it was not practical": too elaborate, too elegant. Clemens got the grim news back in Paris. "It hit me like a thunderclap. It knocked every rag of sense out of my head, and I went flying here and there and yonder, not knowing what I was doing." A dream of ten years shattered, all that money irretrievably lost, all $300,000 of it—well over $8 million in today's currency. (Whitelaw Reid had meanwhile set Mergenthaler's Linotype up in the *Tribune* pressroom back in the mid-1880s, a less refined, bulkier, noisier typesetter that would end by doing all that Clemens had dreamed the magician Paige's would do, and do it robustly in print shops big and small. Ottmar Mergenthaler died early, of tuberculosis, by no means as rich as he should have been; but James Paige died in abject poverty, unknown, buried in a potter's field in Chicago in 1917.)

An even more anguishing event than disasters with the publishing house and the typesetter awaited the Clemens family. They had set out from England on their arduous round-the-world tour, stopping in Elmira to leave the more fragile daughters, Susy and Jean, with Livy's sister, the girls' Aunt Sue. In August of the following year, 1896, the travelers were back in England, at Guildford, their voyage completed, parents and daughter Clara eagerly awaiting a reunion with Clara's sisters, now on their way. But word came that Susy was delayed en route with family friends, indisposed, although nothing serious. Nevertheless, Livy and Clara booked passage at once, to learn on landing in

New York that Susy had died of spinal meningitis three days earlier, on August 18, 1896. And but for a father's imprudent business ventures, might they have been spared all this, all of them still living among loving friends in their beautiful Hartford home? Disconsolate, utterly crushed, Clemens back in England charged himself with "a million things whereby I have brought misfortune and sorrow to this family." Six months later, still in deep grief, he wrote to Joe Twichell, Susy's "Uncle Joe": "I did not know that she could go away, and take our lives with her, yet leave our dull bodies behind. And I did not know what she was. To me she was but treasure in the bank, the amount known, the need to look at it daily, handle it, weigh it, count it, *realize* it, not necessary; and now that I would do it, it is too late; they tell me it is not there, has vanished away in a night, the bank is broken, my fortune is gone, I am a pauper. How am I to comprehend this?"

Livy never did get over the loss of hers and Sam's admittedly favorite daughter, in a less knowledgeable age that saw no reason to hide such preferences. The bereft family lingered in Europe, the world made aware of their loss, as Mark Twain finished his travel book to pay off indebtedness, then wandered restlessly about. In Vienna, Clemens learned that the last payment had been made. "Mrs. Clemens has been reading the creditors' letters over and over again," he wrote to Rogers in March 1898, "and thanks you deeply for sending them, and says it is the only really happy day she has had since Susy died." There had even been money left over, which Rogers (by that time Mark's very dear friend) invested for him, taking advantage of not-then-illegal insider trading. In January 1899: "By grace of you," Clemens wrote to him, "we have had a Christmas and a New Year this time which knocked the gloom out of a season which we have grown accustomed"—since Susy's death—"to anticipate with dread." And in the following year, on the family's return to America, Mark Twain was affluent once more—and more loved than ever by a populace filled with sympathy for his family's ordeals, as well as admiration for the man's courage (his grueling lecture tour begun at age fifty-nine, when average life expectancy for men in America was sixty) and for his integrity in repaying in full debts he could have dodged with pennies on the dollar.

Returned to New York that October 1900, the lecturer-sage was swamped with invitations to speak. Everyone wanted to hear him, and, obliging them when he was able, he spoke his mind. "It is the foreigners who are making all the trouble in China," he told well-fed banqueters, "and if they would only get out how pleasant everything would be! The Boxer is a patriot; he is the only patriot China has, and I wish him success." But that was said in Mark Twain's familiar, drawling voice; so that those who chose need not take the humorist seriously. And to be sure, he was but one anti-imperialist—if the most prominent one—along with Andrew Carnegie, William James, former presidents Harrison and Cleveland, William Dean Howells, Lincoln Steffens, Hamlin Garland, Jane Addams, and William Jennings Bryan, to name a few others.

That last, Bryan, was again a candidate for president this fall of 1900, in an election just a couple of weeks away. Major McKinley was running for a second term, once more from his front porch in Canton, Ohio; but this time the ticket contained someone who could match Mr. Bryan's scampering about—the Democrat yet again traveling the land to deliver his message: now of bimetallism, opposition to trusts, and anti-imperialism.

President McKinley's vice president in his first term, Garret Hobart (who had been renting the Camerons' home on Lafayette Square), had died in office in November 1899—which, incidentally, put John Hay, secretary of state, next in line for the presidency. In June 1900, the Republican convention in Philadelphia was charged with selecting a new vice-presidential nominee. Overwhelmingly it chose New York's governor, the hero of San Juan Hill, Theodore Roosevelt. During the fall campaign that followed, nominee Roosevelt proved even more limber than was candidate Bryan, traveling twenty-one thousand miles through twenty-four states and giving seven hundred speeches, as many as ten a day. About Mr. Bryan's charges, for instance, that the McKinley administration was imperialistic: let the nations of Europe build empires. America, Roosevelt assured the crowds at his many whistle stops, had no interest in empires, although from the beginning we've been an *expanding* nation: across the Alleghenies into Kentucky and onto the Mississippi, into Louisiana, Florida, Texas, over the Rockies into Oregon, California, into Alaska, not long ago to Hawaii. But that was expansion, not empire-building, and those who saw no difference between the two were either ignorant or disingenuous. Thus Roosevelt, campaigning with his usual flair, uttering two words for every one of Bryan's. "I drowned him out," the candidate grinned when the election was over—an election, once more, that William McKinley won, by a larger margin than previously. The major had run on his record of bringing prosperity back from hard times—the "Full Dinner Pail." Bryan's issue of bimetallism no longer counted for much; improved gold-mining techniques in South Africa and the discovery of gold in the Yukon had brought the price of that metal down, even as silver's price had gone up with the depletion of such mines as the Comstock Lode out West. And McKinley had won a war, put the United States on the world map, to the satisfaction of most of his fellow Americans, the great majority not much concerned about whether we were expansionary or imperialistic, as long as we were a power to reckon with. The anti-imperialists, for their part, were never able, despite—or per-haps because of—their distinguished membership, to work in concert effec-tively. And in any case, they were far outnumbered.

The secretary of state all this while had been dealing with other diplomatic issues besides the Boxers, the Open Door Policy, and the threatened dismem-berment of China. Notably, he was engaged in negotiations with England concerning a canal to be built in Central America between the Atlantic and the Pacific. The matter had long been contemplated. Hay himself, as assistant secretary of state in the Hayes administration back in 1880, had served as translator for the Frenchman Ferdinand de Lesseps, builder of the Suez Canal, then in Washington hoping he might persuade the United States to support his plans to cut a similar canal across Panama. But President Hayes had no interest in furthering a French company's efforts; our government meant to build the passageway unaided. And the time to do so came soon; for the Spanish-American War demonstrated the vital importance of such a cross-ing, the battleship *Oregon* in 1898 having required sixty-six days to steam at full speed in wartime from San Francisco around Cape Horn before taking battle station in Admiral Sampson's fleet off Santiago.

A problem, however, that Secretary Hay was obliged to cope with was an earlier treaty between England and America, the Clayton-Bulwer Treaty of 1850, which stipulated that the two countries (England at the time showing considerable interest in the region because of what would become British Honduras)—that both nations, when the time came, would build a canal together, and that the passage through it, open to all at the same rates, would never be fortified. Now, in 1899, Hay and the British ambassador, Lord Julian Pauncefote, devised a treaty that was signed and ready by early 1900 to submit to the Senate for ratification. Hay had persuaded Britain, still full of good feelings for America, to renounce its interest in such a canal, thus effectively abrogating the earlier treaty. The United States was to dig it alone, on the understanding that all nations would be allowed to pass through. And, as in the Clayton-Bulwer Treaty, the canal would be open at the same charges for all in peace and war, and unfortified.

Governor Roosevelt of New York (as he then was) let the press know that the Hay-Pauncefote Treaty contained a grave error: any canal that we build and own we should fortify, and close off to the enemy in wartime. (*"Et tu!"* an irritated Hay wrote his friend in Albany. "Cannot you leave a few things to the President and the Senate, who are charged with them by the Constitu-tion?" Did Roosevelt really think the Clayton-Bulwer Treaty preferable to the one now before Congress? "Please do not answer this—but think about it awhile." The governor did answer, promptly. "I hesitated long before I said anything about the treaty through sheer dread of two moments—that in which I should receive your note, and that in which I should receive Cabot's"—the latter being Senator Henry Cabot Lodge.) Roosevelt's intimate friend sat on the Senate Foreign Relations Committee, which set about amending Hay's treaty in a manner that caused Parliament to refuse to accept it as altered. Hay, delighted earlier at what he had got England to agree to, was furious now at the Senate's tampering, so much so that he submitted his resignation to the president. This provoked McKinley's response, on the same day, March 13, 1900: "I return your resignation. Had I known the contents of the letter you handed me this morning, I would have declined to receive or consider it. Nothing," the president wrote, "could be more unfortunate than to have you retire from the Cabinet. The personal loss would be great, but the public loss even greater." So Hay stayed on, and saw to the treaty's revision in ways that appeased the Senate, the new version omitting any mention of fortifications. Britain and the United States signed the revised Hay-Pauncefote Treaty, and the Senate ratified it near the end of 1901.

That year, 1901, was perhaps the most illustrious in the distinguished career of John Hay—and, personally, the saddest. President McKinley had taken a liking to Hay's son Del and appointed him consul in Pretoria, in the Transvaal, where the Boers were putting up a stout resistance to the English invader of their South African republics. Although still very young—his father's age when John Hay began serving as Lincoln's secretary—Del discharged delicate consular responsibilities to widespread satisfaction, maintaining America's neutral stance between Boers and English, German Americans back in the States strongly favoring the one, Anglo Americans (Secretary Hay among them, although the diplomat held his tongue) just as strongly favoring the other. Del's proud family welcomed the young man home in early 1901, to a future that looked bright. "You have had a very successful year of it," his father said. "I have not heard a word of criticism of you." And over the spring President McKinley chose young Hay to be his private secretary, starting July 1, the position Del's father had held under a previous president in the same White House, on the same upper floor.

Accordingly, Del Hay was on his way from New Hampshire to Washington in mid-June, stopping off on the twenty-third at New Haven to attend alumni festivities at Yale, his third reunion. At midnight the young man retired to his room at the New Haven House. A half-smoked cigarette was found on the wide sill of an open window from which, at 2:30 A.M., a watchman had seen a body fall three stories to the stone flags of the sidewalk below. "Have you heard how it happened?" a mourning, shattered father, trying to cope with the sudden loss of his elder son, wrote to one of the many from all over the world who sent condolences. "The night was frightfully hot and close. He sat on the window-sill to get cool before turning in, and fell asleep. He was the soundest sleeper I ever knew. He probably did not wake." And to the same friend, John Hay allowed himself to wonder: "Why should he go, I stupidly ask, with his splendid health and strength, his courage, his hopes, his cheery smile which made everybody like him at sight; and I be left, with my short remnant of life, of little use to my friends, and none to myself? Yet I know this is a wild and stupid way to wail at fate. I must face the facts. *My* boy is gone, and the whole face of the world is changed in a moment."

Del's death was declared accidental. But had he been drinking? Could it have been a suicide? To Henry Adams, closest of his friends, Hay wrote in mid-July: "I have hideous forebodings. I have been extraordinarily happy all my life. Good luck has pursued me like my shadow. Now it is gone—it seems forever. I expect to-morrow to hear bad news, something insufferable."

Not tomorrow, but soon. In early September, a bit over two months later, President and Mrs. McKinley were attending the Pan-American Exposition, another specimen of those very popular, recurring world's fairs of the late nineteenth and twentieth centuries that celebrated achievements of the industrial age, this one in Buffalo. Before fifty thousand fairgoers the president gave a speech about a prosperous America's need to trade reciprocally with all the world. Next day he and his wife did some sightseeing at Niagara Falls, after which Mrs. McKinley returned to their quarters to rest, while her husband went back to the fairgrounds for a public reception at the Temple of Music. The line to shake the president's hand was long. An unemployed workman in his late twenties stepped forward to take his turn. The young man's right fist was wrapped in a handkerchief. McKinley obligingly extended his left to shake the good hand, but the anarchist, Leon Czolgosz, lifted his right and fired two shots at close range from a revolver hidden by the wrapping. The date was September 6, 1901. In the aftermath, initial reports were favorable, but later the wounded patient's condition took a turn for the worse, and McKinley died, still in Buffalo, on September 14.

"What a strange and tragic fate it has been of mine," wrote Hay, given yet more to grieve over, "—to stand by the bier of three of my dearest friends, Lincoln, Garfield, and McKinley, three of the gentlest of men, all risen to the head of the State, and all done to death by assassins." And to Roosevelt, two days after the vice president had assumed his new office, Hay wrote that if his friend had come by it in any other way, "My sincere affection and esteem for you, my old-time love for your father—would he could have lived to see you where you are!—would have been deeply gratified. And even from the depths of the sorrow where I sit, with my grief for the President mingled and confused with that for my boy so that I scarcely know from hour to hour the true source of my tears, I do still congratulate you, not only on the threshold of an official career which I know will be glorious, but on the vast opportunity for useful work which lies before you."

Yet more grief would follow before September ended. Hay learned from John Nicolay's daughter that her father was near death. The secretary left his mansion at Lafayette Park and proceeded along Pennsylvania Avenue to Capitol Hill, to the far more modest home of his longtime friend and collaborator. Helen Nicolay met him at the door, warning that her father would not recognize him. Hay went up alone, to come down after an interval that must have encompassed retrieved memories reaching as far back as Pittsfield, Illinois, so long ago, when a precocious scholar, John Hay, thirteen years old, met a nineteen-year-old journalist, John George Nicolay. Through all that had happened since, their friendship never wavered.

Nicolay died on September 26. And yet one more: on Christmas Eve, 1901, Clarence King, tubercular, all but penniless except for the checks that his friend Hay remembered to send him from time to time, died in Phoenix, at fifty-nine. "The best and brightest man of his generation," Hay had reflected not long before to Adams, "who with talents immeasurably beyond any of his contemporaries, with industry that has often sickened me to witness it, with everything in his favor but blind luck, hounded by disaster from his cradle, with none of the joy of life to which he was entitled, dying at last, with nameless suffering, alone and uncared for."

On Christmas Day, having learned of King's death: "Dear John, I am very, very sorry," the president of the United States wrote. "I know it is useless for me to say so—but I do feel deeply for you. You have been well within the range of the rifle pits this year—so near them that I do not venture to wish you a merry Christmas. But may all good henceforth go with you and yours. Your attached friend, Theodore Roosevelt."

40. THE THOUGHT OF MY LIFE ENDING

Beginning early in the following year, 1902, the new, young president (youngest to assume the office before or since) fell into a Sunday morning habit of attending St. John's Episcopal Church on Lafayette Square across from the White House, then making his way the short distance to 800 Sixteenth Street, where he passed under the great Romanesque arch into the opulent mansion of his secretary of state for an hour's visit. Roosevelt relished Hay's company—"I think he was the most delightful man to talk to I ever met"—particularly grateful during those Sunday visits for any reminiscences that his older friend might share of days in Lincoln's White House forty years earlier. On an April morning in 1904, for instance—Roosevelt's weekly after-church calls on Hay continuing—"The President came in and talked mostly about the situation in New York, which annoys him greatly and somewhat alarms him. He sees a good many lions in the path—but I told him of the far greater beasts that appeared to some people as in Lincoln's way, which turned out to be only bobcats after all."

The deft turn of phrase would have pleased and reassured Hay's visitor. In these early months of their working together, his secretary of state had made Theodore ("I wish you would always call me Theodore as you used to") a gift of *Abraham Lincoln: A History*, which Roosevelt took to Sagamore Hill and gratefully tore through, all ten volumes of it, at his rapid pace and with his amazing recall. "In reading the great work of you and Nicolay this summer," he reported to Hay, "I have not only taken the keenest enjoyment but I really believe I have profited. At any rate, it has made me of set purpose to try to be good-natured and forbearing and to try to free myself from vindictiveness."

Three years of McKinley's term remained for this new chief executive to practice in, years in which Hay again found himself next in line, uneasily, for the presidency. Yet 1902 was bringing—as even the preceding year, the doleful 1901, had brought—gleams of pleasure as well. In October 1901, for instance (some three months after his son Del's death, a month after McKinley's assassination), Hay and Roosevelt traveled to New Haven to be awarded honorary degrees at Yale's bicentennial celebration. They were but two among a number of other notables similarly robed, including Mark Twain, William Dean Howells, Whitelaw Reid, and Richard Watson Gilder—Hay's close friends all. "It was a splendid and most impressive sight," he recorded afterward of the visit to his late son's alma mater—near the scene of the young man's death. "They were all very good to me, and I had the first day of comfort I have known for ever so long—but always there was the undertone of grief and regret."

More—and equally elaborate—comfort arrived in the early weeks of 1902. Helen Hay, the elder daughter, was marrying Payne Whitney. "They are old friends and playmates and Payne was Del's most intimate friend," Hay explained to Reid. "Mrs. Hay and I have seen a great deal of him this year and we like him very much." Accustomed all her life to wealth, the bride was moving into much more of it, Whitney the heir to gigantic fortunes (oil, tobacco, street railways, real estate) from his father, his mother, and his uncle, the last of whom was providing as a wedding gift the exquisite jewel of a mansion on Fifth Avenue at Seventy-Ninth Street, designed by Stanford White and, as of 1902, still five years from completion. (It stands there in its breath-taking beauty—outside and inside—yet.) The Whitney family had other homes, including one in South Carolina and another on five hundred acres at Manhasset on Long Island; and the wedding that ushered in such plenitude was itself a grand affair, involving a morning reception at the John Hay mansion and a dinner for six hundred guests including many of Washington's elite, among them the president of the United States.

That same year, in late September, in a quieter, more intimate ceremony, the Hays' younger daughter, Alice, was married at the Fells on Lake Sunapee, in the glory of a New Hampshire autumn, her groom also one of brother Del's closest friends at Yale.

Of course neither parent, neither John nor Clara Hay, ever fully recovered from their elder son's death; it made them both old all at once, Hay said. Yet he got on with his work: continuing negotiations over the disputed Alaska-Canada border, negotiations over the Newfoundland fisheries, over Samoa, over the Danish West Indies, and through 1903 most dramatically over Panama. That involved dealing with an unstable, corrupt regime in Colombia, which possessed the isthmus of Panama as a long-discontented department. The tale is complex, although assuredly not without interest, with President Roosevelt and his secretary of state striving to reach a settlement with an ill-governed South American country and with the bankrupt French company that had earlier left on the isthmus heavy machinery and substantial prepara-tory digging. Colombians set their price to lease a passage through, then raised it after Colombia's jefe in Bogotá changed his mind. Meanwhile, off at the distant province (reachable only by sea, not over jungle-clogged land), Pana-manians were plotting to set up their own republic, which would lease the valuable ten-mile-wide, fifty-mile-long corridor between the oceans to Pana-ma's advantage, not to Colombia's. At stake were large sums of money, which brought various emissaries to Washington from the isthmus, from Columbia, and from France, those last hoping to be reimbursed for what De Lesseps's company had abandoned. Colombians under their shifty leadership resorted, in effect, to blackmail. Roosevelt was furious. In Washington, Hay met with Panamanians and conducted himself with his usual discretion. In early

November 1903 the patriots, as they saw themselves, proclaimed a new republic from Panama City on the Pacific. To protect American interests—and
prevent Colombians from interfering—a U.S. warship fortuitously dropped
anchor at Colón on the Caribbean side. In seventeen hours the revolution was
over, with no casualties except for one unfortunate Chinaman and a dog.
Three days later the United States recognized the Republic of Panama. The
Hay–Bunau-Varilla Treaty, signed on November 18, cleared the way for digging to start in 1904, and within a decade the canal was finished, an engineering marvel that Roosevelt regarded as the single greatest achievement of his
presidency.

At the beginning of 1904, Hay resumed keeping a journal, a practice once
pursued—if somewhat fitfully but to our great profit—during the Civil War
and on into the early postwar years. His resumption of the habit would continue until within a few days of the diarist's death. As, for instance, Sunday,
January 17, 1904: "The President came in for an hour and talked very amus-
ingly of many matters. Among others he spoke of a letter he had received from
an old lady in Canada denouncing him for having drunk a toast to Helen at
her wedding two years ago. The good soul had waited two years, hoping that
the pulpit or the press would take up this enormity. 'Think,' she said, 'of the
effect on your friends, on your children, on your own immortal soul, of such
a thoughtless act.'"

Helen was of course Hay's daughter, Mrs. Payne Whitney, who by this time
had given birth to her parents' first grandchild, Joan, now six months old.
During this present year, 1904, Roosevelt—earlier elevated to his high office
only through the national calamity of President McKinley's assassination—
meant to place his name before the voters for his own election to the presidency. Would Hay campaign on his behalf? But the secretary's health was in
question. He felt old—sixty-five—and weary, and had hoped to retire from
office well before this, would have retired when McKinley's second term
began, assuredly when the major was murdered. Yet having been abruptly
hurled into office in Buffalo, Roosevelt insisted that Hay stay on. Of course
under such circumstances the secretary had to. And he did, and served the
new president well, and campaigned to brilliant effect on Roosevelt's behalf
in the summer and fall of 1904, as yet another electoral cycle drew near completion.

In this same autumn of 1904, John Hay was among the earliest seven
elected as charter members of the newly founded American Academy of Arts
and Letters, seven in the fields of literature, art, and music—a most distinguished honor: John Hay, Mark Twain, and William Dean Howells among

the first, the literary, group; Augustus Saint-Gaudens and John La Farge as artists in the second; the composer Edward McDowell in the third. And during the same weeks, the French government let it be known that it wished to present Hay with the Legion of Honor, for services in the interest of peace rendered to the nations of the world—that medal to be added to the honorary degrees already bestowed by Harvard, Yale, Princeton, Brown, Dartmouth, and Western Reserve. The secretary's laurels grew ever more abundant.

As for the autumnal presidential campaign, some, of course, were objecting loudly to the Rough Rider cowboy's bumptious ways, his gunboat diplomacy in Panama, for instance, although John Hay was not among them. Roosevelt had bargained in good faith with the Colombians, but it was (the president said) like trying to nail currant jelly to a wall. Moreover, once the Panamanians had declared for independence, what else could the United States do? Was it to stand by and watch as the tyrant's superior forces sailed forth from Cartagena to trample the nascent little republic into the dust? Hay was in sympathy with the president's policies; and so exalted by now was the secretary of state's reputation around the world as a man of high-mindedness and peace that his mere endorsement gave to Roosevelt's not always orthodox methods in conducting foreign affairs a stamp of temperate fair dealing.

With his countrymen, the secretary's standing was secure. His scrapbooks are full of testimonials to the high regard in which the public held him. A single anonymous specimen from this same 1904: "Dear & Honored Sir, I never hear any one speak of you & of your long roll of illustrious services in other than terms of pride & praise—& out of the heart. I think I am right in believing you to be the only man in the civil service of the country the cleanness of whose motives is never questioned by any citizen, & whose acts proceed always upon a broad & high plane, never by accident or pressure of circumstance upon a narrow or low one. There are majorities that are proud of more than one of the nation's great servants, but I believe, & think I know, that you are the only one of whom the entire nation is proud. Proud and thankful."

Hay's well wisher forbore to sign his name, not wanting to burden a busy public official with responding to the message. For a response would have been warranted: the anonymous correspondent was the secretary's old friend Mark Twain, whose politics contrasted sharply with that of the current administration in Washington. Yet despite the contrast, Clemens never doubted that John Hay acted selflessly and in the interest of peace—unlike his superior: the bellicose, egoistic, jingoistic, self-promoting Theodore Roosevelt, whose politics Sam Clemens abhorred.

Hay did not. Hay and Roosevelt's methods might differ: the latter ebullient, impulsive, impatient; the former composed, conciliatory, diplomatic. But their aims for America as an expansive force for good worldwide (as they understood the good) were the same. And yet Hay was tired. He had long been eager to lay aside the demands of office, with the incessant wrangles it brought him through the treaty-amending powers of the Senate. The secretary thought it no less than a flaw in the Constitution: the State Department charged with conducting tedious, delicate negotiations with a sovereign nation before finally reaching an agreement, only to submit the results (as the founding document obliged be done) for the Senate's approval, where as few as thirty-one legislators were enough to block passage of the treaty, thirty-one prompted by whatever selfish, short-sighted, vindictive, ax-grinding motives polluted their thinking.

He was tired of it. Election Day was November 8. That evening Hay went over to the White House and found the president surrounded by supporters in the Red Room, his hands full of congratulatory telegrams. Against a decent but bland Democrat, New York's judge Alton Parker, the incumbent had won overwhelmingly—more popular votes than any of his predecessors had ever gained, an unmitigated triumph. "I am glad," he told Hay, "to be President in my own right."

From Hay's diary four days later, November 12: "The papers this morning announce on the authority of the President that I am to remain Secretary of State for the next four years. He did it in a moment of emotion,—I cannot exactly see why,—for he has never discussed the matter seriously with me and I have never said I would stay. I have always deprecated the idea, saying there was not four years' work in me; now I shall have to go along awhile longer, as it would be a scandal to contradict him."

Why would Roosevelt prefer a tired old man in his cabinet to someone younger and in better health? Yet on the eve of his inauguration four months later, the president found time to write to Hay in these terms: "I wonder if you have any idea what your strength and wisdom and sympathy, what the guidance you have given me and the mere delight of your companionship, have meant to me these three and a half years." And to his friend Cabot Lodge, Roosevelt would speak more objectively about Hay's contribution after the secretary's death: "His dignity, his remarkable literary ability, his personal charm, and the respect his high character and long service commanded thruout the country, together with his wide acquaintance with foreign statesmen and foreign capitals, made him one of the public servants of real value to the United States."

After Hay's death the president wrote thus—for the end was near. Secretary Hay, wrapped in a heavy coat and scarf against blustery March weather, was able to attend Roosevelt's inaugural ceremonies; but within a very few days, his wife Clara and his friend Henry Adams got him away from Washington. They boarded a ship that took the three to Genoa, for consultations with medical specialists—the issue appeared to be his heart—then on to Nauheim for benefits to be gained from the baths in that German spa. Once there, rulers of Europe urged Hay to call on them: the kaiser, Edward VII, the king of the Belgians. Doctors forbade it. The University of Cambridge desired his presence to receive an honorary degree; the patient was obliged to decline. To old friends whose hospitality Hay had enjoyed on so many earlier trips abroad, he was allowed to write and, on occasions as they appeared, to say goodbye.

Aboard the *Baltic* he and Clara sailed from Liverpool for home on June 7. One night during the passage, John Hay had a curious dream, which his diary records: "I went to the White House to report to the President, who turned out to be Mr. Lincoln. He was very kind and considerate, and sympathetic about my illness. He said there was little work of importance on hand. He gave me two unimportant letters to answer. I was pleased that this slight order was within my power to obey. I was not in the least surprised at Lincoln's presence in the White House. But the whole impression of the dream was one of overpowering melancholy."

The following page, containing the diary's final entry of substance, is dated June 14, 1905. There—with death less than three weeks off—Hay sets down what amounts to his valediction, a testimonial so human, so honest, so eloquent that few considering the totality of the man's rich life have felt free to omit it. "I say to myself," he wrote at the last,

that I should not rebel at the thought of my life ending at this time. I have lived to be old, something I never expected in my youth. I have had many blessings, domestic happiness being the greatest of all. I have lived my life. I have had success beyond all the dreams of my boyhood. My name is printed in the journals of the world without descriptive qualification, which may, I suppose, be called fame. By mere length of service I shall occupy a modest place in the history of my time. If I were to live several years more I should probably add nothing to my existing reputation; while I could not reasonably expect any further enjoyment of life, such as falls to the lot of old men in sound health. I know death is the common lot, and what is universal ought not to be deemed a misfortune; and yet—instead of confronting it with dignity and philosophy, I cling instinctively to life and the things of life, as eagerly as if I had not had my chance at happiness and gained nearly all the great prizes.

One admires the candor—and what a life his was to cling to! The *Baltic* docked in New York on June 15. Clara wanted to take her husband directly to the Fells, but he went south into the heat of summertime Washington instead, to report to the president, to call in at the State Department a final time, and to step once more into his great mansion alongside Adams's. By June 25, Hay was at Sunapee, amid the Fells's cooling breezes. Yet he didn't stay long, having moved beyond any help the doctors summoned from Boston might bring him. Still in office, Secretary of State John Hay, age sixty-six, of Salem, Indiana, and Warsaw, Illinois, died in his bed at the Fells in New Hampshire shortly after midnight on July 1, 1905, Clara in attendance at his side.

John Hay. Portrait by John Singer Sargent, February 1903. Courtesy of Brown University Portrait Collection.

EPILOGUE: 1905–1919

ROOSEVELT, 1905-1910

Ten days after Hay's death, President Roosevelt observed to his intimate friend Cabot Lodge that the late secretary of state's health during the last two years of his life had been such "that he could do very little work of importance. His name, his reputation, his staunch loyalty, all made him a real asset of the administration. But in actual work I had to do the big things myself." That wasn't altogether true, but the stout ego the claim unveils seems characteristic of the speaker. "I took Panama," Roosevelt scribbled in a defiant marginal note in 1912—the celebratory prominence of "I" in his writing commented on by foe, friend (if not to his face), and cartoonist throughout his adult lifetime. I took Panama, even though Secretary Hay had been deeply involved in those complex dealings throughout the busy year 1903. Roosevelt's private, rather ungrateful observation after Hay's death reveals another characteristic of his thinking: his fondness for stances conveyed by "on the one hand . . ." On the one hand, Hay was a real asset; on the other hand, I had to do all the important work myself.

Even so, during the final months of the secretary's life, his president could not have been more generous to him, declining every opportunity to replace the ailing Hay, urging instead that the patient over at his German spa focus only on getting better, in preparation for challenges awaiting the two of them in the fall. Even then, one such challenge was winding down. War had been raging across the Pacific between Russia and Japan, the bloodiest war ever fought on the globe up to that time; it had been Hay's hope in his final days to influence the massive carnage in the direction of peace. He was too ill to do so; it was President Roosevelt who was approached in May to mediate an end to the slaughter on and around Manchuria and the Korean peninsula. In June, emissaries from Moscow and Tokyo arrived at Oyster Bay, where, serving as his own secretary of state, the president received them with due ceremony, on their way to deliberations in Portsmouth, New Hampshire. In September, a bit over two months after John Hay's death, a peace treaty was signed between the two nations, and for his diplomacy in bringing about that outcome, the warrior Roosevelt was awarded the Nobel Peace Prize, the first American to be so honored.

He achieved much more over the seven and a half years of his presidency. The youngest ever to ascend to the office, Theodore Roosevelt was among the best prepared, having served in governments municipal, state, and federal. And temperamentally he was well suited to his duties, although he was a youthful force not seen before in the sedate executive mansion. At the threshold of his responsibilities, Hay had congratulated him "on the vast opportunity for useful work which lies before you," and into that work TR plunged with a tireless zest unequaled by his predecessors. He took on the trusts and holding companies: of the railroads, of oil, beef, tobacco—and instituted proceedings that ended by defending employee and consumer rights against the callous monopolies. He took on the coal mine bosses of Pennsylvania, Christian gentlemen who—God having entrusted them with the miners' welfare—refused to discuss with those humble folk such matters as pay and working hours, even as the long anthracite strike stretched through the summer of 1902 and into the colder nights of fall. Bringing both sides together, Roosevelt hammered out a settlement that markedly improved conditions for the miners—and put coal in the homes of the Northeast just in time. He read Upton Sinclair's *The Jungle* (1906), a horrifying depiction of conditions of filth in the Chicago stockyards: read it, on the one hand, deploring the author's muckraking sensationalism, and on the other hand, vowing to look into problems the book exposed; the Meat Inspection Act and the Pure Food and Drug Act were the beneficial consequences. He got Congress to pass acts prohibiting railroads from charging rates that favored certain (wealthy) customers over others. He moved against those who would despoil America's resources as their God-given right: *our* land, *our* mineral wealth, *our* timber, *our* Grand Canyon. Ours only in trust, the president insisted, to pass on enhanced to America's children's children for generations to come. Of course this made him powerful enemies, so that in Roosevelt's term in office from 1905 to 1909, the Senate fought his reforms about every step of the way. Thus he resorted increasingly to executive orders, having already by those means established the first wildlife sanctuary at Pelican Island in Florida as early as 1903. He had declared Crater Lake a national park in 1902, and thereafter proceeded to introduce irrigation into arid western lands, to set aside 150 million wooded acres—gifts to the public—as national forests, and in 1906 to designate Devils Tower in Wyoming as the first of many such national monuments. Other conservation measures followed.

Politicians who preferred things as they were fought hard against him, but the people loved Roosevelt, whose joy at his work was contagious, whose wife as First Lady appeared in every way admirable, whose half-dozen children were delights to watch growing up, and whose play was as zestful as his labors—the pillow fights with his boys, those regular hunting trips, that trip he and Edith took to Panama to see the canal (the first such venture outside the United States that any sitting president had embarked upon), the boxing, the jujitsu, the journey west to camp in Yellowstone with John Burroughs, tramp through Yosemite and camp out with John Muir.

None of what he did appeared dull; none of it indecisive. As 1908 arrived, Roosevelt bemoaned anew an impulsive pledge he had made not to run for another term; but, in order that the work he had started—his Fair Deal for everyone—might go forward, he made sure to handpick his successor: William Howard Taft, current secretary of war and warm supporter of Roosevelt's progressive program. The incumbent saw Taft successfully elected to the presidency that November and attended his inauguration the following March. Then as a private citizen, the former chief executive, still only fifty, carried through plans to get out of his successor's way by embarking on an extended safari in Africa.

He would start from Mombasa, on the coast of British East Africa (now Kenya). "On March 23, 1909, I sailed thither from New York, in charge of a scientific expedition sent out by the Smithsonian, to collect birds, mammals, reptiles, and plants, but especially specimens of big game, for the National Museum at Washington." It was a mammoth endeavor, thoroughly publicized, supported financially by the likes of Andrew Carnegie, its progress followed worldwide. The party included TR's son Kermit, a nineteen-year-old Harvard freshman, as well as an ornithologist, a zoologist, a field naturalist, a taxidermist, and three hundred porters, horse boys, gunbearers, tent men, and native guards. Supplies were vast: canned goods from home, hundreds of traps, abundant cartridge boxes, four tons of salt to cure skins of animals (their flesh providing food for the hunters), before sending the skins on to the Smithsonian to stuff and display. In the course of the year-long safari—through British West Africa, into the Belgian Congo, then via the Nile up into the Sudan—Roosevelt bagged 296 large animals, including twenty zebras, thirteen rhinos, nine lions, eight elephants, eight warthogs, seven giraffes, seven hippos, six buffalo, five wildebeests, three pythons, two ostriches, and a crocodile. Each evening he would write about the day's adventures, his account published serially in *Scribner's* back home to the great advantage of that magazine's subscription list, the whole appearing in 1910 as a very readable book in two volumes, *African Game Trails* (a signed first edition of which currently sells for $11,000).

That spring, in mid-March, the hunters reached Khartoum in the Sudan, where Edith Roosevelt and daughter Ethel met them by prearrangement. From there the happily reunited family sailed leisurely down the Nile and departed from Alexandria to arrive at Naples on April 2, 1910, poised at the start of a tour of European cities that turned into yet another Rooseveltian triumph.

MARK TWAIN, 1900–1910

In the same month, on April 21, 1910, Mark Twain died at his home, "Stormfield," in Redding, Connecticut, in his seventy-fifth year. Since returning to America in the fall of 1900, the public figure that was Mark Twain had prospered, but the private Samuel Clemens endured events that grieved and embittered him. His beloved wife, Livy, never strong, never fully recovered from the loss of their daughter Susy, sank into invalidism, and over twenty-two months suffered unrelentingly through a variety of ailments that kept her bedridden. After a last visit to Elmira, the Clemenses returned to Italy in search of a more moderate winter climate. There, in June 1904, Livy died in their villa near Florence, at fifty-eight. Sam and his daughter Clara accompanied the body home, Livy's coffin in the hold of the ship—"In these 34 years we have made many voyages together, Livy dear, and now we are making our last. You down below & lonely. I above with the crowd and lonely." The mourners pursued their sad way to New York and by rail to Elmira for the funeral service in the Langdons' parlor, on the spot where Sam and Livy had wed, the Rev. Joe Twichell presiding over both ceremonies. She was buried beside Susy and their infant son. Clara, deeply affected by the loss of her mother, retired to a rest home afterward. Her younger sister Jean, suffering from epilepsy, was herself in and out of institutions. Clemens leased a home on lower Fifth Avenue, and from there he continued writing tirelessly, much of it not to be published in his lifetime.

As Mark Twain he led an active public life, in demand at charitable lectures and at celebratory dinners. Money was not a problem; before the family set off for Italy earlier, his friend from Standard Oil, H. H. Rogers, had helped the author negotiate a lucrative contract with Harper's to publish all of Mark Twain's past, present, and future works. Now in these later years after Livy's death, Clemens resumed dictating his autobiography, not to appear (he thought) until a hundred years after his own death, so that he might speak as from the grave, in honesty and candor. Through morning sessions with a stenographer at his bedside—Clemens propped up on pillows, a posture that the late riser favored—he spoke as the spirit moved him about many subjects, including the president then in the White House. "Mr. Roosevelt," the humorist recorded in January 1906, "is one of the most likable men that I am acquainted with," a man whose "joyous ebullitions of excited sincerity" have made him "the most popular human being that has ever existed in the United States." Yet the speaker's opinion of the politician Roosevelt, as distinct from the person, was decidedly more qualified; he was convinced that Theodore Roosevelt was "far and away the worst President we have ever had."

Years before, the New Yorker had fought for civil service reform, "and in this character," Clemens went on, "he won the strong and outspoken praises of a public sick unto death of the spoils system. This was before he was President." As president, though, Roosevelt had become a full-fledged politician, and like all of them, he had traded principle for expediency. Moreover, this present chief executive was the Tom Sawyer of American politics: "still only fourteen years old after living half a century; he takes a boy's delight in showing off; he is always hugging something or somebody—when there is a crowd around to see the hugging and envy the hugged." It was undignified, unbecoming the office, in the opinion of a now dignified elderly gentleman (Clemens was in his seventies) who had known every president since Grant.

He cared not at all for TR's pose as a great hunter, or for his lunatic glorification of war. But mostly the anti-imperialist Mark Twain lamented the direction in which the cocksure Roosevelt had steered the ship of state in consolidating the American Empire: Puerto Rico, Hawaii, Guam, American Samoa, the Philippines. In Clemens's view, empire and democracy don't mix; Roosevelt's new, imperial America was betraying our founding values: of freedom—of the press, of religion, of assembly; betraying the nation's unique boast that our citizens were equal before the law and that our rulers ruled only with the consent of the governed. Filipinos had not given *their* consent, and certainly were not being treated as equals. Nor did a single Filipino pose the slightest threat to our national security. Yet on March 9, 1906, as late as this very year in which Mark Twain was adjudging TR by far our "worst President," would occur the Moro Crater Massacre, in which American soldiers on the island of Jolo in the southern Philippines, scouting an extinct volcano, came upon a village of just under a thousand Muslim Filipinos, women and children among them, and through a day and a half of firing down from the rim—at the cost of fifteen Americans dead and thirty-two wounded, some only slightly—massacred all but six of the villagers.

"The 20th century is a stranger to me," the author of *Tom Sawyer* and *Huckleberry Finn* (those indelible impressions of agrarian life) would conclude in old age. "I wish it well but my heart is all for my own century. I took 65 years of it," he who had been born in 1835 remarked of the nineteenth century, "just on a risk, but if I had known as much about it as I know now I would have taken the whole of it."

Despite his bitterness, Sam Clemens did find late pleasures in life to enjoy. His friends: Twichell was close to him to the last; and Rogers, with his luxurious yacht and his staunch loyalty; and Howells. Howells's son John, who was becoming an architect of note, built for the humorist a beautiful home in Redding, Connecticut, near New York City, by rail no more than an hour or so away. Clara had a suite of rooms there, and there she was married in the fall of 1909 to a concert pianist, her own musical career as a singer—to Clemens's pleasure and pride—having met with some success. At the wedding the father of the bride almost stole the show by wearing his scarlet Oxford gown. He had been honored with that in June 1907, at a glorious ceremony that occasioned his final return to England and the warmest reception this beloved author—so often warmly received—had been accorded in his lifetime: four weeks of extravagant welcome. Endless ovations, old friends galore to see, luncheons, dinners; and on June 26, alongside Oxford's chancellor Lord Curzon, he accompanied others (Rodin and Kipling among them) to the Sheldonian Theatre to claim their degrees, the joyful crowd erupting with its loudest approval as Sam Clemens of Hannibal, Missouri, stepped forward to be hooded and hear the chancellor's Latin words: "Most amiable and charming sir, you shake the sides of the whole world with your merriment."

Then, the pleasures of Bermuda, which Clemens had first visited in 1867 aboard the *Quaker City* returning from the Holy Land. On an impulse he went back for four days with Joe Twichell in 1877, and returned with him thirty years later, in 1907. Thereafter he returned often, eight times in all—he loved the place, not yet a tourist attraction: its pellucid waters, its sublime weather year-round. No automobiles, no telephones, no newspapers. And he was in Bermuda in the spring of 1910 when a lifetime of cigar smoking brought him back home a feeble old man suffering sharp chest pains. At the New York piers he was carried off the ship, hurried on to Stormfield in

Connecticut, and up to his bedroom into his own bed, where a week later, by
then quite willingly, he died.

ROOSEVELT, 1910-1916

At the start of the same month, April 1910, Theodore Roosevelt and family
began their six-weeks' progress from Naples through Europe. Everyone
wanted to see the American who by that time had become, literally, the most
famous person alive, his cyclonic presidency further adorned now with a year-
long, well-publicized, highly successful safari through darkly exotic lands. To
Rome he went, to call by invitation on King Victor Emmanuel. To Paris, to
address a huge crowd at the Sorbonne, delivering a speech that was much
admired and widely disseminated, in part in praise of the man "in the arena
. . . who strives valiantly," making errors, face sweaty and bloody, coming up
short, but "who at the best knows in the end the triumph of high achievement,
and who at the worst, if he fails, at least fails while daring greatly, so that his
place shall never be with those cold and timid souls who know neither victory
nor defeat." On to Christiania (Oslo), to receive his Nobel Prize. To Berlin to
review the troops with Kaiser Wilhelm II. To London, where, at President
Taft's request, Mr. Roosevelt represented the United States at the pomp-laden
funeral of King Edward VII, amid pretty much all of Europe's uniformed,
bemedaled, helmeted, mounted royalty, TR conspicuous throughout in his
plain republican top hat and black cutaway.

He returned to New York in June to a harbor resounding with ships' horns
and cannon salutes, and on shore to a jubilant, cheering multitude that
mobbed Broadway and Fifth Avenue sidewalks a million strong in welcome,
solid from the Battery five miles up to Fifty-Ninth Street, the avenue alive all
that distance with fans of Roosevelt waving banners and flags and leaning out
of upper windows.

It was a welcome unprecedented in New York annals up to that time. But
TR was troubled. President Taft appeared to be drifting away from the progressive program that his predecessor left him with: one of Roosevelt's most
valued lieutenants Taft had got rid of, his replacement far too friendly with the
special interest he was hired to regulate. The mining interests, the timber
interests out West, the big corporations seemed to be reclaiming their earlier,
untrammeled power; yet Roosevelt had come to believe—as he said not three
months after his return to American soil, in a much noticed speech at Osawatomie, Kansas—that the conflict "between the men who possess more than

they have earned and the men who have earned more than they possess is the central condition of progress. In our day it appears as the struggle of freemen to gain and hold the right of self-government as against the special interests, who twist the methods of free government into machinery for defeating the popular will."

It was those special interests, the robber barons, that President Taft was letting back into power in the Republican Party, as in the earlier unregulated Gilded Age, before progressivism: days of sweat shops and child labor, of twelve-to-eighteen-hour shifts with only Sundays off, of no workers' compensation for injury on the job, no thought of minimum wage, no limits on what railroads could charge, no check on the spoliation that mine owners could wreak on mountains they mined and streams they polluted.

A national election lay not far ahead. Would TR support his party and work for the reelection of his friend, William Howard Taft? In February 1912, Roosevelt announced that he was running against Taft for the Republican nomination—his hat was in the ring!—and he did run hard through that spring and amassed an impressive number of delegates. But when the Republican convention met in June, the Old Guard had it sewed up for the incumbent. TR and his followers stormed out, held their own convention, wrote their platform, and selected their candidate to lead this new Progressive Party, the "Bull-Moose Party." Democrats nominated a former president of Princeton, currently governor of New Jersey, Woodrow Wilson, in a three-way race, one that (with votes for his opponents split between them) Wilson won, by a 42 percent plurality. Roosevelt came in second, with 27 percent—the only time in our history when a third party has defeated a major political party—Taft left with only 23 percent (and a mere 8 electoral votes, to Roosevelt's 88 and Wilson's overwhelming 435).

Although the "Bull Moose" candidate had failed, he had failed "while daring greatly"; his place would never be "with those cold and timid souls who know neither victory nor defeat." Nor would he linger long to lick his wounds. In 1913 Roosevelt went off with Edith to South America to fulfill lecture engagements, and while there he was invited to join a party that proposed to explore an uncharted river in the interior of Brazil—The River of Doubt—following its track (it would prove longer than the Rhine) through the jungle to an unknown outcome. Where did it emerge? It was, TR said, his last chance to be a boy, so he seized the opportunity. Edith returned home, having persuaded their son Kermit to join his father again, in effect to look after him. And it was a good thing, too. The adventure proved a horrific one, plagued with hardships and misfortune. Kermit would end essentially by saving his father's life.

Malaria, fevers, poisonous snakes, swarming loathsome insects, hostile natives in the surrounding jungle who threatened the party's progress, water-logged dugout canoes overladen and ill designed to meet the challenges, portages one after the other—unload the canoes, hack a way through the matted forest, lay down a log trail, emerge days later at the far side of rapids to reload—only to have to unload and repeat the toilsome process a few hundred yards farther on. Torrential sheets of rain. Stinging wasps, biting ants an inch and a half long, biting horseflies the size of bumblebees. Roosevelt came close to dying from a leg wound that abscessed. Very close; he grew delirious, urged his desperate companions to go on without him. Kermit refused to leave his father. At last in late April the battered party reached the Madeira, tributary of the Amazon, with TR gaunt and fifty-five pounds lighter. He never fully recovered from the ordeal.

And just two months after his emergence from that taxing adventure, overseas in the Balkan principality of Herzegovina, on June 28, 1914, a nineteen-year-old Serbian nationalist shot and killed Austria's archduke Franz Ferdinand and his consort Sophie as they rode in an open carriage through Sarajevo. What happened next came as an utter shock to Europeans who had been basking in a peaceful, particularly lovely summer. Austria declared war on Serbia. Russia declared war on Austria. Germany declared war on Russia. France declared war on Germany. Germany in reply drove mercilessly through neutral Belgium to get at France. Britain declared war on Germany for violating Belgium's neutrality. And the nightmarish Great War—which would become World War I in the wake of the nightmarish World War II that it led to—was appallingly under way.

Roosevelt despised President Wilson: Democrat, mincing professor, coward who wouldn't go to war when Germany ruthlessly violated a small nation's neutrality, refused to go to war even after 123 American lives were lost on the British liner *Lusitania*, sunk by a German submarine in May 1915. At the beginning of 1916, still fulminating in periodicals that were eager to publish his writings, Roosevelt was so sickened by the pusillanimous ditherings of "the lily-livered skunk in the White House" (as he termed Wilson privately)—the "white rabbit," "yellow all through"—that all he could do was keep scribbling and coming back to the same bitter reflection: Oh, if I had been president! If only I had been president!

HENRY JAMES, 1900-1916

Early in 1916, Henry James died in London at seventy-two. James had struggled through the 1890s with his declining readership, a change in taste during an era increasingly progressive having made less attractive subtle fiction about the travails of upper-class American expatriates. He kept his devoted readers and won some new ones among the discriminating young, a few of whom came virtually to idolize him as The Master. But even as he went on with his labors, only James's ghost story *The Turn of the Screw* (1898) reached a significantly wider audience. For all that, in early April 1900, the author expressed his gratitude to John Hay for his unflagging support: "I am touched more than I can say by the way you speak . . . of my few recent productions," James wrote. "It seems abject, at my age, to be asking for allowances—but *do*, all the same, give me a little more time. I shall do better stuff—if I can get a few more clear years—than I have ever done before." And, he went on, "you shall, as securely, be there to see if I don't—for it's to you mainly that appeal shall lie. I shall never, never, my dear Hay, forget that you are the person in the world who have said to me the three or four things about my lucubrations that have most uplifted me—and *them*."

What is amazing is that Henry James did indeed, at the then advanced age of fifty-seven, set about to write in succession, into his sixties, three long novels, each one of which is now judged to be among his most glorious achievements: *The Wings of the Dove* (1902), *The Ambassadors* (1903), and *The Golden Bowl* (1904). And busy as Secretary of State Hay was—and ill as he was toward the end—he found time to read and to write to his friend about at least two of them. "My dear Secretary," James responded in mid-December 1902 to one such letter, "Right noble & generous is it of you to have put your so persecuted hand to the beautiful words I have just received from you"—no doubt praising *The Wings of the Dove*—"& which gave me extraordinary joy." They provided the author with encouragement as well. "Give me another chance," James wrote. "I really feel as if I had only now come *into* my chance, & I wish I were ten years younger." *The Ambassadors* appeared the following year, and Hay praised it as "beyond the reach of any writer living. . . . In its scorn of traditions of all sort . . . it is wonderful."

In August 1904, for the first time in two decades, James visited the United States on a leisurely, extended tour through eleven months that took him as far south as Florida, as far west as California, along the way delivering lectures, on Balzac among other subjects, that more than paid his expenses. And en route, on January 10, 1905, the Hays in their Washington mansion entertained their friend at a dinner party for twenty-eight guests, including President and Mrs. Roosevelt. Within two or three days the president was writing a personal note to his host, to "Dear John," in part to ask a favor on behalf of their mutual friend Cecil Spring Rice, but adding, "Mrs. Roosevelt and I are delighted with Henry James. I hope to see something of him when he returns here."

Would the likable president with his astonishing memory have retained any recollection of having once, twenty years earlier, publicly compared the author of *The Portrait of a Lady* to a poodle, "somewhat ornamental, but never useful"? James would have dismissed the affront as nonsense, of course, convinced all his working life that those in his trade of novel-writing were among society's most useful citizens. Very late, in 1915, in a celebrated private exchange of letters with H. G. Wells, who had argued in essence that architecture is the only useful art—the others being decorative, for pleasure, for leisure hours—Henry James vigorously protested. "There is no sense," he insisted, "in which architecture is aesthetically 'for use' that doesn't leave any other art whatever exactly as much so; and so far from that of literature being irrelevant to the literary report upon life, and to its being made as interesting as possible, I regard it as relevant in a degree that leaves everything else behind. It is art that *makes* life, makes interest, makes importance, for our consideration and application of these things, and I know of no substitute whatever for the force and beauty of its process."

It is art that *makes* life: one doubts that Roosevelt, the man in the arena, would have understood the assertion any better than H. G. Wells did; but James believed it fervently, and lived through his industrious, dedicated adulthood accordingly. Out of the chaotic impressions crowding our days, art—all art at its best—strives to fashion form, meaning, significance. It is art that *makes* life, which without it is mere unassimilated chaos—instructs us on how to consider life's myriad impressions and stimuli meaningfully, how to look at sunflowers, say; so that James as a novelist was by no means creating mere ornamental diversions, was on the contrary engaged in work of the highest relevance to living, to "a degree that leaves everything else behind."

Out of his year in America, this artist fashioned his book-length response, *The American Scene* (1907); and back in England through the coming years, he continued to write: novels, short stories, novellas, criticism, memoirs of his childhood, youth, and young manhood. The Great War that burst upon Europe in the summer of 1914 sickened him (the "plunge of civilization into this abyss of blood and darkness"), as it did many other sensitive people: its brutal befouling of all gallantry, of any meaningful sacrifice, of any sense to be made out of trench warfare's rat-infested mud and clay, where tens of thousands of young men were slaughtered advancing a few yards with nothing gained, yards soon yielded after more lives were lost with not a thing to show for it.

James did what war work he could, contributing to war relief, visiting the wounded. He was dismayed that his native land didn't come to England's aid, was dismayed that his status in England after all these years was as an alien who must seek permission to visit his home in Rye near the exposed southern coast. In July 1915 he was granted British citizenship. By year's end he lay ill in his London quarters, his sister-in-law, William's wife now widowed, tending him. On New Year's Day 1916, King George V awarded Henry James the Order of Merit, and at the end of February he died.

James's literary reputation nearly died with him. The cognoscenti, the ultra-literate continued to value his work, but his popularity with general readers declined sharply after his death—it had begun its descent well before. And through the 1920s and 1930s he was virtually unread except by a rare discerning few, Scott Fitzgerald among them. It was only in the mid-1940s, after World War II, with the advent of the New Critics and their close textual readings, that Henry James was rediscovered, and thereafter his reputation soared to where his standing now as among America's greatest writers seems secure. Thus—to cite only one example—the discerning essayist and novelist Cynthia Ozick, assured of general assent among her readers as early as the early 1980s, could in passing refer comfortably to the beams that fly out "from the stupendous Jamesian lantern to keep generations reading in rapture (which is all right), or else scribbling away at dissertation after dissertation (which is not so good)": such beams, specifically, as "the moral seriousness" that permeates his work; as the famous Jamesian prose style, "nuanced, imbricated with a thousand distinctions and observations (the reason H. G. Wells mocked it), and as idiosyncratically and ecstatically redolent of the spirals of past and future as a garlic clove"; as, in sum, the present "sublime position of Henry James in American letters."

ROOSEVELT, 1916–1919

In February 1916, the month of James's death in London, Colonel Roosevelt in New York published a collection of his recent magazine articles called *Fear God and Take Your Own Part*. Several articles berated President Wilson for having done nothing to prepare the United States for a war that had already expanded beyond the borders of Europe, and for remaining neutral in a contest between right and wrong. Germany was blatantly in the wrong for violating Belgium with utter ruthlessness and for waging submarine warfare against merchant vessels at the cost of civilian lives, lives of women and children, lives of Americans. "Individuals and nations who preach the doctrine of milk and water," Roosevelt wrote, "invariably have in them a softness of fiber which means that they fear to antagonize those who preach and practice the doctrine of blood and iron." Indeed, not for more than another year yet—after a presidential campaign that Wilson would conduct on the slogan (a craven slogan, in Roosevelt's view), "He kept us out of war"; a campaign in the fall of 1916 that the incumbent came within a whisper of losing even against such a bearded iceberg of a Republican candidate as the starchy Charles Evans Hughes; a campaign that Roosevelt, had he bided his time in 1912 and, instead of bolting and running against his party, waited and run as the logical Republican candidate these four years later, would almost surely have won— only after the election of 1916 and the inauguration were over, as late as April 1917, did President Wilson at last go before Congress and seek a declaration of war.

Colonel Roosevelt was eager to get to the Western Front, meeting promptly with the president at the White House and presenting his plan to lead a volunteer division into combat. President Wilson was cordial, thanked his visitor, but took no action. The aging colonel must content himself with seeing his four sons in uniform, in active service. Kermit had joined the British army earlier, to fight against the Turk in Mesopotamia; Ted and Archie were in range of combat within weeks after America entered the war. By the late summer of 1917, the youngest, Quentin, had sailed for France as an aviator. "I don't believe in all the United States there is any father who has quite the same right as I have to be proud of his four sons." But the following summer, in July, Quentin at twenty would perish in a dogfight with the Germans. By then, Archie had been severely wounded by shrapnel and, after a lengthy stay in a field hospital, sent home. Ted was wounded in France shortly after news of Quentin's death reached Oyster Bay.

Although characteristically stoic, TR wouldn't recover from the death of his youngest boy. He was unwell in any case, had been hospitalized in early 1918 with a return of ailments suffered four years earlier in Brazil—that leg wound, which needed tissue cut out—complicated by abscesses in the ear. Yet even in duress, he wrote of his sons to a friend: "They have done pretty well, haven't they? Quentin killed, dying as a war hawk should . . . over the enemy's lines; Archie crippled, and given the French war cross for gallantry; Ted gassed once

. . . and cited for 'conspicuous gallantry'; Kermit with the British military cross . . ." To the very last—despite Maxim guns, telescopic sights, flame-throwers, tanks, mustard gas, and the new mass production of gore—this Hero of San Juan Hill clung to the romantic view of war as noble, as sublime, and of battle as gallantry, sacrifice, and glory. "No man," he wrote of his beloved Quentin, "could have died in finer or more gallant fashion; and our pride equals our sorrow."

To the last the warrior found consolations: his deep love for Edith; for his children and their spouses; for his grandchildren, increasing in number. There was, moreover, lively talk of TR's running for president again, in 1920, to retrieve the Republican Party from the Old Guard and give it back to Lincoln's kind of people. Even then political friends were scheming to make that happen.

But it was too late. The war ended on November 11, 1918. On that date, Roosevelt went back into the hospital and wasn't home again until Christmas. And within a month, at Sagamore Hill on the evening of January 15, 1919, the old fighter at age sixty would bid an affectionate good night to his wife and retire to bed feeling a bit odd, short of breath. Before dawn he was dead, found next morning as though "just asleep," Edith reported, "only he could not hear."

AND A VERY FEW OTHERS

Theodore Roosevelt's widow survived her husband nearly thirty years, dying at Sagamore Hill at eighty-seven, in 1948. By then Edith Carow Roosevelt had lived long enough to hold numerous grandchildren in her arms, and to this day the Oyster Bay Roosevelt progeny flourishes in the American census. As (rather less fruitfully) does the family of John Hay. Hay's widow, Clara, lived until 1914, very comfortably, one presumes—after the grief of the loss of her husband had lessened—in their Washington mansion overlooking Lafayette Park, from where she wrote Henry James on March 17, 1909, returning a few of Hay's letters that James had furnished for inclusion in a book she prepared with Henry Adams and privately printed in three volumes, *Letters of John Hay and Extracts from Diary* (1908). In writing to James, Mrs. Hay made mention of "building a house in Cleveland but I do not know that I will ever occupy it. It is more a matter of sentiment than anything else as our old house was to be torn down, and as three of my children had been born there and I wished to preserve some wood carving that had been done by old John Herkomer . . . I am building another."

Of the surviving Hay children, Clarence, the youngest, who would become curator of archaeology at New York's Museum of Natural History, inherited the Fells and with his wife enlarged it, over the years planting quite elaborate gardens on the grounds. The site thrives today as The Fells Historic Estate and Gardens, listed in the National Register of Historic Places. Clarence's older sisters, Helen and Alice, both had married late in their father's lifetime, Helen into quite spectacular wealth. After her husband Payne Whitney's early death in 1927, Helen lived on in the comforts of her beautiful home on Fifth Avenue and her estate on Long Island, pursuing hers and her husband's interests in horse-breeding and -racing and in philanthropy, dying at sixty-nine in 1944. Her daughter Joan grew up to be a philanthropist of note as well, and owner of the New York Mets; and Joan's brother, Helen's son "Jock," became a *Time*-cover celebrity, a thoroughbred horse breeder, polo player, early investor in technicolor, movie producer notably of *Gone with the Wind*, and—like his grandfather—ambassador to Great Britain, in the Eisenhower administration.

A trial involving a humble plaintiff in the New York judicial system in 1933 would have been of interest to Helen Hay Whitney, by then a widow. One Ada King was finally getting her day in court. Mrs. King was in her seventies, accompanied by her grown son Wallace, a jazz musician, tardily to claim her rights as the wife of Clarence King, by that time largely forgotten. In his final days in Arizona, King had written Ada letters (no longer in her possession) explaining that he was not the James Todd he had represented himself as being for the thirteen years of their married life, was not a railway porter, was not African American. She should change the family name to King, with assurances of being provided for by means of a trust fund of $80,000.

She never got the $80,000, but the trial revealed that since King's death, Ada Todd and her family had been receiving a regular monthly stipend from an anonymous source. Only after attorneys representing the plaintiff pressed the matter vigorously was the source revealed. It was John Hay—and, after Hay's death in 1905, his wife Clara until her death in 1914, then their son-in-law Payne Whitney until his death in 1927, then Whitney's widow, Helen Hay Whitney. The amount sounds trivial, $50 a month, although less so when we realize $50 in 1900 corresponds to around $1,400 in 2017. And the same source had paid taxes on the widowed Mrs. King's home in Flushing and seen that it was hers free and clear, as long as she didn't reveal her relationship to Clarence King and thereby jeopardize the health of King's innocent elderly mother, Mrs. Howland. The stipend stopped with the trial; but Ada Copeland Todd King lived on until 1964, to age 103, in some comfort with help from her children. Both daughters (the older of whom died young), Caucasian in appearance and married to white men, remained close to their mother, as did Ada's son Wallace, jazz musician who had been taking whatever gigs came his way.

Henry Adams died in late March 1918, while the Great War raged on through its ghastly devastations of more than thirty-eight million casualties. In 1907, two years after his friend Hay's death, Adams had published privately *The Education of Henry Adams*, a memoir now a classic of American letters. Appearing commercially only after its author's own death, the work was posthumously awarded the Pulitzer Prize in 1919; and in 1999, the Modern Library placed *The Education of Henry Adams* first in a list of the one hundred best English-language nonfiction books of the twentieth century.

Adams's memoir deals admiringly with Clarence King ("the charm of King was that he saw what others did and a great deal more. His wit and humor; his bubbling energy which swept everyone into the current of his interest; his personal charm of youth and manners . . ."). And it deals similarly with Adams's closest friend, John Hay. The author ends his work, in fact, recalling the final voyage to Europe in the spring of 1905 that Hay made in a futile effort to recover his health, Clara Hay and Henry Adams accompanying him. The secretary of state had been morose at leaving so much of his work undone.

"One could honestly help him there," Adams interjects. One could remind Hay "of what was solidly completed. In his eight years of office he had solved nearly every old problem of American statesmanship"—among them the Panama Canal question and the Alaska boundary dispute, along with fishing rights off Newfoundland—"and had left little or nothing to annoy his successor. He had brought the great Atlantic powers into a working system"—through the Open Door—so that even Russia might be ready to make peace with its enemy Japan and join the community of nations. Thus, to one astute observer voyaging at sea with the ailing secretary of state in 1905, it appeared that "for the first time in fifteen hundred years a true Roman *pax* was in sight and would, if it succeeded, owe its virtues to him"—to John Hay. "Except for making peace in Manchuria, he could do no more; and," Adams in the innocence of the Edwardian Age offered dryly as a final comfort for his gravely ill friend, "if the worst should happen, setting continent against continent in arms,—the only apparent alternative to his scheme,—he need not repine at missing the catastrophe."

NOTES

AL is Abraham Lincoln. HJ is Henry James. JH is John Hay.
MT is Mark Twain. TR is Theodore Roosevelt.
Full titles of sources cited are on pages 343–51.

PROLOGUE

xiii. "I am so happy." 12–30–1902. JH papers in Library of Congress. Quoted in Taliaferro, *All the Prizes*, 453.

xiii. "the most delightful man." Morison, *Letters of TR*, 6:1489–90.

xiii. "Proud and thankful." Paine, *MT: Biography*, 3:1249–50.

xiv. "the most important work." JH, *Hay-Howells Letters*, 141.

CHAPTER 1

1. Rising Politician

1. "a high-priced man." 2–21–56. AL, *Speeches and Writings, 1832–58*, 365. The definitive printed source of AL's papers is Basler, *Collected Works of AL*, although in most cases I here cite the selective, equally authoritative, and more accessible two volumes of AL's speeches and writings in the handsome Library of America editions.

2. "the woolly side." Ibid., 749.

2. "so great was the gathering." Wallace, *An Autobiography*, 1:253.

2. "Democratic displays." Schurz, *Reminiscences*, 2:92.

4. "A house divided." AL, *Speeches and Writings, 1832–58*, 426.

4–6. "push it forward." Ibid. Citations that follow to the end of the chapter are from this source, the Lincoln-Douglas debates as there reprinted: 600 ("why cannot this Union exist"), 602 ("restore peace and quiet" and "I agree entirely with him"), 810 ("when these poor tongues"), 810–11 ("soon be an end of it").

2. A Poet in Exile

7. "As we go forth." The poem as originally bound is available online, http://library.brown.edu/cds/lincoln/Lincoln_Hay/img/ligr002771.pdf, at Brown University Library Exhibits > "John Hay's Lincoln & Lincoln's John Hay" > sidebar "About the Exhibit" > "John Hay at Brown." Clicking on that last link takes you to documents, the final one of which is Hay's class poem as a pdf. The lines quoted are at the end of the poem, 42–43.

8. "find only a dreary waste." JH, *Poet in Exile*, 18 (to Nora Perry from Warsaw, 10–12–58).

8. "my first friend and my best." JH, *Letters, Extracts*, 3:321. Letter from JH to TR ("Dear Theodore"), 11–16–1904, about his brother Augustus, who died 11–12–1904: "I owe him everything. He was only four years older than me, but he had a sense of right and of conduct which made him seem much older. He was always my standard." Ibid., 321–22.

8. "He has the talents." Thayer, *JH*, 1:61 (Warsaw newspaper clipping, fall 1858).

9. "luster from my dreams." Ibid., 1:63 (to Sarah Helen Whitman, 12–15–58).

9. "These heavenly asphodels." JH, "Erato," 39. To locate the poem, see note above at p. 7.

10. "twelve months as a student?" Thayer, *JH*, 1:53–54 (from Warsaw, 9–6–58).

10. "a weather-beaten hulk." Dennett, *JH: Poetry to Politics*, 32 (to a college friend, William L. Stone, 5–20–59).

10. "my Daemon has pursued me." JH, *Poet in Exile*, 41–42 (to Nora Perry from Springfield, 5–15–59).

12. "this wonderful man." The eyewitness's response, often cited, may be found online at http://www.abrahamlincolnonline.org/lincoln/speeches/cooper.htm.

12–13. Lincoln's Cooper Union address. AL, *Speeches and Writings, 1859–65*, 111–30.

13. "a pistol to my ear." Ibid., 127.

13. "DARE TO DO OUR DUTY." Ibid., 130.

14. "hang shouts and cheers on." JH, *Lincoln's Journalist*, 1 (in *Providence Journal*, 5–26–60, as from Springfield, 5–21–60).

15. "touching in the last degree." Ibid., 24.

15. "sadness at this parting." AL, *Speeches and Writings, 1859–65*, 199. Holzer, *President-Elect*, 298–302, describes the moving circumstances surrounding AL's farewell address from the train platform and provides the texts both of the president-elect's impromptu remarks and of his revision of them into more formal language as the train

left Springfield. As is customary, the revised version—nearer to Lincoln's intentions—is given here. What he may have actually said, as printed the next day in the *Illinois State Journal*, is similar in meaning but less eloquent in diction; it appears as a note at AL, *Speeches and Writings, 1859–65*, 734.

15. "the crowd stood silent." JH, *Lincoln's Journalist*, 24.

3. From Springfield to Washington, D.C.

16–18. "genuine Son of the West." JH, *Lincoln's Journalist*, 25 (from Indianapolis, 2–11–61). The seven citations that follow are from this source: 25 ("sad, thoughtful" and "bowing to the cheering multitudes"), 28 ("talks like himself" and "magnificent success"), 29 ("one continued wave of cheers" and "intrepid lookers-on"), 31–32 ("a momentary commotion").

18. "My dear little Miss." The letter to Miss Grace Bedell, from Springfield, 10–19–60, is in AL, *Speeches and Writings, 1859–65*, 182, and in Basler, *Collected Works of AL*, 4:129.

18–19. "topic of conversation." JH, *Lincoln's Journalist*, 32. Citations that follow are from this source: 33 ("turbulent ceremonials"), 38 ("they always bellow"), 41 ("unruly, and ill bred"), 42 ("calling for 'Old Abe.'").

19. scholar Harold Holzer. Holzer's detailed, annotated *Lincoln: President-Elect* fleshes out the eleven-day trip from Springfield to Washington fully, 288–396.

4. Inauguration

20. "her entire sovereign powers." *Charleston Mercury*, 12–20–60. The text of the newspaper article is available online at http://www.tulane.edu/~sumter/Dilemmas/Mer21Dec.2.html.

22. "I appear before you." AL, *Speeches and Writings, 1859–65*, 215–24.

25. "will yet again harmonize." Seward's proposed final paragraph, complete with his emendations, is given as a note in Ibid., 735.

25. "I am loth to close." Ibid., 224.

5. Wartime

25. "As you see." Nicolay, *With Lincoln in the White House*, 29 (3–5–61). The two citations that immediately follow are from the same source: 33 ("not the least fear," 4–7–61, and "Don't get alarmed," 4–11–61).

25. "On the 12th day." AL, *Speeches and Writings, 1859–65*, 325–28 ("To the Senate and House of Representatives," 5–26–62).

26. "militia of the several States." Ibid., 232–33 (4–15–61).

26. "Your object." Gov. John Letcher of Virginia to Hon. Simon Cameron, Secretary of War, 4–16–61. The governor's reply may be read online at http://www.nytimes.com/1861/04/22/news/gov-letcher-s-proclamation-his-reply-secretary-cameron-state-affairs-norfolk.html.

27. triumph "of truth and justice." Olsen, *American Civil War*, 78 (*Richmond Dispatch*, 4–15–61: "THE SURRENDER OF FORT SUMTER / GREAT REJOICING AMONG THE PEOPLE / UNPARALLELED EXCITEMENT").

27. "defend Washington." JH, *Inside Lincoln's White House*, 16 (5–1–61).

27. proclamation on the 19th. AL, *Speeches and Writings, 1859–65*, 233–34.

28. "Housekeepers here." JH, *Inside Lincoln's White House*, 8 (4–22–61).

28. "a very anxious suspense." Nicolay, *With Lincoln in the White House*, 38 (to Ozias M. Hatch, 4–26–61).

28. "we shall have no trouble." Ibid., 39.

29. "The solemn midnight march." JH, *Lincoln's Journalist*, 75 (7–22–61).

29. "It was terrible." Ibid., 77.

30. "we went over to McClellans." JH, *Inside Lincoln's White House*, 30.

31. "I wish here to record." Ibid., 32 (11–13–61).

31. "I got there on time." Miller, *Plain Speaking*, 294–96.

32. "so ugly a letter." AL, *Speeches and Writings, 1859–65*, 298–99 (to David Hunter). The six citations that follow are from this source: 313 ("may order what he pleases"), 314 (*"But you must act"*), 315 ("not as plenty as blackberries," to Richard Yates and William Butler), 316 ("call for Parrott guns"), 323 ("Let me hear from you instantly"), 343 ("how to be cured of General Phelps").

32. "I have just read yours." AL, *Speeches and Writings, 1859–65*, 357–58 (8–22–62).

33. "what we require." "Prayer of Twenty Millions." Greeley's open letter, dated the tenth, appears on p. 4 of the *New York Tribune* for 8–20–62.

33. "I would save the Union." AL, *Speeches and Writings, 1859–65*, 358.

34. "social and political equality." AL, *Speeches and Writings, 1832–58*, 732 (10–13–58).

35. "Our soldiers were assaulted." AL, *Speeches and Writings, 1859–65*, 293 (12–3–61).

35. "forever free." Ibid., 368 ("Preliminary Emancipation Proclamation").

6. Domestic Matters

36. "last best hope." AL, *Speeches and Writings, 1859–65*, 415 ("Annual Message to Congress," 12–1–62).

36. "some little items." JH, *Inside Lincoln's White House*, 19.

36. "not an absurdity." Ibid., 20.

36. "naturally anti-slavery." Basler, *Collected Works of AL*, 7:281 (to Albert G. Hodges, 4–4–64).

36–37. "wandering laboring boy." Burlingame, *Inner World of AL*, 42. The two citations that follow are from this source, 39 ("his father taught him" and "I tried to stop it").

38. "beginning to respect him." JH, *At Lincoln's Side*, 5 (to Hannah Angell from Springfield, 1–6–61).

39. "short and simple annals." Thomas Gray, "Elegy Written in a Country Churchyard" (1751), line 32.

39. "this kind of work?" Burlingame, *Inner World of AL*, 276.

40. "a sparkling talker." Baker, *Mary Todd Lincoln*, 114.

40. "came home entranced." Ibid., 197.

41. "milking apparatus." Nicolay, *With Lincoln in the White House*, 216, n. 21. James W. Nesmith was a Democratic senator from Oregon.

42. "one day so kindly." Stoddard, *White House in War Times*, 62.

42. "the Stewards salary." JH, *At Lincoln's Side*, 19–20.

43. "have never fallen out." Baker, *Mary Todd Lincoln*, 196.

7. "What a Man He Is!"

43. "any great intimacy." Quoted in Burlingame, *Inner World of AL*, 60 (Robert Lincoln to J. G. Holland, Chicago, 6–6–65, in *Intimate Memories of Lincoln*, Rufus Rockwell Wilson, ed. Elmira: Primavera Press, 1945).

44. "direction of the law." Burlingame, *Inner World of AL*, 76–77.

44. "silent power of work." T. C. Evans of the *New York World* and friend of JH on the railroad journey east in February 1861, in his "Personal Reminiscences of John Hay," *Chattanooga Sunday Times*, 7–30–1905. Quoted in Editors' Introduction to JH, *Inside Lincoln's White House*, xiv.

44. "put in twenty-four hours." Thayer, *JH*, 1:145 (8–1–62).

45. "we are whipped again." JH, *Inside Lincoln's White House*, 37–38 (9–1–62).

46. "tell that thing again." Stoddard, *White House in War Times*, 93–94.

47. "enemy holds the interior." AL, *Speeches and Writings, 1859–65*, 348 (to Agénor Etienne de Gasparin, 8–4–62).

47–48. "specially good humor." JH, *Inside Lincoln's White House*, 61 (7–11–63). The two citations that follow are from this source: 62 ("whole country is *our* soil," 7–14–63), 63 ("the escape of Lee," 7–15–63).

48. "state of entire collapse." JH, *At Lincoln's Side*, 45 (to Nicolay, 7–19–63).

48. "I was amused." JH, *Inside Lincoln's White House*, 64.

49. "gone some time." Ibid., 48 (to Nicolay, 8–7–63). The two citations that follow are from the same letter: 49 ("in fine whack" and "kept where he is").

49. "to the Soldiers' Home." JH, *Inside Lincoln's White House*, 75–76 (8–23–63).

49–50. "doing the 'Marble Heart.'" Ibid., 110 (11–9–63). The citations that immediately follow are from this source: 111–13 ("Cemetery at Gettysburg," 11–18–63), 113 ("his half dozen lines," 11–19–63).

52. "Falstaff in Henry IV." JH, *Inside Lincoln's White House*, 128 (12–15–63). The citation that follows ("into the office laughing") is from this source, 194 (4–30–64).

53. "I lose my temper sometimes." JH, *At Lincoln's Side*, 92 (2–25–64).

8. Peace Overture

54. Bixby letter. AL, *Speeches and Writings, 1859–65*, 644.

55. "destroyed it in anger." She did so as "an ardent Southern Sympathizer," according to Mrs. Bixby's great-grandson, who heard it as a youth from his father; quoted in Burlingame, "The Trouble with the Bixby Letter," 67. Also see Burlingame's "The Authorship of the Bixby Letter," in JH, *At Lincoln's Side*, pp. 169–84, in particular 177 ff.

55. "not read one in fifty." JH, *At Lincoln's Side*, 110 ("Letter to William H. Herndon, Paris," 9-5-66).

55. "beyond endurance." Burlingame, "The Trouble with the Bixby Letter," 67 ("That month [Nov., 1864] Hay apologized to Charles S. Spencer, a New York Republican leader: 'I regret that the President was literally crowded out of the opportunity of writing you a note for yr. banquet. He fully intended to do so himself & for that reason I did not prepare a letter for him. But the crush here just now is beyond endurance.' ").

57. "industrious, imperious." JH, *Inside Lincoln's White House*, 24 (8 [9]–28–61). For AL's letters to Frémont, see AL, *Speeches and Writings, 1859–1865*, 266, 267 (9–2, 9–11–61).

58. "burlesque of the thing." JH, *At Lincoln's Side*, 34 (to Nicolay, 4–10–63).

58. "handle to my name." Ibid., 37 (to Nicolay, 4–16–63).

59. "a widespread conviction." Seitz, *Greeley*, 248–50. R. C. Williams, *Greeley*, 247–56, places this particular peace effort of Editor Greeley in the larger context of the various peace movements and their advocates during these grim months of the war.

59. "come to me with you." Horner, *Lincoln & Greeley*, 300 (7–9–64).

59. "bring me a man, or men." Ibid., 303 (7–15–64).

59. "down to the parlor." JH, *Inside Lincoln's White House*, 224 (in an undated entry written apparently around 7–22–64).

60. "a personal witness." Horner, *Lincoln & Greeley*, 303 (7–15–64).

60. "the worst man." JH, *Inside Lincoln's White House*, 224.

60. "can send it by mail." Horner, *Lincoln & Greeley*, 304 (7–16–64). The safe conduct that Hay furnished Greeley is quoted at Ibid., 304–5.

60. "I am authorized." Horner, *Lincoln & Greeley*, 305 (7–17–64).

61. "a good deal cut up." JH, *Inside Lincoln's White House*, 225.

61. "half-witted adventurer." Ibid., 229 (after 7–22–64).

61. "interminable letters." Nicolay and Hay, *AL: A History*, 9:185.

61. "halls blooming suddenly." JH, *Inside Lincoln's White House*, 226.

61–62. "To Whom It May Concern." The so-called Niagara Manifesto. Horner, *Lincoln & Greeley*, 312 (7–18–64). The three citations that follow are from this source: 310 ("when he may expect"), 310–11 ("to that gentleman"), 312–14 ("as much indignation as surprise"). The document is given in its entirety on those latter pages.

62. "the purport of this proposal." Nicolay and Hay, *AL: A History*, 9:191–92.

63. "your letters are never so submitted." Horner, *Lincoln & Greeley*, 315.

9. April 1865

65. "constant contact with envy." JH, *Letters, Extracts*, 2:56 (12–25–80).

65. "sick of certain aspects." JH, *At Lincoln's Side*, 103 (3–31–65).

65. "absent at Charleston." Nicolay and Hay: *AL: A History*, 10:301.

65–66. "gossiping in an upper room." Ibid. Citations that immediately follow are from this source: 299 ("bursting through the doors"), 301 ("brought instant death").

67. "His features were calm." Welles, *Diary*, 2:286–87 (4–14–65).

67. "a very different man." JH, *At Lincoln's Side*, 139–40 (in JH, "Life in the White House in the Time of Lincoln," originally published in *Century Magazine* 41, 11–90).

68. "lamplight grew pale." Nicolay and Hay, *AL: A History*, 10:301–2.

68. Stanton's supercilious snub of Lincoln. A rudeness that occurred, but appears to have been considerably embroidered in the retelling. See Thomas and Hyman, *Stanton*, 64–66, and Marvel, *Lincoln's Autocrat*, 72–73, 136.

69. "belongs to the ages." Nicolay and Hay, *AL: A History*, 10:302. The following citation ("with loud outcry") is from this source, same page.

10. From Washington, D.C., to Springfield

70. "horse of the deceased." Shea, *Lincoln Memorial*, 130.

70. "I know his emotion." Welles, *Diary*, 2:293 (4–19–65).

70–71. "I die for my country." Kauffman, *American Brutus*, 320.

71–72. "Messrs. Nicolay and Hay." Shea, *Lincoln Memorial*, 165. The three citations that follow are from this source: 168 ("out-of-the-way places"), 171–72 ("coffin was closed"), 174 ("the entire route").

72. Teedie peering out. Some have speculated that the other blur, rather than Teedie's brother, may be his sister's playmate and future second wife of president Theodore Roosevelt, Edith Carow.

73. "arranging the papers." Nicolay, *With Lincoln in the White House*, 176 (to Therena Bates, 4–24–65).

73. planning to write about their Chief. The two secretaries had earlier spoken with the president about their hopes, and he had been supportive and encouraging.

73. "pleasant place for study." JH, *At Lincoln's Side*, 104 (to Manning Leonard, 4–13–65).

74. "have had no quiet day." Ibid., 109 (to Herndon from Paris, 9–5–66). The letter is printed in its entirety here, 109–11. The citations that follow to the end of the chapter are in those two pages, except for the one immediately below.

74. "beginning to respect." Ibid., 5 (to Hannah Angell, 1–6–61).

74. "greatest character since Christ." JH, *At Lincoln's Side*, 111.

CHAPTER 2

11. Livelihood in the East

77. "stood in the biting air." MT, *Travels with Mr. Brown*, 80.

78. "Everybody knows me." MT, *Letters*, 1:264 (8–19–63).

78. "'call' to literature." Ibid., 322–23 (to Orion and Mollie Clemens, 10–19–65).

79. "'Downhearted,' the devil!" Ibid., 20 (10–26–53).

80. "*not* home again." Notebook entry on day of arrival in San Francisco, 8–13–66, in MT, *Notebooks*, 1:163.

80. "interesting and amusing lectures." Fatout, *MT on the Lecture Circuit*, 40.

81. "fifth death in five days." MT, *Travels with Mr. Brown*, 66. The two citations that follow are from this source: 90 ("piloting women safely"), 9 ("a splendid desert").

82. "possibly taboo it." Kaplan, *Mr. Clemens and MT*, 23.

82–83. "vast amount of enjoyment." MT, *Travels with Mr. Brown*, 111. The two citations that follow are from this source: 113 ("only to enjoy themselves"), 122 ("unspeakably comfortable").

83. "don't hold any intercourse." Ibid., 142 (Letter 14, about St. Louis, written from NYC, 4–16–67). The four citations that follow are from the same source: 143 ("room and to spare"), 154 ("railroads killed it"), 158 ("gorgeous gold frog" and "sumptuously fitted up").

84. "Mark Twain's quaint remarks." *New York Times*, 5–7–67; quoted in MT, *Letters*, 2:43.

84. "a first-rate success." MT, *Travels with Mr. Brown*, 178–79.

84. "moneys to my mother." MT, *Letters*, 2:53.

85. "a spirit that is angry." Ibid., 58.

85. "laughing and carrying on." MT, *Autobiography*, 1:223.

12. Hay Overseas

85. "not very long." JH, *At Lincoln's Side*, 104 (to Manning Leonard, 4–13–65).

85. proceeded directly via overnight train. Thayer says (1:243) that JH spent the day and evening of his landing in New York before "taking the Owl Train for Washington." If so, he might have lingered with friends who also knew Clemens. Or

the two might have met sometime later, Mark Twain's memory not always a reliable faculty.

86. "very much liked." Traubel, *Whitman*, 4:32. Cited in Clymer, "JH and MT," 398.

86. "laughed through his term." Hay, *Inside Lincoln's White House*, 112 (11–18–63).

86. "like a gouty crab." JH, *Letters, Extracts*, 1:265 (from JH's diary, 9–30–66).

87. "spick and span city." quoted in Taliaferro, *All the Prizes*, 109 (to "My Dear Brother," 8–4–65). The citations that immediately follow are from this source.

87. *"stand at the break of day."* JH, *Poems*, 39 ("Sunrise in the Place de la Concorde").

88. in "small clothes." Taliaferro, *All the Prizes*, 111 (JH to "My Dear Father & Mother & Sister," 2–2–66).

88. "no quiet day." JH, *At Lincoln's Side*, 109 (to Herndon from Paris, 9–5–66).

88. "interesting times." Ibid., 104 (to Manning Leonard, 4–13–65).

89. "keen for our book." JH, *Letters, Extracts*, 1:279.

90. "a picture to look at." MT, *Autobiography*, 1:222 (from Florence, 1–31–1904).

90. "my own little orchard of 5 acres." JH, *Letters, Extracts*, 1:280 (6–3–67).

13. The *Quaker City*

91. "tip-top people." MT, *Letters to Bowen*, 20 (6–7–67); quoted in MT, *Mrs. Fairbanks*, xv (editor's introduction).

91. "peal of laughter." MT, *Mrs. Fairbanks*, xxi.

92–94. "butt of small wits." MT, *Innocents Abroad*, 101–2. The citations that follow are from this source: 103 ("Persistence, Enterprise"), 151 ("what a noble forest"), 259 ("gloomy tunnels with lava"), 286–87 ("a colossal church"), 287 ("fresco and a fire-plug"), 200 ("white turnpikes"), 355 ("travel on the Sabbath day"), 429 (Nazareth), 441 (Jerusalem), 481 (Bethlehem).

95. a fifty-eighth letter, for the *New York Herald*. The letter appears as chapter 41 of *The Innocents Abroad*, 513–19.

95. "asked to *write a book*." MT, "The Turning Point of My Life," in MT, *Collected Tales, Sketches 1891–1910*, 935.

95–96. "an immense circulation." MT, *Letters*, 2:120 (11–21–67). The two citations that follow are from this source: 119 ("beyond my comprehension," 12–2–67), 160 ("a splendid contract," 2–24–68).

96. "excuse to go to sea again." MT, *Mrs. Fairbanks*, 23 (3–10–68).

97. "how he *ought* to look." MT, *Innocents Abroad*, 3 ("Preface").

97. "always good-humored humor." Howells, *My Mark Twain*, 107–8.

98. "his flaming mustache." Ibid., 4.

14. Poet and Journalist

99. "the liberty I take." JH, *Hay-Howells Letters*, 3 (from Columbus, Ohio, 6–10–61).

100. " 'disgusting, nasty outrage.' " JH, *Letters, Extracts*, 1:310.

100–101. "three good rooms." Ibid., 1:315 (1,500 florins would have been around $600). The citations that follow are from this source: 339–40 ("entirely satisfactory town"), 341–42 ("roses in full bloom"), 342 ("I hate the water," "presents by hundreds," and "run through Spain"), 338 ("pleasures and hollow splendors"), 345 ("skeletons of his friends"), 361 ("I came for a flyer"), 363 ("she talks in her sleep").

101. "a fat office." Kushner and Sherrill, *John Milton Hay*, 64 (to Nicolay, 12–8–68). On these pages (63–65) the authors go into some detail concerning Hay's discreet but diligent soliciting among his Washington contacts in the fall of 1868 to secure a diplomatic position.

101–2. "absence of trepidation." JH, *Letters, Extracts*, 1:372 (diary entry from Buffalo, 1–27–69). The three citations that follow are from this source: 386 ("I have seen a great deal"), 390 ("my pecuniary circumstances," 5–1–70), 391 ("a curious year," 6–30–70).

103. "diplomatically extravagant habits." Thayer, *JH*, 1:330–31.

103. "début with 240." JH, *Letters, Extracts*, 2:1 (to Nicolay, 10–13–70).

103. "Chaps the likes of you." Taliaferro, *All the Prizes*, 133 (J. T. Fields to JH, 12–9–70).

103. "that ridiculous rhyme." JH, *Letters, Extracts*, 2:5 (12–12–70).

104–5. "Little Breeches." JH, *Poems*, 13–16.

105–6. "Jim Bludso, of the Prairie Belle." Ibid., 9–12.

107. "no more songs." JH, *Letters, Extracts*, 2:6 (12–29–70).

107. "I am no poet." Ibid., 2:9 (to Richard Henry Stoddard, 10–5–71). Citation in original reads "poets are not of them," clearly a slip of the pen.

15. Wedding in Elmira

107. "wishy-washy squibs." MT, *Mrs. Fairbanks*, 14 (from Hartford, 1–24–68).

107. "Hay was not afraid." MT, *Autobiography*, 1:222.

108. "the wrong room." Ibid., 1:145.

109. "a visiting *Spirit*." Wecter, *Love Letters*, 43 (1–6–69).

110. "*always* grateful to you." MT, *Mrs. Fairbanks*, 58 (from Lansing, Mich., 12–24–68).

110. "splendidest man in the *world!*" Steinbrink, *Getting to Be MT*, 41 (12–2–68).

110. "*Mrs. Samuel L. Clemens.*" MT, *Letters to Bowen*, 20.

110. "mar our joy." Quoted in Steinbrink, *Getting to Be MT*, 111 (4–16–70).

111. "vials of hellfire." MT, *Letters to Publishers*, 60 (3–17–71).

111. "ten men in America." MT, *Roughing It*, 559–60.

113. "my vile temper." MT, *Mrs. Fairbanks*, 112–13 (from Amenia, N.Y., 1–6–70).

113. "forbidden things." Ibid., 107 (from Buffalo, 9–27–69).

114. "this splendid compliment." Wecter, *Love Letters*, 179 (9–28–72).

16. John Hay Marries

116. "three or four times." MT, *Autobiography*, 1:222.

117. "*voilà tout*." Quoted in Taliaferro, *All the Prizes*, 155 (7–12–73; at Brown University).

117. "fresh and beautiful life." Ibid. (to Flora Stone, 8–9–72).

118. "convenient residence." *Cleveland Leader*, 1–7–59.

118. "I respected you more." Taliaferro, *All the Prizes*, 160 (to Clara Stone, 5–4–73). The two citations that follow are from the same source: 159 ("mark the admiration," 12–24–72), 161 ("Ah think what you give," 5–4–73).

119. "estimable young person." JH, *Letters, Extracts*, 2:14 (to Nicolay, 8–27–73). The two citations that follow are from this source: 12–13 ("great deal of coin," JH to Reid, 8–14–73), 19 ("hold the baby").

120. "immediate wealth." Kushner and Sherrill, *John Milton Hay*, 154–55 (to Alvey A. Adee, 11–28–74).

120. "first class gold pen." Teliaferro, *All the Prizes*, 163 (6–19–73). The citations that follow are from this source: 167 ("read and yawn," 12–14–75), 165 ("so desirable a wife," to Alvey A. Adee, 11–28–74).

17. *The Gilded Age*

121. chapters of *Gilded Age* to reconsider. MT, *Mrs. Fairbanks*, 184 (from Hartford, 2–25–74).

126. "oddest looking buildings." "Mark Twain in Hartford: The Happy Years." The *Hartford Daily Times*, 3–24–74. Quoted in *American Heritage* 12–1959 (Vol. 1, Issue 1).

126. "the loveliest home." Wecter, *Love Letters*, 312 (from Hartford, 3–20–95).

127. "complete show in itself." C. Clemens, *My Father*, 43.

127. "happy, happy home." K. Leary, *Lifetime with MT*, 73.

128. "You don't know about me." MT, *Huckleberry Finn*, 625.

18. Summer 1877

128. "they were more dangerous." *Report of Joint Committee*, 81, 84.

129. "bemoaning her wounds." *New York Tribune*, 20–3–79; quoted in Cashman, *America in the Gilded Age*, 203.

130–131. Railroad strike of 1877. My account draws principally on Bellesiles, *1877*, and Bruce, *Year of Violence*.

131. "Pittsburgh Delivered Up." Bellesiles, *1877*, 158.

131. "that is the simple truth." Thayer, *JH*, 2:1–2 (4–24–77).

132. Paris Commune. John Merriman's *Massacre* (2014) is a comprehensive retelling of the months of the Commune and the fearsome reactions those months provoked.

133–35. "spoiling at the Depot." Thayer, *JH*, 2:2 (4–24–77). The two citations that follow are from this source: 5 ("This is disgraceful," 4–25–77; and their sympathies "with the laboring man," 8–17–77).

136. "Today was an important one." Taliaferro, *All the Prizes*, 185 (11–25–79).

136. "one of those rare natures." Ibid., 190.

136. "now one-half over." JH, *Letters, Extracts*, 2:46–47.

136. "not going back on Democracy." Ibid., 2:55 (to President-elect Garfield, 12–25–80).

19. "My Friendship with Mr. Hay"

137. "attar of roses." Smith and Gibson, *MT-Howells Letters*, 1:277 (10–27–79).

137. Mark Twain on 1877 strike. MT, *Mrs. Fairbanks*, 208.

138. "You will have a good wife." JH, *Letters, Extracts*, 2:60–61.

139. "very strict about Sunday." MT, *Autobiography*, 1:223.

139. "38 years without impairment." Paine, *MT: Biography*, 3:1249.

139. "one permanent ambition." MT, *Life on the Mississippi*, 253.

140. "two greatest gifts of the writer." Smith and Gibson, *MT-Howells Letters*, 1:55–56 (12–18–74).

141. "Mecca of our rural fancies." JH, *Addresses*, 244–45 ("The Press and Modern Progress," delivered 5–19–1904 at opening of Press Parliament of the World at the Louisiana Purchase Exposition, St. Louis).

141. "'S-t-e-a-m-boat a-comin'!" "Old Times on the Mississippi." *Atlantic Monthly* 35 (1–75): 69–70.

142. "we imagine he would talk of them." Howells, *My Mark Twain*, 110–11.

142. "definitive in American literature." Trilling, *The Liberal Imagination*, 115–17.

20. Mark Twain's Midas Touch

143. "and oh the language!" S. Clemens, *Papa*, 106–7.

144. "the thing was dreadfully funny." Quoted in Franklin J. Meine's introduction to Project Gutenberg eBook verbatim text of "1601."

144. "a grete scandal did ye world heare thereof." MT, "1601" (Golden Hind Press edition), 16–17.

145. Hay's letters to Gunn. Quoted in Franklin J. Meine's introduction to Project Gutenberg eBook verbatim text of "1601." On Howells's part in encouraging Mark Twain to send "1601" to Hay, see Smith and Gibson, *MT-Howells Letters*, 1:271–72 (MT to Howells, late Sept. or early Oct., 1879).

146. "made a Comanche blush." MT, *Connecticut Yankee*, 241–42.

147. "You don't know about me." MT, *Huckleberry Finn*, 625.

149. whatever Mark Twain touched. Paine, *MT: Biography*, 2:830.

CHAPTER 3

21. Apprenticeship of an Author

151. "an eye . . . upon the *Tribune*." Monteiro, *James & Hay*, 81–82.

155. "a collective opacity." Quoted in Edel, *HJ*:1 (*The Untried Years, 1843–1870*), 36. At the same site, same page, Howells is quoted further regarding Henry James Sr.'s writing style, which lighted up his thought "with flashes of the keenest wit and bathed it in the glow of a lambent humor, so that it is truly wonderful to me how it should remain so unintelligible."

156. Henry James Jr.'s "obscure hurt." See Edel, *HJ*:1 (*The Untried Years, 1843–1870*), 173–83, for a full, authoritative discussion of this much-discussed matter.

158. "whatever credit." Monteiro, *James & Hay*, 82–83 (7–21–75).

22. Journalist in Paris

159. "all Parisian things." Monteiro, *James & Hay*, 81 (7–21–75).

160. "pretty sure of my ground." Ibid., 82.

160. "For, say, $20 or $25." Ibid., 14–15 (to Whitelaw Reid, 7–24–75). JH's letter to Reid is in "The Record of a Friendship," pp. 3–49, George Monteiro's valuable essay that accompanies his collection of JH's and HJ's correspondence that has survived.

161. "I summon philosophy." Monteiro, *James & Hay*, 83 (8–5–75).

161. "not to return, I fancy." JH, *Hay-Howells Letters*, 21 (Howells to JH, 12–18–75).

161. "it is remarkably cheap." Edel, *Letters of HJ*, 2:6 (to Henry James Sr., 11–18-[75]).

162. "the poorest I can do." HJ, *Parisian Sketches*, xxix (editors' introduction).

162. "Is not 'The American' astonishing." JH, *Hay-Howells Letters*, 22 (JH to Howells, 2–20–77).

163. "good sense and right feeling." Howells, "Henry James Jr.," *Century Magazine*, Vol. 35 (11–82), 28.

163–65. on a beautiful summer day. HJ, *Daisy Miller*, 16. The citations that follow to the end of the chapter are from this source: 24 ("decidedly charmed"), 30 ("meddle with little American girls"), 43 ("I think you're horrid!"), 44 ("she rackets about"), 63 ("you may be flirting"), 72 ("I *am* engaged"), 73 ("be at pains to respect"), 78 ("appreciated one's esteem").

23. Big Job Well Begun

166–67. "the silly criticisms." Monteiro, *James & Hay*, 62–63. Citations that follow are from this source: 63 ("I have read every word"), 64 ("At Naples, one evening").

167. "very clever foreign lady." HJ, *Daisy Miller*, 78.

168. "the whole story." JH, *Letters, Extracts*, 2:22 (to Nicolay, 6–23–76).

168. "have Lincoln inaugurated." Ibid., 26–27 (to Nicolay, 8–9–77).

169. "for her benefit." Baker, *Mary Todd Lincoln*, 317.

169. "big job well begun." JH, *Letters, Extracts*, 2:28–29 (2–14–78).

169. "I am used up." Ibid., 2:31 (4–6–78).

169. "my first friend and my best." Thayer, *JH*, 1:14–15.

169. "quietest summer of my life." JH, *Letters, Extracts*, 2:38 (1–11–79).

170. "wine unto water." Edel, *HJ:2* (*The Conquest of London, 1870–1881*), 394.

170. "something on a larger scale." Ibid., 401.

170. "comforting delusion." JH, *Letters, Extracts*, 2:40–41 (to Whitelaw Reid, 6–9–79).

171. "No work printed in recent years." JH, "James's *The Portrait of a Lady*," in Monteiro, *James & Hay*, 69. Citations that follow to the end of the chapter are from this source, 69–76.

24. Hay Writes a Novel

171. "John Hay wrote it." MT, *Mrs. Fairbanks*, 256 (from Hartford, 1–30–84).

172. "always bred well." Hay, *Bread-Winners*, 6 (Ch. 1). The three citations that follow are from this source: 183 ("meetings all over town," Ch. 11), 215 ("riot and plunder," Ch. 14), 218–19 ("the sweat of the poor," Ch. 14).

172. "big blast furnace shut down." *New York Times*, 5–12–82.

173. "no disturbances have occurred." Ibid.

173–74. "assessment." Hay, *Bread-Winners*, 226 (Ch. 14). The three citations that follow are from this source: 188 ("Veterans, Attention!" Ch. 12), 133 ("her red full lips," Ch. 9), 82 ("most incapable workmen," Ch. 5).

174. "ignorant and lazy dupes." Edward J. Shriver, " 'The Bread-winners.' A Comment." *Century* 27 (11–83): 157–58.

175. "murder, arson, and rapine." Ibid., 158 ("Reply by the Author").

175. "never seen in print." Ibid., 27 (3–84): 294–96.

175. "had done no work." JH, *Bread-Winners*, 6 (Ch. 1).

176. "got on beautifully." Anesko, *Letters, Fictions*, 236 (HJ to Howells, 11–27–82).

177. "being twenty-one again." JH, *Letters, Extracts*, 2:78 (3–8–83).

177. "so much to live for." Ibid., 2:84–85 (5–2–83).

25. "The Art of Fiction"

177. "How odd and strange." Smith and Gibson, *MT-Howells Letters*, 1:431–32.

177. "dreary, dreadful journey." Monteiro, *James & Hay*, 92–93 (5–24–83).

179–80. "person who tells stories." Besant, "Art of Fiction," 5. Citations that immediately follow are from this source: 6 ("strong man for the weak"), 7–8 ("a real Art"), 12 ("beneath the rags and filth" and "Poetry alone is the rival"), 8 ("at our own sweet will"), 14 ("Rules must be learned").

180. "I should not have affixed." HJ, "The Art of Fiction," *Longman's Magazine*, 4 (9–84): 502. I cite from the essay as it originally appeared. "The Art of Fiction" is more readily available in HJ, *Partial Portraits* (1888), the book version reprinted in HJ, *Henry James, Literary Criticism: Essays on Literature, American Writers, English Writers*, 44–65, although—as was usual between magazine and book versions with this author—the latter is revised, on occasion substantially.

180–82. "upon experiment, upon curiosity." Ibid. The citations that follow are from the same essay in *Longman's Magazine*: 506 ("one would say that being good"), 509 ("unaccommodating to disagree"), 507 ("have done with it at once"), 509 ("but they are not exact" and "what kind of experience is intended"), 510 ("a rather tantalizing monition").

182. HJ and Fanny Kemble. HJ, *Notebooks*, 11–12 (2–21–79).

182–83. "supreme virtue of a novel." HJ, "The Art of Fiction," as in *Longman's*, 4 (9–84): 510. Citations that immediately follow are from this source: 503–4 ("his torment, his delight"), 511 ("cannot possibly take enough"), 512 ("bad novels and good novels"), 511 (it is "a living thing"), 517 ("an adventure—an immense one").

183–84. "*le donnée*." Ibid., 513. The citations that follow are from this source: 507 ("that it be interesting" and "the bad is swept"), 520 ("the magnificence of the form").

185. "as for the Bostonians." Smith and Gibson, *MT-Howells Letters*, 2:534 (7–21–85).

26. Capturing Reality, 1885

185–86. Bunyan's heaven. *The Pilgrim's Progress*, available in many editions. My imagery derives from late pages in Part the First.

186. "as full of Boston." HJ, *Complete Notebooks*, 19.

186. "air of reality." HJ, "The Art of Fiction," *Longman's Magazine*, 4 (9–84), 510.

186–87. "a burning resentment." W. D. Howells, *My Mark Twain*, 135 ("Mark Twain," here reprinted on pp. 134–44 from *The Century Magazine*, 9–82). Citations that follow are from the reprint source: 141 ("indefinitely short of knowing Mark Twain"), 143 ("that stuff is terrible," "an artist of uncommon power," and "force and truth of drawing that makes them permanent").

187. "complete show in itself." C. Clemens, *My Father*, 43.

188. "Would you take it?" W. D. Howells, "Henry James, Jr.," *Century*, 35 (11–82), 25. Citations immediately following are from this source: 25 ("I admired, as we must in all that Mr. James has written," "they had to 'learn to like' it," and "the tears of rage which bedewed our continent"), 26 ("he is decidedly not on humorous terms with his reader" and "I read him with a relief").

189. "most salient and peculiar point." HJ, *Complete Notebooks*, 20.

190. "this fatuous agitation." HJ, *The Bostonians*, 1113.

191. "something to worship." Wecter, *Love Letters*, 43 (1–6–69).

191–92. "history of feminine anguish." HJ, *The Bostonians*, 969. The four citations that follow are from this source: 978 ("infinitely tiresome"), 1115–16 ("you regard us as perfectly inferior?"), 1218–19 ("Ah, now I am glad!" and "these were not the last").

193–94. "the pursuit and not the end." W. D. Howells, "Henry James, Jr.," *Century*, Vol. 35 (11–82), 26. Citations that follow to the end of the chapter are from this source: 26 ("No other novelist, except George Eliot"), 28 ("a finer art in our day," "human nature much more in its wonted aspects," and "its chief exemplar in Mr. James"), 29 ("truly grieve us when it ceases").

27. Nicolay and Hay

196. "a pretty bad business." Lubbock, *Letters of HJ*, 1:117 (quoted in HJ to William James, 2–14–85).

196. "not seen Miss Peabody." Ibid., 115–18.

196. "an exquisite production." W. James, *Letters of . . .* , 1:250–52 (from Cambridge, Mass., 5–9–86).

197. "more matter and less art." The allusion is to *Hamlet* (II, ii, 97), Gertrude's complaint about Polonius's rhetoric-laden speechifying.

197. "meekness of your reply." Gard, *HJ:Critical Heritage*, 159–60.

198. "whose charity began." HJ, *Bostonians*, 825.

198. "when I was young." Ibid., 1169–70.

199. "working like a Turk." Thayer, *JH*, 2:29 (7–18–85).

199–200. "package of documents." Ibid., 2:27 (7–17–[no year]). The citations that follow are from this source: 34 ("I find *Murfreesboro*," 12–17–[85?] and "Now there is certainly," 4–22–85), 35 ("Mexico and Diplomacy," 8–29–85).

201. "gall and bitterness." Thayer, *JH*, 2:32 (8–10–85). The citations that immediately follow are from the same letter to Nicolay: 33 ("blubbering sentiment," "everlasting angels," "Lincoln men all through").

201. "My paramount object." AL, *Speeches and Writings, 1859–65*, 358.

202. "nor did he believe." Lamon, *Life of Lincoln*, 486.

202. his "overweening ambition." Ibid., 483.

203. "nothing to explain or apologize for." Mearns, *Lincoln Papers*, 1:75 (1–6–86).

28. The Five of Hearts

204. "delightful little party." Monteiro, *Correspondence of HJ and H. Adams*, 1.

204. "Son of C.F.A." Ibid., 2.

204. The Adamses' honeymoon. Dykstra, *Clover Adams*, 58–70.

204–5. "germs of typhus fever." Monteiro, *Correspondence of HJ and Henry Adams*, 2. The four citations that follow are from this source: 7 ("entitled *Ann Eliza*"), 3 ("abusing the Britons," HJ to Elizabeth Boot, 6–28–79), 4 ("good American *confidents*" and "then to the *cirque*").

206. "bid farewell to my friends." Edel, ed., *Letters of HJ*, 2:307 (to Grace Norton, 9–20–80).

206. the Five of Hearts. Patricia O'Toole's very readable book of that title, which bears the subtitle *An Intimate Portrait of Henry Adams and His Friends, 1880–1918*, concentrates on Adams, Clover Adams, Hay, Clara Hay, and Clarence King. See 68–73 and passim for an introduction to the world that the Adamses gathered about them in Washington in the 1880s.

207. the Colorado diamond field. See above, p. 108.

207. "very easy and genial." Edel, *HJ:3* (*The Middle Years, 1882–1895*), 30 (to E. L. Godkin).

208. "I would stand on that." Dykstra, *Clover Adams*, 204.

209. "goodly fellowship is broken up." Thayer, *JH*, 2:59–60 (JH to Adams, from the Brunswick Hotel, NYC, 12–9–85).

209. "hurry on your house." Levenson et al., *Letters of Henry Adams*, 2:640 (12–8–[85]).

29. Elevating Lincoln

211. "name of the hall fireplace." Taliferro, *All the Prizes*, 244. My description of Hay's mansion is indebted to this source.

211. "mermaids with funny tails." Ibid., 244. The guest was Elizabeth Cameron.

213. "dedicated to you." Thayer, *HJ*, 2:45. The citation that follows is from this source: 46 ("like a dray-horse of late," 1–22–90).

213. "To fix last page." Ibid., 49. Hay's addition appears in *AL: A History*, 10:350 (with added word *almost*: "after having met the rulers of almost every civilized country on earth"—the added word creating a new, one-word line to end the paragraph).

214. "the most important work." JH, *Hay-Howells Letters*, 141.

214. "by you & not by others." R. T. Lincoln to Hay, Chicago, 4–14–88, Evelyn Symington Collection, Library of Congress. In Burlingame, "Nicolay and Hay: Court Historians," 12.

214. "greater than ever we imagined." Mearns, *Lincoln Papers*, 1:75 (1–6–86).

214. "'this country's greatest President.'" Thayer, *JH*, 2:42.

214. "In nine cases out of ten." Ibid., 2:47 (to Howells, 1–23–90).

215. "a young girl named Ann Rutledge." Nicolay and Hay, *AL: A History*, 1:191–92.

215. "sad, gloomy, and melancholic." Hertz, *The Hidden Lincoln*, 162–63 (Herndon to Jesse W. Weik, 1–20–87).

215. "a marriage license was issued." Nicolay and Hay, *AL: A History*, 1:200.

215. "they in their turn play *hush*." Hertz, *The Hidden Lincoln*, 152, 158 (Herndon to Jesse W. Weik, 1–2–87, 1–22–87).

215. "enough for us to know." Nicolay and Hay, *AL: A History*, 1:201.

216. "We deny that it is partizanship." H. Nicolay, *Lincoln's Secretary*, 297.

216. "illuminate his inner life." Burlingame, "Nicolay and Hay: Court Historians," 16.

30. James and the Theater

218. "farewell to Parnassus." Montiero. *James & Hay*, 105 (6–5–90). HJ's answer, from Garmisch, Bavaria, 6–23–90, is in this source, 106 ff.

218. "a most charming creature." Ibid., 176 (note 5 to Letter 24, JH to HJ, 6–5–90).

220. "but one more book." S. Clemens, *Papa*, 187.

220. "world has got to buy them." Webster, *Mark Twain, Business Man*, 251.

221. "it has fallen flat." Edel, ed. *Letters of HJ*, 3:102 (10–9–85).

221. "works of Victorian fiction." Leavis, *Great Tradition*, 161.

221. "the way it treats James." JH, *Hay-Howells Letters*, 66 (to Howells, 10–20–82).

222. "going every night, or almost." HJ, *Complete Plays*, 37.

222. "extract the simplest." HJ, *Notebooks*, 53 (5–12–89).

222. "become Mr. Newman's *wife!*" HJ, *Complete Plays*, 252.

223. "make my fortune." Ibid., 179 (to Henrietta Reubell, 4–20–90; editor's foreword).

223. "a little from the nose." HJ, *Complete Plays*, 180 (from Edel's editorial introduction to the play). The three citations that follow are from this source: 181 ("abject, lonely fear"), 182 ("select as well as numerous" and "his work applauded").

223. obscure horseshoe of seats. The image, cited by Edel in his introduction to *The American* in his *Complete Plays of HJ*, is from Ch. 2 of HJ's short story "Nona Vincent," written soon after the event here described and published in 1892; it appears in HJ, *Complete Stories, 1892–1898.*

223. "I have larger hopes." HJ, *Complete Plays*, 183 (HJ to Mrs. Hugh Bell).

CHAPTER 4

31. A Commonplace Childhood?

225. "This is Mr. John Hay." Robinson, *My Brother*, 8–9.

225. "absolutely commonplace." Quoted in Wagenknecht, *Seven Worlds*, 149.

226. "simple annals of the Poor." Thomas Gray, "Elegy Written in a Country Churchyard" (1751), line 32.

226–27. "the best man I ever knew." TR, *Autobiography*, 258. The citations that follow ("He would not tolerate in us," "the same standard of clean living," "I was ever really afraid") are from the same source, same page.

227. tales of life on the plantation. McCullough, *Mornings on Horseback*, 43–46.

227. "would walk up and down with me." Bishop, *TR and His Time*, 1:3 (to Edward S. Martin, 11–26–1900).

229. "by no means robust." E. Morris, *Rise of TR*, 32.

230. "prowess, or even ordinary capacity." Wagenknecht, *Seven Worlds*, 149.

32. Tragedies and Consequences

230. "the only small waders." TR, *Diaries of Boyhood*, 300.

231. "know what idleness was." E. Morris, *Rise of TR*, 49.

231. "all the eight subjects." Cowles, *Letters*, 5 (7–25–75).

232–33. "when I kissed the dear dead face." Putnam, *TR: Formative Years*, 148, quoting from TR's private diary, 7–11/14–78. The citations that follow are from this source: 150 ("oh, how my heart pains me"), 151 ("something to keep up his name"), 188 ("so pure and sweet and beautiful"), 209 ("profanation to touch her"). See also E. Morris, *Rise of TR*, 70 ff.

234. "distrust of public life." E. Morris, *Rise of TR*, 124.

234. "one of the governing class." TR, *Autobiography*, 310.

234. "rose like a rocket." Kerr, *Bully Father*, 9–10.

235. "with bankers and bricklayers." E. Morris, *Rise of TR*, 227.

236. "The light has gone out of my life." Putnam, *TR: Formative Years*, 388.

236. "nothing left for me." Morison, *Letters of TR*, 1:65–66 (to Andrew Dickson White, 2–18–84).

236. "I should go mad." Ibid., 66 (to Carl Schurz. 2–21–84).

33. Hay Discontented

242. "Our little set." Levenson et al., *Letters of Henry Adams*, 3:233 (to Lucy Baxter, 4–13–90).

243. "I like *The Tragic Muse*." Monteiro, *James & Hay*, 105 (6–5–90).

244–45. "never do it again." Taliaferro, *All the Prizes*, 269 (5–2–91). The four citations that follow are from this source: 269 ("the Cameron clan," 5–15–91), 269–70 ("felt wicked and improper," Elizabeth Cameron to Henry Adams, 5–26–91), 270 ("last year of his life" and "that night in Paris").

245. "Fascinate John Hay." Levenson et al., *Letters of Henry Adams*, 3:510 (7–31–91).

245. "I walk on air." Tehan, *Henry Adams in Love*, 124.

245. "a ten-year-old boy." Levenson et al., *Letters of Henry Adams*, 3:510 (7–31–91).

245. "opal and diamond necklaces." Ibid., 3:557 (11–5–91).

245. series of extraordinary letters. The correspondence is at the Massachusetts Historical Society in Boston. Adams's letters to Elizabeth Cameron alone extend over a thirty-five year period and number just under nine hundred, the earliest of them dated 5–19–83, the day that the Camerons set off on what was Lizzie's first, year-long trip to Europe.

246. "you dear and splendid friend." Taliaferro, *All the Prizes*, 276–77.

246. "talk to whomever I pleased." Tehan, *Henry Adams in Love*, 115.

246–48. "I found just the one." Quoted in Taliaferro, *All the Prizes*, 271 (to Clara, 5–31–91). The citation that follows ("I give it up") is from the same source, 276.

248. "the bottom of your mind." Levenson et al., *Letters of Henry Adams*, 3:557 (11–5–91).

34. The Uses of Wealth

248. "estimable young person." Thayer, *JH*, 1:351 (to Nicolay, 8–27–73).

250. "How can I ever repay you?" Kushner and Sherrill, *John Milton Hay*, 79 (McKinley to JH, 2–26–93. Hay Papers, Brown University).

250. "To kiss a woman." quoted in Taliaferro, *All the Prizes*, 255 (Clarence King to Henry Adams, 9–27–87).

250. "I thank God." Sandweiss, *Passing Strange*, 203. Additional passages from the letters, which were entered as evidence in the court trial dealt with below, are quoted in this rich source, passim.

251. "his obstinate silence." Taliaferro, *All the Prizes*, 286 (1–1–94). The citation that follows ("a bijou of a house," 1–21–94) is from the same source, same page.

252–53. "weight off my spirit." Monteiro, *James & Hay*, 110 (1–28–94). The citations that follow are from the same letter to JH, 110–12. See Gordon, *Private Life of HJ*, for details of HJ's dealings with two important women in his life, his young cousin Minnie Temple and his later friend Constance Woolson.

253. "buried poor . . . Woolson." Thayer, *HJ*, 2:107 (to Henry Adams, 2–5–94).

253. Attendees at the funeral. Gordon, *Private Life of HJ*, 278–79 ("Clara Hay listed the small group of mourners" to her sister Flora Mather, 1–31–94). This source points out that the window from which Constance Woolson fell was too high from the floor to have allowed for an accidental fall.

254. "down on all fours." Montiero, *James & Hay*, 113.

254. "Beloved John Hay." Ibid., 112.

254. "bloody good thing y'are." HJ, *Complete Plays*, 475 (editor Leon Edel's foreword to *Guy Domville*, to which I'm much indebted).

255. "my mere literary modesty." Montiero, *James & Hay*, 113.

255. "most detestable incidents." HJ, *Complete Plays*, 483 (to Elizabeth Robins).

255. "the wretched tragic facts." Edel, *Letters of HJ*, 3:521 (to Mrs. Edward Compton, 3–15–[95]).

35. Degradation and Reform

255. "still has for his idols." Morison, *Letters of TR*, 1:277 (to Cecil Spring Rice, 5–3–92).

256. "none of the robuster virtues." "Mr. Roosevelt's Creed," *New York Times*, 10–19–84, p. 2. The speech as it appears in posthumous collected works of TR omits any reference to HJ.

256. "a miserable little snob." Morison, *Letters of TR*, 1:390 (to James Brander Matthews, 6–29–94).

259. "Well, it is over now." Brands, *TR*, 260.

261. "vicious as the Paris Commune." Williams, *Bryan*, 184, 185.

261. "it is a trifle wearing." Brands, *TR*, 218–19.

36. "You Might Do Worse Than Select Me"

262. "that system of dishonesty." Williams, *Bryan*, 187.

262. "beg for a pie." Taliaferro, *All the Prizes*, 306 (to Whitelaw Reid, 9–23–96).

262. "yesterday with the Majah." JH, *Letters, Extracts*, 3:78 (10–20–96).

263. "moral earnestness." Dennett, *JH: Poetry to Politics*, 177.

264. "We are at sea here." Taliaferro, *All the Prizes*, 308 (11–16–96).

264. "you might do worse than select me." Ibid., 311 (JH to McKinley, n.d. [1–97]).

265. "diplomatist by natural gifts." Monteiro, *James & Hay*, 181 (Letter 32, n. 2).

265. "This is tremendous and delicious." Ibid., 115 (2–22–97).

266. "The scale of expenditure." Quoted in Taliaferro, *All the Prizes*, 316; to this informative source I'm indebted for the description of JH's embassy quarters.

267. "he is too pugnacious." E. Morris, *Rise of TR*, 578.

267. "All the great masterful races." TR, *Works*, 13:184.

268. "'Desertion' never looks pretty." Taliaferro, *All the Prizes*, 321 (8–5–[97]).

37. Cuba, 1898

268. "explained my object." McCullough, *Mornings on Horseback*, 59.

269. "putting down $5 a month." Ibid., 61.

269. "something to keep up his name!" Putnam, *TR: Formative Years*, 151.

269. "a set of desperadoes." E. Morris, *Rise of TR*, 336 (8–86).

269. "For two nickels." JH, *Letters, Extracts*, 2:235–36 (1–6–92).

270. "we would take Canada." Morison, *Letters of TR*, 1:500 (12–20–95).

271. "all the fervor and zeal I possessed." TR, *Rough Riders*, 11.

272. "the great day of my life." E. Morris, *Rise of TR*, 681 (to Herman Hagedorn, 8–14–1917).

272. "the most magnificent soldier." Quoted in ibid., 674.

273. "a splendid little war." Thayer, *JH*, 2:337 (7–27–98).

274. "little holes in their heads." TR, *Rough Riders*, 112.

274. "eyes put out, flesh wounds." JH, *Lincoln's Journalist*, 77.

276. "CABLE ANSWER." Thayer, *JH*, 2:173.

38. The Beneficent Work of the World

277. "I loafe and invite." Whitman, "Song of Myself," line 4.

277. "pick and choose." Thayer, *JH*, 2:183 (to Samuel Mather from the Fells, 9–24–98).

277. "a match with Corbett." Ibid.

277. "like and respect him." Clymer, *JH*, 123 (n. 38, "Spanish American War").

277. "to resist by every means." Daniel, "Monroe Doctrine," 12–13.

278. "the imposition of irresistible hands." Dennett, *JH: Poetry to Politics*, 189 (4–21–98).

280. "benevolent assimilation." Pres. McKinley's term. Gould, *Spanish-American War*, 115–16 (12–21–98).

282. "a rioting, murdering mob." Taliaferro, *All the Prizes*, 378. The citation that follows ("besieged in British Legation") is from this source, 382.

283–84. "Mr. Clemens never looked better." This and the three citations that follow ("the courtesy of the port," "that's a long story," and "everybody's glad you're back") are from the article on p. 3 of the *New York Times* for 10–16–1900, reporting on the Clemenses' return to America.

284. "I am an anti-imperialist." Scharnhorst, *MT: Complete Interviews*, 353 ("Mark Twain Home, an Anti-Imperialist," *New York Herald*, 10–16–1900).

39. Family Griefs

284. "tear-blinded." C. Clemens, *My Father*, 87–88.

285. "it was not practical." Paine, *MT: Biography*, 2:991.

285. "like a thunder-clap." L. Leary, *MT's Correspondence with H.H. Rogers*, 90 (12–22–94).

286. "sorrow to this family." Wecter, *Love Letters*, 320–21.

286. "treasure in the bank." Paine, *Letters*, 2:641 (1–19–97).

286. "reading the creditors' letters." Ibid., 2:654 (3–7–98).

286. "knocked the gloom out." Leary, *MT's Correspondence with H. H. Rogers*, 384.

286. "Boxer is a patriot." Gibson, "Mark Twain and Howells," 447.

287. "I drowned him out." Quoted in Dalton, *TR: A Strenuous Life*, 195.

288. a grave error. Roosevelt's statement ("I most earnestly hope that the pending treaty concerning the Isthmian canal will not be ratified unless amended . . .") was published on the front page of the *New York Sun*, 2–12–1900.

288. *"Et tu!"* Thayer, *JH*, 2:225 (2–12–1900).

289. "I hesitated long." Ibid., 2:339 (2–18–1900). TR's letter goes on to assert that JH has been "the greatest secretary of state I have seen in my time—Olney comes second—but at this moment I cannot, try as I may, see that you are right."

289. "I return your resignation." Thayer, *JH*, 2:227–28. JH's letter of resignation is on 226–27, exemplary in representing this author's gift of apt expression.

289. "a very successful year." Quoted in Taliaferro, *All the Prizes*, 401.

290–91. *"My* boy is gone." Thayer, *JH*, 2:262–63 (6–30–1901). The three citations that follow are from that source: 263 ("I have hideous forebodings," 7–11–1901), 266 ("a strange and tragic fate," 9–14–1901), 344 ("the true source of my tears," 9–15–1900).

291. Hay's last sight of Nicolay. H. Nicolay, *Lincoln's Secretary*, 342.

291. "alone and uncared for." Adams, *Education*, 1100 (Ch. 28); Sandweiss, *Passing Strange*, 229 (8–9–1901).

291. "very, very sorry." Thayer, *JH*, 2:347–48 (12–25–1901).

40. The Thought of My Life Ending

292. "most delightful man." Morison, *Letters of TR*, 6:1489–90.

292. "bobcats after all." Thayer, *JH*, 2:354 (4–10–1904).

292. "call me Theodore." Hay had written to "Mr. Roosevelt," congratulating him on his nomination as vice president. The request is in TR's response, in June 1900. Quoted in Taliaferro, *All the Prizes*, 390.

292. "free myself from vindictiveness." Morison, *Letters of TR*, 3:300 (7–22–1902).

292. "first day of comfort." Taliaferro, *All the Prizes*, 412 (to Clarence King, 10–27–1901).

292. "They are old friends." Ibid., 413 (11–18–1901; Whitelaw Reid Correspondence, Library of Congress).

294. "'such a thoughtless act.'" Thayer, *JH*, 2:351.

295. "the entire nation is proud." Paine, *MT: Biography*, 3:1249–50.

296. "President in my own right." Thayer, *JH*, 2:359.

296. "I am to remain Secretary of State." Ibid. (JH's diary, 11–12–1904).

296. "mere delight of your companionship." Taliaferro, *All the Prizes*, 531–32 (TR to JH, 3–3–1905).

296. "high character and long service." Morison, *Letters of TR*, 6:1490 (to Lodge, 1–28–1909).

297. "to the White House to report to the President." Thayer, *JH*, 2:405 (6–13–1905).

297. "I cling instinctively to life." JH, *Letters, Extracts*, 3:350 (6–1905); Thayer, *JH*, 2:408–9; Kushner and Sherrill, *John Milton Hay*, 164; Zeitz, *Lincoln's Boys*, 336–37; Taliaferro, *All the Prizes*, 543.

EPILOGUE

301. "I had to do the big things." Morison, *Letters of TR*, 4:1270–71 (to Lodge, 7–11–1905).

301. "I took Panama." Abbott, *Impressions*, 67. TR in an address at the University of California (3–23–1911): "I took the canal zone." Dennett, *JH*, 381.

302. "opportunity for useful work." Thayer, *JH*, 2:344 (9–15–1900).

303. "thither from New York." TR, *African Game Trails*, in *Works*, 4:5.

304. "many voyages together, Livy dear." Wecter, *Love Letters*, 349.

305. "one of the most likable men." MT, *Autobiography*, 1:259 (1–10–1906).

305. "worst president we have ever had." DeVoto, ed., *Mark Twain in Eruption*, 34. Citations that follow are from this source: 29 ("the spoils system"), 12 ("see the hugging").

305–6. Moro Massacre. MT, *Autobiography*, 1:203. See, in addition, Zwick, *MT's Weapons of Satire*, 168–78 (MT, "Comments on the Moro Massacre").

306. "I wish it well." Paine, *MT's Notebook*, 372.

306. "you shake the sides of the whole world." Paine, *MT: Biography*, 3:1394.

307. the man "in the arena." TR, *Letters and Speeches*, 781–82 ("Citizenship in a Republic," Paris, 4–23–1910).

308. "machinery for defeating the popular will." TR, *Works*, 17:9 ("The New Nationalism," Osawatomie, Kans., 8–31–1910).

309. "the lily-livered skunk." E. Morris, *Colonel Roosevelt*, 480 ("Even the lily-livered skunk in the White House may not be able to prevent Germany from kicking us into war." TR in a letter to his son Kermit at the time of the Zimmerman telegram.)

310. "I shall do better stuff." Monteiro, *James & Hay*, 124–25 (4–3–1900). The two citations that follow are from this source: 127–28 ("gave me extraordinary joy"), 37 ("in its scorn of traditions of all sort," 4–3–1904).

311. "delighted with Henry James." Morison, *Letters of TR*, 4:1102 (1–13–1905).

311. "somewhat ornamental." "Mr. Roosevelt's Creed," *New York Times*, 10–19–84, p. 2.

311. "It is art that *makes* life." Edel and Ray, *James and Wells*, 267.

311. "plunge of civilization." Lubbock, *Letters of HJ*, 2:384 (to Howard Sturgis, [4–4–1914]).

312. "sublime position of Henry James." Ozick, "The Lesson of the Master," *New York Review of Books*, 8–12–1982.

313. "doctrine of milk and water." TR, *Fear God*, in *Works*, 18:261 ("America First: A Phrase or a Fact").

313. "proud of his four sons." To Richard Derby, his daughter Ethel's husband, 7–1–1918; Brands, *TR*, 793.

313. "They have done pretty well." Renehan, *Lion's Pride*, 200, quoting from Geoffrey C. Ward, *A First-Class Temperament: The Emergence of Franklin Roosevelt* (New York: Harper & Row, 1989), 389.

314. "our pride equals our sorrow." TR to Kermit, 7–21–1918; quoted in Brands, *TR*, 800.

314. "he could not hear." S. J. Morris, *Edith*, 433 (Edith Roosevelt to son Kermit, 1–12–1919).

315. "I am building another." Monteiro, *James & Hay*, 137.

316. "the charm of King." Adams, *Education*, 1004 (Ch. 20).

316. "he need not repine." Ibid., 1180 (Ch. 35).

BIBLIOGRAPHY

Abbott, Lawrence. *Impressions of Theodore Roosevelt*. Garden City, N.Y.: Doubleday Page, 1919.

Adams, Henry. *The Education of Henry Adams*. In *Henry Adams: Novels, Mont Saint Michel, The Education*. New York: Library of America, 1983.

———. *History of the United States of America during the Administrations of James Madison*. New York: The Library of America, 1986.

———. *History of the United States of America during the Administrations of Thomas Jefferson*. New York: The Library of America, 1986.

———. *Letters of Henry Adams*, J. C. Levenson et al., eds. 6 vols. Cambridge, Mass., Belknap Press, 1982–1988.

Anderson, Quentin. *The American Henry James*. New Brunswick, N.J.: Rutgers Univ. Press, 1957.

Anesko, Michael. *Letters, Fictions, Lives: Henry James and William Dean Howells*. New York: Oxford Univ. Press, 1997.

Angle, Paul M. *"Here I Have Lived": A History of Lincoln's Springfield, 1821–1865*. Springfield, Ill.: The Abraham Lincoln Association, 1935.

Baker, Jean H. *Mary Todd Lincoln: A Biography*. New York: W. W. Norton, 2008, 1987.

Basler, Roy P., ed. *The Collected Works of Abraham Lincoln*. 9 vols. New Brunswick, N.J.: Rutgers Univ. Press, 1953–1955.

Bellesiles, Michael A. *1877: America's Year of Living Violently*. New York: The New Press, 2010.

Besant, Walter. *The Art of Fiction: A Lecture Delivered at the Royal Institution on Friday Evening, April 25, 1884 (with Notes and Additions)*. London: Chatto and Windus, 1884.

Bigelow, John. *Retrospections of an Active Life*. 5 vols. New York: Baker & Taylor, and Garden City, N.Y.: Doubleday, Page, 1909–13.

Bishop, Joseph Bucklin. *Theodore Roosevelt and His Time Shown in His Own Letters.* 2 vols. New York: Charles Scribner's Sons, 1920.

Brands, H. W. *TR: The Last Romantic.* New York: Basic Books, 1997.

Bruce, Robert V. *1877: Year of Violence.* Chicago: Elephant Paperbacks: Ivan R. Dee, Inc., 1989 (originally published by Bobbs-Merrill Co. in 1959).

Burlingame, Michael. *Abraham Lincoln: A Life.* 2 vols. Baltimore: Johns Hopkins Univ. Press, 2008.

———. *The Inner World of Abraham Lincoln.* Urbana: Univ. of Illinois Press, 1994.

———. "Nicolay and Hay: Court Historians." *Journal of the Abraham Lincoln Association*, Vol. 19, Issue 1 (Winter 1998): 1–20.

———. "The Trouble with the Bixby Letter." *American Heritage*, Vol. 50, Issue 4 (July–August 1999): 64–67.

Cady, Edwin Harrison. *Realist at War: The Mature Years, 1885–1920, of William Dean Howells.* Syracuse, N.Y.: Syracuse Univ. Press, 1958.

———. *Road to Realism: The Early Years, 1837–1885, of William Dean Howells.* Syracuse, N.Y.: Syracuse Univ. Press, 1956.

Canby, Henry Seidel. *Turn West, Turn East: Mark Twain and Henry James.* Boston: Houghton Mifflin, 1951.

Cargill, Oscar. *The Novels of Henry James.* New York: Macmillan, 1961.

Cashman, Sean Dennis. *America in the Gilded Age: From the Death of Lincoln to the Rise of Theodore Roosevelt.* New York: N.Y. Univ. Press, 1984.

Clemens, Clara. *My Father Mark Twain.* New York: Harper & Bros., 1931.

Clemens, Susy. *Papa: An Intimate Biography of Mark Twain by His Daughter, Thirteen.* Charles Neider, ed. Garden City, N.Y.: Doubleday, 1985.

Clymer, Kenton J. *John Hay: The Gentleman as Diplomat.* Ann Arbor: Univ. of Michigan Press, 1975.

———. "John Hay and Mark Twain." *Missouri Historical Review*, Vol. 67, No. 4 (1974): 397–406.

Courtney, Steve. *"The Loveliest Home That Ever Was": The Story of the Mark Twain House in Hartford.* Mineola, N.Y.: Dover Publications, 2011.

Cowles, Anna Roosevelt. *Letters from Theodore Roosevelt to Anna Roosevelt Cowles, 1870–1918.* New York: Charles Scribner's Sons, 1924.

Dalton, Kathleen. *Theodore Roosevelt: A Strenuous Life.* New York: Vintage Books, 2002.

Daniel, John Warwick. "The Monroe Doctrine." Speech of Hon. John W. Daniel of Virginia in the Senate of the United States, Thursday, January 23, 1896. Vol. 563, Issue 7. Washington, 1896.

Davidson, Rob. *The Master and the Dean: The Literary Criticism of Henry James and William Dean Howells.* Columbia: Univ. of Missouri Press, 2005.

Davis, Rodney O., and Douglas L. Wilson, eds. *The Lincoln-Douglas Debates.* Urbana and Chicago: The Knox College Lincoln Studies Center and the Univ. of Illinois Press, 2008.

Dennett, Tyler. *John Hay: From Poetry to Politics*. New York: Dodd, Mead & Co., 1933.

DeVoto, Bernard, ed. *Mark Twain in Eruption: Hitherto Unpublished Pages about Men and Events*. New York: Harper & Bros., 1940.

Donald, David Herbert. *Lincoln*. New York: Touchstone, 1996.

———. *Lincoln's Herndon*. New York: Knopf, 1948.

Duff, John J. *A. Lincoln, Prairie Lawyer*. New York: Rinehart, 1960.

Duncan, Bingham. *Whitelaw Reid: Journalist, Politician, Diplomat*. Athens: Univ. of Georgia Press, 1975.

Dykstra, Natalie. *Clover Adams: A Gilded and Heartbreaking Life*. Boston: Houghton Mifflin Harcourt, 2012.

Edel, Leon. *Henry James*, 5 vols. (1. *The Untried Years, 1843–1870*; 2. *The Conquest of London, 1870–1881*; 3. *The Middle Years, 1882–1895*; 4. *The Treacherous Years, 1895–1901*; 5. *The Master, 1901–1916*). Philadelphia: Lippincott, 1953–1972.

———. Introduction to *The Bostonians*, Vol. 3 in The Bodley Head Henry James. London: The Bodley Head, 1967.

———, ed. *Letters of Henry James*. 4 vols. Cambridge, Mass.: Harvard Univ. Press, 1974–1984.

Edel, Leon, and Gordon N. Ray, eds. *Henry James and H. G. Wells: A Record of Their Friendship, Their Debate on the Art of Fiction, and Their Quarrel*. Edited with an introduction by Leon Edel and Gordon N. Ray. Urbana: Univ. of Illinois Press, 1958.

Ensor, Allison. *MT and the Bible*. Lexington: Univ. of Kentucky Press, 1969.

Epstein, Daniel Mark. *Lincoln's Men: The President and His Private Secretaries*. New York: HarperCollins, 2009.

Fatout, Paul. *Mark Twain on the Lecture Circuit*. Bloomington: Indiana Univ. Press, 1962.

Fehrenbacher, Don E. *Prelude to Greatness: Lincoln in the 1850's*. Palo Alto: Stanford Univ. Press, 1962.

Gale, Robert L. *John Hay*. Boston: Twayne Publishers, 1978.

Gard, Roger, ed. *Henry James: The Critical Heritage*. London: Routledge & Kegan Paul, 1968.

Geismar, Maxwell. *Henry James and the Jacobites*. Boston: Houghton Mifflin, 1963.

Gibson, William M. "Mark Twain and Howells: Anti-Imperialists." *The New England Quarterly* 20 (1947): 435–70.

Goodwin, Doris Kearns. *The Bully Pulpit: Theodore Roosevelt, William Howard Taft, and the Golden Age of Journalism*. New York: Simon & Schuster, 2013.

Gordon, Lyndall. *A Private Life of Henry James: Two Women and His Art*. New York: W. W. Norton, 1998.

Gould, Lewis L. *The Spanish-American War and President McKinley*. Lawrence: Univ. Press of Kansas, 1980.

Hay, John. *Addresses of John Hay*. New York: Century Co., 1906.

———. *At Lincoln's Side: John Hay's Civil War Correspondence and Selected Writings*. Edited by Michael Burlingame. Carbondale: Southern Illinois Univ. Press, 2000.

———. *The Bread-Winners: A Social Study*. New York: Harper & Brothers, 1884.

———. *Inside Lincoln's White House: The Complete Civil War Diary of John Hay*. Edited by Michael Burlingame and John R. Turner Ettlinger. Carbondale: Southern Illinois Univ. Press, 1997.

———. *John Hay-Howells Letters: The Correspondence of John Milton Hay and William Dean Howells 1861–1905*. Edited with an Introduction and Annotations by George Monteiro and Brenda Murphy. Boston: Twayne Publishers, 1980.

———. *Letters of John Hay and Extracts from Diary*. 3 vols. Washington, 1908. Printed but not Published. c. Clara S. Hay, 1908.

———. *Lincoln's Journalist: John Hay's Anonymous Writings for the Press, 1860–1864*. Edited by Michael Burlingame. Carbondale: Southern Illinois Univ. Press, 1998.

———. *Poems*. Boston: Houghton Mifflin, 1899.

———. *A Poet in Exile: Early Letters of John Hay*. Edited by Caroline Ticknor. Boston: Houghton Mifflin, 1910.

Hertz, Emanuel, ed. *The Hidden Lincoln: From the Letters and Papers of William H. Herndon*. New York: Viking, 1938.

Holzer, Harold. *Lincoln, President-Elect: Abraham Lincoln and the Great Secession Winter 1860–1861*. New York: Simon & Schuster, 2008.

Horner, Harlan Hoyt. *Lincoln and Greeley*. Champaign: Univ. of Illinois Press, 1953.

Howells, Mildred, ed. *Life in Letters of William Dean Howells*. 2 vols. Garden City, N.Y.: Doubleday, Doran, 1928.

Howells, William Dean. "Henry James, Jr." *Century Magazine*, 35 (Nov. 1882): 25–29.

———. *John Hay-Howells Letters*. See Hay, John.

———. *My Mark Twain*. With a new Introduction by Thomas Wortham. Mineola, N.Y.: Dover Publications, 1997 (unabridged republication of the volume by Harper & Bros. in 1910 under the title *My Mark Twain: Reminiscence and Criticisms*). The volume contains Howells's essay "Mark Twain," originally published in *The Century Magazine*, 24 (9–82): 780–82.

Jaher, Frederic Cople. "Industrialism and the American Aristocrat: A Social Study of John Hay and His Novel, *The Bread-Winners*." *Journal of the Illinois State Historical Society*, 65 (Spring 1972): 69–93.

James, Henry. "The Art of Fiction." *Longman's Magazine*, Vol. 4, No. 23 (9–84). London: Longmans, Green, 1884.

———. *The Bostonians*. HJ, *Novels 1881–1886, Washington Square, The Portrait of a Lady, The Bostonians*. New York: Library of America, 1985.

———. *The Complete Notebooks of Henry James*. Edited with introductions and notes by Leon Edel and Lyall H. Powers. New York: Oxford Univ. Press, 1987.

———. *The Complete Plays of Henry James*. Edited by Leon Edel. Philadelphia: Lippincott, 1949.

————. *Complete Stories, 1892–1898.* New York: Library of America, 1996.

————. *Daisy Miller.* The Bodley Head Henry James, Vol. 11: *Daisy Miller; The Turn of the Screw.* Introduction by Leon Edel. London: The Bodley Head, 1974.

————. *Letters* (Edel). See Edel, Leon, ed. *Letters of Henry James.*

————. *Parisian Sketches: Letters to the New York Tribune 1875–1876.* Edited with an introduction by Leon Edel and Ilse Dusoir Lind. New York: New York Univ. Press, 1957.

James, William. *Letters of . . .* Edited by his son Henry James. 2 vols. Boston: Atlantic Monthly Press, 1920.

Kaplan, Justin. *Mr. Clemens and Mark Twain: A Biography.* New York: Simon and Schuster, 1966.

Kauffman, Michael W. *American Brutus: John Wilkes Booth and the Lincoln Conspiracies.* New York: Random House, 2004.

Kerr, Joan Patterson, ed. *A Bully Father: Theodore Roosevelt's Letters to His Children.* New York: Random House, 1995. An introduction, illustrations, and commentary accompany this reprinting of *Theodore Roosevelt's Letters to His Children,* first published posthumously in 1919, the year of TR's death.

Kushner, Howard I., and Anne Hummel Sherrill. *John Milton Hay: The Union of Poetry and Politics.* Boston: Twayne Publishers, 1977.

Lamon, Ward H. *The Life of Abraham Lincoln; from His Birth to His Inauguration as President.* Boston: James R. Osgood and Co., 1872.

Leary, Katy. *A Lifetime with Mark Twain: The Memories of Katy Leary, for Thirty Years His Faithful and Devoted Servant.* Transcribed by Mary Lawton. New York: Harcourt, Brace, 1925.

Leary, Lewis, ed. *Mark Twain's Correspondence with Henry Huttleston Rogers, 1893–1909.* Berkeley: Univ. of Calif. Press, 1969.

Leavis, F. R. *The Great Tradition: George Eliot, Henry James, Joseph Conrad.* London: Chatto and Windus, 1948.

Levenson, J. C. et al., eds. *The Letters of Henry Adams.* 6 vols. Cambridge, Mass.: Belknap Press, 1982–1988.

————. *Mind and Art of Henry Adams.* Boston: Houghton Mifflin, 1957.

Lewis, R. W. B. *The Jameses: A Family Narrative.* New York: Farrar, Straus and Giroux, 1991.

Lubbock, Percy, ed. *The Letters of Henry James.* 2 vols. London: Macmillan, 1920.

Mark Twain. "1601"; or, Conversation as It Was at the Fireside in the Time of the Tudors, *& Sketches Old and New.* n.p.: Golden Hind Press, 1933.

————. *Adventures of Huckleberry Finn.* In MT, *Mississippi Writings.* New York: Library of America, 1982.

————. *Autobiography of Mark Twain.* Vol. 1. Edited by Harriett Elinor Smith. Berkeley: Univ. of Calif. Press, 2010.

————. *Collected Tales, Sketches, Speeches, & Essays, 1852–1890.* New York: Library of America, 1992.

———. *Collected Tales, Sketches, Speeches, & Essays, 1891–1910*. New York, Library of America, 1992.

———. *A Connecticut Yankee in King Arthur's Court*. In *Historical Romances: The Prince and the Pauper. A Connecticut Yankee in King Arthur's Court. Joan of Arc.* New York: Library of America, 1994.

———. *The Innocents Abroad*. In *The Innocents Abroad. Roughing It*. New York: Library of America, 1984.

———. *Letters to His Publishers, 1867–1894*. Edited by Hamlin Hill. Berkeley: Univ. of Calif. Press, 1967.

———. *Letters, Volume I: 1853–1866*. Edited by Edgar Marquess Branch et al.. Berkeley: Univ. of Calif. Press, 1988.

———. *Letters, Volume II: 1867–1868*. Edited by Harriet Elinor Smith et al.. Berkeley: Univ. of Calif. Press, 1990.

———. *Life on the Mississippi*. In MT, *Mississippi Writings*. New York: Library of America, 1982.

———. *Mark Twain's Letters to Will Bowen: "My First & Oldest & Dearest Friend."* Edited by Theodore Hornberger. Austin: Univ. of Texas Press, 1941.

———. *Mark Twain to Mrs. Fairbanks*. Edited by Dixon Wecter. San Marino, Calif.: Huntington Library, 1949.

———. *Mark Twain's Travels with Mr. Brown: Being Heretofore Uncollected Sketches Written by Mark Twain for the San Francisco Alta California in 1866 & 1867 . . .* Collected and Edited with an Introduction by Franklin Walker and G. Ezra Dane. New York: Knopf, 1940.

———. *Notebooks & Journals, Volume I (1855–1873)*. Edited by Frederick Anderson et al. Berkeley: Univ. of Calif. Press, 1975.

———. *Roughing It*. In *The Innocents Abroad. Roughing It*. New York: Library of America, 1984.

Marvel, William. *Lincoln's Autocrat: The Life of Edwin Stanton*. Chapel Hill: Univ. of North Carolina Press, 2015.

McCullough, David. *Mornings on Horseback*. New York: Touchstone, 1981.

Mearns, David C. *The Lincoln Papers: The Story of the Collection with Selections to July 4, 1861*. Introduction by Carl Sandburg. 2 vols. Garden City, N.Y.: Doubleday, 1948.

Merriman, John. *Massacre: The Life and Death of the Paris Commune*. New York: Basic Books, 2014.

Miller, Merle. *Plain Speaking: An Oral Biography of Harry S. Truman*. New York: Berkeley, 1974.

Monteiro, George, ed. *The Correspondence of Henry James and Henry Adams, 1877–1914*. Baton Rouge: Louisiana State Univ. Press, 1992.

———. *Henry James and John Hay: The Record of a Friendship*. Providence: Brown Univ. Press, 1965.

Morison, Elting E., et al. *Letters of Theodore Roosevelt*. 8 vols. Cambridge, Mass.: Harvard Univ. Press, 1951–1954.

Morris, Edmund. *Colonel Roosevelt.* New York: Random House, 2010.

———. *The Rise of Theodore Roosevelt.* New York: The Modern Library, 2001.

———. *Theodore Rex.* New York: The Modern Library, 2002.

Morris, Sylvia Jukes. *Edith Kermit Roosevelt: Portrait of a First Lady.* New York: Coward, McCann, 1980.

Nagel, Paul C. *Descent from Glory: Four Generations of the John Adams Family.* Cambridge, Mass.: Harvard Univ. Press, 1983.

Nicolay, Helen. *Lincoln's Secretary: A Biography of John G. Nicolay.* New York: Longmans, Green, 1949.

Nicolay, John G. *With Lincoln in the White House: Letters, Memoranda, and Other Writings of John G. Nicolay, 1860–1865.* Edited by Michael Burlingame. Carbondale: Southern Illinois Univ. Press, 2000.

Nicolay, John G., and John Hay. *Abraham Lincoln: A History.* 10 vols. New York: Century Company, 1890.

Olsen, Christopher J. *The American Civil War: A Hands-On History.* New York: Hill and Wang, 2006.

Ozick, Cynthia. "The Lesson of the Master." *New York Review of Books*, August 12, 1982.

Paine, Albert Bigelow, ed. *Mark Twain: A Biography.* 3 vols. New York: Chelsea House, 1980, reprint of the 1912 edition published by Harper & Bros., New York.

———. *Mark Twain's Letters.* 2 vols. New York: Harper, 1917.

———, ed. *Mark Twain's Notebook: Prepared for Publication with Comments by Albert Bigelow Paine.* New York: Harper and Brothers, 1935.

Perosa, Sergio. *Henry James and the Experimental Novel.* Charlottesville: Univ. of Virginia Press, 1978.

Putnam, Carleton. *Theodore Roosevelt: Vol. I: The Formative Years, 1858–1886.* New York: Charles Scribner's Sons, 1958.

Renehan, Edward J., Jr. *The Lion's Pride: Theodore Roosevelt and His Family in Peace and War.* New York: Oxford, 1999.

Report of the Joint Committee Concerning the Ashtabula Bridge Disaster, under Joint Resolution of the General Assembly. Ohio General Assembly, Joint Committee on Ashtabula Bridge. Columbus, Ohio: Nevins and Myers, State Printers, 1877.

Robinson, Corinne Roosevelt. *My Brother, Theodore Roosevelt.* New York: Charles Scribner's Sons, 1921.

Roosevelt, Theodore. *African Game Trails: An Account of the African Wanderings of an American Hunter-Naturalist.* New York: Charles Scribner's Sons, 1910. In TR, *Works*, Vol. 4.

———. *An Autobiography.* In *The Rough Riders* and *An Autobiography.* New York: Library of America, 2004.

———. *Diaries of Boyhood and Youth.* New York: Charles Scribner's Sons, 1928.

———. *Fear God and Take Your Own Part.* In TR, *Works*, Vol. 18.

———. *Letters and Speeches.* New York: The Library of America, 2004.

————. *The Rough Riders*. In *The Rough Riders* and *An Autobiography*. New York: Library of America, 2004.

————. *The Works of Theodore Roosevelt*. National Edition. Hermann Hagedorn, ed. 20 vols. New York: Charles Scribner's Sons, 1926.

Rowe, John Carlos. *Henry Adams and Henry James: The Emergence of a Modern Consciousness*. Ithaca, N.Y.: Cornell Univ. Press, 1976.

Sandweiss, Martha A. *Passing Strange: A Gilded Age Tale of Love and Deception across the Color Line*. New York: Penguin Press, 2009.

Scharnhorst, Gary, ed. *Mark Twain: The Complete Interviews*. Tuscaloosa: Univ. of Alabama Press, 2006.

Schurz, Carl. *The Reminiscences of . . .* 3 vols. New York: The McClure Co., 1907–1908.

Seitz, Don C. *Horace Greeley: Founder of the* New York Tribune. Indianapolis: Bobbs-Merrill, 1926.

Shea, John Gilmary, ed. *The Lincoln Memorial: A Record of the Life, Assassination, and Obsequies of the Martyred President*. New York: Bunce & Huntington, 1865.

Smith, Henry Nash, and William M. Gibson, eds. *Mark Twain-Howells Letters: The Correspondence of Samuel L. Clemens and William D. Howells*. 2 vols. Cambridge, Mass.: Harvard Univ. Press, 1960.

Smith, Theodore Clarke. *The Life and Letters of James Abram Garfield*. 2 vols. New Haven, Conn.: Yale Univ. Press, 1925.

Starr, John W., Jr. *Lincoln and the Railroads*. New York: Dodd, Mead & Company, 1927.

Steinbrink, Jeffrey. *Getting to Be Mark Twain*. Berkeley: Univ. of Calif. Press, 1991.

Stoddard, William O. *Inside the White House in War Times: Memoirs and Reports of Lincoln's Secretary*. Edited by Michael Burlingame. Lincoln: Univ. of Nebraska Press, 2000 (orig. ed., 1890).

Stowe, William W. *Balzac, James, and the Realistic Novel*. Princeton, N.J.: Princeton Univ. Press, 1983.

Taliaferro, John. *All the Great Prizes: The Life of John Hay, from Lincoln to Roosevelt*. New York: Simon & Schuster, 2013.

Tehan, Arline Boucher. *Henry Adams in Love: The Pursuit of Elizabeth Sherman Cameron*. New York: Universe Books, 1983.

Thayer, William Roscoe. *The Life and Letters of John Hay*. 2 vols. Boston: Houghton Mifflin, 1915.

Thomas, Benjamin P., and Harold M. Hyman. *Stanton: The Life and Times of Lincoln's Secretary of War*. New York: Knopf, 1962.

Traubel, Horace. *With Walt Whitman in Camden*. 5 vols. Boston: Small, Maynard 1906 [and various imprints, as for vol. 4: Carbondale: Southern Illinois Univ. Press, 1959].

Trilling, Lionel. *The Liberal Imagination: Essays on Literature and Society*. New York: Viking Press, 1950.

Wagenknecht, Edward. *The Seven Worlds of Theodore Roosevelt*. New York: Longmans, Green, 1958.

Wallace, Lew. *An Autobiography*. 2 vols. New York: Harper & Brothers, 1906.

Weber, Carl J. *The Rise and Fall of James Ripley Osgood: A Biography*. Waterville, Maine: Colby College Press, 1959.

Webster, Samuel Charles. *Mark Twain, Business Man*. Boston: Little, Brown, 1946.

Wecter, Dixon. *The Love Letters of Mark Twain*. New York: Harper, 1949.

Welles, Gideon. *Diary of Gideon Welles, Secretary of the Navy under Lincoln and Johnson*. 3 vols. Edited and with an introduction by Howard K. Beale. New York: Norton & Co., 1960.

Williams, Robert C. *Horace Greeley: Champion of American Freedom*. New York: New York Univ. Press, 2006.

Williams, Wayne C. *William Jennings Bryan*. New York: G. P. Putnam's Sons, 1936.

Yeazell, Ruth Bernard, ed. *The Death and Letters of Alice James: Selected Correspondence Edited with a Biographical Essay*. Berkeley: Univ. of Calif. Press, 1981.

Zeitz, Joshua. *Lincoln's Boys: John Hay, John Nicolay, and the War for Lincoln's Image*. New York: Viking, 2014.

Zwick, Jim. *Mark Twain's Weapons of Satire: Anti-Imperialist Writings on the Philippine-American War*. Syracuse, N.Y.: Syracuse Univ. Press, 1992.

Zwonitzer, Mark. *The Statesman and the Storyteller: John Hay, Mark Twain, and the Rise of American Imperialism*. Chapel Hill, N.C.: Algonquin, 2016.

ACKNOWLEDGMENTS

Such a book as this would not have been possible within the constraints that circumstances imposed had not scholars already done their extraordinary work on the five principals of the narrative. In particular, the work of Michael Burlingame on Lincoln and his private secretaries, of the collective work of the Mark Twain Project on Mark Twain, of Leon Edel on Henry James, of Edmund Morris on Theodore Roosevelt, and of the several scholars of John Hay, including William Roscoe Thayer, Tyler Dennett, and George Monteiro—all emboldened me to undertake what of necessity is not a formal biography (or five formal biographies) but, rather, a meditation on interlocked lives in four pivotal decades of our history.

John Taliaferro's informative *All the Great Prizes*, the first, detailed, full-length biography of Hay in eighty years, appeared while my own manuscript was laid out as a scheme and well along in the writing, but not so far along that I was unable to profit from the wealth of material that Mr. Taliaferro has gathered together in his compelling narrative. My notes seek to acknowledge my indebtedness to him. Mark Zwonitzer's *The Statesman and the Storyteller*, about Hay and Mark Twain, appeared only after my own book was completed; I have read it with pleasure, but because of our different emphases—mine on Mark Twain in the 1870s, his on Mark Twain from the 1890s on—I found less reason to lament the late arrival of his excellent study than might have been the case otherwise.

My bibliography acknowledges some of the many other works that have enlarged my understanding of so rich a field, so richly peopled. I'm indebted as well, as always, to specific individuals for their kindness and helpfulness: among them Melissa Martin at the Mark Twain Project, the Bancroft Library,

University of California, Berkeley; to Mallory Howard at the Mark Twain House and Museum in Hartford; to Heather Cole at the Houghton Library, Harvard University, Cambridge; to Ben Tyler and Holly Snyder at the John Hay Library, Brown University, Providence; and to the ever-obliging staff of the Boston Athenaeum, with special thanks to Mary Warnement, head of reader services (including, invaluably, its rare-book room and its interlibrary-loan service), and to the cheerful, knowledgeable James Feeney, trusty guide at the circulation desk throughout my protracted, fulfilling involvement with that sterling institution.

P.M.
Lexington, Massachusetts
January 2017

INDEX

Ben Hur (Wallace), 2
Bennett, James Gordon, 107
Besant, Walter, 178, 182–84; and "The
    Art of Fiction," 178–80
Bigelow, John, 88
Bismarck, Otto von, 132, 279
Bixby, Lydia, 54–55
Blaine, James G., 237, 239, 241, 255–56
Bliss, Elijah, 107; Clemens's dissatisfac-
    tions with, 127–28, 146; death of,
    146; proposes that Mark Twain write
    a book, 95–96
Booth, John Wilkes, 49, 66, 70–71
The Bostonians (James), 186, 189–92,
    220–21, 253; contrasted with *The
    Bread-Winners,* 193; and contrasting
    viewpoints on women's rights,
    190–92; F. R. Leavis's favorable
    critical opinion of, 221; and Miss
    Birdseye, 196, 198, 221
The Bread-Winners (Hay, anonymously),
    172–74, 193
Breckinridge, John, 14
Brooks, Van Wyck, 115
Bryan, William Jennings, 261–62, 287
Buchanan, James, 22, 59, 270
Bull Run (battle), 28–30, 45, 274
Bunyan, John, 185–86
Burlingame, Michael, 216
Burnside, Ambrose, 46–47
Burroughs, John, 303
Byron, George Gordon, Lord, 165

Cameron, Donald, 242, 246, 276
Cameron, Elizabeth Sherman: and close
    friendship with Henry Adams, 243,
    246; correspondence with Adams,
    245; and friendship with John Hay,
    244–48; marriage to Donald
    Cameron, 242–43, 246, 276
Cameron, Simon, 242
Carnegie, Andrew, 267, 287, 303;
    opinion of Hay, xiii

Carpenter, Francis, 201
Chancellorsville (battle), 47
Chase, Salmon P., 53, 102, 216
Civil War: cause of, according to Nicolay
    and Hay, 201; commencement of,
    25–26; first casualties, 28; why North
    so often beaten in battle, 47; and
    reconciliation, 129, 201. *See also*
    battles by name, "Bull Run," etc.
Clay, Clement, 59, 61–62
Clay, Henry, 38
Clemens, Clara (daughter), 127, 304,
    306
Clemens, Jean (daughter), 304
Clemens, Langdon (son), 110, 112
Clemens, Olivia Langdon ("Livy," wife),
    126; courtship of, 109–10, 113; last
    years and death of, 304; marriage of,
    110, 119; and Susy's death, 285–86.
    See also Langdon, Olivia
Clemens, Orion (brother), 79
Clemens, Samuel L.: adopts pseudonym
    "Mark Twain," 78; and Bermuda,
    306; birth and early life of, 112, 125,
    187; in Buffalo after marriage,
    110–11; builds home in Hartford,
    126; and Charles L. Webster
    Publishing Co., 147, 219–20,
    284–85; death of, 304, 306–7; on
    death of Hay's father-in-law, 177; and
    Elmira, 109–11, 127; goes west with
    brother Orion, 78, 79; leaves
    Hannibal for good, 79; love for Olivia
    Langdon, 109–10, 113; marries, 110,
    119; military service in Civil War, 78,
    140; moves to Hartford, 112; opinion
    of Theodore Roosevelt, 305–6; as
    riverboat pilot, 139–40; Stormfield,
    304, 306; and typesetting machine,
    149, 220, 285; visits family in St.
    Louis (1867), 82–83. *See also* Mark
    Twain